# Financial and Monetary Policy Studies

Volume 43

More information about this series at http://www.springer.com/series/5982

Nazaré da Costa Cabral • José Renato Gonçalves •
Nuno Cunha Rodrigues
Editors

# The Euro and the Crisis

## Perspectives for the Eurozone as a Monetary and Budgetary Union

Springer

*Editors*
Nazaré da Costa Cabral
CIDEEFF - School of Law, University of Lisbon
Alameda da Universidade
Lisbon, Portugal

José Renato Gonçalves
CIDEEFF - School of Law, University of Lisbon
Alameda da Universidade
Lisbon, Portugal

Nuno Cunha Rodrigues
CIDEEFF - School of Law, University of Lisbon
Alameda da Universidade
Lisbon, Portugal

ISSN 0921-8580 ISSN 2197-1889 (electronic)
Financial and Monetary Policy Studies
ISBN 978-3-319-45709-3 ISBN 978-3-319-45710-9 (eBook)
DOI 10.1007/978-3-319-45710-9

Library of Congress Control Number: 2016960545



Printed on acid-free paper

This Springer imprint is published by Springer Nature
The registered company is Springer International Publishing AG Switzerland

# Acknowledgements

The editors are grateful to the leading scholars and experts in European affairs who have contributed to the chapters and to CIDEEFF's language reviewer, Professor David Hardisty (*Leitor, Universidade Nova de Lisboa*), who also provided comments on several chapters of the Book.

The editors wish to thank to Marta Caldas, CIDEEFF/PhD Researcher, for her invaluable organizational work and scientific support to this project.

# Contents

# About the Editors and Authors

**Syed Ehtisham Ahmad** is Senior Fellow at the Center for Development Research at the University of Bonn and at the LSE (since 2010); member of Academic Committee, Institute of State Governance, Sun Yat-Sen University, Guangzhou, PR China (since 2015); and Pao Yu-Kong Professor at Zhejiang University, PR China (since 2016).

At the IMF during 1990–2010, Dr. Ahmad has been Senior Advisor at the Executive Board; Advisor and Division Chief, Fiscal Affairs Department; and Special Advisor to the Finance Minister, Saudi Arabia, 1996–1998 (on leave from the IMF). He was on the World Bank staff team for the 1990 World Development Report "Poverty"; Director of the Development Economics Research Programme, STICERD, LSE (1986–1990); and Deputy Director of the Development Economics Research Center at Warwick University (1980–1986).

He has written widely on public policy and fiscal reforms, governance, fiscal federalism, and poverty reduction. His recent books include *Multi-level Finance and the Crisis in Europe*, Elgar 2016 (with Giorgio Brosio and Massimo Bordignon); *Handbook of Multilevel Finance*, Elgar 2015; *Handbook of Fiscal Federalism*, Elgar 2006; and *Does Decentralization Enhance Service Delivery and Poverty Reduction?* Edward Elgar 2009 (with Giorgio Brosio).

Some earlier books include *Theory and Practice of Tax Reform in Developing Countries*, CUO 1991 (with Nicholas Stern); *Social Security in Developing Countries*, OUP 1992 (with Jean Drèze, John Hills, and Amartya Sen; *Reforming China's Public Finances,* IMF, 1995 (with Gao Qiang and Vito Tanzi); *Financing Decentralized Expenditures—A Focus on Intergovernmental Grants*, Edward Elgar 1997; and *Managing Fiscal Decentralization*, Routledge 2002 (with Vito Tanzi).

**João Sousa Andrade** is Full Professor at the Faculty of Economics of the University of Coimbra and a researcher affiliated with the Group for Monetary and Financial Studies (GEMF). He has a Doctoratd'État en Sciences Économiques. He is PhD Professor and PhD supervisor in the fields of Macroeconomics and

Monetary Policy. He has 40 years of teaching experience mostly in the field of Macroeconomics, Money, and Monetary Policy. He serves as a reviewer for several international ISI and Scopius publications. He has participated in several international research and teaching programmes and was invited professor at Poitiers and Nice. He is the author or co-author of more than 50 publications in international scientific peer-reviewed journals, book chapters, and conference proceedings.

**Oscar Bajo-Rubio** Professor of Economics at Universidad de Castilla-La Mancha. BA in Economics from Universidad Complutense de Madrid, MA in Economics from University of Warwick, and PhD in Economics (Extraordinary Award) from UNED. Research areas: Macroeconomics, International economics, and Economic integration. Visiting positions, among others, at Harvard University, University of Warwick, University of Oxford, and London School of Economics. Has published papers, among others, in *Economics Letters*, *Economic Modelling*, *European Economic Review*, *Recherches Economiques de Louvain*, *Regional Studies*, *Journal of Policy Modeling*, *Journal of Macroeconomics*, *Applied Economics*, *Post-Communist Economies*, *European Journal of Political Economy*, *Explorations in Economic History*, and *The World Economy*. Founding member of the Spanish Association of International Economics and Finance, and its President between 2009 and 2013.

**Miroslav Beblavý** is a Member of the Slovak Parliament (since 2010) and a Senior Research Fellow at CEPS (since 2009). Until 2014, he was also the Associate Professor of Public Policy at the Comenius University in Bratislava, Slovakia. Between 2002 and 2006, he was the State Secretary of the Ministry of Labour, Social Affairs and Family in Slovakia. His areas of interest include employment and social policy, education policy, fiscal policy, governance, and corruption. He has a PhD in Economics from the University of St Andrews in Scotland.

**Ansgar Belke** is Full Professor of Macroeconomics and Director of the Institute of Business and Economic Studies (IBES) at the University of Duisburg-Essen. Since 2012, he is (ad personam) Jean Monnet Professor. Moreover, member of the Adjunct Faculty Ruhr Graduate School in Economics (RGS Econ), and visiting professor at the Europa-Institute at Saarland University, Saarbrücken, and the Hertie School of Governance, Berlin. AnsgarBelke was visiting researcher at the IMF in Washington/DC, CentER Tilburg, CEPS Brussels, IfW Kiel, DIW Berlin, and OeNB Vienna. Furthermore, he was Research Director for International Macroeconomics at the German Institute for Economic Research (DIW), Berlin, and now is Research Professor at the Centre for European Policy Studies (CEPS), Brussels. He is President of the European Economics and Finance Society (EEFS) and member of the "Monetary Expert Panel" of the European Parliament, the Scientific Advisory Council of IAW Tübingen, the Councils of "ArbeitskreisEuropäische Integration" (AEI), the "InstitutfürEuropäischePolitik" (IEP), the Executive Committee of the International Atlantic Economic Society

(IAES), and the Scientific Committee of the International Network for Economic Research (INFER). He is also Research Fellow of IZA Bonn and CELSI (Bratislava), member of the professional central bank watchers' group "ECB Observer", member of the Bureau of European Policy Analysis (BEPA) Visitors' Programme of the European Commission, external consultant of DG ECFIN of the European Commission, and external consultant of the European Union Committee of the House of Lords (UK), and he successfully conducted research projects on behalf of the German Federal Ministries of Finance and of Labour and Social Affairs.

He serves as editor-in-chief of "Credit and Capital Markets—Kredit und Kapital" and "Konjunkturpolitik—Applied Economics Quarterly"; as co-editor of "International Journal of Financial Studies", "Empirica", "International Economics and Economic Policy", "Journal of Economic Studies", "VierteljahresheftefürWirtschaftsforschung", "Aestimatio—The International IEB Journal of Finance", and "Economics" (Kiel Institute of the World Economy); as editor of the book series "Financial and Monetary Policy Studies", Springer; and as co-editor of the book series "Quantitative Ökonomie", Eul Verlag. He has published widely in international refereed journals and other outlets and has regular appearances in the printed press and in national and international TV broadcasts.

His main areas of interest are in the fields of international macroeconomics, monetary economics, European integration, and applied econometrics.

**Annette Bongardt** is currently a Visiting Senior Fellow at the London School of Economics and Political Science (European Institute). She has been a Senior and SCR Member at St Antony's College, Oxford University, since 2012 and a Visiting Fellow at the Robert Schuman Centre for Advanced Studies of the European University Institute (EUI) in Florence. She has been Associate Professor at *Universidade Fernando Pessoa* and Professor and Head of European Studies at the Portuguese National Institute for Public Administration. After receiving her PhD in Economics at the EUI in 1990, she was a Schuman Fellow of the European Commission at CEPS, Assistant Professor (eq.) at the Rotterdam School of Management, Senior Research Fellow at ICER (Turin), and Academic Visitor and consultant of the European Commission. She was also Visiting Professor at the Universities of Aveiro, Pisa, Roma (II), Victoria, BC, Canada, and Católica, Lisbon. Her publications include several books and articles, which range from industrial organization, EU competition policy, and regional competitiveness/EU cohesion to migration from a single market perspective, sustainable growth, and EU governance. She was a contributor to the handbooks on European Integration by Oxford University Press (2012), Palgrave (2013), and Routledge (2015).

**Fritz Breuss** Austrian Institute of Economic Research

Research area(s): Macroeconomics and European Economic Policy; Analysis of Austrian and international economic developments; European and national economic policy; Economic modelling and policy simulations

Working experience:

1974–2009: Researcher at the Austrian Institute of Economic Research (WIFO)
1981: Lecturer at the WU Vienna University of Economics and Business
1985: Habilitation for international economics and applied macroeconomics
1993: University Professor for European Economics
1993: Occupation or position held Professor for European Integration
WichtigsteTätigkeiten und Zuständigkeiten
1995: Occupation or position held Jean Monnet Professor for Economic Aspects of European Integration
June 2004/05: head of the Research Institute for European Affairs
July 2005: deputy head of the Research Institute for European Affairs
July 2005: head of the European Economy Department
2006: Coordinator of the FIW project (Research Centre International Economics)
2009: Deputy Head of the Institute for European Affairs (Europainstitut), EI Working Papers/Europainstitut
2009: Head of the academic unit "European Economy"

**Giorgio Brosio** is Professor of Public Economics at the Department of Economics and Statistics of the University of Torino, Italy. He has been professor at the Universities of Bari, Italy, and Geneva, Switzerland. He has been the President of the Società Italiana di EconomiaPubblica (Italian Public Economics Association) from 2009 to 2012 and is still member of the Board and was President of the European Public Choice Association (April 1992–April 1993) and member of the Board until 1999. He has worked as a consultant for international institutions (mostly the IMF, the EU, the IADB, and the World Bank) on public sector reform and development, with particular emphasis on taxation, natural resources, and decentralization issues. He has published widely on journals, and his recent books include, inter alia, Handbook of Fiscal Federalism, 2006 (with Ehtisham Ahmad); Cases for and against transparency/obfuscation in intergovernmental relations, The Economics of Transparency in Politics (with Albert Breton, Gianluigi Galeotti, Pierre Salmon, and Ronald Wintrobe); Environmental Governance and Decentralization (with A. Breton, S. Dalmazzone, and G. Garrone), 2007; Governing the environment: Salient institutional issues [with A. Breton, S., Dalmazzone, and G. Garrone (Eds), New Horizons in Environmental Economics], 2009; Does Decentralization Enhance Poverty Reduction and Service Delivery? (with Ehtisham Ahmad), 2009; and Decentralization and Reform in Latin America (with JuanPablo Jimenez), 2012.

**Sérgio Gonçalves do Cabo** Born in Faro/Portugal, September 17, 1966. After his Graduation in Law at the University of Lisbon Law School (1984–1989) and his postgraduate Studies in European Community Law at the Portuguese Catholic University (1989–1990), he completed a master's degree in European Community Law at the University of Lisbon Law School (1990–1996) where he has been Assistant Professor (1991–1998 and 2001–2007), teaching public finance law, economic law, tax law, and European community law. He is attorney at law—admitted to the Portuguese Bar Association—1991 (partner of *Luís Silva Morais/Sé rgioGonçalves do Cabo—Law Firm,* with head office in Lisbon/Portugal); former Legal Adviser to the Portuguese Minister of Finance (1995–1998); former Legal Counsel in the Legal Division of the European Monetary Institute (EMI) and later Legal Counsel in the ECB's Directorate General—Legal Services; member of the Audit Commission of the Portuguese Securities Commission (2006 to present); member of the special Commissions for the Privatization of EDP and REN (2011–2012), EMEF and CP Carga (2015); and member of the Portuguese Association for European Law (member of the International Federation of European Law) and of the Inter-Universities Association for European Studies (member of the European Community Studies Association).

He is author and co-author of several books, articles, and papers in the fields of Economic Law, Public Finance Law, and European Community Law.

**Nazaré da Costa Cabral** is Associate Professor in Lisbon Law School and principal researcher of the Center for European, Economic, Fiscal and Tax Law Research (CIDEFF) of the same University (Group IV on "Crises, Public Policies, Fiscal Policy and the Euro"). Nazaré is vice president of the journal *Revista de FinançasPúblicas e Direito Fiscal (Public Finances and Tax Law Journal),* published by IDEFF and Almedina Editors. She is also a member of the Executive and Editorial Board of the journal *Concorrência&Regulação* (*Competition and Regulation),* published by The Portuguese Competition Authority, IDEFF and Almedina, and a member of the Editorial Board of the journal *Economia&Segurança Social* (*Economics and Social Security*), published by Diário de BordoEditores. Nazaré is author of several books, articles, and working papers, and her research areas are mainly on Public Finances, Public Budgeting, and Social Security.

Currently (since 2015), she is national expert at FreSsco ("Network of Experts on Intra-EU Mobility—Free Movement of Workers and Social Security Coordination") and also of the EU project entitled "National feasibility assessment of the different European unemployment benefit scheme options".

**Carmen Díaz-Roldán** is Professor of Economics at Universidad de Castilla-La Mancha and President of the Spanish Association of International Economics and Finance (aeefi.com). She has a BA in Economics from Universidad de Málaga and a PhD in Economics from Universidad Pública de Navarra. Her research interests include macroeconomics, international economics, European economy, and fiscal policy. She is the co-editor of a book on International Economics and a special issue on Economic Policy and the co-author of two books on Macroeconomics. And she has also published papers in international journals like *Economics Letters*, *Czech Journal of Economics and Finance*, *Regional Studies*, *European Planning Studies*, *Journal of Macroeconomics*, *Journal of Policy Modelling*, *Applied Economics*, *Post-Communist Economies*, *European Journal of Political Economy*, *Journal of Applied Economics*, *The World Economy*, and *Panoeconomicus*.

**Adelaide Duarte** Adelaide Duarte is an Associate Professor at the Faculty of Economics of the University of Coimbra and a researcher affiliated with the Group for Monetary and Financial Studies (GEMF). She is PhD Professor and PhD supervisor in the fields of Economic Growth and Economic Policy. She has 40 years of teaching experience mostly in the field of Macroeconomics (BSc, master's, and PhD). She serves as a reviewer for several international publications. She has participated in several international research and teaching programmes. She is the author or co-author of over 50 publications in international scientific peer-reviewed journals, book chapters, and conference proceedings.

**José Renato Gonçalves** has a PhD in Law (Law and Economics of European Monetary Union) and is Professor of Law and Economics at Lisbon University Law School (Faculdade de Direito da Universidade de Lisboa).

His teaching and research activities focus on European Union and Integration Law, Economic and Financial Regulation, Development, Regional and Local Law, and Public Finance.

Currently, he is member of the board of the Centre for Research in European, Economic, Financial and Tax Law (CIDEEFF), of the board of the European Institute (InstitutoEuropeu), and of the editorial board of the quarterly *Competition and Regulation Journal*(*Revista de Concorrência e Regulação*). He is author of several books and articles on EU Law and Economics, Monetary Union, and Competition and Regulation.

**Yannis M. Ioannides** joined the Tufts faculty in September 1995 as the Max and HertaNeubauer Chair and Professor in Economics. Previously, he taught at the University of California, Riverside, 1973–1974, Brown University, 1974–1980, Boston University, 1980–1986, and Virginia Polytechnic Institute and State University, where he also served as Department Head from 1989 to 1995. He held an appointment as a Professor of Economics at the Athens School of Economics and Business, Athens, Greece, 1983–1986, and was a Research Associate at the National Bureau of Economic Research from 1982 to 1993. He received his Diploma in Electrical Engineering from the National Technical University, Athens, Greece, 1968, and his MS in Engineering-Economic Systems, 1970, and his PhD in Engineering-Economic Systems and Economics, 1974, both from Stanford University.

His current research interests combine social economics and macroeconomics, with special emphasis on social economics, economic growth and inequality, social interactions and networks, and housing markets. He teaches courses in macroeconomics, economic growth, social interactions and social networks, and the economics of the European Union. He has participated widely in conferences and has published articles in numerous edited volumes and leading scholarly journals.

**George Kopits** is a senior scholar at the Woodrow Wilson Center, member of Portugal's Public Finance Council, and advisor at the IMF's Independent

Evaluation Office and teaches at the Central European University. In 2009–2011, he served as the first chair of the Fiscal Council in Hungary—elected unanimously by Parliament. In 2004–2009, he was a member of the Monetary Council, National Bank of Hungary. Previous positions include assistant director at the International Monetary Fund and financial economist at the U.S. Treasury Department. He is the author of more than 80 publications. Most recent titles include “Managing the Euro Debt Crisis” in *Rethinking Fiscal Policy after the Crisis* (Cambridge, forthcoming) and *Restoring Public Finance Sustainability: The Role of Independent Fiscal Institutions* (Oxford, 2013). He has held academic appointments at Bocconi, Budapest, Cape Town, Johns Hopkins, Siena, and Vienna universities. He holds a PhD in economics from Georgetown University and is a member of the Hungarian Academy of Sciences.

**Karolien Lenaerts** joined the Jobs and Skills Unit at CEPS as a researcher in June 2015. She obtained a PhD in Economics from Ghent University in 2014, with a dissertation on the productivity spillovers of foreign direct investment, multinational enterprises, and global value chains using micro-level data. In the past, she wrote a thesis on inequality and social segregation in education to obtain a master’s in economics (major globalization) and worked on a project regarding the trajectories and career perspectives of young researchers (aimed at formulating policy recommendations to support them). Her main research interests and expertise lie in the fields of labour and international economics. As a member of the Jobs and Skills Unit, she contributes to a number of projects on education, employment, and mobility, one of which deals with the possibility to introducing a European unemployment benefit scheme.

**Francisco Louçã** is full professor of Economics, Lisbon University, former deputy of the Portuguese National Parliament (Assembleia da República), and former leader of the Portuguese political party “Bloco de Esquerda”. He has published recently in “The Years of High Econometrics” (Routledge) and, with other authors, “OsBurgueses” (Bertrand) and “A Solução Novo Escudo” (Leya).

**Ilaria Maselli** Research Fellow in the Jobs and Skills unit of CEPS (Centre for European Policy Studies). Her main area of expertise is the analysis of labour markets, in particular in their interaction with education and technological change and their institutions. She is the co-author of the recently published books “Let’s Get to Work! The Future of Labour in Europe—Vol. 1 and 2”. She currently co-leads the research on the possibility to create a European unemployment benefit scheme, on which is published extensively in the last months. She holds a master’s degree in European Affairs from the University of Bologna and undertook further training in economics and statistics at the University of Leuven.

**Herman Matthijs** is full professor (Dutch: gewoonhoogleraar) at the universities of Brussels (VrijeUniversiteitBrussel) and of Ghent (Universiteit Gent). He became his doctorate in 1989 with a dissertation concerning the EU budget. Over the last years, he published several books and articles about this item, the EFTA budget, the NATO funding, and the ESA budget.

The author teaches public budget law, public finances, EU budget, political structures of the USA, and International Economic Organizations. Herman Matthijs is member of the "High Council of Finances" in Belgium, which is the advisory board of the Belgian federal and regional governments concerning the budgets. Also he is a member of the Belgian parliamentary committee in the Federal House of Representatives, which controls the finances and the accountancy of the political parties.

**António Mendonça** Full Professor, Department of Economics, University of Lisbon—Lisbon School of Economics and Management (UL-LSEM).

Former Minister of Public Works, Transport and Communications of the XVIII Constitutional Government of Portugal (26.10.99–22.06.2)

Chairman of the School Council (2015–...)

President of CEsA—Centre for African, Asian and Latin American Studies.

Dean of the Lisbon School of Economics and Management (1999–2002 and 2007–2009).

Research in the fields of Macroeconomics, International Economics, International Financial Economics, and Transport Economics and Policy (since 1976).

Invited/Visiting Professor at the University of Orléans (France), Federal University Fluminense (Rio de Janeiro), Federal University of Bahia and the Federal University of Paraíba (Brazil), University AgostinhoNeto (Angola, Lubango Centre and Benguela Centre), and the new University ManduneYaNdemufayo (Angola-Lubango).

Several teaching missions in France, Brazil, Angola, Cape Verde, and Bulgaria.

**Francesco Paolo Mongelli** is Senior Adviser in the Directorate Monetary Policy at the ECB and honorary Professor at the Johann Wolfgang Goethe University of Frankfurt. He holds a BA in Economics from the Free University for Social Studies (LUISS) in Rome and also a master's degree and a PhD in Economics from the Johns Hopkins University in Baltimore. He has worked at the ECB since 1998 as organizer of the research agenda of Economics and editor of the ECB Occasional Paper Series and the monetary sections of the ECB Monthly Bulletin and in the Directorate Monetary Policy. Prior to that, he spent several years as an economist at the International Monetary Fund in Washington. Mr. Mongelli also teaches Economics of Monetary Unions. His papers have been published in various outlets including the Journal of Money Credit and Banking, the Journal of Common Market Studies, EconomieInternationale, Bancaria, and the Journal of Economic Integration.

**Pierre-Alain Muet,** MP Lyon since 2007, is Vice President of the Finance Commission of the National Assembly. He was professor of economics at the Ecole Polytechnique and the Institute of Political Studies in Paris from 1980 to 2004; he was director at the French Economic Observatory (OFCE) from 1981 to 1997.

Advisor to the Prime Minister Lionel Jospin, he founded the Council of economic analysis in 1997 and was the first Deputy Chairman. From 2001 to 2008, he was deputy mayor of Lyon and Vice President of Greater Lyon in charge of economic development. He is the author of twenty books of economics and economic policy. His last books published include "A citizen tax for a more just society", 2010; "A taxation at the service of sustainable growth", 2010; "Taxing financial transactions", 2011; "Cons-truths and sad realities years Sarkozy" in 2012.

As an economist, Pierre-Alain Mute started his career in 1968: developed the first French econometric model to forecast (DMS), which will serve more than 15 years in the development of plans, and then oriented research projects, at CEPREMAP (economic research centre under Planning Commission); from 1977 to 1981, he published numerous works on modelling and economic forecasting and defended his thesis at the University of Paris 1. From 1981 to 1997, he was director of the Econometrics Department of OFCE (French Economic Observatory), an independent organization and pluralistic university study in the economy, created in Raymond Barre initiative, set up by Pierre Mauroy, and chaired by Jean-Marcel Jeanneney. Alongside his work at the OFCE, he taught economics: Ecole Polytechnique 25 years (1980–2004), the Institut d'Etudes Politiques of Paris (1983–1989), and in many foreign universities, notably in Lausanne and Montreal. He has published twenty books on economic theories of growth, unemployment, and economic policies and more recently on taxation. He was the Board Chair of the French Economics Association in 2004–2005.

**Georgios Papadopoulos** is currently a PhD candidate in Economics at the Democritus University of Thrace in Greece. He holds a BSc in Physics and an MSc in Computational Physics from the Aristotle University of Thessaloniki. He has previously worked at the European Central Bank as a research assistant and as a technical consultant. His research interests are in the field of computational economics and model development. Mr. Papadopoulos' research has been published both in institutional papers series such as the Occasional Paper series at the ECB and in scientific series such as the Physica A.

**Elisa Reinhold** is Technical Consultant for the Eurosystem's Household Finance and Consumption Survey at the Directorate General Research of the ECB. She joined the ECB in 2015 as Research Assistance Trainee. Prior to that, she completed the MPhil graduate programme at Tinbergen Institute and worked as a Student Assistant for the University of Amsterdam. Further she holds master's degrees in Economics and in East European Studies from both Humboldt and Free Universities of Berlin, as well as a bachelor's degree in International Economics with Specialization on Central and Eastern European Countries from the University of Regensburg.

**Nuno Cunha Rodrigues** is a Professor at the Faculty of Law, University of Lisbon.

He earned his PhD in legal and economic sciences and his master's degree and completed his graduation in law from the Faculty of Law, University of Lisbon.

He is also Vice President of the European Institute and a member of the Board of the IDEFF.

He was a visiting Professor at the Law School of Louvain-la-Neuve (Belgium), Salgaocar Law School (Goa—India), International Law Institute (New Delhi—India), Eduardo Mondlane University (Maputo—Mozambique), FundaçãoGetúlio Vargas (São Paolo—Brazil), and Catholic University (Lisbon).

He has published several articles and books, namely in his area of expertise which lies in EU law, Economic law, Competition Law, Public procurement, and Public Finance.

He joined the research group on Globalization, Economic Integration and Development: European and Lusophone Perspectives and the group on Crisis, Public Policies, Taxation Policies and the Euro as a member.

**Sergio Rossi** is Full Professor of Economics at the University of Fribourg, Switzerland, where he holds the Chair of Macroeconomics and Monetary Economics since 2005. His research interests are in macroeconomic analysis, particularly as regards national as well as international monetary and financial issues. He has authored and edited many books, contributed several chapters to books, widely published in academic journals, and is frequently invited to radio and TV talk shows discussing contemporary macroeconomic issues at national as well as international level. He is also a columnist for a variety of newspapers addressing economic policy issues related to the euro-area crisis and a member of the scientific board of the *International Journal of Monetary Economics and Finance*, *Economics and Finance Research*, and the *Review of Keynesian Economics*.

**Luís Máximo dos Santos** Master's degree in law (Legal-Economic Sciences) by the Faculty of Law of the University of Lisbon (FDUL). Graduate in Law, Legal-Economical Sciences, by FDUL.

President of the Board of Directors of BancoEspírito Santo, S.A. (since 3 August 2014, appointed by the Portuguese Central Bank). President of the Liquidation Commission of BancoPrivadoPortuguês, S.A. (since May 2010), and of several of its subsidiaries. Researcher of the European, Economic, Financial and Tax Law Investigation Center of the FDUL.University Lecturer at the European, Economic, Financial and Tax Law Institute (IDEFF) of the FDUL (since October 2009). University Lecturer at the European Institute of FDUL (March 1986 to June 2010. Assistant Professor at FDUL, having lectured several courses in the Legal and Economic Area (October 1985–October 1999).

Professor of International Economics at the Law Faculty of the University of Oporto, under the Protocol with FDUL (January 1997–January 1999). More than 50 works published in areas of expertise.

Award granted by the German Foundation FVS, with head office in Hamburg, awarding works related to European Integration, on the occasion of granting of the Robert Schuman Award to His Excellency the President of the Portuguese Republic, Mr. MárioSoares (1987). Member of the Drafting Commission of the Public Finances and Tax Law—Journal Revista de FinançasPúblicas e Direito Fiscal.

Editor for the financial area of the Competition and Regulation Journal—RevistaConcorrência e Regulação—C&R.

**Marta Simões** is an Assistant Professor at the Faculty of Economics, University of Coimbra, and a researcher affiliated with the Group for Monetary and Financial Studies (GEMF). She holds PhD, master's, and bachelor's degrees in Economics from the Faculty of Economics, University of Coimbra. She is the author or co-author of over 40 publications in international scientific peer-reviewed journals, book chapters, and conference proceedings. She serves as a reviewer for several national and international publications. She has 20 years' teaching experience mostly in the field of Macroeconomics (BSc, master's, PhD, and MBA).

**Joseph Stiglitz** was born in Gary, Indiana, in 1943. A graduate of Amherst College, he received his PhD from MIT in 1967, became a full professor at Yale in 1970, and in 1979 was awarded the John Bates Clark Award, given biennially by the American Economic Association to the economist under 40 who has made the most significant contribution to the field. He has taught at Princeton, Stanford, and MIT and was the Drummond Professor and a fellow of All Souls College, Oxford. He is now University Professor at Columbia University in New York, where he is also the founder and Co-President of the university's Initiative for Policy Dialogue. He is also the Chief Economist of the Roosevelt Institute. In 2001, he was awarded the Nobel Prize in economics for his analyses of markets with asymmetric information, and he was a lead author of the 1995 Report of the Intergovernmental Panel on Climate Change, which shared the 2007 Nobel Peace Prize.

His appointments include the following:

University Professor. Teaching at the Columbia Business School, the Graduate School of Arts and Sciences (Department of Economics), and the School of International and Public Affairs

Co-founder and Co-President of the Initiative for Policy Dialogue (IPD)

Co-chair of the High-Level Expert Group on the Measurement of Economic Performance and Social Progress, Organisation for Economic Co-operation and Development

Chief Economist of The Roosevelt Institute

**Francisco Torres** is a Visiting Senior Fellow in European Political Economy at the London School of Economics and Political Science and a Senior Member of St Antony's College, Oxford, since 2012. He is also Adjunct Professor at UCP, Lisbon. He was a Visiting Fellow at the EUI, Florence, at CEPS, Brussels, and at Oxford University and a Visiting Professor at the universities of Victoria, BC, Canada, Rome, Bolzano, and Aveiro (Associate Professor, 5 years). He is a EU and ESC Steering Committee Member of ECPR and ESC, Oxford, respectively, and a Member of CICP, an inter-institutional FCT research centre, as well as a Research Associate of NIFIP, U. Porto, and of PEFM, Oxford University. He has published various books, numerous articles, and book chapters on EMU and EU governance. On that same topic, he has just edited with Erik Jones a Special Issue of the *Journal* *of European Integration* as well as a Routledge book. He holds a PhD in European Political Economy (UCP), an MSc in Economics (UNL, Lisbon), and a "licenciatura" also in Economics (UCP). He also studied Economics at the EUI (PhD programme) and holds an MA in International Affairs from the Johns Hopkins University.

# List of Figures

# List of Tables

# Overview

**Nazaré da Costa Cabral, José Renato Gonçalves, and Nuno Cunha Rodrigues**

**Abstract** In this chapter ('Overview'), a global outlook of the Book *The Euro and the Crisis* is provided. It starts with a general description of the purposes of this academic project, lead by the Center for Research in European, Economic, Financial and Tax Law of the University of Lisbon, to which the Editors—Nazaré da Costa Cabral, José Renato Gonçalves and Nuno Cunha Rodrigues—are linked as researchers. Then it proceeds with a description of each of the subsequent chapters, distributed along four parts, respectively entitled: Part 1—The Eurozone as a (non) Optimum Currency Area; Part 2—A monetary union relying on fiscal policy coordination: achievements, shortcomings and future perspectives; Part 3—New perspectives for macroeconomic stabilizers in the European Union; Part 4—A Budgetary Union as a way-out of the EMU crisis: is it possible?

## 1 General Description

The *Centre for Research in European, Economic, Financial and Tax Law* (CIDEEFF) of the University of Lisbon was created in 2014–2015 as a university research centre with the aim of monitoring and addressing the academic work (especially the guidance of Doctoral and Post-Doctoral Theses), along with functioning as an academic production hub, through the medium of books, articles, working papers and organization of conferences and other themed events, that are capable of contributing to the advancement of the social sciences, especially in the field of Law and Economics. CIDEEFF, under the general coordination of Professor Eduardo Paz Ferreira, is composed of researchers that are mostly University professors, post-doctoral researchers who have a reputation in scientific and academic planning in their areas of expertise—areas that form the basis of the Centre. These specialised areas correspond to research groups, each led by a principal researcher. One of these groups, Group 4, is entitled "Crisis, Public Policies, Fiscal Policy and

N. da Costa Cabral (✉) • J.R. Gonçalves • N. Cunha Rodrigues
CIDEEFF – School of Law, University of Lisbon, Alameda da Universidade, Lisbon, Portugal
e-mail: nazarecabral@fd.ulisboa.pt; rgoncalves@fd.ulisboa.pt; nunorodrigues@fd.ulisboa.pt

 
N. da Costa Cabral et al. (eds.), *The Euro and the Crisis*, Financial and Monetary Policy Studies 43, DOI 10.1007/978-3-319-45710-9_1

the Euro" aiming to conduct studies on the origins and consequences of the the financial crisis that the Eurozone has faced in recent years, and evaluate the effectiveness of the responses adopted in Europe (from 2008 until the present). Within the framework of these objectives, three of CIDEEFF's members, Nazaré da Costa Cabral (main researcher for Group 4), José Renato Gonçalves and Nuno Cunha Rodrigues (both deputy directors of CIDEEFF and members integrated within Group 4) conceived the idea of organising the Collective Book presented here.

The response to the call made by the Organisers/Editors to renowned academicians and experts in European affairs was immensely positive. The authors (with different nationalities and affiliated to prominent academic or sectorial institutions) accepted the challenge to analyse the effects of the recent crisis and evaluate some possible answers to the gridlock that is currently being faced by the Eurozone and the European Union, concerning both monetary policy and the budgetary (and fiscal) policy arms. The 'Brexit' decision, in the 23 June 2016 referendum, can be seen as a consequence of the fundamental contradictions and insufficiencies concerning the construction of the E(M)U building, and highlights the fact that this is a vital moment to discuss truthful reforms, not mere cosmetic changes, concerning those two framing arms. In fact, this wary political outcome reinforces the uncertainty that has surrounded the E(M)U project, particularly since 2007. What is more, it is precisely this uncertainty that justifies the timeliness of such academic research and discussion, such as the Book presented here. The result is an interdisciplinary work that embraces economic, financial and legal perspectives, although including linked items previously selected to ensure the global coherence of its analysis. The main objectives have been largely attained (not to say surpassed), with the result being a unique and high quality publication that will certainly provide an important academic contribution to the debate about the future and viability of the Euro and of the European integration project as a whole.

In Part I, the authors were invited to discuss, through taking into consideration the history of the E(M)U and its recent evolution, whether the main Optimum Currency Areas (OCA) conditions fail to apply in the case of the EMU (departing from Mundell's conditions—flexibility in prices and wages and factor mobility) and, if so, which improvements can be made. In this stance, a characterisation of the EMU is implied as a territory of different and divergent economic structures and the way in which the successive enlargements have reinforced this divergence, ultimately preventing the construction of a truthful and complete OCA. The consequences of this imperfect construction are of a different nature, and the last (current) financial and debt crisis has highlighted some of its aspects, notably the remaining fragmentation of the European financial markets, despite the implementation of a single monetary policy.

In Part II, the authors were challenged to discuss the political and economic foundations of the European Monetary Union and to discuss the current monetary policy framework, also explaining the nature of the relationships between the single monetary policy and fiscal policy since the creation of the EMU. They were also invited to discuss the design of the fiscal policy coordination system and notably to explain the historical background of the Fiscal Compact and its economic rationale. Another topic brought to light was whether the occurrence of 'debt-restructuring procedures' in some Eurozone member countries may curtail fiscal coordination within the area. Debt restructuring economic effects (for the respective Member countries and for the Eurozone as a whole) have also been examined, and it was analysed their legal and financial conditions and ethical implications (on reputational grounds, bearing in mind future sovereign risk assessment).

In Part III, the authors were asked to discuss and to verify, in the current scenario, the accuracy of the optimistic idea that prevailed in the conception of the E(M)U, notably in the Report 'One Market, One Money' (1990), that a monetary union would minimise the occurrence of adverse shocks, and that asymmetric shocks in particular would become less frequent. Departing from existing problems concerning the practical implementation of monetary and fiscal policies, some instruments of macroeconomic stabilisation can be identified as a way to improve the E(M)U's future performance. These stabilisation devices can work as private insurance mechanisms—as the creation of the Banking Union has been—or as government insurance instruments against asymmetric shocks as is the case with debt pooling funds or the proposed European Unemployment Insurance scheme.

Finally, in Part IV, the authors were instructed to analyse the reinforcement of the Budgetary policy arm within the E(M)U, with eventually the creation of a (complete) Budgetary Union in the EU. They were invited to look at European national experiences of fiscal federalism (fiscal relationships between different levels of Government), and to discuss the transposition of Fiscal Federalism insights to the EU scenario, with specific drawbacks able to be anticipated on either normative or on political grounds in the aforementioned transposition. Another issue in this stance, and departing from the existing system of EU budget resources, is the reinforcement of tax harmonisation and tax assignment in the EU, particularly future perspectives concerning income taxes. Furthermore, fiscal federalism enhancement should also involve the development of a system of grants, not only as a way to prevent or to address cyclical shocks but also as a way to overcome horizontal fiscal gaps between EU Member States (e.g. economic convergence), thus helping to create a new environment for long run, sustained economic growth.

## 2 The Structure of the Book

Part I opens with Joseph Stiglitz's chapter, *The fundamental flaws in the Euro Zone framework,* where the author starts by sustaining that the fundamental flaws of the Eurozone, rather than being due merely to fiscal profligacy of some of its Members (even though this factor cannot be neglected) are first and foremost related to market failures within the zone. The main prescriptions of the neoclassical type fail to apply here because there was not sufficient Government intervention to cope with these failures: notably, free mobility of labour without a common debt issuance and free mobility of capital without tax harmonisation leads to an unstable and inefficient allocation of these same factors. Furthermore the author refers to the wrong conception of the European monetary policy, mostly focused on price stabilization, and this has explained the late and weak response given by the European Central Bank to the severe economic downturn suffered by peripheral European countries from 2009 onwards.

For Annette Bongardt and Francisco Torres, in their chapter entitled *EMU as a sustainable currency area*, conditions for sustainability should rely on a preference convergence within a gradual, learning process, and reflect a perceived need for creating ownership of reforms at a national level, through a process of slow-moving convergence of preferences in institutions. Structural reforms relying on individual/national responsibility are required not only to give credibility to the adjustment programmes (and the crisis has reinforced them as legal commitments based on the principle of conditionality), but most of all because these reforms are a condition for sustainable growth. Reforms should lead Europe to a new paradigm of economic growth, sustained on the idea of environmental protection, notably through the promotion of private green investments. In this domain, EU harmonised environmental regulation (and a new role for taxation) should be able to provide a push for EU green innovation and cost-efficiency.

On the other hand, as mentioned by Sergio Rossi in the chapter entitled *A structural-reform proposal for a two-speed European monetary union*, the EMU is not yet an optimum currency area for various other reasons, notably because the ECB does not work as a European Treasury able to support fiscal policy across the Euro area, by purchasing government bills, bonds, and treasuries in the primary market. Considering the information provided in the course of the TARGET 2 payment system, notably when exhibiting 'different euros' that *effectively* exist within the Euro Area, the author advocates that this system can eventually assume a new role regarding the institution of a two-speed monetary union. This structural reform within the monetary union would transform the euro into a truly international currency, and at the same time would contribute to economic and financial stability and restore an idea of cohesion and solidarity among Member States, which are, as noticed, constitutive principles of the European integration project.

In the two following Chapters—the first, from Francesco Mongelli, Georgios Papadopoulos and Elisa Reinhold, with the title *Are Euro Area economic structures changing?*, and the second from João Sousa Andrade, Adelaide Duarte and Marta Simões, entitled *Differences in human capital and openness to trade as barriers to growth and convergence in the EU*—the topic of convergence/divergence between member countries is brought to light. The former addresses the fundamental economic transformation that has occurred in the Member States, starting even before the E(M)U was launched, notably considering the contribution given to the economy, in terms of gross value added, by certain economic sectors, such as industry, construction and the public sector. Furthermore, the findings concerning the effects of the recent crisis over these economic sectors, which are different for different E(M)U countries, seem to provide a new argument to the *new geography theory*, according to which by promoting trade and factor mobility, deeper integration will produce new economies of scale, activity specialisation and economic agglomeration, ultimately leading to regional disparities and economic divergence. The latter, on the other hand, relying on a regression approach, examines the growth and convergence process of 14 EU member states over the 1960–2014 period. The results confirm that different human capital/trade regimes correspond to different growth performances due to technological catch-up, external competitiveness, the weight of tradable goods, physical capital accumulation, government size and public debt.

In the final Chapter of Part I, entitled *Has the euro any future as part of secular stagnation?*, Francisco Louçã, based on Larry Summers's idea, discusses the reasons for the Euro's failure and the political and economic alternatives to this failed project. The 'exit' hypothesis (notably for small and poor countries as is the case with Portugal) is analysed and the main implications (advantages and losses) are investigated. In Louçã's opinion, permanence in the euro—which notwithstanding everything would be the best solution—will only be possible if based upon a new dimension of solidarity amongst Member States and above all on the basis of a different vision for democracy.

Part II also departs from Democracy (or the lack of it in the European construction). The two initial Chapters—from Luís Máximo dos Santos, entitled *The European Monetary Union: political motivation* and from Pierre-Alain Muet, entitled *The great recession of 2012–2014: the monetary union challenged by national egoisms*—converge in the idea that a project—the construction of a monetary union—that began by being 'political' in its essence (politically sustained), has been progressively captured by national egoisms that the late crisis ended up by exacerbating. Today, the E(M)U is facing this fundamental contradiction: when it requires more political support (both at the national and European levels) it is confronted with growing national-wide scepticism and (democratic) rejection—and again the 'Brexit' solution is quite elucidative about the current 'state of the art'. The European political leaders are now facing these two (real or apparent) opposing demands: on the one hand, to internally respond to voters' expectations, notably by addressing the increasing fear caused by the integration process itself (the side effects of openness and of free movement); on the other hand, to positively respond to the challenge of deeper integration both on economic and political grounds.

Sometimes, policy-type insights can be counter-productive. The 'Deficit Excessive Procedure', implemented by the Stability and Growth Pact—SGP and lying behind the Fiscal Compact framework, is illustrative about this. Since its inception, the SGP has shown itself to be weakly enforceable in certain cases (for certain countries) and strongly binding in others (or at least menacing). The menace of sanctions has greatly depended on political motivations and on the current balance of power existing within the European institutions rather than on the *natural* capability of the SGP to be enforceable. Furthermore, the inherent complexity of its analytical tools, notably GDP data and the notion of structural balance, has fostered some political manipulation. Ansgar Belke, in his chapter entitled *The Fiscal Compact and the Excessive Deficit Procedure—Relics of bygone times?*, puts—in his own words—a finger in this wound. In his view, the road to a sustainable 'economic governance', through fiscal federalism in conjunction with an incentive-compliant banking union, should lead to market-based interest rates able to provide a better incentive and sanction mechanism than the 'Excessive Deficit Procedure' has proven to be.

In the following Chapter, Yannis M. Ioannides proposes *A Conceptual Framework for Reforms versus Debt in the Context of a Fiscal Union within the European Monetary Union*. The author adds this unique insight from International Economics to explain relationships between integrated economies in the presence of debt, claiming that size matters (e.g. the dimension of the population) for decision-making purposes, and notably explains the way in which a small country's *fundamentals* affect its bargaining power, especially over a full range of fiscal policy. The equilibrium model here presented helps for instance to frame the 'Greek case' (a small indebted economy in a monetary union) and the negotiating impasse with the European institutions and the other member States, during the peak of the 2015 political crisis.

Debt, sovereign debt, and debt renegotiation have definitively entered the European political agenda; Greece, in particular, has managed over the successive adjustment programmes to renegotiate the terms and conditions of its debt payment. Sérgio Gonçalves do Cabo, in his Chapter entitled *Sovereign debt restructuring in a monetary union: the case of the euro area Member States* discusses the legitimacy and suitability of debt renegotiation procedures. The author starts out by analysing the concept of debt restructuring and its modalities, and then addresses its main implications and drawbacks. In Cabo's view, restructuring "public debt is at the antipodes of economic policy co-ordination and convergence of euro area Member States sharing a common currency", representing "a major failure of the decentralized economic governance system that underpins the single currency." Furthermore, on the other hand, alternatives already exist—notably the path that was opened by the European Stability Mechanism considered as an *embryo* for a European Treasury and for EU joint issuance of public debt.

Macroeconomic stabilisation is at the heart of the current academic and political EU debate. Part III starts with two Chapters related to the monetary policy arm, and particularly with a characterisation and assessment of the European Central Bank (ECB) policy in the aftermath of the 2007 crisis. Both Fritz Breuss in his Chapter *The Crisis Management of the ECB* and António Mendonça, in a chapter entitled *Unconventional monetary policy of the ECB and the international economic and financial crisis: efficiency versus exhaustion,* refer to the justification for the adoption of 'quantitative easing' measures, notably after 2012, and the main economic and financial shortfalls that can be attached to them.

Further in this stance, Nazaré da Costa Cabral in the Chapter entitled *The Eurozone's Private and Governmental Shock Absorbers: Current Setup and Future Prospects* proceeds to identify and investigate the respective categories within the two main types of shock absorbers—private and governmental shock. As for private shock absorbers (that imply the reinforcement of 'market forces' within the E(M)U), the author indicates certain measures that are intended either to ensure the completion of the internal market or to address sectorial market fragmentation, as is the case with the creation of the Banking Union. As for governmental shock absorbers, the author then distinguishes between macro stabilising measures that can be implemented outside the EU's budget (e.g. the creation of a new 'Debt Agency' or the institution of a new 'European unemployment insurance scheme') and those measures that can be adopted through the current EU budget, with it being stressed though that, for this latter case, significant changes in the design of tax assignment criteria and rules for the allocation of funds would be required.

The preceding Chapter introduces the two subsequent and closing ones. In fact, from the so-called private shock absorbers, the implementation of a Banking Union is considered to be the most important (albeit incomplete) political decision after the crisis and, among the so-called government insurance mechanisms, the creation of a European unemployment insurance scheme is now already, following academic contributions, being discussed and assessed on an institutional basis (by the European Commission and the current Slovakian European Presidency). The Chapter written by Nuno Cunha Rodrigues and José Renato Gonçalves, entitled *The European banking union and the Economic and Monetary Union: the puzzle is yet to be completed,* and the one by Miroslav Beblavý, Karolein Lenaerts and Ilaria Maselli, entitled *The (future) European unemployment insurance and its role as an automatic stabiliser* present the advantages, risks, and main drawbacks that can be found, respectively, in the Banking Union and in the new unemployment scheme—both, in their own ways, aiming to act as macroeconomic stabilisation devices.

The ultimate subject of the debate around the reform of the E(M)U concerns the eventual creation of a Budgetary Union. Is it possible? Is it strictly necessary? The decentralisation experience on a national basis can be elucidative both on economic and political grounds regarding the 'promises and perils' involving the federalist path. In the first Chapter of Part IV, entitled *Achieving accountable governance and structural reforms—lessons from the crisis in Europe*, Ehtisham Ahmad and Giorgio Brosio assess administrative reforms made following the crisis in selected countries—e.g. Spain, France and Denmark. The evidence presented shows that with the exception of Denmark, the restructuring of government levels and numbers has proved difficult. The Chapter highlights pure normative-economic (i.e., achievable scale economies) and political economy arguments, and how they can be transposed by other fiscal federal experiences (as is the case with the EU).

In fact, the idea of fiscal federalism relies on a central budget of a sufficient dimension and making use of a standard set of revenues (taxes) and expenditures able to fulfil conventional fiscal functions—notably, allocation, redistribution and macroeconomic stabilisation. It is commonly recognised that the EU's budget does not have the conditions or dimension to be assigned to these functions. In the subsequent Chapter, entitled *The financing of the European Union Budget,* Herman Matthijs precisely explains and quantifies the evolution of the EU budget (concerning the respective main sources of financing) and refers to its main and persistent transparency and adequacy problems. These problems, as indicated, can condition or prevent a future increase or enlargement. In the subsequent Chapter, entitled *Toward a Closer Union in Europe: Elusive Mirage or Reality within Grasp?*, George Kopits, departing notably from the theoretical insights of Fiscal Federalism literature, investigates the two main branches of the EU budget, the revenue side and the expenditure side, and then explores the prospects and tasks for further political and fiscal integration—in line with well-known guiding principles, such as subsidiarity and solidarity. Last but not the least is the Chapter entitled *The scope for a budgetary union in the European monetary union*, where Oscar Bajo-Rubio and Carmen Díaz-Roldán discuss the macroeconomics of a monetary union focusing on the scope for coordination of budgetary policies. Using public deficit as a policy instrument, they proceed to identify the full cooperation of fiscal policies with a budgetary or fiscal union and to show to what extent the fully coordinated fiscal action of the Eurozone members should be complemented with fiscal discipline, a zone-wide system of transfers, or an automatic mechanism to ensure the stability of the Eurozone.

# Part I
# The Eurozone as a (non) Optimum Currency Area

# The Fundamental Flaws in the Euro Zone Framework

**Joseph E. Stiglitz**

**Abstract** Europe has not done well in the years since the 2008 crisis, with a double dip recession and a recovery far slower than that of the US from whence the crisis came. Among the key reasons for this dismal performance is the euro, or more precisely, the structure of the Eurozone, the institutions, rules, and regulations that were created to ensure growth and stability of a single currency amongst a diverse set of countries—and the failure to do some of the things (like the establishment of a common deposit insurance system) that should have been done. The paper describes how Europe created a divergent system, with increasing disparities between the richer and poorer countries, and the role of certain beliefs, prevalent at the time, but since questioned, about what makes for good economic performance.

The euro was a political project, conceived to help bring the countries of Europe together. It was widely recognized at the time that Europe was not an optimal currency area.[1] Labor mobility was limited, the countries' economies experienced different shocks, and there were different long-term productivity trends. While it was a political project, the politics was not strong enough to create the economic institutions that might have given the euro a fair chance of success. The hope was that over time, this would happen. Bur, of course, when things were going well, there was little impetus to "complete" the project, and when a crisis finally occurred (with the global recession that began in the United States in 2008) it was hard to think through carefully what should be done to ensure the success of the euro.

I and others who supported the concept of European integration hoped that when Greece went into crisis, in January, 2010, decisive measures would be taken that

---

Excerpt of the chapter "Crises: Principles and Policies: With an Application to the Eurozone Crisis," in *Life After Debt: The Origins and Resolutions of Debt Crisis*, Joseph E. Stiglitz and Daniel Heymann (eds.), Houndmills, UK and New York: Palgrave Macmillan, 2014. Permission granted by the Author and rights acquisition to the Publisher.

[1]See Mundell (1961).

J.E. Stiglitz
Columbia University, Uris Hall, 3022 Broadway, Room 212, New York, NY 10027-6902, USA
e-mail: jes322@columbia.edu



N. de Costa Cabral et al. (eds.), *The Euro and the Crisis*, Financial and Monetary Policy Studies 43, DOI 10.1007/978-3-319-45710-9_2

would demonstrate that the European leaders at least understood that further actions would be needed to enable the euro to survive. That did not happen, and quickly, a project designed to bring Europe together became a source of divisiveness. Germans talked about Europe not being a transfer union—a euphemistic and seemingly principled way of saying that they were uninterested in helping their partners, as they reminded everyone of how they had paid so much for the reunification of Germany. Not surprisingly, others talked about the high price they had paid in World War II. Selective memories played out, as Germans talked about the dangers of high inflation; but was it inflation or high unemployment that had brought on the political events that followed?

Greece was castigated for its high debts and deficits, and it was natural to blame the crisis on excessive profligacy, but again there was selective memory: In the years before the crisis bit Spain and Ireland had low debt to GDP ratios and a fiscal surplus. No one could blame the crisis that these countries faced on fiscal profligacy. It was thus clear that Germany's prescription, that what was required were stronger and more effectively enforced fiscal constraints, would not prevent a recurrence of crisis, and there was good reason to believe that stronger constraints—austerity—would make the current crisis worse. Indeed, by so manifestly showing that Europe's leaders did not understand the fundamentals underlying the crisis—or that if they did, by manifesting such enormous resistance to undertaking the necessary reforms in the European framework—they almost surely contributed to the markets' lack of confidence, helping to explain why each of the so-called rescue measures was viewed as only a temporary palliative.

In the remainder of this section, I describe several of the underlying *structural* properties of the Euro Zone that, if they do not make crises inevitable, certainly make them more likely to occur. (What is required is not so much the structural adjustment of the individual countries, but the structural adjustment of the euro framework.) Many of these were rules that reflected the neoclassical model, with the associated neoliberal policy prescriptions, which were fashionable (in some circles) at the time of the creation of the euro. Europe made two fundamental mistakes: first, it enshrined in its "constitution" these fads and fashions, the concerns of the time, without providing enough flexibility in responding to changing circumstances and understandings. And secondly, even at the time, the limits of the neoclassical model had been widely exposed—the problems posed, for instance, by imperfect competition, information, and markets to which I alluded earlier. The neoclassical model failed to recognize the many market failures that require government intervention, or in which government intervention would improve the performance of the economy. Thus, most importantly from a macroeconomic perspective, there was the belief that so long as the government maintained a stable macro-economy—typically interpreted as maintaining price stability—overall economic performance would be assured. By the same token, if the government kept budgets in line (kept deficits and debts within the limit set by Maastricht Convention) the economies would "converge," so that the single currency system would work. The founders of the Euro Zone seemed to think that these budgetary/macro-conditions were necessary and essentially sufficient for the countries to converge, that is, to have sufficient "similarity" that a common currency would work. They were wrong. The founders of the Euro Zone were also focused on government failure, rather than market failure, and thus they circumscribed governments, setting the stage four the market failures that would bring on the euro crisis.

Much of the framework built into the Euro Zone would have enhanced efficiency, *if Europe had gotten the details right and if the neoclassical model were correct*. But the devil is in the detail, and some of the provisions, even within the neoliberal framework, led to inefficiency and instability.

*Free mobility of factors without a common debt leads to the inefficient and unstable allocation of factors*. The principle of free mobility is to ensure that factors move to where (marginal) returns are highest, and if factor prices are equal to marginal productivity, that should happen. But what individuals care about, for instance, is the after-tax returns to labor, and this depends not only on the marginal productivity of labor (in the neoclassical model) but also on taxes and the provision of public goods. Taxes, in turn, depend in part on the burden imposed by *inherited debt*. Ireland, Greece and Spain face high levels of inherited debt. In these countries, the incentive for outmigration, and is especially so, because that debt did not increase to its current levels as a result of investments in education, technology, or infrastructure that is, through the acquisition of assets, but rather as a result of financial and macro-economic mismanagement. This implies migration away from these highly indebted countries to those with less indebtedness, even when marginal productivities are the same; and the more individuals move out, the greater the "equilibrium" tax burden on the remainder, accelerating the movement of labor away from an efficient allocation.[2] (Of course, in the short run, migration may have positive benefits to the crisis country, both because it reduces the burden of unemployment insurance, and as the remittances back home provide enhanced domestic purchasing power. Whether in the short run these "benefits" to migration out-weight the adverse effects noted above is an empirical question. The migration also hides the severity of the underlying downturn, since it means that the unemployment rate is less, possibly far less, than it otherwise would be.)[3]

*Free mobility of capital and goods without tax harmonization can lead to an inefficient allocation of capital and/or reduce the potential for redistributive taxation, leading to high levels of after-tax and transfer inequality*. Competition among jurisdictions can be healthy, but there can also be a race to the bottom. Capital goes to the jurisdiction which taxes it at the lowest rate, not where its marginal productivity is the highest. To compete, other jurisdictions must lower the taxes they impose on capital, and since capital is more unequally distributed than labor, this reduces the scope for redistributive taxation. (A similar argument goes for the allocation of skilled labor.) Inequality, it is increasingly recognized, is not just a

---

[2]Interestingly, this problem has long been recognized in the theory of fiscal federalism/local public goods. See, for example, Stiglitz (1977, 1983a, b).

[3]By the same token, if some of the burden of taxation is imposed on capital, it will induce capital to move out of the country.

moral issue: it also affects the performance of the economy in numerous ways (Stiglitz 2012).

*Free migration might result in politically unacceptable patterns of location of economic activity.* The general theory of migration/local public goods has shown that decentralized patterns of migration may well result in inefficient and socially undesirable patterns of location of economic activity and concentrations of population. There can be congestion and agglomeration externalities (both positive and negative) that arise from free migration. That is why many countries have an explicit policy for regional development, attempting to offset the inefficient and/or socially unacceptable patterns emerging from unfettered markets.

In the context of Europe, free migration (especially that arising from debt obligations inherited from the past) may result in a depopulation not only of certain regions within countries but also of certain countries. One of the important adjustment mechanisms in the United States (which shares a common currency) is migration; and if such migration leads to the depopulation of an entire state, there is limited concern.[4] But Greece or Ireland are, and should be, concerned about the depopulation of their countries.

*The single market principle for financial institutions and capital too can lead to a regulatory race to the bottom, with at least some of the costs of the failures borne by other jurisdictions.* The failure of a financial institution imposes costs on others (evidenced so clearly in the crisis of 2008), and governments will not typically take into account these cross-border costs. That is why either there has to be regulation by the host country (Stiglitz et al. 2010), or there has to be strong regulation at the European level.

Worse still, *confidence in any country's banking system rests partially in the confidence of the ability and willingness of the bank's government to bail it out (and/or to the existence of institutional frameworks that reduce the likelihood that a bailout will be necessary, that there are funds set aside should a bailout be necessary, and that there are procedures in place to ensure that depositors will be made whole).* Typically, there is an implicit subsidy, from which banks in jurisdictions with governments with greater bailout capacity benefit. Thus, money flowed into the United States after the 2008 global crisis, which failures in the United States had brought about, simply because there was more confidence that the United States had the willingness and ability to bail out its banks. Similarly, today in Europe: what Spaniard or Greek would rationally keep his money in a local bank, when there is (almost) equal convenience and greater safety in putting it in a German bank?[5] Only by paying much higher interest rates can banks in those countries compete, but such an action would put them at a competitive

[4]Some see an advantage: buying influence over that country's senators because less expensive.

[5]The exit from Spanish banks while significant—and leading to a credit crunch—has been slower than some had anticipated. This in turn is a consequence of institutional and market imperfections (for example, rules about knowing your customer, designed to limit money laundering), which interestingly the neo-classical model underlying much of Europe's policy agenda ignored. There is far less of a single market than it is widely thought.

disadvantage; and the increase in interest rates that is required may be too great—the bank would quickly appear to be non-viable. What happens typically is capital flight (or, in the current case, what has been described as a capital jog: the surprise is not that capital is leaving, but that it is not leaving faster). But that sets into motion a downward spiral: as capital leaves, the country's banks restrict lending, the economy weakens, the perceived ability of the country to bail out its banks weakens, and capital is further incentivized to leave.

There are two more fallacies that are related to the current (and inevitable) failures of the Euro Zone. The first is the belief that there are natural forces for convergence in productivity, without government intervention. There can be increasing returns (reflected in clustering), the consequence of which is that countries with technological advantages maintain those advantages, unless there are countervailing forces brought about by government (industrial) policies. But European competition laws prevented, or at least inhibited, such policies.[6]

The second is the belief that necessary, and almost sufficient, for good macroeconomic performance is that the monetary authorities maintain low and stable inflation. This led to the mandate of the European Central Bank to focus on inflation, in contrast to that of the Federal Reserve, whose mandate includes growth, employment, and (now) financial stability. The contrasting mandates can lead to an especially counterproductive response to a crisis, especially one which is accompanied by cost-push inflation arising from high energy or food prices. While the Fed lowered interest rates in response to the crisis, the continuing inflationary concerns in Europe did not lead to matching reductions there. The consequence was an appreciating euro, with adverse effects on European output. Had the ECB taken actions to weaken the euro, it would have stimulated the economy, partially offsetting the effects of austerity. As it was, it allowed the US to engage in competitive devaluation against it.

It also meant that the ECB (and central banks within each of the member countries) studiously avoided doing anything about the real estate bubbles that were mounting in several of the countries. This was in spite of the fact that the East Asian crisis had shown that private sector misconduct—even when there is misconduct in government—could lead to an economic crisis. Europe similarly paid no attention to mounting current account balances in several of the countries.

Ex post, many policymakers admit that it was a mistake to ignore these current account imbalances or financial market excesses. But the underlying ideology then (and still) provides no framework for identifying good "imbalances," when capital is flowing into the country because markets have rationally identified good investment opportunities, and those that are attributable to market excesses.

---

[6]Even the World Bank has changed its views on industrial policies; yet views about industrial policies are to a large extent enshrined in the Euro Zone's basic economic framework. See Lin (2012) and Stiglitz and Lin (2013a, b).

## References

Lin JY (2012) New structural economies: a framework for rethinking development policies. The World Bank, Washington, DC

Mundell R (1961) A theory of optimum currency areas. Am Econ Rev 51(4):657–665

Stiglitz JE (1977) Theory of local public goods. In: Feldstein MS, Inman RP (eds) The economics of public services. Macmillan Press, London, pp 274–333 (Paper presented to IEA Conference, Turin, 1974)

Stiglitz JE (1983a) The theory of local public goods twenty-five years after Tiebout: a perspective. In: Zodrow GR (ed) Local provision of public services: the Tiebout model after twenty-five years. Academic, New York, pp 17–53

Stiglitz JE (1983b) Public goods in open economies with heterogeneous individuals. In: Thisse JF, Zoller HG (eds) Locational analysis of public facilities. North-Holland, Amsterdam, pp 55–78

Stiglitz JE (2012) The price of inequality. W. W Norton, New York (Spanish edition published by Taurus)

Stiglitz JE, Lin JY (eds) (2013a) The industrial policy revolution I: the role of government beyond ideology. Palgrave Macmillan, Basingstoke

Stiglitz JE, Lin JY (eds) (2013b) The industrial policy revolution II: Africa in the 21st century. Palgrave Macmillan, Basingstoke

Stiglitz JE, Sen A, Fitoussi JP (2010) Mismeasuring our lives: why GDP doesn't add up. The New York Press, New York

# EMU as a Sustainable Currency Area

**Annette Bongardt and Francisco Torres**

**Abstract** EMU's governance framework was incomplete at its inception. Its institutional fragilities allowed for the building up of competitiveness and fiscal disequilibria in some Member States during its first 10 years and left the Eurozone unprepared to cope with the sovereign debt crisis. While some of those weaknesses have been addressed in response to the crisis EMU's governance framework remains incomplete to date and therefore vulnerable to adverse market and political-economy pressures. This chapter argues that EMU—or at least the membership of individual countries—will not be sustainable without national adjustment capacity and willingness to implement economic reforms. Those reforms are also a pre-condition for promoting sustainable growth and hence a credible crisis exit strategy. Although EMU's resilience could still be guaranteed through other mechanisms in the absence of sufficient national adjustment capacity, notably a banking union with an orderly state bankruptcy regime, even if feasible it would mean a rather different model of European integration.

**JEL Classification** E42 • E61 • E65

---

We would like to thank, without implicating, seminar participants in Oxford (ESC, St Antony's), London (LSE and King's College) and Florence (EUI), and in particular Paul De Grauwe, Charles Goodhardt, Erik Jones, Ramon Marimon, Kalypso Nicolaïdis and Waltraud Schelkle, for valuable comments and discussions.

A. Bongardt (✉)
European Institute, London School of Economics and Political Science, London, UK

UFP, Porto, Portugal

CICP, Minho, Portugal
e-mail: a.bongardt@lse.ac.uk

F. Torres
European Institute, London School of Economics and Political Science, London, UK

CICP, Minho, Portugal

Universidade Nova de Lisboa, Lisbon, Portugal
e-mail: f.torres@lse.ac.uk

 
N. da Costa Cabral et al. (eds.), *The Euro and the Crisis*, Financial and Monetary Policy Studies 43, DOI 10.1007/978-3-319-45710-9_3

# 1 Introduction

At Maastricht, Economic and Monetary Union (EMU) membership was made conditional on the fulfilment of entry criteria that would test whether (or show to those opposing EMU or too large an EMU, that) there was a 'sufficient' prior convergence of preferences with regard to both inflation and budgetary and fiscal discipline. As in the case of the creation of the European Monetary System (EMS) before, a number of institutional questions remained open in order to allow for the establishment of a timescale for the creation of EMU. Moreover, besides the need to allow for the establishment of a timescale to implement EMU, its Maastricht blueprint could not have been complete for a variety of reasons, notably the idiosyncrasy of the European construct, which had no parallel in previous experiences. To be sure, that incompleteness had been pointed out at the time by academics (Giavazzi and Wyplosz 2016), policy makers and politicians but member states could only agree on the lowest common denominator, hoping for preferences to converge (Torres 2009).[1] Open questions primarily concerned how to enforce the convergence/stability (entry) criteria once countries had joined EMU and how to further coordinate budgetary and various other policies in order to guarantee EMU's sustainability. The fiscal (entry) criteria were complemented in 1997 by the establishment of the Stability and Growth Pact (SGP) with regard to the post-entry period. They did not however address institutional and economic gaps in the criteria identified by some economists for an optimum currency area (OCA). Still, endogenous developments could have improved matters over time (see Corsetti 2010; De Grauwe and Mongelli 2005; Torres 2009).[2]

Unlike in the case of a common monetary policy, where national central banks had been made independent as EMU qualifying criteria, there was no parallel establishment at the national level of enhanced fiscal rules or national institutional fiscal arrangements in future Eurozone member countries. As a result, the monitoring of fiscal policies and debt accumulation was not effective: the SGP did not function satisfactorily as a fiscal disciplinary device, as its legalistic approach failed when the European Commission faced national arguments of "special circumstances" (Giavazzi and Wyplosz 2016). No Eurozone institutional mechanisms

[1] Jones et al. (2016) argue that the incompleteness of EMU was both a cause of the euro crisis and a characteristic pattern of the policy responses to the crisis.

[2] Traditional OCA theory states that the condition for a country to surrender its monetary autonomy and join a monetary union is that the (microeconomic) efficiency gains must outweigh the macroeconomic costs of participation. These factors are dependent on the characteristics of the country in question. OCA theory has tended to focus on the stabilization policies (the macroeconomic costs) of a monetary union, namely the loss of the exchange rate as an adjustment mechanism. For an analysis of the role played by OCA theory in the process of European monetary integration, see Krugman (1993), Mongelli (2008, 2010) and Eichengreen (2014). For a critical appraisal (namely of the unreliable role of the exchange rate or of labour mobility as adjustment mechanisms) as part of the more recent transatlantic debate on EMU as a non-OCA, see Schelkle (2016).

were put in place for a systematic detection and correction of private sector imbalances, because those imbalances would be subject to—and thought to be taken care of by—creditor discipline. As Giavazzi and Wyplosz (2016) note, the European Central Bank (ECB) had frequently expressed frustration with governments that were not fiscally disciplined and with financial markets that did not price public debts accordingly[3] but its warnings went ignored. In addition, creditors allowed private imbalances and debts in some cases to reach unsustainable levels.

In 2000, at the Lisbon European Council Member states also committed to an economic reform agenda. Under the heading of the Lisbon Strategy (2000–2010), common EU objectives and benchmarks were established for member state performance, which were to be gauged against agreed targets. The Lisbon Strategy was above all driven by international competitiveness concerns and the objective to make the internal market deliver economic results (growth and employment; sustainable development) in a globalized world economy, rather than by monetary union requirements. Of course, to the extent that structural reforms and economic liberalization promote price and wage flexibility, the Lisbon economic agenda would also contribute to a better functioning of the monetary union.

The way the Lisbon strategy and its successor, the Europe 2020 Strategy, were set up was conducive to preference convergence within a gradual, learning process, and reflects a perceived need for creating ownership of reforms at the national level, through a process of slow-moving convergence of preferences on institutions (Bongardt and Torres 2013b). The implementation of their commitments came to hinge on soft coordination rather than being effected through the Community method. Given that instruments remained a national competence, the convergence of preferences relied on member states' willingness and capacity of putting best practice and mutual learning to good use. Enforcement relied on public and peer pressure, exerted via benchmarking and ranking of member states' performance (Bongardt and Torres 2012). Yet, by and large public opinion in member states failed to take ownership of reforms and exert pressure with a view to institutional modernization, and peer pressure was largely ineffectual and official ranking abandoned.

The remainder of this chapter is organised as follows. The next section shows how EMU incompleteness allowed for the building up of macroeconomic imbalances throughout its first decade. Section 3 examines how the crisis brought to the forefront additional demands on the economic union part of an incomplete EMU. Section 4 focuses on the need for and importance of creating ownership of reforms at the national level. Section 5 argues the case for a sustainable growth strategy with structural reforms at the national level as a pre-condition for a credible exit strategy and a durable recovery. Section 6 operationalizes that strategy. Section 7 concludes.

[3] Barta and Schelkle (2016) address this lack of support from markets (rating agencies) in disciplining budgetary policies during EMU's first decade. Eijffinger et al. (2015) argue that markets had behaved in a rational manner, taking the no bailout clause as unreliable from EMU's inception. Risk weights on sovereign debts of euro members were also set at zero by the official sector.

## 2 EMU's First Decade: The Building Up of Macroeconomic Imbalances

Despite a rather successful first decade by many accounts, EMU's incompleteness—rooted in an incomplete institutional model beyond monetary policy—implied persistent institutional fragilities and allowed for building up (financial, fiscal and competitiveness) disequilibria. The lack of national reforms in some member states also contributed to growing intra-EMU macroeconomic imbalances.[4]

In the EU, the increase in economic integration to a monetary union had brought about a qualitative change, in which different member state conceptions of the mixed economy (with its different state-market relations), when in contradiction with additional monetary union requisites on the economic side, became no longer sustainable. Albeit to different degrees, member states—especially those which were to experience severe problems later on in the sovereign debt crisis—failed (some of them significantly) to internalize what living in a monetary union meant, let alone to internalize the challenges posed by globalization, and delayed long-due reforms. Any proposed remedies—as it were, even more so under time pressure—would necessarily be more 'intrusive' in member state affairs. After all, a country's permanence in EMU requires the compliance with those commitments it made under constrained decentralization, needed to sustain EMU.

The combination of the absence of market pressure during EMU's first decade—when financial markets failed to differentiate between the sustainability of public debt and external imbalances among participants—and non-binding and not enforceable commitments in the case of the Lisbon Strategy and binding but not enforceable rules in the case of the SGP contributed to the procrastination of some of those (economic and institutional) reforms. The same holds true for the announced objectives (various times voted in national and European elections) to which various governments and political parties had subscribed and which were poorly implemented. It is therefore hardly surprising that economic policy coordination, effected through the Lisbon Strategy and the SGP, failed to deliver during EMU's first decade.

The combination of those two factors—the lack of national reforms in some member states, in conjunction with the incapacity of financial markets to distinguish between Eurozone sovereigns—paved the way for increasing intra-EMU macroeconomic imbalances. Apart from its weak enforcement, the Lisbon Strategy also lacked any specific EMU dimension to address the increased interdependencies between members of a monetary union.[5]

---

[4]Most EU countries had failed to internalize the established common objectives of fiscal (SGP) and economic and social governance (the Lisbon and Europe 2020 Strategies).

[5]With the launch of EMU's second phase in 1994, the nature of European integration changed, as developments in any member state could have a much greater impact on the others (Mongelli et al. 2016). The crises have been illustrative in this regard.

# 3 The Crises and Additional Demands on Economic Union

## 3.1 *Towards a* 'Genuine EMU'?

EMU's incompleteness in the economic union part left its (financial, fiscal and economic) governance institutions unable to encompass increasing policy interdependence, let alone capable of dealing with the cumulative effects of the financial and sovereign debt crises.[6] EMU institutions, already affected by the 2008–2009 global financial crisis, were unable to deal with the sovereign debt crisis that began in 2010.[7]

Although the EU moved towards increased coordinated financial supervision in response to the 2008/2009 global financial crisis, it was insufficient. However, in the sovereign debt crisis the large negative spillovers, originating in the economic part of the union where there had been insufficient financial, fiscal and economic policy coordination and domestic adjustments to prevent macroeconomic instability and imbalances, affected the monetary side (Torres 2015). They came to put at risk even the survival of the monetary union. The sovereign debt crisis thereby added urgency to the completion of the economic union side of EMU. Member States responded by seeking to address the causes of the crisis, namely banking sector fragilities, budgetary disequilibria and competitiveness differentials between member states. In order to curb spillovers into the monetary sphere, in particular in the Eurozone, it was most urgent to break the feedback loop between weak banks and over-indebted sovereigns.

The advances in economic governance were triggered in the crisis through successive steps, prompted by the need to ensure the survival of EMU in the light of market pressure. Different measures meant to strengthen fiscal discipline and economic coordination have come to address some of EMU's fragilities since 2010 as a result. These responses, together with the creation of the European Stability Mechanism (ESM) as a permanent rescue fund, new arrangements for financial regulation and supervision and better tools for macro-prudential supervision, arguably reduce the risk of future crises and strengthen the capacity of crisis management.[8] However, and although those incremental steps add up over time and foster

[6]As Bini-Smaghi (2016) points out, Eurozone governance combines a centralization of competences in policy areas such as monetary policy and now banking supervision (the responsibility of the ECB) and competition policy, state aid and external trade (the responsibility of the European Commission) with a form of "constrained" decentralization in other areas, such as fiscal and structural policies.

[7]There were neither financial backstops for stressed sovereigns or strained banks nor for countering sudden stops in financial flows (Mongelli et al. 2016).

[8]A brief summary of the measures taken since 2010 to strengthen EMU's resilience is presented in Juncker et al. (2015a). See also Mongelli et al. (2016) and the European Commission Fact Sheet on "The EU's economic governance explained" 28 November 2014, http://europa.eu/rapid/press-release_MEMO-14-2180_en.htm

further integration, a "complete EMU" seems always beyond reach (Jones et al. 2016; Pisani-Ferry 2016).

The various versions of the EU Presidents' Reports (Van Rompuy et al. 2012; Juncker et al. 2015a, b) seek remedy for the fact that the functioning of an economic and monetary union, as compared to a stand-alone economic union, makes additional demands on the economic side (notably on labour, product and financial markets with regard to flexibility and coordination requirements), which were previously unaccounted for. To make EMU sustainable they advocate the necessity to respond to the Eurozone crisis by completing its economic union part. That means creating a 'genuine EMU' (GEMU) with a banking union, an integrated budgetary framework, an integrated economic policy framework and enhanced democratic legitimacy and accountability of EMU governance.

Thus far the process of creating new institutions and mechanisms has displayed significant political and institutional resilience to the crisis. Nevertheless, efforts to create a 'genuine EMU' have only made limited progress. Considering GEMU's three economic strands, fiscal integration did not progress much since 2011 although financial integration (banking union) advanced substantially (to what can be denominated a half banking union). As far as enhanced democratic legitimacy and accountability of EMU governance is concerned, the institutional steps taken during the crisis appear not to be significant. However, a non-negligible informal bottom-up process of political integration is occurring through the substantially increased politicisation of multi-level governance (Torres 2015).[9] Among GEMU's four strands, it was the integrated economic policy framework that has progressed the least during the crisis (Mongelli et al. 2016; Bongardt and Torres 2016); it is also still far from the level required to sustain EMU.

The various Presidents' reports recognize that policy adjustment in the Eurozone cannot rely on macroeconomic policies alone. Economic integration would have to be pursued along the lines of creating stronger incentives for structural reforms in low-productivity countries. This would help the Eurozone better meet the economic requirements of a currency union by improving the overall stability of EMU to macroeconomic shocks. However, the proposal of creating incentives for promoting structural reforms for member states, such as a system of national reform contracts to be signed with EU institutions in exchange for financial support (Van Rompuy et al. 2012), seems not to have gathered the necessary political support across member states and was abandoned.

Against the background of an integrated economic coordination framework which barely advanced, held back by member state competences, the Five Presidents' report (Juncker et al. 2015b) proposes building on the Euro Plus Pact, with its EMU dimension and focus on interdependencies, rather than on the EU-wide Europe 2020 Strategy. More specifically, they suggest strengthening national

---

[9]Still, governments and citizens were not mobilized around a new impetus for European integration in the midst of the crisis, which in turn raises the question of the longer-term political sustainability of both EMU and the European Union project (see Jones and Torres 2015 and 2016).

reform efforts through competitiveness authorities at the national level and, in a second phase, by moving to a legal base for commitments. This innovation looks like an attempt to increase ownership and the effectiveness of reforms at national levels.[10]

## 3.2 *Urgent Institutional Challenges to Be Addressed*

A growing consensus has emerged on the causes of the crisis (Baldwin et al. 2015) and also on the fragilities that have to be corrected. It is summarized in Baldwin and Giavazzi (2016) and includes: completing the missing one-and-a-half pillars of the currently incomplete banking union; breaking the feedback loop between banks and their over-indebted sovereigns; securing Eurozone-wide risk sharing for dealing with Europe-wide shocks and coordinating fiscal policy/national fiscal policies while reinforcing discipline at the national level; some sort of sovereign debt restructuring mechanism for the Eurozone in order to redistribute the burden of legacy debt ("cleaning up the legacy debt problem"); and advancing structural reforms to push the Eurozone more towards an OCA.

As yet, there is no consensus on the specifics of the additional demands on economic union with respect to macroeconomic stabilization, notably whether fiscal policy needs to be centralised (De Grauwe and Ji 2016a, b; Tabellini 2016) or not (Eichengreen and Wyplosz 2016; Gros 2016). There is also some controversy on the role of the ECB as a lender of last resort.[11] The legacy debt problem seems to be the most important political obstacle that stands in the way of most of the other necessary corrections. There are various proposals for a limited set of measures to be implemented as fast as possible without any need for deepening political or even economic integration for which there is little appetite today.[12] However, all of these proposals encompass the creation of some fiscal space at the level of the Eurozone and some sort of (more or less limited) programme of debt consolidation/restructuring. A second important political obstacle, stressed by Sapir (2016), is the resistance to creating Eurozone-wide risk sharing for Europe-wide shocks (which begs increased fiscal integration) for fear that structural weaknesses in

[10]The proposal of such a legal base in the second phase suggests that the five presidents have little faith in the delivery of national structural reform through non-binding coordination (Begg et al. 2015). Sapir and Wolff (2015) propose the establishment of a European Competitiveness Council composed of national competitiveness councils and the creation of a Euro System of Fiscal Policy to oversee fiscal debt sustainability and an adequate area-wide fiscal position.

[11]See De Grauwe (2013), Eichengreen (2014) and Torres (2013) and Feld et al. (2016) for a discussion.

[12]Corsetti et al. (2016) put forward a mechanism to redistribute the burden of legacy debt over time and only to a minimal extent across countries, not requiring debt mutualisation or a joint debt guarantee.

some countries, in particular in the functioning of labour markets, may lead to structural rather than temporary fiscal transfers.

Today it has become more or less consensual that the one fundamental ingredient for a sustainable monetary union is banking union (Baldwin and Giavazzi 2016; Eichengreen and Wyplosz 2016; Gros 2016; Gros and Belke 2016). However, the question is whether such a banking union can materialise without a fiscal backstop requiring a significant move towards a fiscal union.

Member states have resisted the centralization of competences on the economic side of EMU and it is uncertain whether this will change any time in the future. It nevertheless remains urgent to address those challenges and make the necessary institutional changes. Independently of those necessary changes, however, it is the adjustment capacity and the willingness to implement economic reforms at the member-state level that is crucial for a better functioning monetary union and for promoting sustainable growth and hence a credible crisis exit strategy.

## 4 Beyond Institutional Reform: The Need to Create Ownership of Reforms

Regardless of the completion of a banking union and progress towards fiscal integration and other necessary changes, any attempts at moving the Euro area closer to an OCA, or to at least transform it into a sustainable currency area (SCA), require reforms in areas where competencies have remained national.[13] For the time being, this is therefore only possible through structural reform and adjustment capacity at the member state level.

Throughout the sovereign debt crisis market pressure surfaced as an additional source of pressure for increasing lagging member states' reform efforts. In addition, conditionality made an appearance through the access to funds for those countries that were cut off from capital markets for their financing needs. To a certain extent, this has been a game changer for softly coordinated economic reforms.[14] The new crisis-enacted mechanisms and the conditionality-linked availability of funds have started to positively affect the implementation of structural reforms. In fact, there has been an acceleration of structural reforms in laggard countries—including Greece, at least until 2014—as a result of market and peer pressure and of formal and informal conditionality (Schmieding and Schulz 2014; OECD 2015).

The relevance of economic reforms rises in a context where fiscal policy is also constrained by the need to ensure a proper adjustment of the budgetary imbalance, which is due to the need for an enduring correction of the budgetary imbalance. This is because structural reform can increase the credibility of the adjustment programme whereby a more gradual fiscal adjustment can be achieved

[13]For a discussion of the concept of SCA in contrast to OCA, see Torres (2009).

[14]Arguably, by buying time for reform the ECB also alleviates market pressure on member states.

(Bini-Smaghi 2016). As Draghi (2016) emphasizes, even supporting demand is not just a question of the budget balance, but also of its composition, especially the tax burden and the share of public investment—that is, fiscal policy can be used as a microeconomic policy tool in that it can enhance growth even when public finances require consolidation.

Without efforts by member states to create ownership of reforms, there may however be a political backlash.

As Gros (2015) and Gros and Belke (2016) show for the case of Puerto Rico, even a 'genuine' economic and monetary union (with a well-functioning banking union) like the US cannot prevent regional failures. The case of Puerto Rico in the US bears many similarities with the case of Greece in the Eurozone. Both delayed over-due reforms and arrived at the brink of bankruptcy. The only difference is that in the case of Puerto Rico there seems to be little criticism of the US dollar for the failure and of the US government for lack of solidarity (Puerto Rico is left to the mercy of the markets). However, Puerto Rico, member of a financially integrated monetary union, did not put the monetary union at risk. It did not receive any help from the US either, and entered into default (see Gros 2015). In the case of Greece, Eurozone partners paid the country's debts to the IMF (which were over due) and to the ECB.

The case of Greece has illustrated that, without increased sovereignty sharing, the new governance framework still remains vulnerable to adverse market and political-economy pressures. So far Cyprus, Ireland, Portugal and Spain seem not to have succumbed to the Greek disaster, although the jury is still out also for these countries as well as for other member states, notably Italy and France. Therefore, even if macroeconomic stability was to substantially improve, the as yet incomplete recasting of the governance of EMU leaves it at risk without structural reforms.

One might ask what the implications were if a member state opted for not honouring its 'constrained' commitments to sufficiently reform and modernize its economy and society to be part of a dynamic economic and monetary union. That member state should assume the responsibility for its choice of following a different economic model and do so without putting at risk the Eurozone's common good of monetary and financial stability and of other Eurozone members' budgetary sustainability. That would imply leaving the Eurozone, but Euro exit is not foreseen in the Treaties; they allow for voluntary exit from the EU but not for Euro exit alone. The question then becomes whether there is any alternative to make EMU function regardless of a lack of member state progress on economic reform. It is possible but requires a monetary union that is no obstacle to an orderly restructuring of the sovereign debt of one of its members (see Philippon 2015 for a more complete proposal). It amounts to a credible non-bailout regime. There is also the possibility of a drastic form of banking union *à la* Buiter (2015), which makes it possible to rescue the banks without rescuing the sovereign. The EU would thereby move towards US practice. In the above scenarios member states would be free to choose whether or not to comply with reform commitments. They alone would suffer the dire consequences (lower living standards and, most likely, a more unfair type of society) of their political choices (Giavazzi 2015; Phelps 2015).

In fact, the lack of ownership of economic reform by the national government in Greece has proven disastrous for the country and has carried a high cost for the other members of the Union (Bongardt and Torres 2016). In the end Greece, or for that matter any other EU member state, has the choice between addressing structural reforms in order to move on to sustainable growth (and, therefore, to a fairer model of society) or be prepared to continuously deteriorate living standards and internal social cohesion and quality of life vis-à-vis its partners.

## 5 A Durable Exit from the Crisis: Sustainable Growth

Apart from EMU resilience, structural reforms are also important for higher potential growth (Draghi 2015, 2016) and hence for dealing with legacy costs and with exit from the crisis. Still, whereas appropriate structural reforms are growth enhancing in the long run, they often fail to bring about immediate benefits (IMF 2015), while causing frictions at a high political cost when they collide with entrenched interest groups or affect vulnerable social groups. The common objectives put down in the Europe 2020 Strategy have, with the sovereign debt crisis, come to encompass increasingly salient political and distributional issues, not only in but also between member states. The enforcement, under market and peer pressure and conditionality, of objectives to which the member states already committed risks being perceived as intrusive as competencies have remained national.[15]

If one is concerned with long-term sustainability, a sustainable growth strategy with structural reforms at the national level is a pre-condition for a credible exit strategy and a durable recovery. According to the ECB (2015), the smooth functioning of EMU warrants growth that is sustainable in the long run, which implies that any economic recovery from the crisis needs to be durable. Sustainable (not only economically but also environmentally) growth thereby offers both a crisis exit strategy and adds to the wider benefits from EU integration. As we suggested elsewhere (Begg et al. 2015), EMU can be sustained both in the more immediate crisis context and in the long run as part of a political sustainable integration project, which envisages high-quality growth and respects longer-term budgetary challenges.

Even on purely economic grounds, economic growth will not be sustainable—and any recovery not durable—unless environmental damages and resource depletion and long-term, inter-generational effects are internalized; nor would it be politically sustainable. Any general call for growth ('whatever kind of growth'), and one which makes do with sustained rather than sustainable growth, ignores the economic case for environmental protection and with it environmental constraints

[15]This is especially complicated when conditionality in adjustment countries coincides with EU institution building (Nicolaïdis and Watson 2016).

on growth, let alone the EU's commitment to a model of development with quality sustainable growth[16] and a moral obligation (towards the less well off and future generations) of dealing with climate change.[17]

The need for long-term sustainable growth for EMU sustainability first of all begs the question whether it is possible to promote sustainable growth within the crisis context given a one-fits-all monetary policy and budgetary constraints. As for monetary policy, it can smoothen cyclical shocks but it is unable to solve structural problems. The European Central Bank, to which the conduct of monetary policy has been delegated in the EU, has consistently stressed the importance of structural reform for EMU's smooth functioning (see for instance ECB 2015).[18] ECB actions (just like a more expansionary fiscal policy stance in the Eurozone) can only buy time for member states to address their structural problems; they cannot solve them. Structural reforms are therefore a precondition for generating sustainable growth and for putting countries on a higher potential growth trajectory (ECB 2015; Draghi 2016).

As for budgetary constraints, one should note that a fiscal stimulus (even if feasible) is a crude instrument. As such it is unlikely to result per se in quality growth, unless it deals with the causes of competitiveness problems. Incentives for growth can be provided not only through the level but also and perhaps more importantly the composition of expenditure and incentives on the revenue side, notably taxation (Giavazzi and Wyplosz 2016; Begg et al. 2015; Bongardt and Torres 2016; Draghi 2016).

## 6 Operationalizing Sustainable Growth

It is probably fair to say that the more immediate concerns with economic results somewhat eclipsed long-term sustainability concerns and their implications for future growth in the EU policy discussion (Bongardt and Torres 2013a). This was more the case after the crisis, when many economists and politicians proposed fiscal expansions, which risked perpetuating unsustainable consumption and production patterns. In our view, the need to stimulate domestic demand in surplus countries—which is not irrespective of the composition of expenditure and taxation, rather the

[16]Sustainable development has been an objective of the EU for about three decades (the concept goes back to the so-called Brundtland report, World Commission on Environment and Development 1987). The 2009 Lisbon Treaty goes further, committing the EU to a high level of protection and improvement of the quality of the environment in the management of the single market (Art.3 (3) TEU).

[17]In this respect, see the encyclical letter on the environment by Pope Francis (2015) and Stern (2015).

[18]See Torres (2013) for an explanation of this 'invasion of other policy domains' by the ECB: it became a guardian of EMU given that the EU's political system per se seemed incapable of providing timely and consistent solutions.

opposite—goes hand-in-hand with the need to implement structural reforms in order to reduce built-up disequilibria in deficit countries. Structural reforms that modernize the economy are a precondition for a shift to sustainable growth.

The overall European objective of transforming its economy into a low-carbon green economy produces important economic benefits in the long run, but rather obviously the cost-benefit balance depends on how well it is implemented in the shorter term (Bongardt and Torres 2013b). Apart from the adequacy of policies and instruments, it will also be much conditioned by the characteristics of the EU Energy Union that is being created. In the crisis context, public opinion in Europe has been concerned first and foremost with dealing with the effects of the immediate economic crisis, although longer-term environmental concerns have for long and consistently been among European citizens' priorities.[19] It is important to communicate that such a dichotomy is unfounded since addressing both can be mutually reinforcing with regard to economic and political resilience of the European project.

With regard to the political sustainability of structural reforms, sequencing ought to be a relevant concern: those reforms that are growth enhancing in the short run should be prioritized, and private investment encouraged in ways compatible with fiscal constraints. This will avoid that structural reform and austerity do not mingle in such a way that it may push countries into problems they did not have.[20] As for sustainable growth, appropriate taxation and tighter regulation to promote green investments are a case in point (Pisani-Ferry 2014). The use of fiscal instruments opens up the perspective of promoting sustainable growth by shifting taxation onto inefficiencies (like pollution), away from taxing productive factors (such as labour). Taxes carry a double dividend, in that they provide receipts for the state and discourage inefficient behaviour.[21] The abolition of incentive-distorting inefficient subsidies (negative taxes), like the ones on coal (IEA 2014), likewise reduces government expenditure and improves the state of the environment by lowering carbon emissions. Economic instruments (like taxes and transferable emission licences) have dynamic efficiency properties, promoting innovation, and provide least cost abatement of pollution; as such they are very much in tune with the Europe 2020 goals of (green) growth. In addition, regulation (market rules) can be used to foster private green investments without incurring fiscal expenditure. Demanding EU harmonized environmental regulation can provide a push for EU green innovation and cost-efficiency.[22] For that it needs to be perceived as part of a

[19]Environmental protection and combatting climate change reflect European citizens' values and priorities, as Eurobarometer surveys (http://ec.europa.eu/public_opinion/archives/eb/eb82/eb82_first_en.pdf) have consistently indicated.

[20]We thank Paul De Grauwe for calling our attention to this point.

[21]EU level fiscal instruments require unanimity in the Council of the EU. While member states can impose taxes or cut subsidies at the national level they will be reluctant to do so if that implies competitiveness disadvantages in the internal market.

[22]EU environmental regulation provides for minimum standards with a view to avoiding a race to the bottom in member state regulation standards. Conversely, demanding EU harmonized

sustainable growth strategy rather than as constituting red tape. The circular economy package is a case in point where demanding EU regulation can promote growth and employment creation (EEA 2015).[23] Its success will be indicative for the EU's resolve in implementing sustainable growth. The same can be said for the Commission's European Fund for Strategic Investment, where much will depend on whether it will be oriented towards long-term sustainable growth.

## 7 Conclusion

This chapter focuses on the need for national reforms and for completing EMU. Their importance in the monetary union context derives on the one hand from market requisites for pushing EMU towards a sustainable currency area and on the other hand from institutional modernization being a pre-condition for promoting growth and hence a credible exit strategy from the crisis.

While ECB actions have been buying time they are no substitutes for either the EU completing the economic side of EMU or for member states to enact economic reforms. Monetary policy can smoothen cyclical shocks but it is unable to solve structural problems. It is member states that need to implement long-due structural reforms. In fact, ECB actions, with all their positive effects, even have the (negative) side effect to alleviate pressures for reform. Experience has shown the difficulties in implementing economic reforms without external pressure.

Furthermore, the relevance of economic reforms rises in a context where fiscal policy is also constrained by the need to ensure fiscal consolidation, as structural reform can increase the credibility of the adjustment programme whereby a more gradual fiscal adjustment can be achieved. Fiscal policy can also be used as a microeconomic policy tool in that, if properly employed, it can enhance (sustainable) growth even when public finances require consolidation.

It is true that structural reform has become also more politically charged. The reason is that economic reform became entangled with austerity in the public debate, particularly so in countries that underwent (or are still undergoing) adjustment programmes and did not use structural reforms to achieve a more gradual fiscal adjustment (clearly the case of Greece). What this increased politicization highlights is the need for creating ownership of reforms. Ownership of reforms can contribute to more sustainable and high quality growth that in turn also reduces the need for austerity. Without economic modernization countries will not prosper in an

---

environmental regulation can be used as an instrument to foster EU green innovation and cost-efficiency.

[23]The circular economy package, aimed at making the European economy more resource-efficient by increasing recycling levels and tightening the rules on incineration and landfill, was withdrawn by the Juncker Commission in December 2014 amidst wide-ranging concerns and protests, among which EU environment minsters, MEPs, NGOs.

economic environment in which competitiveness factors changed significantly notably due to globalization, let alone be able to deal with crisis legacy costs.

Ownership and implementation of structural reforms are hence a precondition for generating sustainable growth and for putting countries on a higher potential growth trajectory. It will also increase the acceptance of economic reforms against the background of wider benefits from EU integration.

## References

Baldwin R et al (Rebooting Consensus Authors) (2015) Rebooting the Eurozone: step 1 – agreeing a crisis narrative. VoxEU.org, 20 Nov 2015

Baldwin R, Giavazzi F (eds) (2016) How to fix Europe's Monetary Union: views of leading economists. CEPR Press, London (VoxEU.org eBook)

Begg I, Bongardt A, Nicolaïdis K, Torres F (2015) EMU and sustainable integration. J Eur Integr 37(7):803–816

Bini-Smaghi (2016) Governance and conditionality: towards a sustainable framework? In: Jones E, Torres F (eds) Governance of the European Monetary Union. Routledge, London

Bongardt A, Torres F (2012) The Lisbon strategy. In: Jones E, Menon A, Weatherill S (eds) The handbook on the European Union. Oxford University Press, Oxford, pp 469–483

Bongardt A, Torres F (2013a) Economic governance and sustainability. In: Verdun A, Tovias A (eds) Mapping European economic integration. Palgrave Macmillan, Basingstoke

Bongardt A, Torres F (2013b) Forging sustainable growth: the issue of convergence of preferences and institutions. Intereconomics 48:72–77

Bongardt A, Torres F (2016) EMU and structural reform. In: Talani LS (ed) Europe in crisis: a structural analysis. Palgrave Macmillan, Basingstoke, pp 37–64

Buiter W (2015) There is a way past the insanity over Greece. Financial Times 21 June

Corsetti G (2010) A modern reconsideration of the OCA theory. In: Buti M, Deroose S, Gaspar V, Martins JN (eds) The Euro. The first decade. Cambridge University Press, Cambridge, pp 143–180

Corsetti G, Feld L, Koijen R, Reichlin L, Reis R, Rey H, di Mauro BW (2016) Reinforcing the Eurozone and protecting an open society. Monitoring the Eurozone 2. CEPR Press, London

De Grauwe P (2013) Design failures in the Eurozone: can they be fixed? LSE 'Europe in Question. Discussion Paper Series no. 57/2013

De Grauwe P, Ji Y (2016a) Correcting for the Eurozone design failures: the role of the ECB. In: Jones E, Torres F (eds) Governance of the European Monetary Union. Routledge, London

De Grauwe P, Ji Y (2016b) How to reboot the Eurozone and ensure its long-term survival. In: Baldwin R, Giavazzi F (eds) How to fix Europe's Monetary Union: views of leading economists. CEPR Press, London, pp 137–150 (VoxEU.org eBook)

De Grauwe P, Mongelli F (2005) Endogeneities of optimum currency areas: what brings countries sharing a single currency closer together? ECB WP 468, April 2005

Draghi M (2015) Structural reforms, inflation and monetary policy. ECB Forum on Central Banking, Sintra (introductory speech)

Draghi M (2016) On the importance of policy alignment to fulfil our economic potential. In: 5th Annual Tommaso Padoa-Schioppa, Brussels Economic Forum, Brussels, 9 June 2016

Eichengreen B (2014) The Eurozone crisis: the theory of optimum currency area bites back. Notenstein Academy White Paper Series

Eichengreen B, Wyplosz C (2016) Minimal conditions for the survival of the Euro. In: Baldwin R, Giavazzi F (eds) How to fix Europe's Monetary Union: views of leading economists. CEPR Press, London, pp 34–46 (VoxEU.org eBook)

Eijffinger S, Kobielarz M, Uras B (2015) Sovereign debt, bail-outs and contagion in a Monetary Union. CEPR DP n° 10459, March 2015
European Central Bank (2015) Progress with structural reforms across the Eurozone and their possible impacts. Economic Bulletin 2. ECB, Frankfurt
European Environment Agency (2015) European environment state and outlook. EEA, Copenhagen
Feld L, Schmidt CM, Schnabel I, Wieland V (2016) Maastricht 2.0: Safeguarding the future of the Eurozone. In: Baldwin R, Giavazzi F (eds) How to fix Europe's Monetary Union: views of leading economists. CEPR Press, London, pp 46–61 (VoxEU.org eBook)
Francis P (2015) Laudato Si'. On Care for our Common Home. Encyclical Letter, Libreria Editrice Vaticana, Vatican City
Giavazzi F (2015) Greeks chose poverty, let them have their way. Financial Times, June 9 2015
Giavazzi F, Wyplosz C (2016) EMU: old flaws revisited. In: Jones E, Torres F (eds) Governance of the European Monetary Union. Routledge, London
Gros D (2015) Puerto Rico and Greece: a tale of two defaults in a Monetary Union. CEPS High-Level Brief, Brussels (updated 30 June 2015)
Gros D (2016) Completing the Banking Union. In: Baldwin R, Giavazzi F (eds) How to fix Europe's Monetary Union: views of leading economists. VoxEU.org eBook. CEPR Press, London, pp 88–99
Gros D, Belke A (2016) Banking Union as a shock absorber: lessons for the Eurozone from the US. Rowman & Littlefield, Lanham
International Energy Agency (2014) World energy outlook 2015. IEA, Paris
IMF (2015) Where are we headed? Perspectives on potential output. In: World economic outlook: uneven growth—short- and long-term factors. International Monetary Fund, Washington, DC
Jones E, Torres F (2015) An 'Economics' window on an interdisciplinary crisis. J Eur Integr 37:7
Jones E, Torres F (eds) (2016) Governance of the European Monetary Union. Routledge, London
Jones E, Kelemen RD, Meunier S (2016) Failing forward? The Euro crisis and the incomplete nature of European integration. Comp Polit Stud 49:1010–1034
Juncker J-C, Tusk D, Dijsselbloem J, Draghi M (2015a) Preparing for next steps on better economic governance in the Euro area. Analytical Note prepared for the Informal European Council, Brussels, 12 Feb 2015
Juncker J-C, Tusk D, Dijsselbloem J, Draghi M, Schulz M (2015b) Completing Europe's economic and Monetary Union. European Commission, Brussels, 22 June 2015
Krugman P (1993) Lessons of Massachusetts for EMU. In: Torres F, Giavazzi F (eds) Adjustment and growth in the European Monetary Union. Cambridge University Press, Cambridge, pp 241–261
Mongelli F (2008) European economic and Monetary integration and the optimum currency area theory. DG ECFIN, Economic Papers, 302, Feb 2008
Mongelli F (2010) The OCA theory and the path to EMU, chapter 4. In: Buti M, Deroose S, Gaspar V, Martins JN (eds) The euro. The first decade. Cambridge University Press, Cambridge, pp 115–142
Mongelli F, Dorruccci E, Ioannou D, Terzi A (2015) Responses to the Euro area crisis: measuring the path of European Institutional Integration. J Eur Integr 37:7
Mongelli F, Dorruccci E, Ioannou D, Terzi A (2016) Responses to the euro area crisis: measuring the path of European Institutional Integration. In: Jones E, Torres F (eds) Governance of the European Monetary Union. London and New York, Rutledge
Nicolaïdis K, Watson M (2016) Sharing the Eurocrat's dream: a demoi-cratic approach to EMU governance. In: Chalmers DMJ, Joerges C (eds) The post-crisis era and the end of the EUrocrat's dream. Cambridge University Press, Cambridge, pp 50–77
OECD (2015) Economic policy reforms 2015: going for growth. OECD, Paris
Phelps ES (2015) What Greece needs to prosper. Project Syndicate, 6 Aug 2015
Philippon T (2015) The state of the Monetary Union, published on VOX, CEPR's Policy Portal (http://www.voxeu.org), 31 Aug 2015
Pisani-Ferry J (2014) How to climb a mountain with both hands tied. VoxEU.org, 7 Nov 2014

Pisani-Ferry J (2016) The Eurozone's Zeno paradox – and how to solve it. In: Baldwin R, Giavazzi F (eds) How to fix Europe's Monetary Union: views of leading economists. CEPR Press, London, pp 75–85 (VoxEU.org eBook)
Sapir A (2016) The Eurozone needs less heterogeneity. In: Baldwin R, Giavazzi F (eds) How to fix Europe's Monetary Union: views of leading economists. CEPR Press, London, pp 180–187 (VoxEU.org eBook)
Sapir A, Wolff G (2015) Euro-area governance: what to reform and how to do it. Bruegel Policy Brief 2015/01, Feb 2015
Schelkle W (2016) Krugman's Argument that the Eurozone is not an optimum currency area could easily be applied to the US. EUROPP–European Politics and Policy, London School of Economics. http://blogs.lse.ac.uk/europpblog/2016/04/29
Schmieding H, Schulz C (2014) Euro pact plus monitor 2014. Leaders and Laggards. The Lisbon Council, Brussels
Stern N (2015) Why are we waiting? The logic, urgency, and promise of tackling climate change. MIT Press, Cambridge
Tabellini G (2016) Building common fiscal policy in the Eurozone. In: Baldwin R, Giavazzi F (eds) How to fix Europe's Monetary Union: views of leading economists. CEPR Press, London, pp 117–131 (VoxEU.org eBook)
Torres F (2009) The role of preferences and the sustainability of EMU. In: Talani S (ed) The future of EMU. Palgrave Macmillan, Basingstoke, pp 54–74
Torres F (2013) The EMU's legitimacy and the ECB as a strategic political player in the crisis context. J Eur Integr 35(3):287–300
Torres F (2015) The political economy of economic and Monetary Union. In: Magone J (ed) Handbook on European politics. Routledge, London, pp 764–777
Van Rompuy H, Barroso JM, Juncker J-C, Draghi M (2012) Towards a genuine economic and Monetary Union ("Four Presidents' Report" – Report by the Presidents of the European Council, European Commission, Eurogroup and the ECB), Brussels, 5 Dec 2012

# A Structural-Reform Proposal for a Two-Speed European Monetary Union

**Sergio Rossi**

**Abstract** This chapter presents a structural–monetary reform to transform the euro into a factor of European integration rather than representing a straightjacket for member countries that are suffering from the crisis without any likelihood to resolve it. This requires transforming the European Central Bank to make it become a settlement institution for those national central banks that participate in the TARGET2 system, enabling those member countries that are suffering most from the crisis to reintroduce their own national currencies for their domestic payments. This will transform the euro into a truly international currency, thereby providing for both an orderly working euro-area payments system and the possibility to steer domestic interest rates policy with the aim of contributing to economic as well as financial stability. Such a structural–monetary reform will be instrumental in enhancing at both economic and institutional level the integration of euro-area countries, with a view to do justice to the original project of European union.

## 1 Introduction

This chapter presents a structural–monetary reform to transform the euro into a factor of European integration rather than representing a straightjacket for member countries that, at the time of writing, are suffering from the crisis without any likelihood to resolve it in a foreseeable future. The next section recalls that the European Monetary Union (EMU) is obviously not an optimum currency area (OCA), as it has become plain after the euro-area crisis burst at the end of 2009. As a matter of fact, this area lacks both international labour mobility and fiscal transfers that would make it similar to the United States with regard to the OCA criteria pointed out by Mundell (1961), among others. An ancillary but relevant issue refers to the 'optimal policy-mix' for such an area, which is so only if there

S. Rossi, Ph.D.
Department of Economics, University of Fribourg, Boulevard de Pérolles 90, 1700 Fribourg, Switzerland
e-mail: sergio.rossi@unifr.ch



N. de Costa Cabral et al. (eds.), *The Euro and the Crisis*, Financial and Monetary Policy Studies 43, DOI 10.1007/978-3-319-45710-9_4

exists a Treasury—empowered to tax and spend—opposite the relevant central bank (Kenen 1969, 45–6). The third section elaborates on this, explaining that the euro-area governance should be improved in light of the critical issues pointed out by OCA literature and largely noticed after the eruption of the euro-area crisis. This implies transforming the European Central Bank (ECB) into a settlement institution for all those national central banks (NCBs) that participate in the Trans-European Automated Real-time Gross-settlement Express Transfer (TARGET2) payments system across the euro area, enabling those EMU member countries that actually are suffering most from the crisis to reintroduce their own national currencies—to be used by their residents for the payment of all their transactions. This will transform the euro into a truly international currency, thereby providing for an orderly working euro-area payments system and the renewed possibility to steer domestic interest rates policy with the aim of contributing to economic as well as financial stability both within and across the euro-area member countries. The fourth section expands on this to explain that such a structural–monetary reform will be instrumental in enhancing at both economic and institutional level the integration of euro-area countries, with a view to do justice to the original project of European union, which is indeed encapsulated in article 3, paragraph 3, of the Treaty on the European Union (TEU).[1] This will imply a transfer of some taxation powers to a supranational Treasury, the issuance of eurobonds by it, as well as a fiscal equalisation mechanism that supports those countries or regions most in trouble, particularly when the performance of the global economy is affected by an asymmetric shock or a severe financial crisis—two events that have become more likely to occur frequently as a result of economic globalisation.

## 2 The EMU Is Not an Optimum Currency Area

The official political reason to adopt a single European currency in 1999 was that the euro was expected to increase trade as well as economic convergence between euro-area member countries. A reduction in transactions costs elicited by abolishing exchange-rate volatility between an array of different currencies and the external constraints resulting from euro adoption by would-be EMU member countries were meant to spur both economic growth and the countries' 'competitiveness', particularly as regards 'catching-up' EMU countries with respect to Germany—whose foreign trade was also going to benefit from the process of European monetary unification. To support these arguments on scientific grounds, many economists referred to OCA literature, both as concerns the original Mundell approach and with a view to so-called 'endogenous' OCA criteria (see Frankel and Rose 2002). At that time, however, an increasing number of authors were pointing

[1]According to article 3, paragraph 3, of the TEU, the European Union (EU, including the EMU) "shall promote economic, social and territorial cohesion, and solidarity among Member States".

out that the EMU was not an OCA in light of Mundell's (1961) analysis as well as considering many other criteria brought to the fore in the aftermath of that analysis (see for instance McKinnon 1963; Kenen 1969). As a matter of fact, when the EMU project was being discussed at EU level, as well as when the euro replaced a number of national currencies in 1999, the then would-be EMU member countries were not forming an OCA: neither international labour mobility, nor national economic structures and performance were up to the task—as argued for instance by Dahrendorf (1997), Échinard (1999), and Hankel et al. (2001). Further, the so-called convergence criteria enshrined in the 1992 Maastricht Treaty were ignoring real economic performance focusing just on some nominal magnitudes with no theoretical argument in economic analysis justifying the (in)famous limits for the public sector's debt and deficit with regard to Gross Domestic Product (GDP) (Wyplosz 1991; Buiter et al. 1993; Pasinetti 1998).

The most difficult OCA criterion to be met is clearly labour mobility across national boundaries. Even after the euro-area crisis burst in 2009, the geographical mobility of EMU workers remained very low in comparison to the United States. As the European Commissioner for Employment, Social Affairs and Inclusion observed in an official speech, "approximately 8.1 million EU citizens work and live in another Member State today, representing 3.3 % of the total EU labour force" (Andor 2014, 1). Since Andor gave his speech, the situation on this front has been worsening: rather than increasing as a result of the persistent euro-area crisis, international labour mobility across the EU has been reduced below 3 % of the total EU labour force. This is particularly dramatic within the euro area (Barslund et al. 2015). As a matter of fact, "the [EMU] economic and financial crisis has affected mobility patterns by redirecting flows away from the periphery, thus showing the limits to the potential of labour mobility within the current eurozone—largely due to the negligible mobility of nationals from large countries hit by the crisis. Second, east-west mobility has not been fundamentally affected by the [EMU] crisis, and ten years after the eastern enlargement the number of East Europeans living in [the] EU15 should be of no overall concern" (Barslund et al. 2015, 1).[2]

In light of the very tiny share of international labour mobility across the EMU, which is a mark of the euro-area lack of 'optimality' as a currency union, there should exist some mechanism for fiscal transfers from the best-performing member countries to those EMU countries whose economic performance is worst, in order to make the euro area viable—as this occurs, for instance, in the United States, where a fiscal equalisation system is in place with regard to the different unemployment rates across the federation of US States with a view to reduce the gaps in this respect between them. In fact, the euro area lacks to date such fiscal transfers, which further corroborates the argument that considers the EMU not an OCA at all. Indeed,

[2]EU15 refers to the 15 member countries of the EU before the EU enlargement in 2004. It includes Austria, Belgium, Denmark, Finland, France, Germany, Greece, Ireland, Italy, Luxembourg, the Netherlands, Portugal, Spain, Sweden, and the United Kingdom.

Draghi (2014, Internet) pointed this out in a speech at the University of Helsinki, when he explained that a monetary union needs permanent fiscal transfers to be viable over the long run: "[i]n all national economies, permanent transfers take place from richer to poorer regions; from more densely populated to more sparsely populated areas; and from those better endowed with natural resources to those less endowed. This is true in the United States, where those transfers occur through the federal budget. It is true within Germany, within Italy, within Finland. Fiscal transfers, so long as they remain fair, often help cement social cohesion and protect against the temptation of secession". In the same speech, Draghi also observed that, in the current institutional set-up of the euro area, where there are no public (fiscal) transfers across its member countries' borders, their role has been carried out by private capital flows from rich to poor countries, until the euro-area crisis erupted at the end of 2009. In particular, German banks were more than happy to lend to Greek (public and private sector) agents a large part of those savings that corresponded to the German trade surplus, in order for the Greek economy to pay for its net imports from Germany and further inflate the trade imbalances between these two countries (Rossi 2013, 2015). There is, nevertheless, an important difference between a mechanism of fiscal transfers and private capital flows between EMU member countries: the latter flows come with the obligation to reimburse the relevant (public or private) debts, which are also charged with interest payments and the relevant spread (see Rossi and Dafflon 2012), while fiscal transfers are unilateral flows without any interest payment associated to them.

In this regard, another major difference is striking—and in fact was already pointed out before the euro changeover (see for example Rossi 1997, 328). Contrary to the US Federal Reserve (Fed), which must and does support the US federal government policy by purchasing government bills, bonds, and treasuries on the primary market, the ECB does not support fiscal policy across the euro area—both as a result of its own statutes and because, so far, there is no European Treasury in front of it. Actually, the so-called 'dual mandate' of the Fed, which ought "to promote effectively the goals of maximum employment, stable prices, and moderate long-term interest rates" (Board of Governors of the Federal Reserve System 2014, Section 2A) also through continued purchases of government bonds, must be considered, particularly by political leaders in 'peripheral' EMU countries, in order to revise the statutes of the ECB so that the latter has a similar mandate for the euro area as a whole. This will be necessary at the latest when the EMU will set up a European Treasury, with the power to tax and spend, as recalled by Bibow (2016). Only then, indeed, will the EMU move in the direction of becoming an OCA as explained above. So far, in fact, it represents a hybrid (hence a heterogeneous) currency area, because it has a single European currency by name without the necessary settings, both at institutional and at structural–monetary level, which would make it an OCA, or at least a viable and resilient monetary union. Let us expand on this in the next section.

# 3 The Euro Must Become the Common Currency of EMU Member Countries

Despite the appearances, the euro, as it stands, is not the single European currency that the EMU member countries' residents can use to settle any domestic or foreign debt in the euro area. In fact, in spite of the singleness of their denomination, the euros actually issued in two different EMU member countries remain heterogeneous, as long as their national payment systems are not really integrated into a homogeneous monetary space. To be sure, the TARGET2 payments system lacks payment finality between the national central banks involved thereby (Rossi 2013). This is so, because the ECB does not act—to date—as a settlement institution for the participating national central banks, contrary to the logic of money emission and the orderly working of any payments infrastructure. A simple look at Fig. 1 suffices to grasp the structural–monetary problem at hand.

In each country, there is a Real-Time Gross-Settlement (RTGS) protocol used by local payment systems, to process large-value payment orders and settle them finally by the end of the day if not earlier than that (see Rossi 2007, 64–79). This protocol is run by the payment infrastructure's owner, and implies the emission of central bank money always and everywhere, in order to pay finally any debt positions between participating financial institutions, notably commercial banks. As a result, the national central bank (NCB) is a technically necessary institution that issues the means of final payment that banks need to settle their debts during or at the end of any banking day. Using Keynes's image in his *Treatise on Money*,[3] the central bank is at the centre of the banking system, as the sun is at centre stage of the solar system, around which planets (banks) gravitate. This two-tier banking system existing within each EMU member country provides for a domestic monetary order, as it makes sure that all payments are finalised, that is to say, each of them leaves the seller of commercial or financial items with no further claims on the buyer (Goodhart 1989, 26). By contrast, between any two euro-area countries, to date, payments are not final for the countries concerned, as they leave the 'receiving' country with a claim on the set of TARGET2 participating countries (see Rossi 2013). Indeed, as Fig. 1 shows, the ECB is not acting as the central bank of NCBs—which is what one would expect considering the economic logic of payments, as explained above—since the TARGET2 payments system implies two tiers rather than three: the first and second tiers are those of domestic payments systems, implying commercial banks (first tier) and the NCB (second tier). Now, instead of representing the third tier by itself, the ECB is part of the second tier in TARGET2, because it does not issue the means of final payment that NCBs would need to settle their debt across the TARGET2 system finally. The European Central Bank (2007, 34) explained this unequivocally: "[c]ross-border TARGET[2] payments are processed via the national RTGS systems and

[3] "The typical modern banking system consists of a sun, namely the central bank, and planets, which, following American usage, it is convenient to call the member banks" (Keynes 1930/1971, 8).

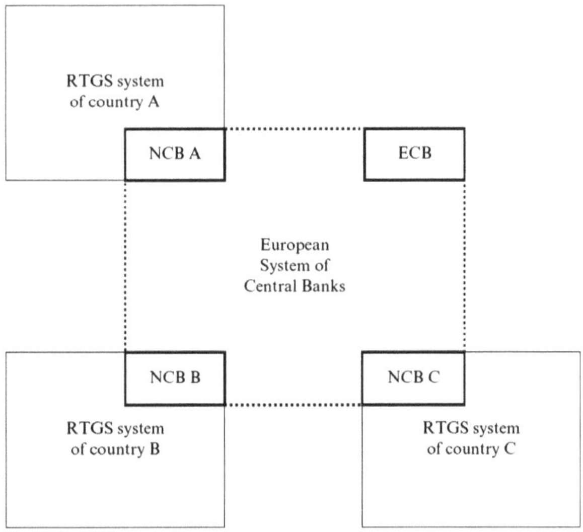


**Fig. 1** The two-tier payment infrastructure of TARGET2

exchanged directly on a bilateral basis between NCBs". This means that, "[o]nce the sending NCB has checked the validity of a payment message and the availability of funds or sufficient overdraft facilities, the amount of the payment is debited irrevocably and without delay from the RTGS account of the sending credit institution and credited to the Interlinking account of the receiving NCB" (p. 35).[4] If so, then the ECB does not act as a settlement institution between the NCBs involved, as it issues no units of (central bank) money for such a settlement to occur. As a result, the payment is just promised, not final, for the relevant countries, although their residents pay, and are paid, finally, when there is an international transaction across the euro area whose result is recorded by TARGET2. This explains why, so far, the structural–monetary problem of TARGET2 has remained unnoticed, even though various authors have been proposing different explanations for the mushroom growth of TARGET2 imbalances as a result of the euro-area crisis (see Rossi 2012a for analytical elaboration on this point).

To address the lack of TARGET2 payment finality at international level, a structural–monetary reform must be designed and implemented. Contrary to the arguments raised notably by Sinn and Wollmershäuser (2012)—who attribute the origin of TARGET2 imbalances to profligate government spending in the euro-area 'periphery'—and those pointed out by Buiter et al. (2011), De Grauwe and Ji (2012), and Westermann (2012)—who consider TARGET2 imbalances the result of capital flight in the aftermath of the euro-area crisis—the origin of these

[4]The "Interlinking account" is an account that each NCB holds within the Interlinking mechanism, which designates "the infrastructures and procedures which link domestic RTGS systems in order to enable the processing of inter-Member State payments within TARGET[2]" (European Central Bank 2011, 58).

imbalances is structural rather than behavioural. It is thus necessary to go beyond agents' forms of behaviour to understand and eradicate the problem structurally.

Waiting for the ECB to play the technical role that it should play as the central bank for euro-area NCBs, let us consider setting up a two-speed EMU: on the one hand, there are a number of countries willing and able to continue using the euro as single currency, but on the other hand there might be some countries, such as Greece, Spain or Portugal, that could benefit from the possibility to reintroducing their own national currencies because this will be instrumental in improving their economic performance considerably, whilst making sure that all their international payments are final for the countries concerned (a major advance with regard to the current situation, as explained above). Let us consider a stylised case, involving two countries, say Germany and Portugal, epitomising in turn those countries that use the euro as their single currency and those other countries using the euro as their common currency.[5]

Suppose that a Portuguese firm imports some equipment from Germany, for an amount of $x$ euros. In the current TARGET2 payments system, the payment of this transaction as regards the Portuguese importer and the German exporter is final but gives rise also to a debt–credit relationship between the two NCBs involved thereby: the Banco de Portugal (the Portuguese NCB) has a negative balance in TARGET2, while the German NCB has a positive balance in TARGET2, both for an amount of $x$ euros. Unless German savers—or German banks in their place—purchase some commercial or financial items from the Portuguese economy up to this amount, the relevant imbalance in TARGET2 remains. It records therefore the promise of payment delivered by Portugal (the country as a whole, represented by the Banco de Portugal) to the set of TARGET2 participants, among them Germany still having to receive the object of that payment—namely, a produced output, delivered by the originator of the promise of payment (to wit, Portugal). To avoid such a payment deficit (Machlup 1963, 256) between the paying and the receiving countries (in our stylised case Portugal and Germany respectively), the NCB of the country where the payer resides must split its books into two departments, thereby reintroducing in fact its domestic currency (the Portuguese escudo, PTE) for its agents' transactions (Table 1).

As Table 1 shows, the Banco de Portugal enters the relevant payment for the import in two separate departments, one recording the result of this payment in national currency, while the other records the result of the same payment in euros—which thus becomes a common currency for the Portuguese economy with regard to its trade with other EMU member countries. This is enough, but instrumental, in order for Portugal to recover its monetary sovereignty, that is to say, the capacity for

[5]Note in passing that the large majority of economists, politicians, journalists, and central bankers do not distinguish, conceptually, a single currency from a common currency, using these two expressions as if they were synonymous. The mistake in this regard is plain, if one considers the famous analogy between 'money' and 'language' (see Tobin 1992). If English is our common language in this chapter, this is not our single language, as each of us can speak different languages, say French and Portuguese, particularly with one's own friends and family.

**Table 1** The result of a cross-border payment from a non-euro EMU member country

| Banco de Portugal | | | |
|---|---|---|---|
| Domestic department | | External department | |
| Assets | Liabilities | Assets | Liabilities |
| Bank B1 (importer) +$z$ PTE | External department +$z$ PTE | Domestic department +$x$ euros | Bundesbank +$x$ euros |

*Note*: we assume that $z$ PTE = $x$ euros

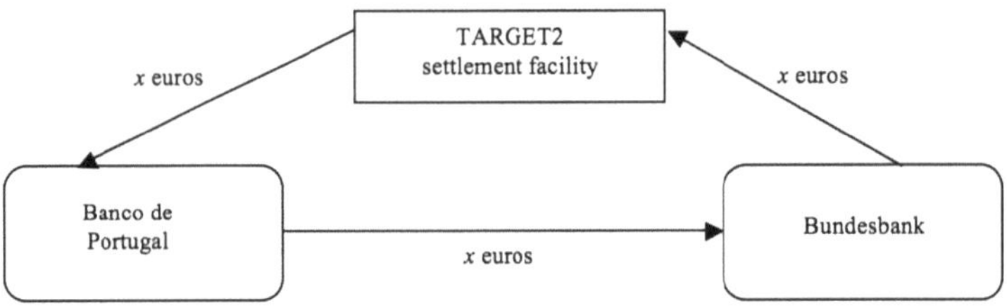


**Fig. 2** The international circuit of euros

the Banco de Portugal to carry out again its monetary policy, including exchange-rate policy, according to the needs of the domestic economy—which are not really taken into account by the ECB, whose policy decisions are largely influenced by the economic performance of Germany (Feldstein 2000; Lee and Crowley 2009; Krugman 2011).

Indeed, the two double-entries in Table 1 do not amount to double counting one and the same object. They are necessary in order to separate the circuit of euros from the circuit of Portuguese escudos. If the former does not intrude the latter, then Portugal as a whole recovers its monetary sovereignty, becoming thereby part of the international monetary space defined by the circuit of euros between the NCBs involved by this (Fig. 2).

Although there is no technical obligation to refer to the TARGET2 payments system in order for Portugal to adopt the euro as a common currency in the international monetary space, because this settlement facility could be set up autonomously by the Portuguese NCB, let us imagine that the EMU member countries are willing to set up such a facility within the TARGET2 payments infrastructure. Indeed, this solution would make sure it works multilaterally rather than just bilaterally (that is, between two particular countries in the euro area, such as Portugal and Germany in our stylised case). Be that as it may at the institutional level, we must not forget that money is, always and everywhere, just the means and not the object of the payment. In the case at hand, this means that Portugal as a whole must dispose of some commercial or financial items, to pay Germany finally in order to have no further debt. If Portugal reintroduces its national currency, therefore, its central bank must be obliged to settle, at least once per year, the Portuguese debt against the TARGET2 settlement facility, by disposing of financial assets for an amount equal to the country's trade deficit within the relevant period.

**Table 2** The result of the settlement of a non-euro EMU member country's trade deficit

| Banco de Portugal | | | |
|---|---|---|---|
| Domestic department | | External department | |
| Assets | Liabilities | Assets | Liabilities |
| Financial assets<br>$-z$ PTE<br>External department<br>$+z$ PTE | | Bundesbank<br>$+x$ euros | Domestic department<br>$+x$ euros |

*Note*: we assume that $z$ PTE $= x$ euros

**Table 3** The result of payment finality for a trade deficit non-euro EMU country

| Banco de Portugal | | | |
|---|---|---|---|
| Domestic department | | External department | |
| Assets | Liabilities | Assets | Liabilities |
| Bank B1 (importer)<br>$+z$ PTE<br>Financial assets<br>$-z$ PTE | | 0 euros | 0 euros |

These (or other) financial assets will be transferred to those countries whose central banks have a positive balance with the TARGET2 settlement facility, such as Germany in our stylised case. As a result of this transfer, the Banco de Portugal will be credited with the corresponding amount of $x$ euros (Table 2).

All in all, the Portuguese trade deficit ($x$ euros) is paid finally, by an export of financial assets representing Portugal's (current or future) output, whose property rights are thus transferred from the set of Portuguese residents to the trade surplus country (Germany). This makes sure that (the external department of) the Banco de Portugal has no further debt against the TARGET2 settlement facility, hence against other countries (Table 3).

Now, if no German economic agents, including German banks and non-bank financial institutions, intend to buy those financial assets that the Portuguese central bank has to sell in order to pay the country's trade deficit, the TARGET2 settlement facility might be asked to intervene in this regard. If so, then this facility will act thereby as a financial intermediary at international level, lending to trade deficit countries (like Portugal) the euro balances saved by trade surplus countries (such as Germany). In fact, this is not at all akin to introducing an international lender of last resort, as the TARGET2 settlement facility would not grant an *ex-nihilo* credit to the NCB of a trade deficit country (such as Portugal in our stylised case). As a matter of fact, no NCB has been operating to date as a lender of last resort—be it for the banking sector or the general government sector—as it merely transfers to deficit-spending agents an income that is saved by other agents. As Table 4 shows, this financial intermediation may occur also between countries, provided that EMU member countries agree to set up a TARGET2 settlement facility as pointed out above.

**Table 4** An international financial intermediary is not a lender of last resort

<table>
<tr><td colspan="4">Banco de Portugal</td></tr>
<tr><td colspan="2">Domestic department</td><td colspan="2">External department</td></tr>
<tr><td>Assets</td><td>Liabilities</td><td>Assets</td><td>Liabilities</td></tr>
<tr><td>Financial assets sold to the TARGET2 settlement facility<br>–z PTE<br>External department<br>+z PTE</td><td></td><td>TARGET2 settlement facility<br>+x euros</td><td>Domestic department<br>+x euros</td></tr>
<tr><td colspan="4">TARGET2 settlement facility</td></tr>
<tr><td>Assets</td><td colspan="3">Liabilities</td></tr>
<tr><td></td><td colspan="3">Bundesbank (External department)<br>–x euros<br>Banco de Portugal (External department)<br>+x euros</td></tr>
<tr><td colspan="4">Bundesbank</td></tr>
<tr><td colspan="2">Domestic department</td><td colspan="2">External department</td></tr>
<tr><td>Assets</td><td>Liabilities</td><td>Assets</td><td>Liabilities</td></tr>
<tr><td>Financial assets bought from the TARGET2 settlement facility<br>+x euros</td><td>External department<br>+x euros</td><td>Domestic department<br>+x euros</td><td>TARGET2 settlement facility<br>+x euros</td></tr>
</table>

*Note*: we assume that $z$ PTE $= x$ euros

As Table 4 shows, the Bundesbank disposes of $x$ euros (the amount corresponding to the German trade surplus in our stylised case) to pay those financial assets that it purchases from the TARGET2 settlement facility. The latter can therefore transfer to the Banco de Portugal the purchasing power that its country needs to pay its trade deficit finally, via a sale of financial assets to the TARGET2 settlement facility. All in all, as Fig. 3 shows clearly, this facility acts just as an international financial intermediary, since it transfers to a trade deficit country (Portugal, in our case) the purchasing power earned by a trade surplus country (Germany)—without adding any units of purchasing power by a stroke of the pen (or the keyboard).

Eventually, the lender of last resort is the NCB of the trade surplus country (namely, the Bundesbank in our stylised case), which—through the intermediation of the TARGET2 settlement facility—provides a loan to the NCB of the trade deficit country (the Banco de Portugal in our case) for an amount that allows the latter country to pay finally, thus disposing of the TARGET2 imbalances problem that actually epitomises the structural–monetary flaw of the euro area.

## 4 Making the EMU a Viable Monetary Union

Transforming the euro into the common currency of EMU member countries needing to reintroduce their own national currencies to carry out an appropriate 'exit strategy' from the crisis will be instrumental to transform the euro area into a

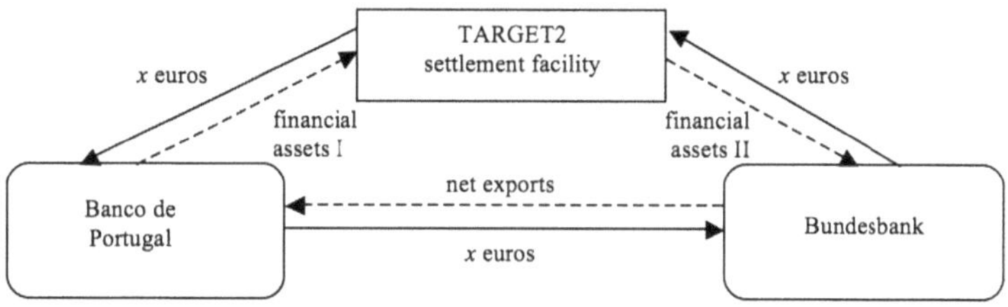


**Fig. 3** The TARGET2 settlement facility as an international financial intermediary

viable monetary union. It will enlarge the policy room for manoeuvre for those member countries that can thereby steer their own monetary policy with the aim to contributing to economic growth, fiscal revenues and job creation, thereby also impacting on intra euro-area trade favourably. It will not be enough, however, to rebalance the macroeconomic imbalances observed—to date—across the euro area. A further contribution in that respect may come from fiscal transfers from rich to poor regions or countries, as Draghi (2014) pointed out cogently. As noted above, there should be a European Treasury—empowered to tax and spend—opposite the ECB. In order to achieve this goal, EMU member countries should proceed by blending 'policies, politics, and polity' to fulfil the objectives laid down in article 3, paragraph 3, of the TEU (see above). The first step in this direction is to design and then agree on a series of pan-European taxes,[6] levied by the European Treasury. Part of their revenues must be distributed to EMU member countries with a view to reduce their own imbalances. Such a fiscal equalisation mechanism will reduce real economic divergence between all EMU countries (measured notably by per-capita income levels in real terms, and by unemployment rates for the most problematic categories of wage earners, such as the young, women, and senior workers, particularly when they are unskilled, are not mobile, or have a reduced capacity to work).

If the European Treasury can collect taxes for an amount corresponding (at least) to 10 % of the euro-area GDP, it may then issue various types of eurobonds[7] to gather a relevant amount of savings that could finance a variety of investment projects across the EMU—for which euro-area banks would also be interested in opening credit lines—and particularly in the member countries most in need of them. As pointed out by Holland (2010, 53), "if the investments [financed by the issuance of eurobonds] were in the social domain, in areas such as health, education, urban renewal and the environment, they could lift the cost of this from national budgets and enhance the ability of lower-income member states to align their investment, employment and welfare levels with those of more advanced member states, without recourse to a common fiscal policy."

[6]Natural candidates for such pan-European taxes would be bank-based financial transactions and uses of non-renewable resources across the euro area (see Rossi 2012b).

[7]Various authors have proposed different types of eurobonds, called eurobills, blue bonds, red bonds, or stability bonds. See Claessens et al. (2012) for a summary and an assessment of these (and other types of) eurobonds.

The ECB will also be able to buy eurobonds without infringing its own statutes or the TEU, because eurobonds issuance does not imply mutualising the public debt of EMU member countries. The ECB could notably purchase eurobonds through a variety of its open-market operations—as the Fed does with regard to the US federal government, as explained above. By intervening on the eurobonds primary market, the ECB will send a clear signal to market participants that these securities may be used as eligible assets for those refinancing operations that euro-area banks need to carry out on a regular basis. It will thereby much increase eurobonds' liquidity as well as circulation, thus contributing to make its own monetary policy decisions and interventions more efficient all over the EMU.

The issuance of eurobonds by a European Treasury will also make it easier to finance a fiscal equalisation mechanism to make sure that the poorer EMU member countries can reduce if not close the gap separating them from the richer EMU countries. This will be instrumental in enhancing real economic convergence between these two types of euro-area countries, through sustainable economic growth and solidarity between all of them (Pisani-Ferry 2014 elaborates on this). It thereby alleviates the burden on a number of national governments' budgets, thereby freeing up financial resources to be invested in those countries most in need of an economic recovery, which will therefore be also in a position to reimburse their maturing debts and finally pay for those goods and services they need to import in order for their domestic economy to grow and develop further—in a virtuous circle including all euro-area countries for the common good.

## 5 Conclusion

This chapter has addressed the structural–monetary flaw of the EMU, that is, its lack of payment finality as regards those countries (represented by their NCBs) participating in the TARGET2 payments system. Even though this flaw has remained unnoticed so far—since it has nothing to do with agents' behaviour and does not impede payment finality at their level—it is a major factor of systemic crisis for the euro area as a whole. To get rid of such as flaw, a structural–monetary reform is in order. It consists in making sure that EMU countries pay, and are paid, finally, owing to the issuance of the euro as their common (rather than single) currency by an international settlement facility that can be assigned to the TARGET2 payments protocol. This will allow various countries, namely those actually most suffering from the euro-area crisis, to reintroduce their own national currencies, thereby recovering monetary sovereignty and thus the capacity to steer their own interest rates policy with a view to contribute to economic growth. This structural–monetary reform will not be enough to dispose of the euro-area crisis, but in fact will be instrumental in order to transform the EMU into a viable monetary union, so much so if it is accompanied by a euro-area fiscal equalisation mechanism to reduce real economic divergence between its poorer and richer member countries. This mechanism can easily be financed with a number of pan-European taxes, to be collected ideally by a European Treasury with the power to spend part of the relevant tax revenues in order to contribute to such a goal—which is indeed clearly spelt out in article 3, paragraph 3 of the TEU. A two-speed monetary union represents a step forward, rather than backward, for Europe: by transforming the euro into their common currency, it allows all those EMU countries that are unable to use a single currency not to lose ground with those other countries for which the 'one-size-fits-all' monetary policy carried out by the ECB does not represent a major problem. Our proposal will thus enhance the support provided by the euro-area population to a project—the EMU—that the 'founding fathers' of the EU considered as instrumental to avert war and disruption—at social and economic level—across Europe.

## References

Andor L (2014) Labour mobility in the EU: challenges and perspectives for a genuine European labour market, lecture at the European University Institute, Florence, 24 June, available at http://europa.eu/rapid/press-release_SPEECH-14-491_en.htm

Barslund M, Busse M, Schwarzwälder J (2015) Labour mobility in Europe: an untapped ressource? Centre for European Policy Studies Policy Brief, No. 327

Bibow J (2016) Making the euro viable: the Euro treasury plan. Eur J Econ Econ Policies: Interv 13(1):72–86

Board of Governors of the Federal Reserve System (2014) Federal Reserve Act. Federal Reserve System, Washington, DC, available at http://www.federalreserve.gov/aboutthefed/fract.htm

Buiter WH, Corsetti G, Roubini N (1993) Excessive deficits: sense and nonsense in the Treaty of Maastricht. Econ Policy 8(16):58–100

Buiter WH, Rahbari E, Michels J (2011) The implications of intra-euro area imbalances in credit flows. Centre for Economic Policy Research Policy Insight, No. 57

Claessens S, Mody A, Vallée S (2012) Paths to eurobonds. International Monetary Fund Working Paper, No. WP/12/172

Dahrendorf R (1997) Perché l'Europa? Riflessioni di un europeista scettico. Laterza, Rome

De Grauwe P, Ji Y (2012) What Germany should fear most is its own fear: an analysis of Target2 and current account imbalances. Centre for European Policy Studies Working Document, No. 368

Draghi M (2014) Stability and prosperity in monetary union, speech at the University of Helsinki, 27 November, available at https://www.ecb.europa.eu/press/key/date/2014/html/sp141127_1.en.html

Échinard Y (ed) (1999) La zone euro et les enjeux de la politique budgétaire: une monnaie, onze budgets.... Presses Universitaires de Grenoble, Grenoble

European Central Bank (2007) Payment and securities settlement systems in the European Union, Volume 1: Euro Area Countries. European Central Bank, Frankfurt

European Central Bank (2011) TARGET annual report 2010. European Central Bank, Frankfurt

Feldstein M (2000) Europe can't handle the euro. Wall Street J, 8 February, available at http://www.nber.org/feldstein/wj020800.html

Frankel J, Rose A (2002) An estimate of the effect of common currencies on trade and income. Q J Econ 117(2):437–466

Goodhart CAE (1989) Money, information and uncertainty, 2nd edn. Macmillan, London (first published 1975)

Hankel W, Nölling W, Schachtschneider KA, Starbatty J (2001) Die Euro-Illusion: Ist Europa noch zu retten? Rowohlt-Taschenbuch-Verlag, Reinbek
Holland S (2010) Financial crises, governance and cohesion: can governments learn up? In: Richardson J (ed) From recession to renewal: the impact of financial crises on public services and local government. Policy Press, Bristol, pp 50–68
Kenen PB (1969) The theory of optimum currency areas: an eclectic view. In: Mundell RA, Swoboda AK (eds) Monetary problems of the international economy. University of Chicago Press, Chicago, pp 41–60
Keynes JM (1930/1971) A treatise on money (vol. I The pure theory of money). Macmillan, London (Reprinted in The Collected Writings of John Maynard Keynes, Vol. V, Macmillan, London)
Krugman P (2011) One size fits one, redux (wonkish). NY Times, 15 June, available at http://krugman.blogs.nytimes.com/2011/06/15/one-size-fits-one-redux-wonkish/?_r=0
Lee J, Crowley PM (2009) Evaluating the stresses from ECB monetary policy in the euro area. Bank of Finland Discussion Paper, No. 11
Machlup F (1963) Reform of the international monetary system. In: Grubel HG (ed) World monetary reform: plans and issues. Stanford University Press/Oxford University Press, Stanford/London, pp 253–260
McKinnon RI (1963) Optimum currency areas. Am Econ Rev 53(4):717–725
Mundell RA (1961) A theory of optimum currency areas. Am Econ Rev 51(4):657–665
Pasinetti LL (1998) The myth (or folly) of the 3 % deficit/GDP Maastricht 'parameter'. Camb J Econ 22(1):103–116
Pisani-Ferry J (2014) The euro crisis and its aftermath. Oxford University Press, Oxford
Rossi S (1997) Modalités d'institution et de fonctionnement d'une banque centrale supranationale: le cas de la Banque Centrale Européenne. Peter Lang, Paris
Rossi S (2007) Money and payments in theory and practice. Routledge, London
Rossi S (2012a) The monetary–structural origin of TARGET2 imbalances across Euroland. In: Gnos C, Rossi S (eds) Modern monetary macroeconomics: a new paradigm for economic policy. Edward Elgar, Cheltenham, pp 221–238
Rossi S (2012b) Replacing recession and austerity with growth and solidarity across Euroland. In: Méaulle M (ed) Austerity is not the solution! Contributions to European economic policy. FEPS, Brussels, pp 33–40
Rossi S (2013) Financialization and monetary union in Europe: the monetary–structural causes of the euro-area crisis. Camb J Reg Econ Soc 6(3):381–400
Rossi S (2015) The euro-area crisis: structural origins and possible exit strategies. In: Bitzenis A, Karagiannis N, Marangos J (eds) Europe in crisis: problems, challenges, and alternative perspectives. Palgrave Macmillan, Basingstoke, pp 143–154
Rossi S, Dafflon B (2012) Repairing the original sin of the European Monetary Union. Int J Monet Econ Financ 5(2):102–123
Sinn H-W, Wollmershäuser T (2012) Target loans, current account balances and capital flows: the ECB's rescue facility. Int Tax Public Financ 19(4):468–508
Tobin J (1992) Money. In: Newman P, Milgate M, Eatwell J (eds) The new Palgrave dictionary of money and finance, vol 2. Palgrave, London, pp 770–779
Westermann F (2012) Two types of capital flight: will a common deposit insurance help to stabilise the TARGET2 imbalances? In: Beck T (ed) Banking Union for Europe: risks and challenges. Centre for Economic Policy Research, London, pp 57–64
Wyplosz C (1991) Monetary union and fiscal policy discipline. In: Commission of the European Communities (ed) The economics of EMU: special edition of "European Economy". Office for official publications of the European Communities, Luxembourg, pp 165–184

# Are Euro Area Economic Structures Changing?

**Francesco Paolo Mongelli, Georgios Papadopoulos, and Elisa Reinhold**

**Abstract** Euro area countries have exhibited modest convergence prior to the financial crisis, but have started to follow diverging paths thereafter. Such divergence has been examined from many angles, and diverse narratives of the crisis have developed. Surprisingly, the gradual transformation of economic structures of euro area countries over the last 15–20 years has instead received less attention. This chapter presents evidence of ongoing changes in the allocation of countries' resources across sectors. Some of such changes even preceded the launch of the euro.

**JEL Codes** E01 • F45 • J21 • O47

## 1 Introduction

Over the past years, the euro area has confronted a mutating crisis which started with the Financial Turmoil in 2007, followed by Lehman's Bankruptcy in 2008, the Global Financial Crisis, and the Great Recession. One fact that went initially unnoticed is that the financial crisis outside the euro area exacerbated the fiscal, macro and financial imbalances that were already accumulating in several euro area countries.

Some years later, the immediate causes of the euro area crisis were an auditing of Greek statistics, and then Greece sovereign default in May 2010. This was quickly followed by a "sudden stop" and reversal of financial flows with loss of market access for Ireland and Portugal. Diverse amplifying factors played an important role such as a lack of a crisis management and resolution framework, and a lack of

The views expressed in this article are those of the authors and do not necessarily reflect those of the ECB or the Eurosystem. We are responsible for any errors or omissions.

F.P. Mongelli (✉)
European Central Bank (ECB) and Goethe University, Frankfurt, Germany
e-mail: Francesco.Mongelli@ecb.int

G. Papadopoulos • E. Reinhold
European Central Bank (ECB), Frankfurt, Germany

 
N. da Costa Cabral et al. (eds.), *The Euro and the Crisis*, Financial and Monetary Policy Studies 43, DOI 10.1007/978-3-319-45710-9_5

financial backstops. Contagion fed an "adverse feedback loop" that spread among weakening sovereigns, fragile banks and shrinking economies.

Several underlying explanations for the euro area crisis have been put forward, including the "*competitiveness narrative*" (Sinn and Valentinyi 2013), "*fiscal narrative*" (Schuknecht et al. 2011; Sinn 2012), and "*banking narrative*" (Constâncio 2013; Chen et al. 2012).[1] It has been argued that the EMU's governance could not prevent—and in part endogenously fuelled—the accumulation of public and private debt in several countries. When the sovereign crisis erupted in 2010, neither a crisis management framework, nor financial backstops for sovereigns or banks to contain the propagation of shocks was in place. This so-called "*institutional narrative*" of the crisis is discussed in Dorrucci et al. (2015). All narratives have been widely examined jointly or in isolation. Each helps to understand how the euro area came so close to breaking-up—the ultimate form of divergence.

*Yet, despite the richness of these explanations, could something important still have been missed?* Yes. The transformation of economic structures of euro area countries over the last 15–20 years comes to mind. In this chapter we present some preliminary evidence about such transformation, set it in the context of the vast literature that preceded the launch of the euro. There were optimistic views, sceptical assessments, critical warnings, and agnostic predictions about countries specialising along their comparative advantages, some of which help to explain diverse initial findings.

The chapter is organised as follows. Section 2 sets the context by reviewing diverse prediction preceding the launch of the euro. This will help rationalising some of the later findings. In order to judge the foresight of some predictions, Sect. 3 presents evidence about income per capita before and after the launch of the euro. This indicates some convergence prior to the launch of the euro, and definitely divergence thereafter. *What might be driving such divergence?* Income per capita is decomposed into developments in labour productivity, employment, participation, and working age ratios to find that different dynamics in labour productivity explain a large share of income divergence. *But what do countries produce, and how is their labour employed?* Section 4 presents a macro-perspective of the changes in economic structures of euro area countries. This is based on the analysis of changes in Gross Value Added-shares. The economic transformation that emerges is significant for several sectors, such as Industry, Construction and the Public sector. In the case of Industry, transformation started well before the launch of the euro. Instead, in some other sectors, such as Construction, and in some countries, excesses appear after the launch of the euro). Section 5 draws some preliminary final remarks, and lists various ways forward for research in this area.

[1]Moreover, households, and to a lesser extent firms, took advantage of cheap and abundant liquidity (Fernández-Villaverde et al. 2013). When the euro area crisis hit, stressed euro area countries experienced "*sudden stops*" and there was financial fragmentation (Camba-Méndez et al. 2014). A "doom loop" ensued (Schambaugh 2012).

The chapter focuses on the 12 initial members of the euro area—i.e., Austria, Belgium, Germany, Greece, France, Finland, Ireland, Italy, Luxembourg, The Netherlands, Portugal, and Spain—as these countries are the most likely to be fully impacted by the EMU project, the preparation for the single currency, and its launch in 1999 (and physical introduction in 2002).

## 2 EMU-Optimists Versus EMU-Pessimists

*What did many academics and experts think about the EMU-project when plans were put forward at the end of the 1980s? What did they expect from the euro?* Before the launch of the new single currency in 1999, there were diverse opinions concerning the future of the euro area, and the prospect for further convergence. At the risk of oversimplifying, they might be summarised as follows.

### 2.1 EMU-Optimism

The consensus view among EMU-optimists was that economic and monetary integration—and the new single currency, the euro—would foster deeper links between countries, and convergence. This view evolved over time. Initially, the "*One Market, One Money*" report assumed that the euro would complement the EU Single Market (Emerson Report 1992), and prevent disruptive competitive devaluations. The euro was also expected to enhance price transparency, discourage price discrimination, promote intra-euro area trade in goods and services, and support economic and financial integration and thus overall convergence.

Some saw the euro as the "cherry on the pie", i.e., the single market pie. Coe and Helpmann (1995) noted instead that integration facilitates "technology spillover", which fosters more similar supply sides, thus supporting symmetry of output fluctuations. McCallum (1995) noted that a single currency facilitates cross-country foreign direct investment (FDIs), building of long-term relationships, supports economic and financial integration, and fosters business cycle synchronisation.

Some years later, the literature on "*One Money, One Market*" changed the perspective about the effects of monetary integration, and postulated that the euro lowers trading costs and removes an important trade barrier, i.e., national currencies and the exchange rate risk that stems from international business relations. It was argued the common currency would steadily catalyse further economic integration, and not just complement the Single Market. This would in turn spur further convergence among euro area countries (Gaspar and Mongelli 2003).[2]

[2]Today we know that the euro has been accompanied by more reciprocal trade between euro area countries (and with no "fortress Europe"). Estimates on the higher degree of openness range from a few percentage points to a more significant increase in intra-euro area trade.

Convergence can develop endogenously, as the "*OCA Endogeneity*" theory predicts. According to this line of reasoning, the euro area may turn into an optimum currency area (OCA) after the launch of monetary integration even if it wasn't an OCA before, or "*countries which join EMU, no matter what their motivation may be, may satisfy OCA properties ex-post even if they do not ex-ante!*" (Frankel and Rose 1998). Summing up, all in all greater integration, more synchronised demand shocks, and further convergence were expected by EMU-optimists.[3]

## 2.2 EMU-Scepticism and Selected Criticisms

The idea of the euro—and the creation of a European Economic and Monetary Union (EMU)—was accompanied by scepticism from the beginning. A large number of US-based academics, including Paul Krugman and Martin Feldstein, were doubtful that the euro area could function as a viable economic and monetary union. In their view, euro area countries, as a group, failed the Optimum Currency Area (OCA) tests[4]: for example, the euro area exhibits little labour mobility, shares no supranational fiscal arrangement comparable to the US Federal Budget (which can buffer asymmetric economic shocks hitting US States), and shares no political union. Feldstein (1999) added that, eventually, the EMU may even lead to war amongst its member countries.

Other EMU-critical academics, such as Barry Eichengreen, Maurice Obstfeld, Kenneth Rogoff, Michael Bordo and Paul Garber, were somewhat more nuanced. They pointed to specific flaws in EMU's institutional framework, such as the lack of a lender of last resort for banks and/or sovereigns, the lack of centralised decision-making, and the lack of a single banking supervision. Chris Sims (1999) asked whether EMU's institutions were equipped to deal with "stress". He observed that "*[...] fiscal institutions as yet unspecified will have to arise or be invented in order for EMU to be a long-term success*".

Another group of critics, both in the US and Europe, felt that an economic and monetary union cannot be viable without a greater degree of political union. In the view of these critics, the EMU's political economy was born weak and would need strengthening (which is happening today with various institutional reforms). In the meantime, the implication of these combined criticisms is that the euro area would

---

[3]Consequently, the borders of new currency unions could be drawn larger in expectation that trade integration and income correlation would augment once a currency union is created. For some qualifications see Wyplosz (2006), and Mongelli and Wyplosz (2008). Then, more recently these early findings were completely overturned when Glick and Rose (2015) re-run a new set of gravity models using a dataset including the euro and found no significant effect of currency union on trade.

[4]For a survey of early EMU scepticism, see "*It Can't Happen, It's a Bad Idea, It Won't Last: U.S. Economists on the EMU and the Euro, 1989–2002*" by Jonung and Drea (2010).

neither have backstops nor political procedures to tackle and contain idiosyncratic shocks.

There is also the *Walter Critique*. With a unified money and bond market, upon the launch of the euro nominal interest rates were equalised. Mechanically, therefore, real interest rates were lower in countries with high inflation, and were also expected to remain at elevated levels. This observation is encapsulated in the *critique* that is named after Sir Richard Walter. The critique held that the effects of the common monetary policy would be more expansionary in euro area countries with high inflation rates, and more contractionary in countries with low inflation. As a result, growing disequilibria may occur, with inflation rising in countries that joined the EMU with higher inflation and declining in low-inflation countries. However, this is not what materialised (Mongelli and Wyplosz 2008). With a fixed exchange rate, higher inflation also means an appreciating exchange rate, which caused competitiveness to deteriorate and reduced demand. Thus any expansionary effects of low real interest rates were partly offset by the contractionary effects of an appreciating real exchange rate.

## 2.3 Predictions About Specialization of Euro Area Countries

"Specialization" is about the emergence of endogenous patterns altering economic structures of euro area countries. Individual euro area countries producing a wide range of products and services 15–20 years ago would over time concentrate on fewer activities, and their economies would become more dissimilar from each other (which is another OCA property). Incomes across countries could become less correlated, and there might even be persistent divergence. This might make euro area countries increasingly vulnerable to idiosyncratic shocks. However, divergence is not a necessary outcome in the presence of compensating risk-sharing channels.

Two complementary channels might foster specialization: the New Trade Theory, and income insurance. With the *New Trade Theory*, Paul Krugman and Anthony Venables argue that the removal of an important trade barrier—i.e., legacy currencies—encourages economies to specialize in a limited variety of productions in order to take advantage of economies of scale. This might not necessarily follow differences in their endowments as postulated in the neoclassical theory (Krugman and Venables 1996). Industrial agglomeration and industry concentration are the likely results, leading to more specialised euro area countries and persistently diverging economic patterns.

Another channel fostering specialisation might also be at work: income insurance. Kalemli-Ozcan et al. (2003) argued that higher financial integration strengthens risk-sharing opportunities. This renders specialisation in production more attractive, and macroeconomic fluctuations less symmetric. Members of a currency union would then become less diversified and more vulnerable to asymmetric shocks. Correspondingly their incomes will become less correlated.

Kalemli-Ozcan et al. (2003) provide empirical evidence that financial integration enhances specialisation in production based on US data.

## 2.4 Predictions on Trade Patterns

Fidrmuc (2004) makes a case that *intra-industry trade* has risen the most among euro area countries thus far. Ceteris paribus, this raises symmetry of business cycles, a point also highlighted by Mélitz (2004). Fontagné and Freudenberg (1999) find that the elimination of exchange rate variability has fostered product differentiation in European trade: i.e., intra-industry trade is occurring more in horizontally differentiated goods (two-way trade in varieties) than in vertically differentiated goods (two-way trade in qualities). On the other side, inter-industry trade would do the opposite. Fontagné and Freudenberg (1999) also argue that even if agglomeration and inter-industry trade may occur in some industries this tendency may be counteracted by overall more intra-industry trade—i.e., trade in diversity.

There is one consideration supporting the view that economic integration may after all not lead to full country specialisation and increased asymmetric shocks within a monetary union. This has to do with the rising importance of services. Economies of scale do not seem to matter as much for services as for industrial activities. As a result, economic integration does not lead to regional concentration of services in the way it does with industries. As services become increasingly important, and today they account for about 70 % or more of GDP in many EU countries, the trend towards regional concentration of economic activities may stop even if economic integration moves forward.

## 2.5 Takeaways from EMU/Euro Predictions

Plans for EMU, and the subsequent launch of the euro, stirred great interest and spurred a wide range of research contributions. With hindsight, diverse criticisms of EMU's architecture are being addressed by a slew of institutional reforms since the onset of the crisis, such as the Fiscal Compact, the Macroeconomic Imbalances Procedures (MIP), the setting up of the Single Supervisory Mechanisms (banking union). There is also a drive towards four-Unions: economic, capital market, fiscal and political unions. The questions of countries' specialisation, and convergence versus divergence, are instead an empirical matter and are discussed in the rest of this chapter, keeping in mind that it may take a long time to see the full effects of the euro.

# 3 Macro Evidence: Convergence Versus Divergence

This section provides a first look into the evolution of income per capita across euro area countries. *Which drivers can help explain the initial modest euro area convergence, and then divergence in recent years?*

## 3.1 Was There Income Convergence?

A good point to start is to look at *β-convergence* among euro area countries. Did countries with an initially lower level of income (measured by the log of real GDP per capita in 1995) experience higher per capita growth in GDP? The sample period is split into three segments: the first pre-euro period from 1995 to 1998, the second period covers the early years of the monetary union from 1999 until 2007, and the last period encompasses the years after the start of the global financial crisis in 2008 until 2014. Hence, we distinguish between convergence/divergence that might have taken place before the launch of the euro, after the launch of the euro, and during the crisis period.

Figure 1 shows the evidence of income convergence or divergence for our sample of 12 Euro area countries. When the entire time period between 1995 and the latest included data (as of 2014) is considered, there is no evidence of income convergence. On the contrary, the pre-euro period shows some weak evidence of beta convergence with a positive coefficient β. Dispersion is high though. One can clearly identify a cluster of middle income countries (as of 1995), which experienced relatively low income growth over the pre-EMU period. Further, both the countries with highest initial income (i.e. Luxembourg) and the countries with lowest initial income in 1995 (i.e. Portugal, Greece and Spain) experienced similar rates of growth in GDP per capita. Ireland is an outlier with the highest per capita income growth over the period analysed. In addition it becomes evident that income in Italy grew at a lower rate than in countries that had comparable income levels in 1995. In fact, real income per capita in Italy was almost the same in 2014 as in 1995.

Income growth continued after the launch of the euro. However, countries that experienced the lowest income growth prior to EMU, such as Germany or Italy, were still growing slowly. Ireland was, again, an outlier with a continued strong growth performance, as were Finland and Greece. The previously identified cluster of middle- to high-income countries can still clearly be identified, so that any attempt to fit a linear model will be driven by countries that are "scattered" around this grouping of countries. There is no evidence of beta convergence during the early EMU period; on the contrary, a linear regression model would show an increasing slope indicating that high income countries grew faster during this period. One should however regard this as weak inference on divergence only, as it is driven by the performance of Luxembourg and others.

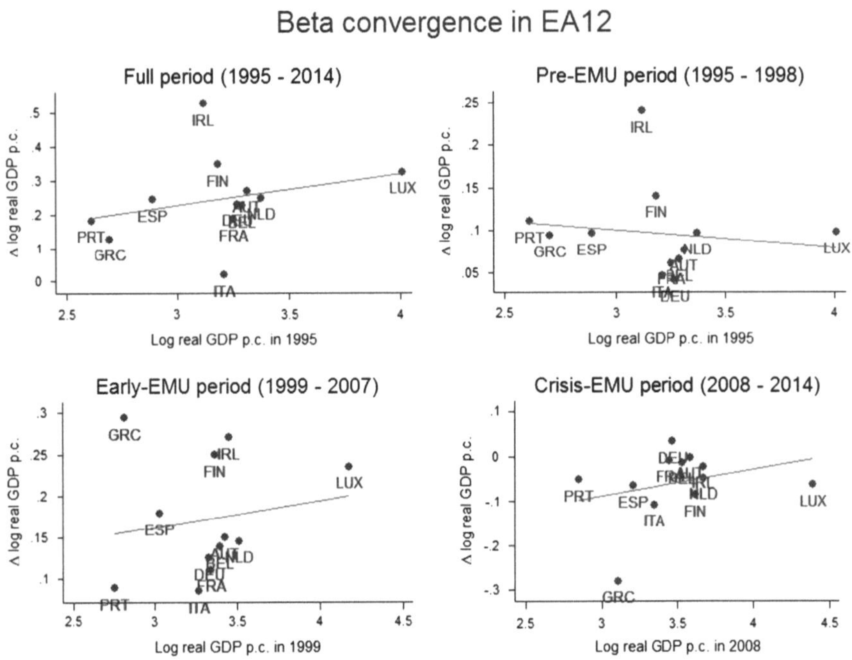


**Fig. 1** Income convergence/divergence in the Euro Area. *Source*: AMECO and authors' calculation

During the crisis period from 2008 to 2014, the picture shows divergence of per capita income within the Euro Area 12, but this time the EA12 countries are grouped relatively close together with one notable exception, which is again Greece. Log real GDP per capita declined for almost all countries in this period, however, the decline was most pronounced in Greece, erasing previous gains. Although the boom-bust experience of Greece stands out (Ireland recovered somewhat in the most recent years), income per capita actually declined in diverse euro area countries and over a protracted period. Such declines were considerable in the cases of Portugal and Italy. Only Germany posted positive growth.[5]

What is also apparent in Fig. 2 is that after an initial decline in the standard deviation of real GDP per capita in the beginning of the sample period, dispersion increased to 0.38 by the end of the second sub period in 2007. During the financial crisis, income differences decreases for about 2 years, probably because economic activity and income declined across the board, after which the standard deviation increases again to above 0.40 toward the end of the sample. Income dispersion within the EA 12 is higher than in the beginning of our sample period, contradicting the hypothesis of sigma convergence.

[5]There is instead some early evidence of income convergence when looking at all EU 27 countries: i.e., when the faster growing new EU members are added, see ECB (2015).

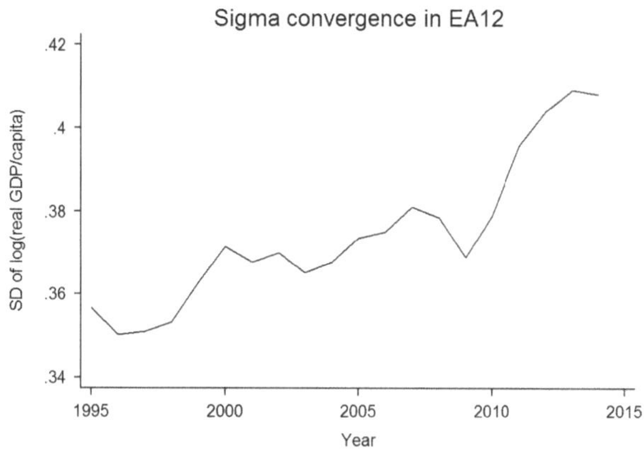


**Fig. 2** Income dispersion. *Source*: AMECO and authors' calculation

*What is happening?* Prima facie, this evidence seems to back the view of diverse EMU critics: that EMU would spur divergence among euro area countries. However, this evidence is not statistically robust, it's just indicative. To shed some light, the rest of this section decomposes the main drivers of income per capita across euro area countries, as well as the changes in economic structures that play a critical role over long periods of time. The search for clues starts by decomposing growth of GDP per capita.

## 3.2 Decomposing Growth of GDP per capita

The evolution of GDP per capita discussed in the previous section, can be decomposed statistically in four main components: the output of those employed (*labour productivity*), the number of people with a job (*employment rate*), the share of people that actually opted to be in the labour market and would like to work (*participation rate*), and the total share of people that might be eligible to work if they wanted to (*working age ratio*).[6]

$$\frac{GDP}{population} = \frac{GDP}{employment} \cdot \frac{employment}{labour force} \cdot \frac{labour force}{population^{working\,age}} \cdot \frac{Population^{working\,age}}{population}$$

[6]In fact, economic growth is the combination of various additional factors such as demographics, capital endowment, human capital, natural resources, comparative advantages, a trained labour force that is able to work, and so on. Several of these factors are beyond the scope of this chapter.

$$GDP\,per\,capita = labour\,productivity \cdot employment\,rate \cdot participation\,rate \cdot working\,age\,ratio$$

Among these four components, labour productivity carries the largest weight and is the one we focus on in the rest of this chapter (see Table 1). Changes in employment rates, participation rates, and working age ratios are handled as exogenous and remain beyond the scope of this chapter. In all euro area countries, annual growth of GDP per capita is positive in the first two sub-periods. Euro area countries grew by about 3.2 % per year on an unweighted basis during 1995–1998, and by about 1.9 % during 1999–2007, i.e, growth slowed down somewhat in the first 9 years with the euro, but still remained at historical averages. Yearly gains in labour productivity account respectively for 1.7 % during 1995–1998 (explaining more than half of annual income growth), and for about 1.1 % during 1999–2007 (explaining a slightly higher share of annual income growth). During 2008–2014 GDP per capita shrank on average by 0.7 % per year, whereas labour productivity still grew, if only by 0.1 %.

Thus, albeit the decline in income growth, labour productivity plays a relatively more substantial role in the "convergence versus divergence" debate. Differences across countries are substantial as euro area countries which underwent IMF/EU/ECB adjustment programmes outgrew all other upon the launch of the euro during 1999–2007 (with the exception of Portugal). Italy is an underperformer in both sub-periods accounting for the smallest growth in labour productivity during 1995–2007.

The picture changed since the start of the global financial crisis in 2008 and then the euro area crisis in 2010. Growth in income per capita slowed down or reverted in all countries with the exception of Germany and Austria. In formerly stressed euro area countries—Greece, Ireland, Portugal, Spain and Italy—income contracted by over 2 % per year on an unweighted basis during 2008–2012. In most countries, income growth rebounded in the last 3 years with a few exceptions. Figure 3 provides a graphical representation of some of the results in Table 1, namely the importance of labour productivity (shown in red) and labour market conditions for growth in per capita income. For the sake of space we focus on Portugal, Italy, Germany and Austria-four countries that we will follow also in the next sections for other indicators.

### 3.3 Takeaways on Income Divergence and Drivers of Growth

This section makes two points. The first is that there is evidence of income divergence across euro area countries: in fact, divergence has been rising—on an irregular path—since launch of the euro. It retrenched somewhat during the Great Recession, but picked up upon the euro area crisis. Income per capita actually fell back in diverse stressed countries. In the meantime, income also rebounded in

**Table 1** Decomposition of GDP growth

| | Percent growth of | 1995–1998 | 1999–2007 | 2008–2015 | | |
|---|---|---|---|---|---|---|
| | | | | | **2008–2012** | **2013–2015** |
| DEU | **GDP/capita=** | **4.1** | **12.4** | **5.0** | **2.3** | **2.7** |
| | *Labour productivity* | *3.4* | *9.4* | *0.6* | *−0.7* | *1.8* |
| | + Employment rate | −1.1 | −0.1 | 2.9 | 1.9 | 0.9 |
| | + Participation rate | 1.9 | 6.0 | 1.2 | 1.1 | 0.0 |
| | + Working age ratio | −0.1 | −2.8 | 0.2 | 0.1 | 0.0 |
| FRA | **GDP/capita=** | **6.1** | **11.1** | **−0.2** | **−0.6** | **0.5** |
| | *Labour productivity* | *4.1* | *9.0* | *2.9* | *1.6* | *0.8* |
| | + Employment rate | −0.2 | 1.8 | −3.2 | −2.6 | 0.0 |
| | + Participation rate | 2.4 | 0.3 | 3.2 | 1.9 | 0.7 |
| | + Working age ratio | −0.1 | 0.0 | −3.1 | −1.5 | −0.9 |
| BEL | **GDP/capita=** | **6.5** | **13.8** | **−1.3** | **−2.3** | **1.2** |
| | *Labour productivity* | *4.5* | *9.4* | *1.3* | *−0.6* | *1.3* |
| | + Employment rate | 0.6 | 0.4 | −1.6 | −0.2 | 0.0 |
| | + Participation rate | 2.0 | 3.5 | 0.8 | −0.7 | 0.6 |
| | + Working age ratio | −0.6 | 0.5 | −1.8 | −0.8 | −0.7 |
| NLD | **GDP/capita=** | **9.7** | **14.5** | **−3.4** | **−4.1** | **1.7** |
| | *Labour productivity* | *3.8* | *9.7* | *1.4* | *−1.1* | *1.9* |
| | + Employment rate | 2.2 | −2.1 | −3.4 | −1.5 | 0.1 |
| | + Participation rate | 4.1 | 7.7 | 1.6 | 0.1 | 0.4 |
| | + Working age ratio | −0.5 | −0.8 | −2.9 | −1.6 | −0.7 |
| LUX | **GDP/capita=** | **9.7** | **23.5** | **−4.8** | **−6.4** | **1.9** |
| | *Labour productivity* | *3.6* | *5.6* | *−4.6* | *−6.2* | *1.6* |
| | + Employment rate | 6.0 | 13.2 | −0.3 | −0.3 | 0.5 |
| | + Participation rate | 1.0 | 3.3 | −1.3 | −1.3 | 0.1 |
| | + Working age ratio | −0.9 | 1.3 | 1.3 | 1.5 | −0.3 |
| ITA | **GDP/capita=** | **4.6** | **8.6** | **−10.8** | **−8.0** | **−0.6** |
| | *Labour productivity* | *2.8* | *0.4* | *−4.2* | *−3.8* | *−0.4* |
| | + Employment rate | −0.1 | 5.6 | −6.7 | −4.3 | −0.6 |
| | + Participation rate | 2.9 | 5.4 | 2.1 | 1.2 | 1.1 |
| | + Working age ratio | −1.0 | −2.9 | −2.0 | −1.0 | −0.6 |
| IRE | **GDP/capita=** | **24.3** | **27.1** | **0.5** | **−6.6** | **7.1** |
| | *Labour productivity* | *10.0* | *15.2* | *13.0* | *10.2* | *4.9* |
| | + Employment rate | 5.9 | 0.2 | −2.3 | −8.3 | 3.3 |
| | + Participation rate | 5.6 | 8.4 | −4.3 | −4.9 | 0.3 |
| | + Working age ratio | 2.8 | 3.4 | −5.9 | −3.6 | −1.4 |
| GRC | **GDP/capita=** | **9.4** | **29.4** | **−27.1** | **−25.3** | **1.6** |
| | *Labour productivity* | *7.9* | *21.0* | *−7.6* | *−7.6* | *0.0* |
| | + Employment rate | −4.0 | 3.6 | −20.1 | −19.0 | 2.5 |
| | + Participation rate | 4.9 | 6.5 | 3.1 | 3.2 | −0.8 |
| | + Working age ratio | 0.5 | −1.7 | −2.4 | −2.0 | −0.1 |

(continued)

**Table 1** (continued)

| | Percent growth of | 1995–1998 | 1999–2007 | 2008–2015 | 2008–2012 | 2013–2015 |
|---|---|---|---|---|---|---|
| ESP | **GDP/capita=** | **9.6** | **17.2** | **−4.5** | **−8.1** | **4.6** |
| | *Labour productivity* | *1.1* | *0.5* | *9.7* | *8.2* | *0.0* |
| | + Employment rate | 4.3 | 1.4 | −12.8 | −16.2 | 5.0 |
| | + Participation rate | 3.8 | 14.5 | 2.5 | 2.0 | 0.5 |
| | + Working age ratio | 0.4 | 0.8 | −3.7 | −2.1 | −0.9 |
| PRT | **GDP/capita=** | **11.1** | **8.9** | **−4.1** | **−6.7** | **3.7** |
| | *Labour productivity* | *5.4* | *9.5* | *5.1* | *3.2* | *0.5* |
| | + Employment rate | 0.0 | −6.2 | −4.3 | −6.7 | 3.4 |
| | + Participation rate | 5.4 | 6.8 | −3.5 | −2.2 | −0.3 |
| | + Working age ratio | 0.2 | −1.1 | −1.4 | −1.1 | 0.1 |
| AUT | **GDP/capita=** | **7.7** | **15.0** | **0.0** | **0.6** | **−0.2** |
| | *Labour productivity* | 5.9 | *11.1* | *−2.3* | *−1.5* | *−0.4* |
| | + Employment rate | 2.6 | −0.8 | −0.4 | 0.2 | −0.2 |
| | + Participation rate | −1.1 | 4.4 | 3.2 | 1.7 | 0.7 |
| | + Working age ratio | 0.2 | 0.2 | −0.4 | 0.1 | −0.3 |
| FIN | **GDP/capita=** | **14.1** | **24.9** | **−8.9** | **−6.5** | **−0.7** |
| | *Labour productivity* | *8.3* | *16.5* | *−3.1* | *−3.6* | *0.4* |
| | + Employment rate | 5.6 | 6.3 | −2.0 | −0.5 | −1.0 |
| | + Participation rate | 0.1 | 2.7 | 1.0 | −0.1 | 1.6 |
| | + Working age ratio | 0.0 | −0.5 | −4.8 | −2.2 | −1.7 |

Ireland, Spain and also Portugal. The second point, is that the main driver of changes in income, are changes in labour productivity which also swing by wide margins and develop unevenly across countries. Yet, this analysis has limitations in telling us what is happening at the level of economic structures. In order to search the root causes of euro area divergence, the chapter now turns to the analysis of sectoral specialisation of euro area countries.

## 4 Evidence of Sectorial Specialisation in the Euro Area

This section focuses on shares in Gross Value Added (GVA) along the main sectors of the economy. GVA-shares measure the contribution to the economy of each sector, and sum up to the Gross Domestic Product (GDP).[7] Changes in GVA-shares

[7]Technically, the relation is the following: the sum of GVA-shares at current basic prices, plus taxes on goods and services, less subsidies on goods and services provides a measure of GDP at current market prices.

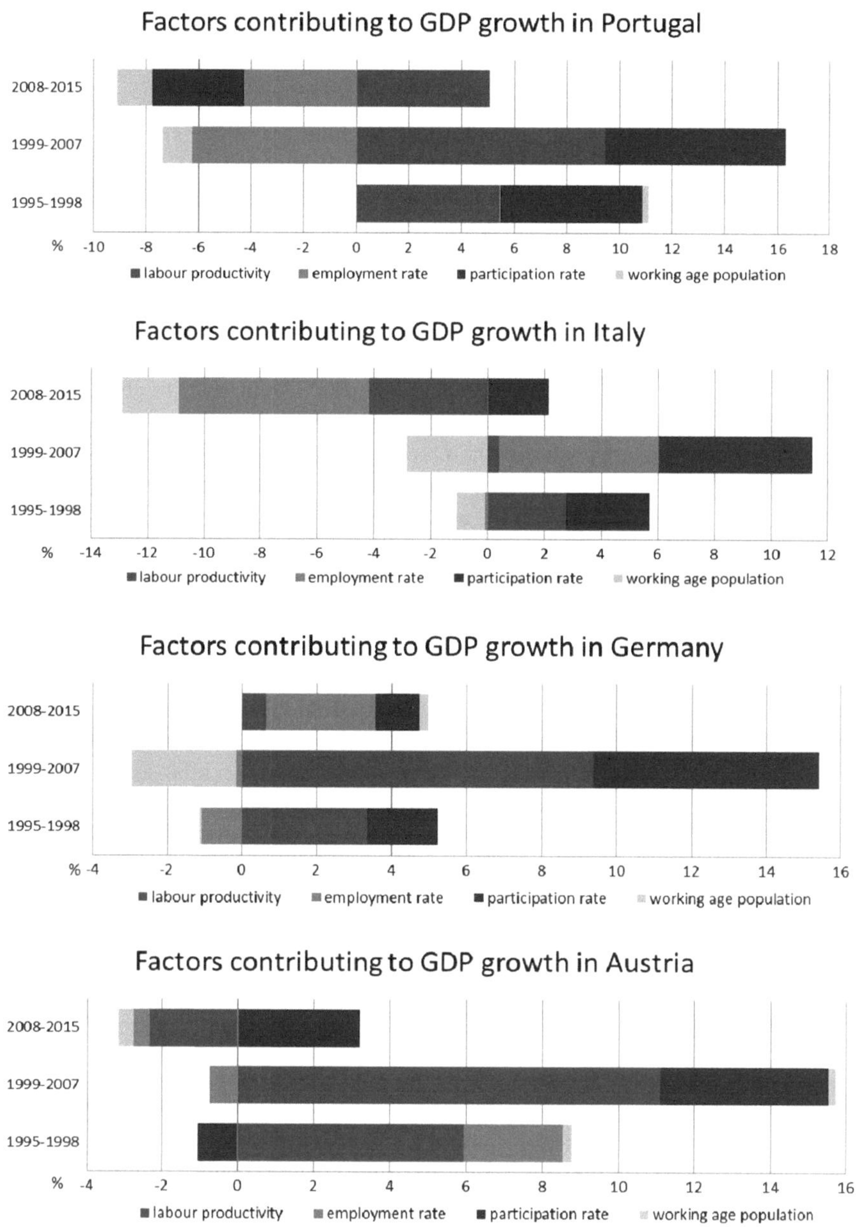


**Fig. 3** Examples of GDP growth decomposition

provide an initial magnitude of change in economic structures. This section also plots the sub-sectors of manufacturing as a share of industrial Gross Value Added, and discusses possible explanations, as well as implications, of the main findings.

## 4.1 *Slow, but Steady, Changes in Euro Area Gross Value Added-Shares*

Changes in GVA-shares of the euro area as a whole are rather gradual. Figure 4 depicts the share of the ten sectors out of total gross value added (GVA). These are: Industry, Construction, IT, Professional, Agriculture, Public Sector, Financial Sector, Real Estate, Trade, and Arts. While the weights of the Wholesale and Retail Sale Sector as well as the sector of Real Estate activities do not change significantly over time, the size of other sectors clearly vary over the period 1995–2014. The size of the sector of Professional, Scientific and Technical Activities as well as the ICT (Information and Communication Technology) sector steadily rises. The ICT especially sector increases over time, growing from 3 % in 1995 to almost 6 % in 2014. Construction and the Financial Sector grow until the onset of the crisis, but retrenched somewhat in the aftermath in recent years. In addition, the industrial and public sectors are clearly affected by the crisis, even though the effect appears to work in opposite directions. Until the crisis, the size of the industrial sector steadily declines to around 20 % of total GVA.

During the crisis, the share of industrial output initially fell, relative to total GVA and, despite a small bounce back, still has not returned to the pre-crisis level. The average share of Industry in gross value added in the EA12 declined from over 23 % in 1995 to around 19 % in 2014. Yet, interestingly, the share seems to have stabilised in early 2011. Might the crisis have spurred changes bucking the declining trend? To stabilize the economy, the Public Sector share increased during the crisis and has stabilized on this elevated level. Construction exhibits a slow decline at the beginning of our sample period, and a more pronounced fall after the outset of the crisis in 2007. We don't see a discontinuity around the time of the launch of the euro or the early years of the single currency, i.e. until 2007.

## 4.2 *Changes in Sectoral GVA-Shares Across Euro Area Countries*

This section looks at the evolution of some specific sectors over the sample period, starting with the industrial sector (Fig. 5). The only countries that did not experience a decline in Industry shares before the crisis were Germany and Austria, while Finland experienced a modest fall. During the Global Financial Crisis and Great Recession—i.e. between 2008 and 2010/2011—the share of Industry experienced a sharp decline. A partial rebound took place after 2012 followed by a stabilisation thereafter: looking at euro area as a whole, might this be trend reversal? Yet there are national stories. Whereas most countries' shares had recovered or at least stabilized by 2011, they continued to decline in Finland, Belgium and Luxembourg. When the entire sample period is taken into account, from 1995 up to 2014, Finland suffered the most severe decline in overall industry (8.5 %), followed by Belgium

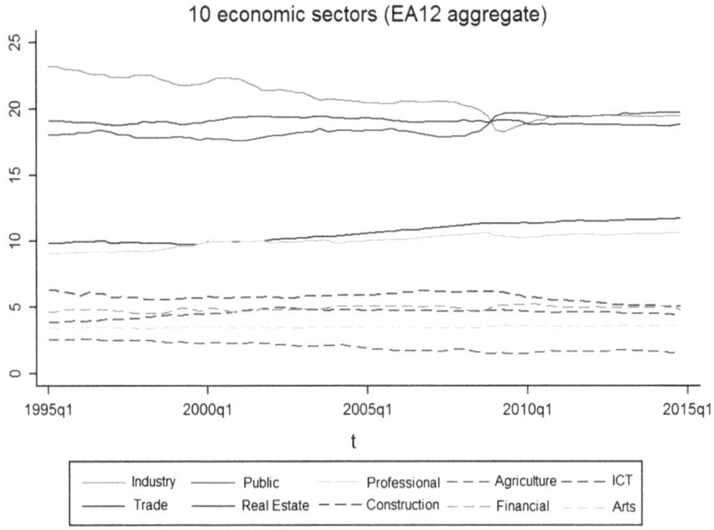


**Fig. 4** Share of economic sectors in total GVA (in percent), 1995–2014. *Source*: Eurostat. Data is adjusted seasonally and by working days

(7.1 %) and by Ireland (5.8 %). Austria and Germany, Ireland, and Finland (until recently) managed to maintain a high industry share. Other countries, such as Belgium, the Netherlands, France, Spain, Greece, Portugal and Luxembourg saw their industrial sector decline. The Coefficient of variation shows that dispersion of industry shares in GVA was low before the Euro introduction, but started to increase afterwards.

Figure 6 illustrates the importance of the construction sector for the EA12 countries. Its share in total GVA was well above average in Ireland, Portugal, Austria, and roughly twice the EA average in Spain. While its importance started to decline in the early 2000s for Portugal and Austria, the bubbles in both the Spanish and Irish construction sectors continued to grow until the financial crisis. At this point, both countries experienced a rapid drop in construction GVA of 5 %–6 % respectively. Instead, over the past decade, Germany has been the EA12 country with the lowest share of construction in GVA (ranging between 4 and 4.5 %), a level that is now only undercut by Ireland and Greece. Variation of construction shares increased during the early-EMU period, but dropped with the crisis.[8]

As seen in Fig. 7, the Financial Sector is overwhelmingly important in Luxembourg accounting for about 25 % of economic activity, whereas the GVA share of this sector is considerably lower in all other countries. The Dutch financial sector

[8]The opposite picture arises when we examine at the sale and rental of properties as captured by the Real Estate Sector share in GVA (see Annex). Spain, as well as Portugal and Ireland had lower shares than the other EA countries. An above average increase in the importance of this sector can be noted in Greece. Extreme developments in Greece and Ireland also drive the increasing coefficients of variation.

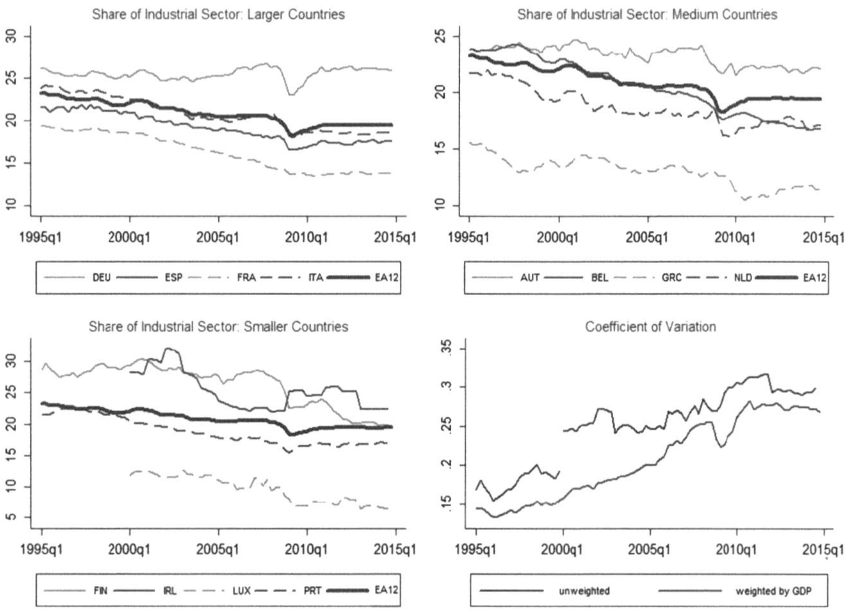


**Fig. 5** GVA shares of industrial sector for euro area (in percent), 1995–2014. *Note*: The figure compares the share of the industrial sector out of total GVA for the EA12 as a whole with the shares computed for the member states (*upper panels* and *lower left panel*). The *lower right panel* shows the coefficient of variation for this sector using data for the founding members of the euro area (for Ireland and Luxembourg the data start in 2000q1). The weighted coefficient of variation is computed by taking the GDP of member states into account

importance increased throughout the crisis, as did the sector's shares in Belgium and Italy.

Prior to the crisis, the importance of the Public Sector remained generally stable hovering around 18 % (see Fig. 8). The exceptions were the Netherlands and Portugal where public sector shares increased before 2008. During the crisis, the share of the public sector leapt to and now hovers around 20 %. Thus, on average, its share is now substantially higher than 20 years ago.

## 4.3 Aggregation of Sectors into Tradable and Non-tradable

Were there different patterns across tradable versus non-tradable sectors in GVA? The 10 economic sectors are roughly divided according to whether the sectors can mainly be regarded as tradable or not[9] (see Fig. 9). Following a conventional

[9]We regard Construction, Financial and Real estate services, as well as Public administration as not tradable. Classifying an entire sector as either tradable or non-tradable is a very crude measure.

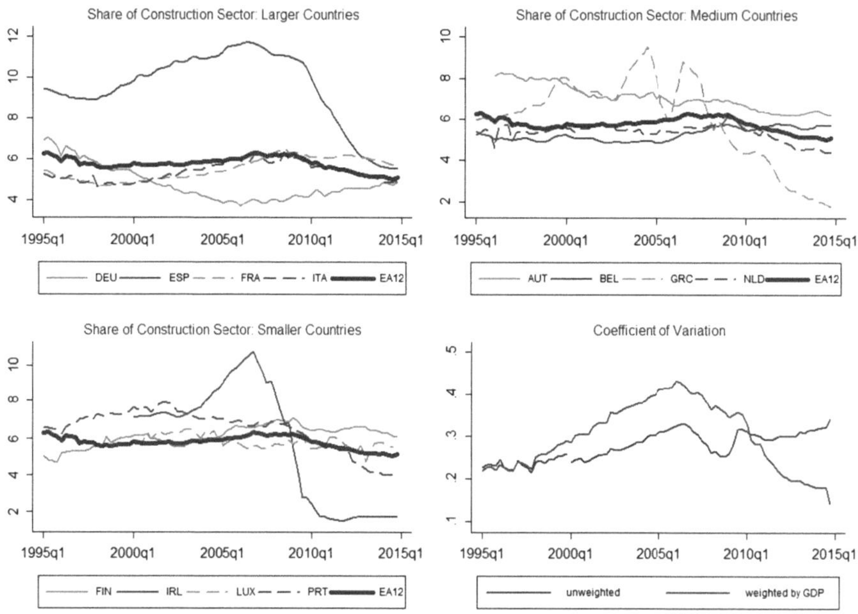


**Fig. 6** GVA share of Construction (in percent), 1995–2014

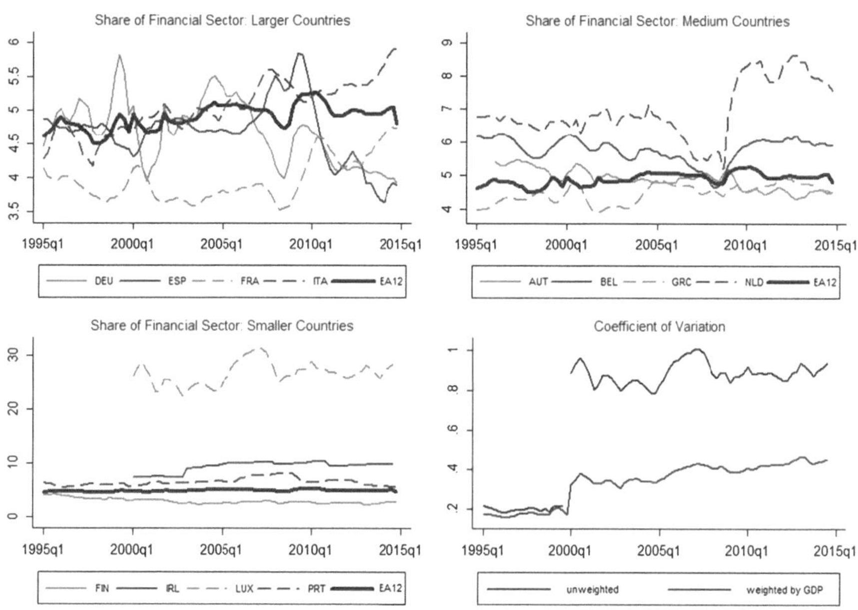


**Fig. 7** GVA share of Financial sector (in percent), 1995–2014

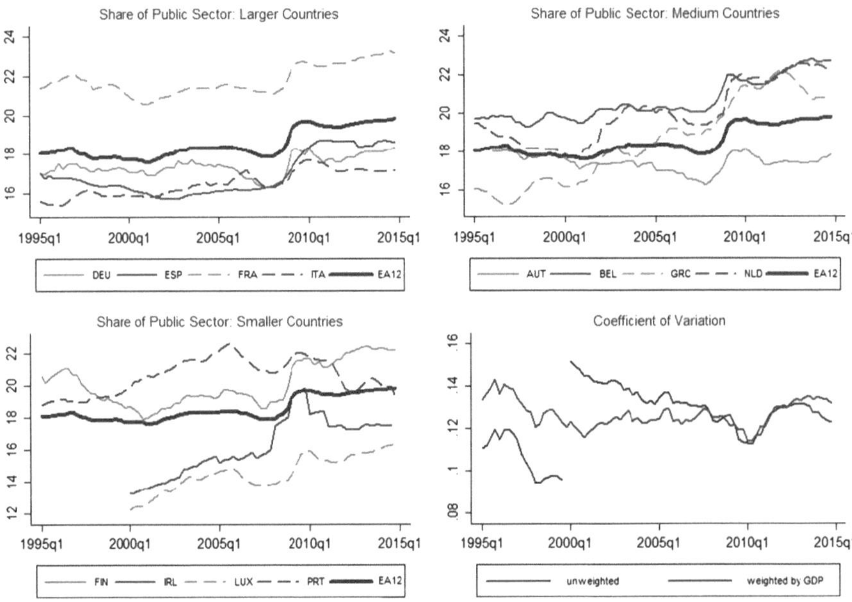


**Fig. 8** GVA share of Public Sector (in percent), 1995–2014

practice (as in Zeugner (2013), Construction, Financial and Real estate services, as well as Public administration are classified as not tradable. Admittedly, classifying entire sectors as either tradable or non-tradable is a very crude measure that should be revisited. The share of non-tradables has been on the rise even before the crisis, notably in France, Greece, Spain, Italy, and Portugal. The high share of non-tradables in Luxembourg is clearly driven by the important role played by the financial sector in the country (and thus due to our classification of sectors). Figure 10 shows the aggregation of GVA sectors that can be classified as market services: confirming the increasing role of services in euro area economies.

## *4.4 A Deeper Look into Sub-industrial Sectors*

What are the main industries across euro area countries? This section provides a comparison of GVA shares of 18 subsectors of manufacturing for a few sample countries from 1995 until the present, depending on the latest available data (see Fig. 11). This analysis is partial and simply indicative: i.e., further work might be very helpful in this area.

In 1995, industries in Austria were relatively specialized in the manufacturing of food and beverages and metal. Over the past 20 years, machinery and metal production became even more important in terms of GVA shares in total manufacturing. The German manufacturing sector looked rather similar in 1995,

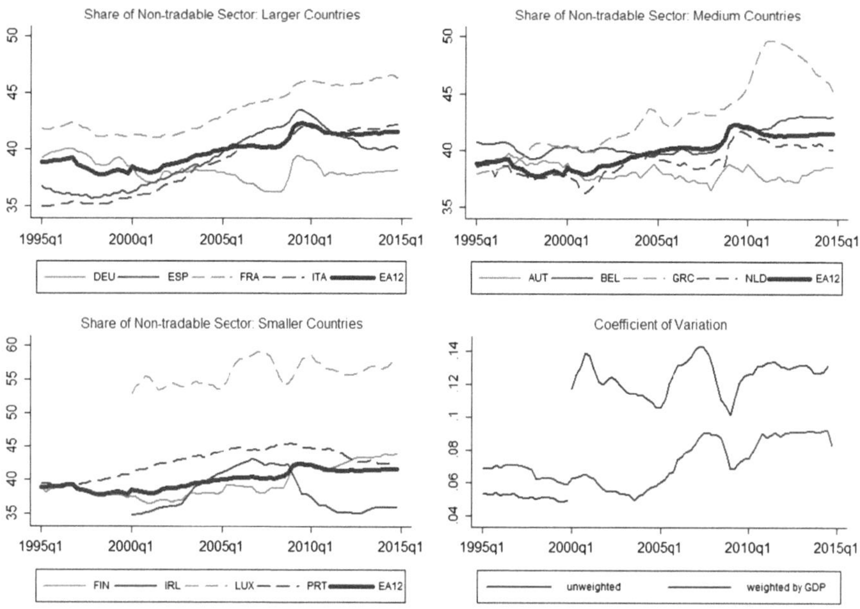


**Fig. 9** GVA share of Tradable and Non-Tradable sectors

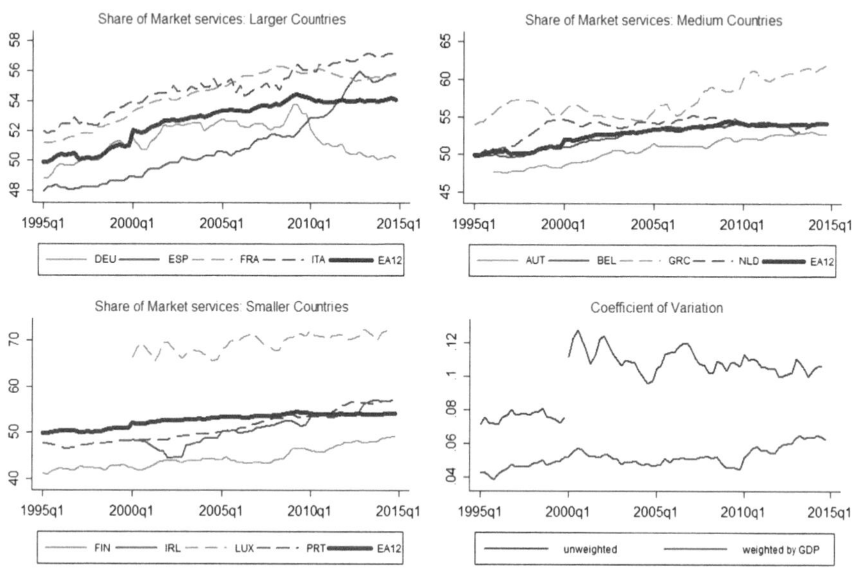


**Fig. 10** GVA share of Market services. *Note*: Market services include NACE sectors G to N and R to U: Wholesale and retail trade, ICT, Financial, Real estate and Professional and technical services, Arts

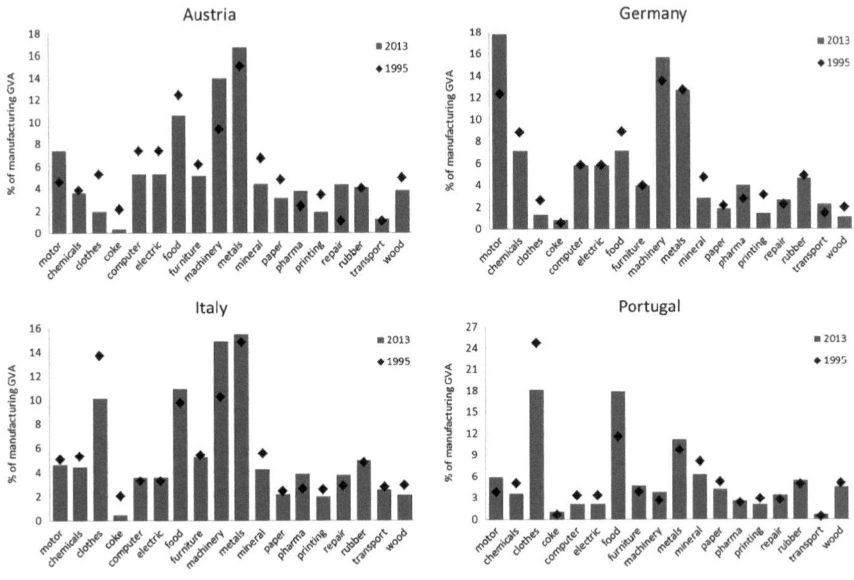


**Fig. 11** Sub-sectors of manufacturing (in percent of total manufacturing GVA). *Source*: Eurostat and authors' calculation

with high GVA shares of machinery and metal, but also of motor vehicles and chemical products. While the automotive, as well as machinery subsectors became relatively more important, the metal industry has remained relatively flat, while food production and chemical production have declined.

Clothing has always played in important role in the Italian and Portuguese economies and while still important, the share of clothing in GVA has declined in recent years. It should be considered that the bulk of clothing manufacturing shifted to Asia in recent decades. Machinery and the processing of food have become relatively more important in Italy. The Portuguese manufacturing sector has drastically increased its reliance on food production and also increased its metal and motor industries somewhat.

## *4.5 Takeaways on Sectorial Specialisation in the Euro Area*

There is evidence that the economic structures of euro area countries have changed substantially over the last 20 years. Specialisation has risen, albeit at different paces across countries and sectors. For some sectors, these changes preceded the launch of the euro (as in the case of Industry): This is also a sign that the single currency is not the only force reshaping European economies. The financial crisis was instead a disruptive event which affected some sectors more than others: for example Construction, Real Estate, and the Public Sector. Industry, that was already on a slow declining path, was heavily impacted by the Global Financial Crisis and in particular the decline in global trade during the Great Recession. Eventually, Industry recovered some ground in the most recent period, but remains below pre-crisis period. There might be timid evidence that the prolonged crisis might have bucked the declining trend, even though it is too early to draw any conclusions on this matter.

The cross country evidence is also striking. To start with, there is a high level of heterogeneity across euro area countries. In other words, euro area countries have very different economic structures (which in and by itself is advantageous with high trade integration). Overall, such heterogeneity seems to be increasing over time in many, but not all, sectors. The dispersion is substantially higher at the end of the sample period in the case of Industry and Real Estate; whereas, in the case of Construction, dispersion rises up to the crisis and then declines, returning to a long-term average.

## 5 Some Final Remarks

The transformation of economic structures of euro area countries over the last 15–20 years has received only modest attention. This chapter finds evidence suggesting that such transformation is underway: gross value added (GVA) shares of Industry and Agriculture started declining already prior to the launch of the euro, while GVA shares of Professional Services and ICT have been steadily rising across euro area; and Financial Sector and Construction rise till the crisis and then retrench. Heterogeneity across countries and most sectors is on the rise.

Such incipient specialisation becomes even more apparent when looking at the dispersion across the 18 manufacturing sectors. Thus, the prediction of Krugman, Venables, Kalemly-Ozcan, Yosha and Soerensen about increasing specialisation and differentiation across countries is corroborated. But how shall these developments be interpreted?

Changing economic structures of euro area countries should not be judged in isolation but understood in the context of several perspectives which we did not explore in this chapter, like:

- The role of financial frictions and financial fragmentation especially during the crisis (see Durre et al. 2014). The vast risk-sharing and income insurance literature suggests to investigate ex-ante and ex-post channels of risk-sharing and the feedback loop with financial deepening.
- The New Trade Theory/Economic Geography suggest a deeper look into the role of "borders" and postulates that a "*polycentric geography is also sustainable*" (Krugman and Venables 1996).
- The degree of business cycle synchronisation across euro area countries, and transmission of monetary policies is seen by some as a meta-OCA property. While economies of scale and agglomeration effects may enhance asymmetries,

the net effect of financial integration on specialisation and shock absorption are more complex to decipher.

Hence we end up with a research agenda and more questions.

## Annex: Additional Graphs and Tables

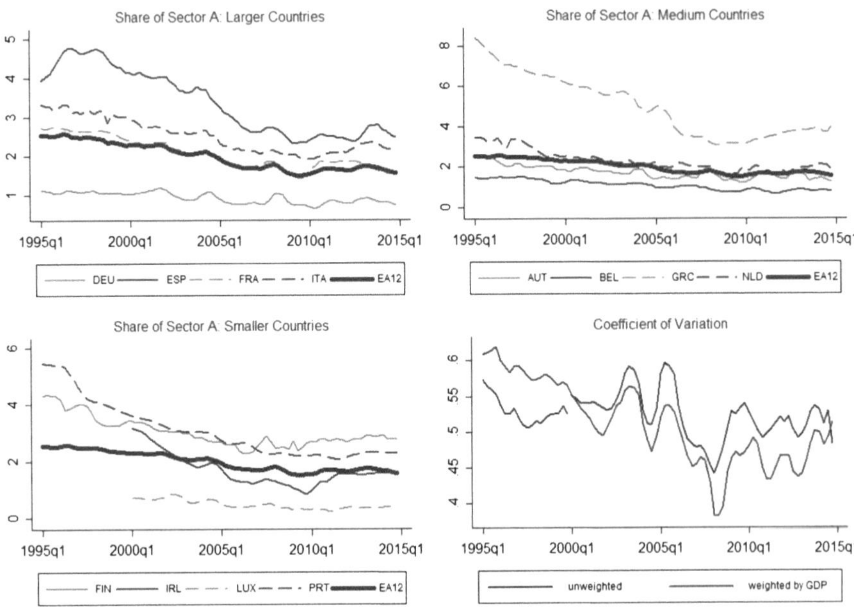


**Fig. 12** GVA Share of Agricultural Sector (in percent), 1995–2014

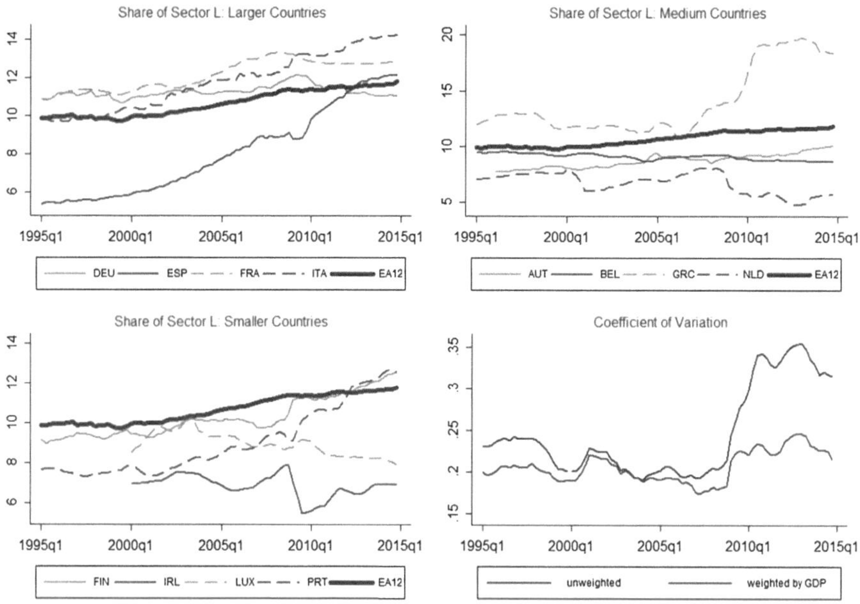


**Fig. 13** GVA Share of Real Estate Sector (in percent), 1995–2014

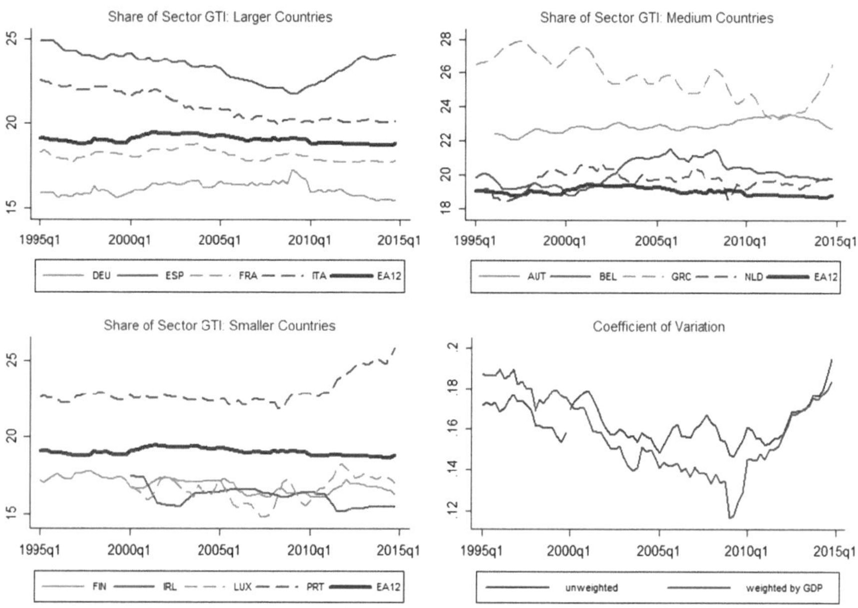


**Fig. 14** GVA Share of Wholesale and Retail Trade Sector (in percent), 1995–2014

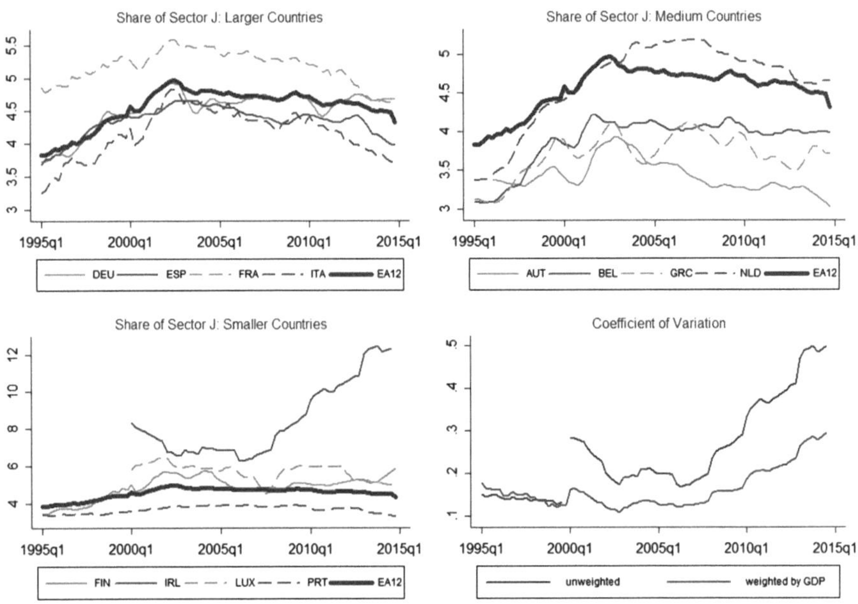


**Fig. 15** GVA Share of ICT Sector (in percent), 1995–2014

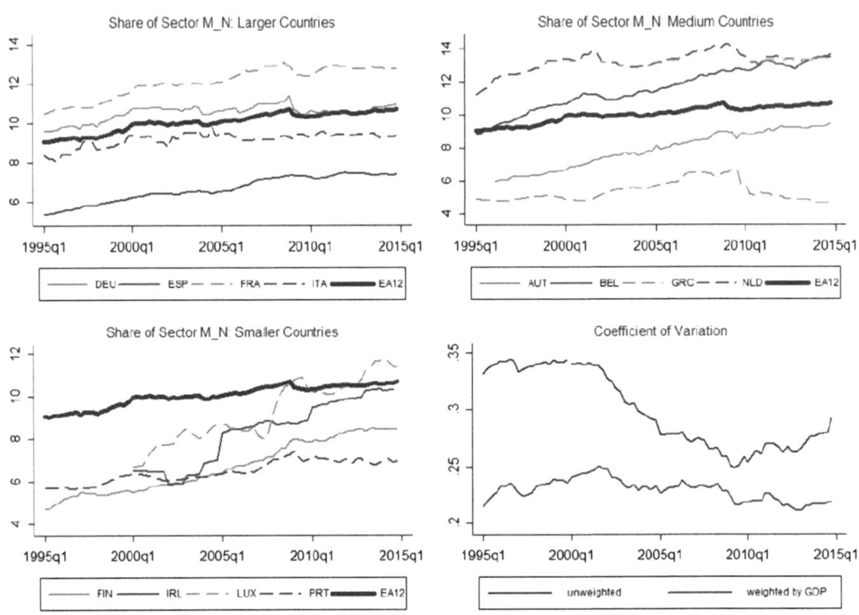


**Fig. 16** GVA Share of Professional Sector (in percent), 1995–2014

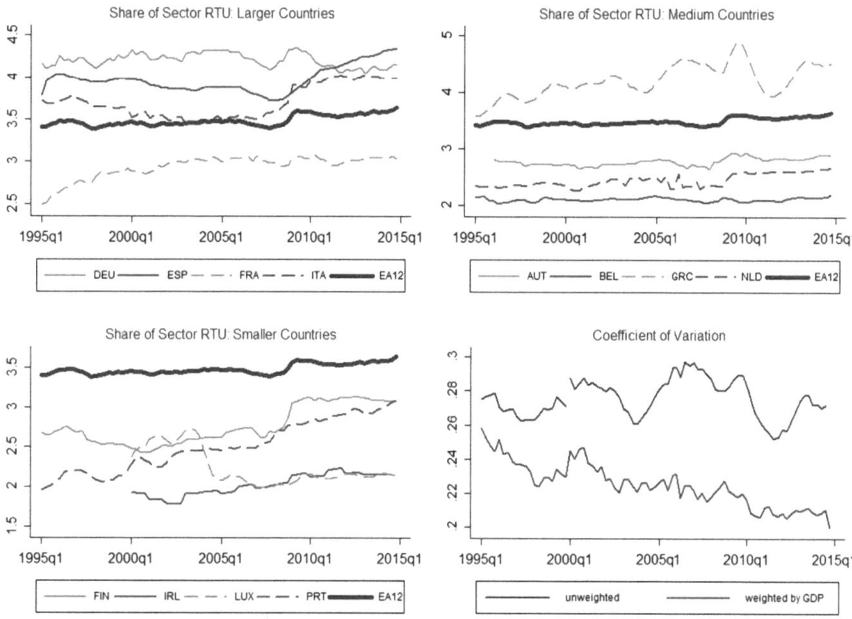


**Fig. 17** GVA Share of Arts, Entertainment and Recreational Activities (in percent), 1995–2014

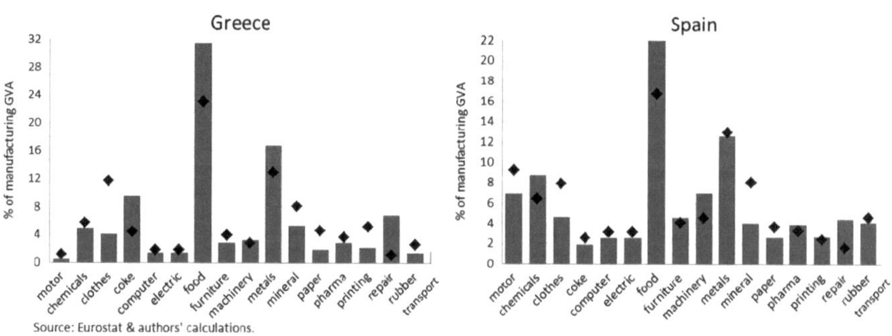


**Fig. 18** Sub-Sectors of manufacturing (in percent of total sub-sector GVA). *Source*: Eurostat and authors' calculation

# References

Camba-Méndez G, Carbó-Valverde S, Rodriguez-Palenzuela D (2014) Financial reputation, market interventions and debt issuance by banks: a truncated two-part model approach. European Central Bank

Chen R, Milesi-Ferretti MG-M, Tressel MT (2012) External imbalances in the Euro area. International Monetary Fund, Washington, DC

Coe DT, Helpman E (1995) International R&D spillovers. Eur Econ Rev 39(5):859–887
Constâncio V (2013) Establishing the single supervisory mechanism. Speech at the BAFT-IFSA 2013 Europe Bank-to-Bank Forum, 29 Jan 2013 (see ECB website)
Dorrucci E, Ioannou D, Mongelli FP, Terzi A (2015) The four Unions 'PIE' on the Monetary Union 'CHERRY': a new index of European Institutional Integration. ECB Occasional Paper (160)
Durre A, Maddaloni A, Mongelli F (2014) Financial fragmentation and ECB monetary policy. Comp Econ Stud 56(3):396–423
Emerson M (1992) One market, one money: an evaluation of the potential benefits and costs of forming an economic and monetary union. Oxford University Press, Oxford
European Central Bank (2015) Real convergence in the euro area: evidence, theory and policy implications. Economic Bulletin Issue 5/2015
Feldstein M (1999) The euro risk. Time Europe Magazine
Fernandez-Villaverde J, Garicano L, Santos T (2013) Political credit cycles: the case of the euro zone. National Bureau of Economic Research
Fidrmuc J (2004) The endogeneity of the optimum currency area criteria, intra-industry trade, and EMU enlargement. Contemp Econ Policy 22(1):1–12
Fontagné L, Freudenberg M (1999) Endogenous symmetry of shocks in a monetary union. Open Econ Rev 10(3):263–287
Frankel JA, Rose AK (1998) The endogenity of the optimum currency area criteria. Econ J 108(449):1009–1025
Gaspar V, Mongelli FP (2003) Monetary unification and the single market. Economic convergence and divergence in Europe: growth and regional development in an enlarged European Union, 24
Glick R, Rose AK (2015) Currency unions and trade: a post-EMU mea culpa. National Bureau of Economic Research
Jonung L, Drea E (2010) It can't happen, it's a bad idea, it won't last: US economists on the EMU and the Euro, 1989–2002. Econ J Watch 7(1):4–52
Kalemli-Ozcan S, Sørensen BE, Yosha O (2003) Risk sharing and industrial specialization: regional and international evidence. Am Econ Rev 93(3):903–918
Krugman P, Venables AJ (1996) Integration, specialization, and adjustment. Eur Econ Rev 40(3-5):959–967
McCallum J (1995) National borders matter: Canada-US regional trade patterns. Am Econ Rev 85(3):615–623
Mélitz J (2004) Risk-sharing and EMU. J Common Mark Stud 42(4):815–840
Mongelli FP, Wyplosz C (2008) The euro at ten–unfulfilled threats and unexpected challenges. In: Paper presented at the 5th ECB central banking conference. ECB
Schuknecht L, Moutot P, Rother P, Stark J (2011) The stability and growth pact: crisis and reform. ECB Occasional Paper (129)
Shambaugh JC (2012) The Euro's three crises Brookings papers on economic activity Spring 2012
Sims CA (1999) The precarious fiscal foundations of EMU. De Economist 147(4):415–436
Sinn HW (2012) Europe's path to disunity. Project Syndicate, http://www.project-syndicate.org/commentary/why-a-united-states-of-europe-has-become-impossible-by-hans-werner-sinn
Sinn HW, Valentinyi A (2013) European imbalances. VoxEU, http://www.voxeu.org/article/european-imbalances
Wyplosz C (2006) European Monetary Union: the dark sides of a major success. Econ Policy 21(46):208–261
Zeugner S (2013) Tradable vs. non-tradable: an empirical approach to the classification of sectors. http://www.zeugner.eu/studies/research/TradedShares_zeugner.pdf

# Differences in Human Capital and Openness to Trade as Barriers to Growth and Convergence in the EU

**Marta C.N. Simões, João A.S. Andrade, and Adelaide P.S. Duarte**

**Abstract** Growth in Southern European EU member states has been weak and is resulting in divergent growth paths relative to the richer EU countries. Convergence in terms of income levels requires more rapid growth in the economically weaker member states but it can succeed or fail depending on possessing necessary human capital and openness to trade levels, fundamental determinants of innovation and diffusion activities that drive productivity growth and thus long-run per capita income growth and convergence. We apply a thresholds regression approach to examine the growth and convergence process of 11 EU member states over the period 1960–2014 using human capital and openness to trade proxies as thresholds identification variables allowing us to determine specific policy implications for different human capital/trade regimes. Our findings confirm the existence of different regimes according to trade levels corresponding to different growth performances due to technological catch-up, external competitiveness, the weight of tradable goods, physical capital accumulation, government size and public debt.

**JEL Classification** C23 • F10 • I25 • O47 • O52

## 1 Introduction

Economic integration in the EU has been viewed by poorer member states such as Southern European countries as a guarantee of convergence with the income levels of the richer older member states (Crespo-Cuaresma et al. 2008; Campos et al. 2014). The objective of convergence is also part of the official treaties described as promoting economic cohesion (Dauderstädt 2014). However, growth in the Southern periphery has been weaker since around the year 2000 and as a consequence of the crisis and the austerity policies implemented this group of

M.C.N. Simões (✉) • J.A.S. Andrade • A.P.S. Duarte
GEMF – Group for Monetary and Financial Studies and Faculty of Economics, University of Coimbra, Av. Dias da Silva 165, 3004-512 Coimbra, Portugal
e-mail: mcsimoes@fe.uc.pt; jasa@fe.uc.pt; maduarte@fe.uc.pt

 
N. da Costa Cabral et al. (eds.), *The Euro and the Crisis*, Financial and Monetary Policy Studies 43, DOI 10.1007/978-3-319-45710-9_6

countries has recorded zero or even negative growth rates in recent years, which are resulting in divergent growth paths relative to the older and richer EU member states (Kaitila 2013). Convergence in terms of income levels requires more rapid growth in the economically weaker member states. However, income convergence and catch-up processes can succeed or fail, depending on possessing relevant and necessary structural characteristics, namely in what concerns human capital availability and openness to trade. Human capital and trade are fundamental determinants of innovation and diffusion activities that drive productivity growth and thus long-run per capita income growth and convergence (Romer 1990; Nelson and Phelps 1966; Abramovitz 1986; Benhabib and Spiegel 2005; Comin and Mestieri 2014; Dar and Amirkhalkhali 2003; Awokuse 2008). The absence of the necessary human capital and trade openness levels can compromise sustained economic growth and convergence.

This paper applies a thresholds model to estimate a growth regression for a sample of 11 EU member states over the period 1960–2014 in order to assess the importance of differences in human capital and trade levels across European countries for growth and convergence in the region. Our main aim is to identify the relevant growth determinants for the EU, assuming that the sign and magnitude of relevant growth determinants will vary with human capital and trade levels. For this purpose we apply an estimation methodology aiming to capture non-linearities in the growth relationships, the Hansen thresholds model. This estimation approach allows for the identification of different impacts of the explanatory variables according to different regimes defined by different values of human capital and/or trade. Given the initially low levels of human capital and trade in the initially poorer member states and its potential negative growth impact both directly and through other growth determinants this seems a suitable approach. Bruce Hansen proposed an estimation methodology for the identification of different regimes based on tests for the existence of "thresholds", with bootstrap (Hansen 1999). This method allows us to identify different human capital and trade regimes selected according to statistical criteria. The threshold model enables splitting the sample into different groups thus potentially capturing a nonlinear effect of different explanatory variables on growth and determine specific policy implications for different regimes.

The chapter proceeds as follows. Section 2 discusses how growth and convergence can be related to human capital and trade. Section 3 is concerned with the estimation strategy and the presentation and discussion of the results. We conclude in Sect. 4.

## 2 Growth and Convergence: The Role of Human Capital and Trade

This section provides an overview of the potential role played by differences in human capital and trade on the process of growth and convergence across countries. While exogenous growth models emphasize the role of capital accumulation in explaining differences in income levels and growth rates across countries in the medium-term, new growth theory views technological change as the main source of growth and differences in the rate of technological change as the principal cause of income differences across countries.

Human capital formation is an essential ingredient in many growth models, exogenous and endogenous, and formal education is viewed as the main source of human capital. Human capital can be described as "(...) the knowledge, skills, competences and other attributes embodied in individuals that are relevant to economic activity" (OECD 1998: 9). Formal education gives rise to an increase in the human capital stock available in the economy thus allowing an expansion of output since it is a major input into the production of final goods (Mankiw et al. 1992). In what is known as the augmented Solow model, Mankiw et al. (1992) introduce human capital as a factor of production of final goods, along with physical capital and labour, with its accumulation explained by the decisions of economic agents in terms of consumption and savings. In a neoclassical framework, the authors show that differences in human capital availability are key in explaining the differences in income levels across countries, with higher human capital accumulation also leading to faster growth, at least in the short to medium-run. But in advanced knowledge-based economies the importance of human capital for the growth process emerges from its fundamental role in the production of new ideas. The endogenous growth models originally developed by Lucas (1988), Romer (1986, 1990), Aghion and Howitt (1992), and Jones (1995) predict that a higher investment in human capital will change the long run path of an economy making it grow faster since human capital drives the domestic rate of innovation. However, since most countries depend on imitation for technological progress, education also influences economic growth by speeding up the rate at which inventions developed by the leaders are adopted. Human capital is viewed as one of the major determinants of the absorptive capacity of an economy that enables it to fully exploit the advantages from technological backwardness (Nelson and Phelps 1966; Abramovitz 1986; Benhabib and Spiegel 1994). Benhabib and Spiegel (1994) pioneer empirical study of the different mechanisms of transmission of education human capital—both as a factor of production of final goods and as a crucial input in the creation of new ideas (inventions), but also for the imitation and absorption of existing technologies—concluded that the relative importance of these different channels depends mainly on the level of development of countries, with the role of human capital in the generation of technological change more important for advanced economies, as expected. Engelbrecht (2003) was concerned with the lack of significance of the technology diffusion variable in the richest third of the sample in the Benhabib and Spiegel (1994) study which, in his opinion, invalidated the Nelson and Phelps approach. The author replicates the former study for the sample of OECD countries and performs a sensitivity analysis of the results to the use of alternative human capital data sets and the presence of outliers. He concludes that the use of these alternative human capital data sets leads to a higher significance of the technology diffusion component.

The role of human capital in technological progress through both innovation and imitation activities is usually modelled as in Eq. (1):

$$\frac{\dot{A}}{A} = g(H) + c(H)\left(\frac{A_{\max}(t) - A(t)}{A(t)}\right), \qquad g_H,\ c_H > 0 \tag{1}$$

where the growth rate of A, the level of technology, is given by $\frac{\dot{A}}{A}$; g(H) and c(H) are non-decreasing functions of H, human capital, corresponding to the idea that the level of education not only enhances the ability of a country to develop its own technological innovations, but also its ability to adapt and implement technologies developed elsewhere. Amax represents the technology level of the technological leader, i.e. the country with the highest A. Thus $\left(\frac{A_{\max}(t)-A(t)}{A(t)}\right)$ represents the distance to the technological leader also known as the technological gap. In this equation human capital and the technological gap are the engines of the growth of technology, with higher levels of human capital allowing for faster technological diffusion (higher impact of the technological gap).

Human capital can thus be particularly important for the post crisis economic recovery, not only by helping workers to find new job opportunities and thus accelerate recovery, but also from a long-run perspective since rapid technological change requires a highly educated workforce if the EU countries are to succeed in sustaining economic growth. The European education systems should thus provide education of sufficient quality and relevant to recover, sustain and even accelerate pre-crisis economy growth rates and promote convergence among its member states.

Additionally, technology diffusion can take place through different channels that involve the transmission of advanced technologies across countries, where international trade can act as an important pathway for the absorption of foreign knowledge. Modelling this role of international trade in imitation activities thus leads to the following extension of Eq. (1):

$$\frac{\dot{A}}{A} = g(H) + f(H; Trade)\left(\frac{A_{\max}(t) - A(t)}{A(t)}\right), \qquad g_H,\ f_H; f_{Trade} > 0 \tag{2}$$

where now the impact of the technological gap on the growth rate of A, the level of technology, depends also on international trade levels as it appears interacted with a function $f$ that depends positively not only on human capital (H) but also on a measure of openness to trade (Trade).

This idea that international trade is associated with faster economic growth is strongly rooted in economic analysis with the positive relationship being justified on the basis of different channels, where accelerating technology diffusion is one of several possible mechanisms of transmission. According to the model developed by Perla et al. (2015), opening to trade affects firms' technology choices and thus has aggregate consequences for growth. Trade liberalization produces reallocation effects by changing firms' incentives to adopt a better technology (copying and implementing the technology of the leaders) resulting in low productivity firms contracting or exiting the market and high productivity exporting firms expanding. The aggregate consequence is faster economic growth since those choices lead to more technology adoption/technology diffusion and thus faster productivity improvements.

On an empirical level, Lewer and Berg (2003) review the existing literature in order to grasp the quantitative gains from trade in terms of economic growth. The authors conclude that the evidence supports a predominantly positive and statistically significant relationship between international trade and growth. Additionally, the average estimates for the coefficients of the growth of trade variables in the cross-section and time-series growth regressions suggest that the growth effects of trade are quite substantial.

To shed additional light on the empirical identification of the relationship, Papageorgiou (2002) uses Hansen's threshold estimation methodology and initial GDP, literacy and the trade share as threshold variables to identify different groups of countries to estimate a growth regression for a cross-country sample composed of 96 countries over the period 1960–1985. The dependent variable is the growth rate of real GDP per capita over the period 1960–1985 and the explanatory variables considered are initial GDP per capita, investment in physical and human capital and the effective population growth rate. The results obtained by the author indicate a particularly striking heterogeneity of coefficient estimates between regimes defined according to the trade threshold variable for middle-income economies, while at the same time indicating that openness may not be as crucial in the growth process of low and high-income countries. In the more open middle-income countries, human capital has a positive and statistically significant growth influence and the convergence mechanism also only applies to this regime, while there is divergence in the less open middle-income countries. Given the controversies concerning the measurement of openness to trade, Serranito (2009) uses ten different indicators, divided in trade intensity ratios and measures of trade restrictions, to investigate the link between trade and output growth and convergence by applying a threshold methodology to standard growth regressions. The sample covers the period 1970–1997 and is composed of 74 countries. As in Papageorgiou (2002), the author uses different threshold variables: initial per capita GDP, the initial level of human capital and the various trade variables. The different rounds of threshold model selection indicate that when trade in the growth regression is measured by a tariff variable the linearity hypothesis applies, whatever the threshold variable used, so the author goes on to compare the OLS results for three different regimes defined according to trade intensity ratios together with the population growth rate or initial income per capita, so with no imposition of a threshold variable a priori. The results obtained indicate that the relationship between growth and its determinants is different for each regime with only the countries in the middle openness regime showing convergence. Another interesting result concerns the growth influence of trade barriers that is only significant in countries belonging to the second regime, while the influence of human capital is always insignificant for less open countries. Both Papageorgiou (2002) and Serranito (2009) however dot not explore the growth effects of the time series variation in trade indicators given the cross section nature of their samples.

# 3 Empirical Model, Methodology and Results

We replicate here estimations of empirical growth models that have been carried out in a large number of previous empirical growth studies in order to identify the relevant growth determinants for our sample of 11 EU member states taking into account parameter heterogeneity. We accomplish this by applying a thresholds methodology. The factors driving growth and convergence included in our empirical model are those highlighted by the theoretical and empirical literature on growth and convergence that developed over recent decades (e.g. Doppelhofer et al. 2004; Durlauf et al. 2005; Sala-i-Martin 1997; Barreto and Hughes 2004; Crespo-Cuaresma et al. 2011). Our ultimate goal is to derive potential implications of the results obtained for a better understanding of the growth and convergence process of Portugal as a member of the EU, based on our sample of 11 EU countries.

## 3.1 Growth Regression Specification

We estimate what is known in the literature as an ad hoc growth regression (e.g. Barro and Lee 1994; Crespo-Cuaresma et al. 2011) that encompasses the neoclassical, technological diffusion and endogenous growth models explanations. As Crespo-Cuaresma et al. (2011) point out this implies that it is not possible to establish a single clear link between the selected variables and a unique growth theory since the same variable can have an important role in different growth theories.[1]

The estimated growth regression is given by Eq. (3):

[1]For example, exogenous growth models emphasize the importance of human capital for growth through factor accumulation to be used in final goods production (see Mankiw et al. 1992), while more recent endogenous growth models emphasize its importance for productivity growth (Lucas 1988; Romer 1990; Nelson and Phelps 1966).

$$g_{it} = \alpha_0 + \beta_1 tfp_{it-1} + X'_{it}\beta_x + \varepsilon_{it} \quad (3)$$

where the real GDP per capita annual growth rate (g_it) depends on technological catch-up/convergence (tfp) and a vector X that includes a set of control variables found to be relevant growth determinants in previous theoretical and empirical growth models through factor accumulation and productivity and or efficiency gains[2]; $\alpha_0$ is the constant term and $\varepsilon$ the error term.

The choice of the explanatory variables was determined by theoretical predictions and previous empirical evidence. The expectations concerning growth and real convergence of the Portuguese economy after EU membership are supported by exogenous and technological diffusion growth models predictions (e.g. Solow 1956; Mankiw et al. 1992; Nelson and Phelps 1966; Barro and Sala-i-Martin 1997). According to exogenous growth models, poorer countries grow faster than initially richer countries through faster factor accumulation since marginal productivities are higher in the former. However, catch-up only occurs if the countries possess the same structural characteristics. In technology diffusion models, real convergence occurs through technological catch-up of the followers, where imitation is less costly than innovation. This assumption implies that the growth rate of technology will be higher in the countries further away from the technological frontier. We consider the USA as the technological leader in order to emphasize the technological convergence mechanism for the sample, so the variable tfp corresponds to the level of technology in country i relative to the level of technology in the USA lagged one period. We expect the estimated coefficient to be negative.

The final vector of control variables X includes the growth rate of the investment rate, measured as GFCF as a percentage of GDP (dlk) with a predicted positive growth impact; public consumption as a percentage of GDP (csh_g) with a predicted negative growth impact; public debt change (dPD) with a predicted negative growth impact; the real exchange rate (rer) with a predicted negative impact on growth since an increase in this variable implies a decrease in price competitiveness in external markets; and the share of the tradable sector in total value added (trad) measured as the value added of industry excluding building and construction (val1) over total value added of industry (val2). We expect that a higher share of non-tradables is detrimental to growth based on its negative impact on productivity. For theoretical arguments and empirical results supporting the previous predictions see for example Baumol (1967), Mankiw et al. (1992), Barro (1990), Karras (1997), Sala-i-Martin (1997), Aghion et al. (1999), Barro (2000), Doppelhofer et al. (2004).

Our database consists of a group of 11 EU countries (Austria, Belgium, Finland, France, Germany, Greece, Ireland Italy, Netherlands, Portugal and Spain), covering

[2]We considered a wide set of potential control variables besides the ones retained in our preferred regressions, such as different proxies of human capital, openness to trade, the capital stock, different shares for non-tradables, and price deflators. Details on these variables and associated estimated regressions can be obtained from the authors.

**Table 1** Variables included in the preferred regressions

| Notations | Description | Source |
|---|---|---|
| g | First difference of logs of GDP (rgdpo) in PPP | PWT 8.1 |
| hc | Index of human capital per person, based on years of schooling and returns to education | PWT 8.1 |
| k | Capital stock in PPP | PWT 8.1 |
| cshx | Share of merchandise exports | PWT 8.1 |
| tfp | TFP level at current PPPs (USA = 1) | PWT 8.1 |
| cshi | Share of gross capital formation at current PPPs | PWT 8.1 |
| cshg | Share of government consumption at current PPPs | PWT 8.1 |
| trad | Value added of industry excluding building and construction (val1) over total values added of industry (val2) | AMECO |
| rer | Real exchange rate based on unit labour costs relative to the rest of the former EU-15 with double exponential weights | AMECO |
| PD | Public debt values relative to GDP | AMECO |

*Notes*: The values of val1 and val2 were not available in AMECO so they were computed applying a simulation process assuming an AR process with a maximum order of 3, allowing to estimate these values based on the BIC criterion. The simulations were done country by country with missing data

the period from 1960 to 2014. Table 1 summarizes the information about the variables included[3] in our preferred regressions and respective sources.

The following variables from PWT8.1 and PWT7.0 were extended until 2014 using the growth rates of the corresponding variables from the World Bank WDI database: cshi with NE.GDI.FTOT.ZS, cshg with NE.CON.GOVT.ZS, cshx and cshm with NE.EXP.GNFS.ZS and NE.IMP.GNFS.ZS. We did the same for the capital series from the PWT8.1, ck, based on the series available in AMECO, the same for the GDP growth rate, rgdpo, and the constant prices GDP (in ppp) from AMECO. For the tfp variable (tfp relative to the USA) from PWT8.1 we used the behaviour of tfp available in AMECO. For hc we built a simple OLS model of hc with SE.XPD.CTOT.ZS from WDI.[4]

## 3.2 Empirical Methodology

Our main objective is to identify non-linearities that might explain different growth regimes associated with differences in human capital and openness to trade. For this purpose we implement a two stage econometric strategy: first, we test for the existence of panel unit roots using the cross-section ADF test (CIPS), Im et al. (2003) and Pesaran (2007), and the panel instrumental generating function

[3]Notice that new variables such as first difference variables or variables with lags of order one or two were not included in Table 1 for economy of space reasons.

[4]Data will be available upon request from the authors.

test (PIGF), (Chang 2002); second, we estimate threshold models following the methodology proposed by Hansen (1999). The second stage is composed of two distinct phases: the identification of the static panel model that best fits our data and of the thresholds and different regimes associated with those models.

The first generation of panel unit root tests may produce inconsistent results since it ignores the presence of cross-sectional dependence assuming that individuals were cross-sectionally independently distributed. The first correction proposed to these tests was to demean the series, which implied assuming that pair-wise cross-section covariances of the error term was the same across individual series. These hypothesis were in clear contradiction with strong co-movements among variables especially in a time of growing integration of economies.

According to Hurlin and Mignon (2007) the tests we apply in this study belong to the second generation of panel unit root tests. They are based on developments of Eq. (4) that characterizes ADF tests for heterogeneous individuals with the unit root hypothesis corresponding to $\alpha_i = 1$.

$$\Delta y_{i,t} = (\alpha_i - 1) \cdot y_{i,t-1} + \sum_{k=1}^{p_i} \alpha_{i,k} \cdot \Delta y_{i,t-k} + \epsilon_{i,t} \tag{4}$$

Pesaran (2007) augmented Eq. (4) with the cross-section averages of lagged levels and first-differences of the individual series. The individual CADF (cross-section ADF) can be averaged from the N cross-sectional units to obtain the CIPS test as $CIPS_n = \frac{1}{\sqrt{N}} \sum_{i=1}^{N} t_i$, where $t_i$ is the cross-section ADF t-ratio for testing $\alpha_i = 1$ for ith unit. Its distribution is not a standard one and the critical values were computed by us.

Chang (2002) proposes an instrumental variable (IV) estimation method for the ADF equation in levels and, to solve for the presence of cross-sectional dependency, he uses a non-linear function F for the lagged level values of y. Finally, for the lagged difference, the augmented part of the ADF equation, he takes as instruments the variable y and respective lags in levels. This transformation is named IGF. The average IV t-ratio statistic is defined as $S_n = \frac{1}{\sqrt{N}} \sum_{i=1}^{N} Z_i$ for the N cross-sectional units and $Z_i$ is the cross-sectional non-linear IV t-ratio statistic for testing $\alpha_i = 1$ for the ith unit. Chang (2002) test presents several advantages: it is suited for balanced and unbalanced panels; it is asymptotically Normal; it is a standardized sum of individual IV t-ratios; and the non-linear transformations take into account the possibility of contemporaneous dependence among cross section units (see Chang 2002; Hurlin and Mignon 2007; Breitung and Pesaran 2005).

Hansen (1999) suggested an econometric methodology to estimate different economic regimes based on statistical tests using bootstrap techniques to account for the existence of different thresholds. Let us consider that the static panel model underlying the threshold model is a fixed effects model and suppose that the dependent variable is the growth rate of y (g) and that we have two kind of regressors: those that are independent from the regimes established by the thresholds, the $x_k$ variables (with k = 1, . . ., j), and those that depend on the regime defined by the threshold indicator variable, the $z_m$ variables (with m = 1, . . ., n), so that the respective impact can vary across thresholds. Additionally, consider that the threshold variable (D) is not included in the equation as a regressor (but it could well be) and that we have three thresholds identified by (d1, d2 and d3) and, consequently, we have four economic regimes. I denotes the indicator function that assumes the value 1 when its condition is respected and 0 otherwise. Under these assumptions the coefficients for the four economic regimes are given by $\beta_{1m}$, $\beta_{2m}$, $\beta_{3m}$ and $\beta_{4m}$, respectively, as represented in Eq. (5):

$$\begin{aligned} g_{it} = \alpha_i + \sum_{k=1}^{j} \delta_k x_k + \sum_{m=1}^{n} \beta_{1m} z_m . I(D \leq d_1) + \sum_{m=1}^{n} \beta_{2m} z_m . I(d_1 < D \leq d_2) \\ + \sum_{m=1}^{n} \beta_{3m} z_m . I(d_2 < D \leq d_3) + \sum_{m=1}^{n} \beta_{4m} z_m . I(d_3 < D) + \mu_{it} \end{aligned} \tag{5}$$

We investigate the existence of three thresholds, at the most, for the whole sample, using Tsung-wu (2015) pdR package for R.[5] In order to test for the existence of the thresholds we apply the likelihood ratio test (F-test), where the null hypothesis accounts for the inexistence of thresholds, LR denotes the test statistic and SL is the level of significance associated to, respectively, 100, 200 and 300 (bootstrap simulations).

## 3.3 *Unit Root Tests Results*

Unit root tests results are presented in Tables 2 and 3. Results from the IPS (Im et al. 2003) test corrected for cross-sectional dependence following Pesaran (2007) are included in Table 3 and the computations were performed by using the package PLM de Croissant and Millo (2008) for R.

In Table 3 we present the results for the Chang (2002) test that includes a correction to the standard ADF test by applying non-linear estimation with instrumental variables that allow for cross-sectional dependence. We used the package pdR from Tsung-Wu (2015) for R to perform the tests.

The results presented in Tables 2 and 3 reveal that the variables g, lhc, dlk, dope, trad, dPD, dtfp, cshi are stationarity and, eventually, also cshg. Since the variable tfp in levels is our key variable to account for the technological catch-up convergence process and not dtfp, stationary, we have not used the first difference

[5] See also Robert Hansen's homepage: http://www.ssc.wisc.edu/~bhansen/

**Table 2** CIPS unit root tests results

| | CIPS (w, C) | | CIPS (C) | | CIPS (C, T) | |
|---|---|---|---|---|---|---|
| g | −4.10 | *** | −4.43 | *** | −4.58 | *** |
| lhc | −1.56 | | −3.06 | *** | −2.99 | ** |
| dlk | −3.27 | *** | −3.29 | *** | −3.74 | *** |
| op | −1.51 | | −2.08 | | −2.25 | |
| dop | −4.93 | *** | −4.98 | *** | −5.06 | *** |
| trad | −2.26 | *** | −2.87 | *** | −3.24 | *** |
| PD | −1.17 | | −1.41 | | −1.49 | |
| dPD | −3.94 | *** | −3.98 | *** | −4.20 | *** |
| tfp | −1.34 | | −1.68 | | −2.25 | |
| dtfp | −4.03 | *** | −4.07 | *** | −4.24 | *** |
| cshi | −1.47 | | −1.47 | | −2.05 | |
| dcshi | −4.89 | *** | −4.96 | *** | −5.07 | *** |
| cshg | −1.15 | | −1.73 | | −1.99 | |
| dcshg | −4.50 | *** | −4.53 | *** | −4.61 | *** |
| rer | −2.35 | *** | −2.22 | * | −2.57 | *** |

*Notes*: CIPS (wC), CIPS (C), CIPS (C, T)—unit root test statistic resulting from the unit root equation without constant, with constant and with constant and trend, respectively, with H0 corresponding to the presence of a unit root in all series against the alternative that at least one of the series is stationary. (***), (**) and (*) indicate a significance level of 1 %, 5 % and 10 %, respectively. The prefix d denotes the first difference of the variable

**Table 3** PIGF unit root tests results

| | PIGF (wC) | | PIGF (C) | | PIGF (C, T) | |
|---|---|---|---|---|---|---|
| g | −6.83 | *** | −8.96 | *** | −10.01 | *** |
| lhc | −3.34 | *** | −3.60 | *** | −1.54 | |
| dlk | −6.87 | *** | −7.30 | *** | −7.94 | *** |
| ope | 6.98 | | −0.38 | | −2.26 | ** |
| dope | −14.74 | *** | −15.29 | *** | −15.80 | *** |
| trad | 2.31 | | 0.07 | | −1.68 | ** |
| PD | 3.07 | | 0.72 | | −0.55 | |
| dPD | −7.85 | *** | −8.21 | *** | −8.51 | *** |
| tfp | 1.35 | | 0.71 | | −1.35 | |
| dtfp | −9.57 | *** | −10.40 | *** | −11.24 | *** |
| cshi | −2.18 | ** | −4.29 | *** | −4.88 | *** |
| cshg | 0.59 | | −0.76 | | −1.53 | * |
| dcshg | −11.66 | *** | −11.90 | *** | −12.09 | *** |
| rer | −1.98 | ** | −3.49 | *** | −4.06 | *** |

*Notes*: PIGF (wC), PIGF (C), PIGF (C, T)—unit root test statistic resulting from estimating the unit root equation without constant, with constant and with constant and trend, respectively, with H0 corresponding to the presence of a unit root in all series against the alternative that at least one of the series is stationary. When applied to panel data this test is the mean of the individual tests, with an asymptotic Normal standard distribution. (***), (**) and (*) indicate a significance level of 1 %, 5 % and 10 %, respectively dtfp = tfpt − tfpt in the estimations but the difference estimated by the model, $tfp_t - \hat{\beta} tfp_{t-1}$.

## 3.4 Evidence from Differences in Human Capital as a Barrier to Growth and Convergence

Our main objective was to test whether human capital and openness of trade constitute barriers to growth and convergence in our sample. We apply a strategy of non-linearities identification corresponding to the estimation of a threshold model following Hansen (1999). Since the threshold test never rejected the null hypothesis of a zero number of thresholds for the human capital variable we adopted a different though very simple strategy with respect to the identification of the influence of human capital on growth.

The estimation of the baseline models reveal that the estimated coefficients for the human capital variables (hc and lhc) were negative in all cases, a sign that goes against the theoretical predictions. We thus assumed that the effect of this variable on growth is not homogenous but depends on reaching a certain minimum amount (lhc*) and accordingly we estimated the following growth Eq. (6):

$$\begin{aligned} g &= F\left(tfp_{-1}, tfp_{-2}, dlck, dPD, cshg, rer, I^{lhc}.lhc\right) && (1) \\ I^{lhc} &= 1, lhc \geq lhc^{*} \wedge = 0,\ lhc < lhc^{*} && (2) \end{aligned} \quad (6)$$

The indicator I was obtained by the minimisation of the sum of the squared deviations using the least squares estimator. The value obtained for lhc* was 2.63 % and corresponds to percentile 0.542 of the growth rate distribution. The results from the estimation of this model 1 are presented in Table 4.

According to the results presented in Table 4, the null hypothesis of the Hausman test was rejected leading us to accept the fixed effects model. This model confirms: (a) the catch-up/convergence process (the overall estimated coefficient on tfp1 and tfp2 is negative), and also; (b) the negative relationship between an increase in public debt (dPD) and growth and between government size, proxied by (cshg), and growth that we think are due to the phenomenon of financial as well as real crowding out; (c) the negative relationship between the real exchange rate and growth due to external competitiveness deterioration; (d) the positive relationship with human capital in the economies that experienced higher growth rates, and finally (e) a positive relationship with the tradable goods share, or conversely, a negative relationship with the nontradable goods share, and growth. We highlight the fact that the estimated coefficient for the variable rer is negative and statistically different from zero but its magnitude is very small. Based on the former result identified as (d) we have used the corresponding human capital proxy associated with higher growth rates in the estimation of all the models that follow.

**Table 4** Estimation results for baseline model 1

| Vars. | Coefficients | SL |
|---|---|---|
| tfp_1 | 5.76e-02 | * |
| tfp_2 | −9.46e-02 | *** |
| dlk | 9.10e-02 | *** |
| dPD | −1.01e-03 | ** |
| cshg | −2.09e-01 | *** |
| rer | −2.40e-04 | *** |
| lhc* | 3.16e-02 | *** |
| trad | 7.47e-02 | *** |
| R2 = 0.63; RSS = 0.17 | HT(8) = 32.4*** | |

*Notes*: (***), (**) and (*) indicate statistical significance at the levels 1 %, 5 % and 10 %, respectively. White heteroscedasticity correction; HT(8) is the Chi-Squared statistic with 8 degrees of freedom for the Hausman test applied to select between fixed effects and random effects models. lhc* stands for the variable $I^{lhc}lhc$. R2 stands for R squared and RSS for the residual sum of squares

**Table 5** LR test results for different thresholds (d = cshx) applied to model 1

| H0/H1 | Statistics | SL |
|---|---|---|
| 0/1 | 31.04 | * |
| 1/2 | 21.98 | |

*Notes*: LR test is the likelihood ratio test. The first column identifies the hypotheses that were tested where 0/1 means the null hypothesis of 0 thresholds against 1, and 1/2 the null hypothesis of 1 threshold against 2. The star has the usual meaning: (*) indicates statistical significance (SL) at the 10% level; these statistics were obtained by bootstrap using 100 simulations for 0/1 and 200 for 1/2

In the remainder of this study we present the results from the estimation of two threshold models (models 1 and 2). The estimations were performed using a fixed effects model and for the set of variables included in the model we have estimated different combinations of dependent and independent variables relative to the threshold indicator. Threshold regimes correspond to splits associated to the estimated thresholds, which are selected using a likelihood test and the critical values are calculated by bootstrap simulations. Models that included the variable lhc* have always presented a better fit than the models estimated with the variable lhc.

## *3.5 Evidence from Differences in Openness to Trade as a Barrier to Growth and Convergence*

To test whether openness of trade constituted a barrier to growth and convergence in our sample we use as the threshold indicator variable the share of exports in total output (cshx) and we use the LR test to select between the existence of one threshold and two thresholds. The respective test statistics are presented in Table 5.

**Table 6** Estimation results of model 1 with two threshold regimes

| Var. | Indep. Var. | | Dep. Var. (1) ≤d1 | | Dep. Var. (2) >d1 | |
|---|---|---|---|---|---|---|
| dPD | −1.03e-03 | *** | | | | |
| rer | −2.91e-04 | *** | | | | |
| trad | 8.23e-02 | *** | | | | |
| dlck | 8.47e-02 | *** | | | | |
| lhc* | 3.15e-02 | *** | | | | |
| tfp_1 | | | −1.69e-01 | | 5.26e-02 | * |
| tfp_2 | | | 7.72e-02 | | −8.07e-02 | ** |
| cshg | | | 5.37e-01 | ** | −1.64e-01 | *** |
| RSS = 0.16 | | | | | | |

*Notes*: See notes to Table 4. Dependent (independent) variables are explanatory variables that (do not) depend on the threshold indicator. The value of the threshold indicator is d1 = 0.1690343

At the 6 % significance level we reject the null hypothesis of the existence of zero thresholds against the existence of one threshold. The null hypothesis of the existence of one threshold against the existence of two thresholds is not rejected so we retained the model with one threshold that corresponds to the existence of two regimes that we thus apply to model 1. The threshold value estimated is d1 = 0.1690343.

According to the results presented in Table 6, the values of the estimated coefficients of the independent variables for the two regimes are very similar to those obtained in baseline model 1. As expected, the estimated coefficients for the threshold dependent variables are very different from those obtained for the baseline model. These results do not support the existence of a catch-up/convergence process for the countries with a lower degree of openness to trade (first regime), while in this regime the estimated coefficient on government size is positive (first regime for values ≤ d1). On the contrary, for countries that are more open to trade (second regime) there is evidence of convergence and also of a negative relationship between government size and growth (second regime for > d1). In fact, the prediction that government size is inversely related to growth is not rejected when we estimate baseline model 1 and is only confirmed in the case of the second regime. When we take into account the results from the two regimes we find that the economies belonging to the first regime experienced an external constraint that is weaker when compared to that of the countries belonging to the second regime. The economies belonging to the first regime seem thus to be able to more efficiently stabilise output in face of external shocks since government size is not detrimental for growth.

Table 7 presents the results from the estimation of model 2 an extension of model 1 that includes as an additional explanatory variable the share of exports on output whose growth impact was found to depend on the threshold indicator.

The results of the estimation of the baseline model 2 (see Table 7) confirm the theoretical predictions on the sign of the relationship between the different covariates and economic growth: there is evidence of convergence (overall

**Table 7** Estimation results of baseline Model 2

| Vars. | Coefficient | t | SL |
|---|---|---|---|
| tfp_1 | 5.66E-02 | 1.80 | * |
| tfp_2 | −9.49E-02 | 2.85 | *** |
| cshx | 2.85E-03 | 0.42 | |
| dPD | −10.0E-04 | 2.03 | ** |
| rer | −2.31E-04 | 2.44 | ** |
| trad | 8.33E-02 | 2.88 | *** |
| cshg | −2.07E-01 | 5.15 | *** |
| lhc* | 3.16E-02 | 18.68 | *** |
| dlk | 9.16E-02 | 4.02 | *** |
| R2 = 0.63 | HT(9) = 38.82 | RSS = 0.17 | |

*Notes*: See notes to Table 4

**Table 8** LR test results for different thresholds (d = cshx) in model 2

| H0/H1 | Statistics | SL |
|---|---|---|
| 0/1 | 34.52 | * |
| 1/2 | 37.81 | ** |
| 2/3 | 69.64 | *** |

*Notes*: See notes to Table 4

estimated negative coefficient on tfp) and of a negative relationship between growth and public debt growth, higher real exchange rate values (lower external competitiveness), as well as with government size. A positive sign is found for the estimated coefficients on the tradable goods share, human capital and investment. We highlight the fact that the estimated coefficient on the exports share is statistically different from zero but, as we will see below, this last result is not maintained in the framework of the thresholds regimes that consider as the indicator variable the share of exports on output.

According to the results from the LR test for the determination of the number of thresholds applied to model 2 presented in Table 8, there are three thresholds according to the values of the exports' share, which implies that there are four growth regimes according to the different thresholds. The values of the exports' share that correspond to the three thresholds are: d1 = 0.06723173, d2 = 0.1159999 and d3 = 0.6225656 (Table 9).

The independent variables for the four regimes have values similar to those of the model without thresholds (baseline model 2). The exception concerns the estimated coefficient for the investment rate that presents a slightly lower estimated coefficient. In what concerns the results for the thresholds dependent variables there are however substantial differences. The estimated coefficient on the exports share is only statistically significant for the second regime with a positive sign. The estimated coefficient on government size is negative for the second, third and fourth regime, but presents a positive estimated coefficient in the first regime. Possible explanations for this latter result that goes against theoretical predictions have already been pointed out when we discussed the results for model 1. The

**Table 9** Estimation results of model 2 with four thresholds regimes

| Var. | Indep. Var. | | Dep. Var. (1) ≤d1 | | Dep. Var. (2) d1 < d ≤ d2 | | Dep. Var. (3) d2 < d ≤ d3 | | Dep. Var. (4) d > d3 | |
|---|---|---|---|---|---|---|---|---|---|---|
| tfp_1 | 4.59e-02 | | | | | | | | | |
| tfp_2 | −7.24e-02 | ** | | | | | | | | |
| dlk | 7.92e-02 | *** | | | | | | | | |
| lhc* | 3.14e-02 | *** | | | | | | | | |
| rer | −2.83e-04 | *** | | | | | | | | |
| cshx | | | −5.40e-01 | | 5.98e-01 | *** | −7.48e-03 | | 7.80e-03 | |
| cshg | | | 8.32e-01 | *** | −2.65e-01 | *** | −1.27e-01 | *** | −1.25e-01 | ** |
| trad | | | −1.47e-01 | ** | −1.53e-02 | | 9.96e-02 | *** | 7.11e-02 | * |
| dPD | | | −3.26e-04 | | −2.84e-03 | *** | −1.20e-03 | *** | 7.10e-05 | |
| RSS = 0.145 | | | | | | | | | | |

*Notes*: See notes to Table 6. Threshold values are the following: d1 = 0.06723173, d2 = 01159999 and d3 = 0.6225656

estimated coefficient on the tradable goods share is negative for the first and second regimes (but not statistically significant in the latter) and positive for the third and fourth regimes. Finally, the estimated coefficient on public debt growth has a negative and statistically significant estimated coefficient for the intermediate regimes (second and third) and is not statistically significant in the other two (first and fourth regimes).

## 3.6 *Potential Implications for Portugal, a Southern Peripheral Economy of the EU*

In order to examine the potential implications for Portuguese economic growth from our previous threshold analysis we have to identify the threshold regimes that characterise the Portuguese economy over the period under analysis. To do this we calculate and allocate the number of Portuguese observations across the number of regimes identified: two in the case of model 1 and four in the case of model 2. Additionally, we also take into consideration the distribution over time of the observations belonging to each regime in order not to arrive at misleading

**Table 10** Distribution of the observations across the two regimes in model 1

| Regimes (d = cshx) | d ≤ d1 | d1 > d |
|---|---|---|
| Total number of observations | 29 | 554 |
| Number of obs. for PRT | 0 | 53 |

*Notes*: PRT denotes Portugal; Total obs.—total number of observations for the whole sample; d denotes the threshold indicator cshx; the value of the threshold is d1 = 0.1690343

conclusions about the current importance of each regime and therefore to inaccurate policy recommendations.

Recall that for model 1 the threshold value estimated for the exports' share is d1 = 0.1690343. The observations for Portugal in our sample are distributed in accordance to the information presented in Table 10.

According to the information presented in Table 10, all the observations for Portugal belong to the second regime (>d1) and for the whole sample the number of observations belonging to this second regime is 19 times higher than the number of observations belonging to the first regime. As for the distribution of the observations over time, the median in the first regime is the year 1969 and the most recent observation occurs in year 1979. The histogram with the years covered by this first regime illustrates the distribution over time of the observations belonging to this regime (see Fig. 1). There is a clear decrease in the number of observations as we move forward in time and the probability of an observation belonging to this regime after 1978 is zero.

Table 11 contains information on the number of observations by regimes according to model 2 for the whole sample and for Portugal alone. We can see that the distribution for Portugal is similar to that of the overall sample with the majority of observations belonging to the third regime. In particular, Portugal has no observations in the first and fourth regimes. In what concerns the distribution over time of the observations belonging to each regime, we have already concluded for model 1 that the first regime is a regime from the past. The same applies to the second regime although at later years: in this regime the median is year 1979 and the most recent observations were recorded in year 2011. For the second and third regimes the median occurs at years 1987 and 2003, respectively, and both regimes record observations in year 2014. We can thus consider that these last two regimes are almost current times regimes. These findings are illustrated with the histograms for the second, third and fourth regimes in Figs. 2, 3, and 4, respectively. Portugal is mainly represented by the third threshold regime since it is the one where this country's observations are most concentrated.

Based on the information on the distribution of the observations for Portugal across the thresholds regimes in models 1 and 2, this country's growth rate behaves according to the second regime in model 1 and the third regime in model 2. If we analyse jointly the results for the different regimes in models 1 and 2 that Portugal belongs to we come to the conclusion that increasing openness to trade allowed Portugal to grow faster due to technological convergence and also enabled this country to benefit in terms of faster growth from a higher tradable goods share. On

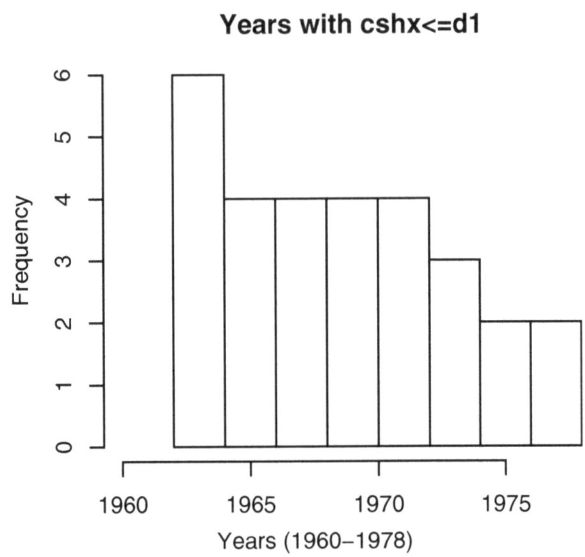


**Fig. 1** Histogram for the distribution over time of the observations belonging to the first regime in models 1 and 2

**Table 11** Distribution of the observations across the two regimes in model 2 four regimes

| Regimes (d = cshx) | d ≤ d1 | d1 < d ≤ d2 | d2 < d ≤ d3 | d > d3 |
|---|---|---|---|---|
| Total obs. | 29 | 77 | 376 | 101 |
| PRT obs. | 0 | 21 | 32 | 0 |

*Notes*: See notes to Table 10. The values of d are now: d1 = 0.06723173, d2 = 01159999 and d3 = 0.6225656

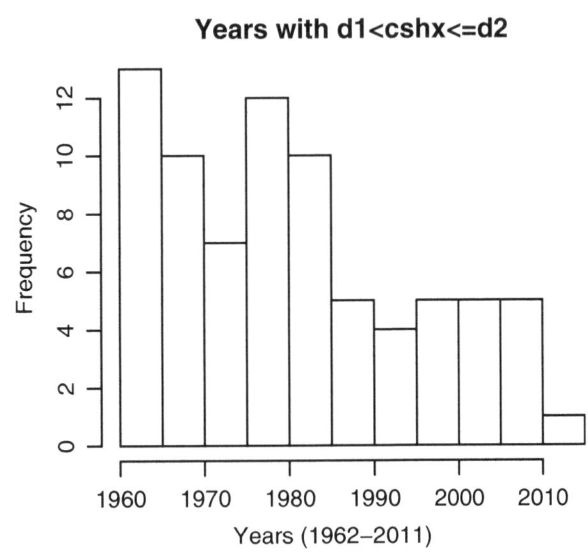


**Fig. 2** Histogram for the distribution over time of the observations belonging to the second regime from model 2

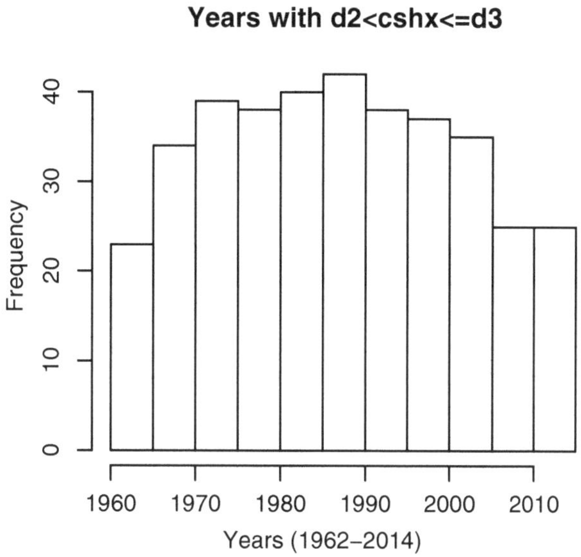


**Fig. 3** Histogram for the distribution over time of the observations belonging to the third regime from model 2

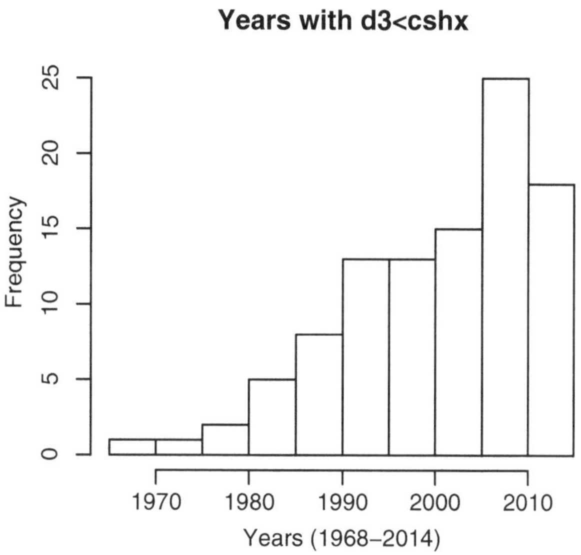


**Fig. 4** Histogram for the distribution over time of the observations belonging to the fourth regime from model 2

the other hand, the growth rhythm and convergence trajectory of the Portuguese economy was negatively affected by government size and public debt probably due to crowding-out effects exacerbated by the higher openness to trade. According to these results, policy-making can foster growth in a variety of ways in countries relatively open to trade such as Portugal. In particular, fostering the tradable goods sector and reducing government intervention and public debt will promote growth.

# 4 Conclusion

We investigated the existence of thresholds defined according to the importance of openness to trade for the verification of the convergence hypothesis and the confirmation of the predicted nexus between other potentially important growth determinants and output growth using annual data for 11 EU countries from 1960 to 2014 and applying the Hansen methodology. This methodology seems to be richer when applied to panel data instead of sectional data. It allows the identification of different economic regimes and thus overcomes the limits of linear econometric models that assume homogeneity of the coefficients of the explanatory variables. It is expected to lead to more accurate and promising policy implications since it goes beyond the estimation of the coefficients of the right hand side variables conditional to the mean. The estimation of different threshold regimes uncovers countries distinct behaviour from the average economy and in this way gives support to the design and implementation of policies suited to each type of country. The use of panel data information that combines sectional (country) variation with times series variation is richer since the latter allows for the identification of past and current threshold regimes reinforcing the accuracy of growth policies. However, the interpretation of the estimations based on panel information is more complex since the same country may belong to several threshold regimes.

The results obtained lead us to identify different regimes, characterized by different relationships between growth and its determinants. The results support the predicted theoretical signs between growth and the retained determinants and also confirm the technological convergence hypothesis. Human capital was not confirmed as a threshold indicator, nonetheless we were able to find evidence indicating that for higher growth rates human capital is a significant (positive) growth determinant. On the other hand, for stagnant economies the impact of human capital on growth is not significant, indicating that economies that remain stagnant for some time will suffer a loss of human capital which will hinder their future growth. The threshold estimation results lead to a two regimes and to a four regimes thresholds models. We focus on the latter since it contains more information and the observations for the Portuguese economy are concentrated in the second and mostly in the third regime. For the latter, the degree of trade openness is a growth incentive for economies with intermediate openness levels. Tradable goods are a positive growth factor for economies that exhibit a higher degree of openness and government size has a less harmful effect on those economies than on the economies represented by intermediate regimes. Notice that the first regime is different from the remaining ones: it is a regime from the past corresponding to a smaller degree of openness to trade where government size has a positive effect on growth. Public debt has no effect on growth under the first and fourth regimes, but exerts a negative influence in the intermediate regimes, which is smaller in the third regime.

Finally, we derived some potential implications of the above described results for understanding the growth and convergence situation of Portugal as a Southern

EU peripheral economy. We focused on the third regime which concentrates the largest number of Portuguese observations and on the coefficient estimates for the variables dependant on the threshold indicator: government size and public debt have a negative effect on growth and the tradable goods share has a positive effect. As for the threshold independent variables (technological convergence, human capital and external competitiveness), the predicted theoretical signs are confirmed.

## References

Abramovitz M (1986) Catching up, forging ahead and falling behind. J Econ Hist 46(2):385–406

Aghion P, Howitt P (1992) A model of growth through creative destruction. Econometrica 60 (2):323–351

Aghion P, Caroli E, García-Peñalosa C (1999) Inequality and economic growth: the perspective of the new growth theories. J Econ Lit 37(4):1615–1660

Awokuse TO (2008) Trade openness and economic growth: is growth export-led or import-led? Appl Econ 40(2):161–173

Barreto RA, Hughes AW (2004) Under performers and over achievers: a quantile regression analysis of growth. Econ Rec 80(248):17–35

Barro RJ (1990) Government spending in a simple model of endogenous growth. J Polit Econ 98 (5):S103–S126

Barro RJ (2000) Inequality and growth in a panel of countries. J Econ Growth 5(1):87–120

Barro RJ, Lee J-W (1994) Sources of economic growth. Carn-Roch Conf Ser Public Policy 40:1–46

Barro RJ, Sala-I-Martin X (1997) Technological diffusion, convergence, and growth. J Econ Growth 2(1):1–26

Baumol WJ (1967) Macroeconomics of unbalanced growth: the anatomy of urban crisis. Am Econ Rev 57(3):415–426

Benhabib J, Spiegel M (1994) The role of human capital in economic development: evidence from aggregate cross-country data. J Monet Econ 34(2):143–173

Benhabib J, Spiegel MM (2005) Human capital and technology diffusion. In: Aghion P, Durlauf S (eds) Handbook of economic growth. Elsevier, North-Holland, pp 935–966

Breitung J, Pesaran M (2005) Unit roots and cointegration in panels. Deutsche Bundesbank Discussion Paper No. D 42

Campos NF, Coricelli F, Moretti L (2014) Economic growth and political integration: estimating the benefits from membership in the European Union using the synthetic counterfactuals method. IZA Discussion Paper No. 8162

Chang Y (2002) Nonlinear IV unit root tests in panels with cross-sectional dependency. J Econ 110:261–292

Comin D, Mestieri M (2014) Technology diffusion: measurement, causes, and consequences. In: Aghion P, Durlauf SN (eds) Handbook of economic growth. Elsevier, North-Holland, pp 565–622

Crespo-Cuaresma J, Ritzberger-Grünwald D, Silgoner MA (2008) Growth, convergence and EU membership. Appl Econ 40(5):643–656

Crespo-Cuaresma J, Foster N, Stehrer R (2011) The determinants of regional economic growth by quantile. Reg Stud 45(6):809–826

Croissant Y, Millo G (2008) Panel data econometrics in R: the PLM package. J Stat Softw 27 (2):1–51

Dar A, Amirkhalkhali S (2003) On the impact of trade openness on growth: further evidence from OECD countries. Appl Econ 35(16):1761–1766

Dauderstädt M (2014) Convergence in crisis: European integration in jeopardy. Friedrich-Ebert-Stiftung International Policy Analysis Working Paper, October 2014
Doppelhofer G, Miller RI, Sala-I-Martin X (2004) Determinants of long-term growth: a Bayesian averaging of classical estimates (BACE) approach. Am Econ Rev 94(4):813–835
Durlauf S, Johnson PA, Temple J (2005) Growth econometrics. In: Aghion P, Durlauf S (eds) Handbook of economic growth. North-Holland, Amsterdam, pp 555–677
Engelbrecht H-J (2003) Human capital and economic growth: cross-section evidence for OECD countries. Econ Rec 79(2):S40–S51
Hansen B (1999) Threshold effects in non-dynamic panels: estimation, testing and inference. J Econ 83:345–368
Hurlin C, Mignon V (2007) Second generation panel unit root tests. HAL, Hal
Im K, Pesaran MH, Shin Y (2003) Testing for unit roots in heterogeneous panels. J Econ 115:53–74
Jones CI (1995) R&D-based models of economic growth. J Polit Econ 103(41):759–784
Kaitila V (2013) Convergence, income distribution, and the economic crisis in Europe. ETLA Working Papers No. 14
Karras G (1997) On the optimal government size in Europe: theory and empirical evidence. Manch Sch 65(3):280–294
Lewer JJ, Berg HVD (2003) How large is international trade's effect on economic growth? J Econ Surv 17(3):363–396
Lucas R (1988) On the mechanics of economic development. J Monet Econ 22:3–42
Mankiw NG, Romer D, Weil D (1992) A contribution to the empirics of economic growth. Q J Econ 107(2):407–437
Nelson RR, Phelps ES (1966) Investment in humans, technological diffusion and economic growth. Am Econ Rev 56(1/2):69–75
OECD (1998) Human capital investment. An international comparison. OECD, Paris
Papageorgiou C (2002) Trade as a threshold variable for multiple regimes. Econ Lett 77:85–91
Perla J, Tonetti C, Waugh ME (2015) Equilibrium technology diffusion, trade, and growth. NBER Working Paper Series No. 20881
Pesaran MH (2007) A simple panel unit root test in the presence of cross-section dependence. J Appl Econ 22:265–312
Romer P (1986) Increasing returns and long-run growth. J Polit Econ 94(5):1002–1037
Romer P (1990) Human capital and growth: theory and evidence. Carn-Roch Conf Ser Public Policy 32:251–286
Sala-I-Martin X (1997) I just run two million regressions. Am Econ Rev 87(2):178–183
Serranito F (2009) Trade, catching-up and divergence. Int Rev Appl Econ 23(3):239–264
Solow RM (1956) A contribution to the theory of economic growth. Q J Econ 70(1):65–95
Tsung-Wu H (2015) Pdr: Panel data regression: threshold model and unit root tests: R-package version 1.3

# Has the Euro Any Future Under Secular Stagnation?

**Francisco Louçã**

**Abstract** This chapter investigates the dynamics of the world economy and the political constraints in 2016, and then discusses the effects of the Portuguese integration in the euro. As the financial crash and then the recession unfolded, the difficulties of the European peripheral economies were amplified by austerity measures leading to social and political unrest. Finally, the chapter reviews some of the debates on the alternative strategies and considers the conditions and difficulties for a negotiation on the reduction of the external debt and namely for an exit from the Eurozone.

**JEL Classification** E58 • E60 • G38 • H63

## 1 Introduction

In this brief text I reflect on the international context and the European crisis on the basis of the experience of Portugal under the Troika and the political change that has happened since then. The first part presents a map for 2016, the second deals with Europe, the struggle for the restructuring of the debt and the question of exit from the Euro. The reader will excuse this blunt presentation of my views, and in particular this exercise on economic and political strategy, but why should I or we shy away from a debate that is so consequential for our lives?

---

F. Louçã
ISEG, Lisbon University, Lisboa, Portugal
e-mail: flouc@iseg.ulisboa.pt

 
N. da Costa Cabral et al. (eds.), *The Euro and the Crisis*, Financial and Monetary Policy Studies 43, DOI 10.1007/978-3-319-45710-9_7

## 2 A Prolonged Stalemate that Feeds Successive Crises

1. The world economy is stagnant. The international system is under transformation and in crisis. In transformation, because new centres of profitability of capital and therefore of political power arise, with the Chinese economy being the most powerful newcomer while that of Brazil is experiencing a sharp fall. In crisis, because this mediocre growth maintains a high rate of unemployment in the more developed countries and because the difficulty in the recovery of the rate of accumulation precipitates austerity measures and modification of the distribution of income between capital and labour, with effects that are socially regressive and economically recessive. This results in the weakening or disturbance of political regimes, as shown in the instability in France, in the referendum in the United Kingdom, the governmental impasse in Spain and the emergence of xenophobic populism, in Hungary and Poland as well as in Belgium or the Netherlands. Finally, the centre of the empire, Washington, is a decadent power, with a decomposing hegemony and as such is even more dangerous. The world economy and power is at a stalemate.
2. The USA represents one third of the global economy. In the political arena, more than that. In demography and geography, much less. In currency, still almost everything but it is no longer the single power. In military technology, total control. This monumental power, which dominated the last century and that is now slowly degrading in the twenty-first century, is one of the greatest threats to global stability. This is due to three reasons: its external action accentuates conflict, its policy is dangerous, and its economy is extractive and therefore decadent.
3. Foreign policy was the main factor in President Obama's election. He promised decompression (the closure of Guantanamo) and multilateralism (a minimum form inclusion of allies), in order to provide peace solutions in old conflicts. However, neither one nor the other has transpired and in all these areas of intervention, he has retreated. In Europe, he has drawn Germany into a conflict in the East, in Ukraine, trying to place the boundary of NATO at the edge of Russia. Meanwhile, the three pillars of the US's relationship in the Middle East have suffered serious disturbance or increasing risks: in Egypt, with a popular uprising and then with a military coup, while Israel and Saudi Arabia both risking writing a suicide note through complacency or support for the Daesh. The foreign policy of the USA has failed because in the first case, it allowed the resurgence of Russia as a military power and in the second Iran's assertion as a regional force, and because it prolonged the regional conflicts President Obama claimed to be able to solve.
4. The biggest problem, however, is that for the USA, from its privileged position, foreign policy is determined by internal politics (in Europe it is the opposite). This is imposed by the drift to the right of the US political system with the emergence of isolationist populism in the two major parties, moving from an imposing imperial leadership towards a hesitant government, with brutal and disjointed disciplinary actions that inflame the world. Even if this is more obvious in the case of the Republican Party, divided between the Tea Party sect (represented by Senator Ted

Cruz) and the unpredictable acrobatics of Donald Trump, such derivation also has a systemic impact on the ability of the US political system and Congress to decide upon international matters. In addition, the US no longer has control as a territorial power. The defeat in Vietnam seems to have closed an epoch. Attack and withdrawal has become the US practice, so that internal politics becomes volatile in its external actions. This is a “drone militarism”. The technology allows air wars, with null military perspectives and the immediate effect of amplifying the conflict and facilitating conditions for the globalization of terror, from Afghanistan to Iraq, Libya and Syria.

5. Since internal politics is closed in on itself, the US can no longer lead the world: President Obama cannot enforce a treaty on climate change because it would be rejected by the House of Representatives or by the Senate, starting with his own party—and he would be forced to seek legal solutions based on a weak compromise. That is to say, if foreign policy is determined by internal politics, the US also abdicates from offering an external leadership, even when needed for the international system. The world is dominated by a state that cannot lead international decisions.

6. The extractive economy is at the root of this contradiction in internal policy. The sovereign privilege of the dollar has begun to be undermined by the existence of a basket of currencies of reference for the creation of a trade reserve, although none can yet compete in the supreme role that the US preserved to ensure accumulation. Only the yuan has the support of a state that can aspire to such a role, but China still does not have a sufficiently powerful financial market to absorb enough income from savings and direct the financial funds that are the nerve of capital accumulation. Thus, it is still what the US decides that conditions globalization.

7. The US benefits and will continue to benefit from globalization, standing in a privileged and comfortable position to be the first hegemonic leader that imports capital rather than exporting it, making this anomaly one of its forms of domination. This is something unprecedented in history. This engineering of power requires the dollar to be the reference currency (without being the only privileged international reserve currency) and requires control of the main productive forces (without the US being the productive motor of goods or possibly knowledge), of natural resources (although the powder keg of the Middle East threatens this guarantee), of innovative capacity (where space has been opened up for other powers with the change of energy pattern and new essential goods, as in medicine) and even the control of savings and investment (although China will soon have sufficient resources to overtake the US). That is to say, the reason for its strength today is the cause of its fragility tomorrow, inasmuch as this advantage is transient.

8. Some US economists, alarmed by these vulnerabilities, launched a debate 2 years ago on “secular stagnation” (Summers 2014), retrieving a term used in 1939 by a president of the American Association of Economists, Alvin Hansen, 10 years after the start of the crisis of 1929, to describe demographic stagnation, the deficit in demand and therefore a perspective of degradation of investment with consequent reduction in potential growth. Following this analogy, we would now, having

entered the twenty-first century, be in a new secular stagnation for reasons similar to those of the Great Depression.

Hansen (1939) argued that "Not until the problem of full employment of our productive resources from the long-run, secular standpoint was upon us, were we compelled to give serious consideration to those factors and forces in our economy which tend to make business recoveries weak and anaemic and which tend to prolong and deepen the course of depressions. This is the essence of secular stagnation—sick recoveries which die in their infancy and depressions which feed on themselves." In his view, the demographic menace was that slow population growth would leave a chronic shortage of demand, undermining incentives for investment. In this sense, "secular stagnation", the term he proposed specifically for this demographically induced slowdown, would lead to a "hard and seemingly immovable core of unemployment" with, at most, a jobless recovery, or "depressions feeding on themselves". In the same sense, he insisted, "The great transition, incident to a rapid decline in population growth and its impact upon capital formation and the workability of a system of free enterprise, calls for high scientific adventure along all the fronts represented by the social science disciplines."

9. It is known how the Great Depression precipitated two major transformations in the world economy, with the first being that of the US. It mobilized expansionary measures in order to generate employment and fight the depression: the standard of anti-cyclic policies was set as monetary, budgetary and fiscal action in order to expand demand in the short term. Furthermore, and as important, the paradigm in economic thinking moved from the disastrous liberal doctrines, which had implied the passive reaction of president Hoover and therefore the contamination of the economy and the spread of the recession, to Keynesian views on public strategy for boosting demand and Rooseveltian policies.

Instead, the current crisis has generated alternatives doomed to deepen it even more. Recessive policies are designed to respond to recession and more liberal economics is erected as the standard in order to compensate for the failures of neoliberalism and deregulation. Therefore, fuel is added to the fire.

10. The actual numbers seem to confirm this fear of secular stagnation. The IMF revised their forecasts for 2020 at the end of last year, anticipating a GDP for China 14 % lower than its previous forecast, with Europe and the US being 6 % lower. A previous study by the National Bureau of Economic Research, a research institute in Cambridge, Massachusetts, had already registered this pessimism, subsequently worsened, stating that the production potential of the major economies of the world because of the crash of the sub-primes in the recessions in 2008–2009 would be of the order of 9 % or, as summarized in The Economist (June 14, 2014), would be "as if the entire German economy had evaporated".

11. Hence the extractive economy, in which financial income is parasitic on the system: a shadow banking that absorbs savings, a political system which imposes austerity on workers, central banks that guarantee the socialization of losses to banking, a voracious capitalism that commodifies social services and that, above all, wishes to privatize social security. Ideologically, the academy, the institutions and the US leaders direct this process. Politically, it is multi-polar, highlighting the

growing strength of Chancellor Merkel in the European Union. Strategically, nobody knows what will happen really, because the financial system of the most powerful economies, if they had a heart, would have reasons that reason ignores. Without knowing about these reasons we do not know anything. The future is not what it used to be.

12. Europe is at risk in this whirlwind. It is living through a relentless process, where its leader, Angela Merkel, now takes advantage of the signs of European disintegration, because it provides the best conditions for attracting capital, with the issuing of securities at negative interest, in advantageous conditions for her electoral hegemony; in return, the spiral of debt in the peripheral countries or austerity in the others leads, by the rules of the Euro, to unstoppable processes of internal devaluation, or, in other words, to an increase in the absolute exploitation and the transfer of surplus value of national economies to the international capitalist rentiers. Consequently, the political regimes of Greece, Portugal, Spain, Italy and France lose their capacity for cohesion, or the main parties are eroded or are wrenched apart, with possible sudden electoral changes, favouring in certain cases forces that represent the anti-systemic revolt of the working population or in other cases populist forces that seek to condition the population with xenophobic politics.

13. Lawrence Summers, a paradoxical economist who, as Secretary of the Treasury, imposed some of the more devastating neoliberal measures favouring the financial system against regulation, is currently one of the advocates of unorthodox measures including deficit spending and the expansion of central-bank balance sheets because "it is an irony of today's secular stagnation that what is conventionally regarded as imprudent offers the only prudent way forward" (Summers 2014). Krugman (2013) had already argued the same.

Summers identifies multiple factors accounting for deficient demand and long-term low interest rates: slower population growth; innovation slowdown; the reduced capital intensity of the new technologies ("Google isn't General Motors"); and high inequality concentrating wealth among people with the lowest propensity to spend, arguing that these forces reduce the demand for capital goods and reduce aggregate demand altogether. This is of course not consensual in the profession: Robert Lucas, a Nobelized economist, had instead argued that the "central problem of depression prevention has been solved, for all practical purposes, and has in fact been solved for many decades" (Lucas 2003), although the facts have not been kind to this extraordinary claim. Instead, the facts prove that stagnation and recession under regimes of financial instability and extraction have been the immediate danger.

14. Can the euro resist another general recession and, in particular, a financial crash? The current writer doubts it can came out unscathed, even if the resourcefulness of the European Union construction proved to be effective and its structure resilient, as it systematically added more concentration of power to any challenge it met. In any case, monetary policy was the only effective tool used after the recession—although quantitative easing by the European Central Bank, saving the euro, was only used 6 years after similar programmes in the US—but it is ineffective after reaching the liquidity trap. As such, only an expansionary fiscal

policy could avoid a long period of stagnation and therefore speculation against the euro, but the European authorities and, first of all, the German prime minister, have been consistently hostile to the idea.

The disgrace of the euro is that its unbalanced effects favour the power of Angela Merkel (since they create an image of contrasting instability in other countries) and the emergence of the financial centre in Germany (moving financial institutions from the City to Frankfurt), while destroying convergence processes and therefore the promise of any Union, and imposing never-ending austerity on the societies most affected by prolonged recession. The euro is a fabric of unemployment and social destruction for most of Europe.

## 3 Europe and Portugal and the Debt and the Euro

15. The Portuguese problem, as with some of the other countries in the EU, is in the first place a democratic issue because it is social in nature. An immediate response to this problem is a democratic struggle against the blackmail of the debt and the austerity that results from it, with a social impact that is destroying Portugal, in particular under the impact of the disarrangement of the international system, the pressure of the extractive economy and the danger of a long recession, presented as "secular stagnation". That is the problem of all problems.

16. Without vanquishing the debt, Portugal and other countries in the same situation will experience a period of social disintegration, driven by the transfer of financial revenue guaranteed through present and future taxes, thus accentuating the neo-liberal project of the imposition of reducing incomes for labour to the benefit of those for capital, and drain the area of deliberation and the struggle for hegemony in this country. That is to say, either the left leads the opposition and mobilizes the popular classes, or populism will occupy its space.

17. In recent years, it was in response to the debt problem that major changes have taken place in terms of social mobilization and in the perception of Portuguese public opinion [the massive "Que se lixe a Troika" ("Screw the Troika") demonstrations in 2012 and 2013, or the 2014 manifesto of 74 personalities arguing for public debt renegotiation, including ex-finance ministers of both centre and right wing governments], and this is one of the elements explaining the change that occurred in the elections of October 2015, with the left parties enjoying a large electoral increase.

18. None of these changes would have been possible with another political platform that was not centred on the rejection of the blackmail of the debt. It should be recalled that the programme of the left parties included not only concrete proposals on the debt but also explicit declarations stating that, if negotiations with creditors and the European institutions did not permit a solution, exit from the Euro would be the only remaining alternative.

19. To form a majority against the debt, i.e., a government that rejects austerity and the debt in favour of wage earners, public services and investment, requires an

alliance. Such a government can only emerge from this alliance. To work towards such a government, it is necessary to defeat the political right, mobilize the workers, win hegemony over the centre and submit a viable solution to the people that changes the political landscape. For such a transformation, it is necessary to concentrate forces on an understanding between the parties and on an engagement, namely the rejection of the debt.

20. As the strategy of Syriza in Greece showed, the struggle for an anti-austerity government can gather around a flag, the rejection of the debt. As the Greek experience reflected, the right and the radical centre will use the fear of exit from the Euro as its main political argument because this fear can swing elections. As the experience of Syriza showed, a government can only advance if it acts with tactical rigour, with clarity to formulate proposals, within an alliance and concentrating on the decisive argument: the debt. As the third rescue plan showed, to have the strength to negotiate it is necessary to have a plan B that is concrete and viable. As has been exemplified in Greece, there is only one plan B to support the restructuring of the debt, and that is exit from the Euro. The failure of the Tsipras government was the consequence of its lack of alternative.

21. There is a huge amount of work to be done to bring positions more closely together and articulate proposals. The left, in the past, has barely addressed this task. It must be carried out at a European level as quickly and intensely as possible. This road can only be taken through a break with the debt and austerity. This path is viable and it is possible to build such an alliance.

22. The exuberant proposal of a plan A (for political federalism, in the hope of resolving the difficulties of the peripheral states through acceptance of the increased power of Berlin) has disappeared from Portuguese political debate. This proposal started from the principle that a better solution for Portugal and Europe consisted in a constitution for a European state, in a federal form. That is to say that Portugal should be part, as a province of that state, of course led by the German government or some of its extensions in central Europe. Such a solution is neither good nor acceptable: it would be a historical regression from which the only exit for Portugal, or any other country of the European periphery, would be a high intensity conflict for its independence. At best.

23. The federalist proposal, the proposal for the creation of a European State, remains a farce because neither a doubling of the budget to 2 % (and the European trend is, the other way round, to decrease the EU budget), nor the management of a single currency necessarily requires the European government of a European state, but it creates the expectation of having one. In any case, it certainly calls for common rules and reinforced cooperation, and therefore a hegemonic sovereign authority. In this sense, the federalist proposal intends to submit the countries to the acceleration of the authoritarian project of the European bourgeoisie. This is why the left that opposes federalism neither can nor should desist from struggle at the European level. Nor can it expect the forces of federalist centralism to see the reason for egalitarian cooperation, which would go against their social interests. The anti-austerity left cannot oppose a cordial federalism with a fierce federalism. It has to overcome any form of federalism, which reduces

democracy to formalism, since legitimate elected national bodies cease to have the power of decision on national matters.

24. The experience of blackmail of the European authorities in breaking down the Greek government and imposing endless austerity shows that a decision that leads to conflict will always be political and the fruit of a relationship of forces, both local and European. However, the Greek experience also shows that all the discourses on "another Europe" are fragile and empty. To appeal to otherness when the dominant forces in Europe are applying austerity and locking European institutions to strengthen the extractive economy and its austerity, is simply an exercise in distraction. It only prospers among political fields that have been disoriented for too long with vain promises of European unity. It is necessary to abandon the discourse of "another Europe" and to focus on concrete measures to overcome the present-day institutions.

25. To achieve a new relationship of European forces it is necessary that anti-austerity governments be elected in the polls, being faithful to the population by mandating them to anti-austerity action. To achieve such a government it is necessary to know where pressure should be concentrated, because this path requires clarifying alternatives to change both parties and policies. All the pressure should focus on the requirement for the contending parties to submit a plan to cancel the debt, via European negotiation or, if necessary, the unilateral imposition of a moratorium and cancellation, which can lead to an exit from the Euro. This is only possible with a radical change in the relationship of forces, so popular mobilization is determinant.

26. An anti-austerity government will not be constituted by the centre or by a new formation of political forces of the centre. The meaning of socially oriented politics is based on this conviction: to overcome it is necessary to want to win and know how to win; it is necessary to reject financial income that strangles wages, pensions and public services. An anti-austerity left-wing government requires that the left have a new policy. The democratic problem of Portugal is the blackmail of financial capital and it is this financial capital that the left government must confront.

27. There is no intelligent or expansionary austerity (as proposed by Alesina et al. 2015). Nor means of austerity that are worth it. A new government which accepts financial blackmail will create more austerity and more destruction because every day the imposition of the rules of the Budgetary Treaty will be worse: as it is already clear, its solution for the fire of austerity is to blow on the embers of the fire.

28. The amiable hypothesis of alleviating the conditions of financial blackmail to strengthen Chancellor Merkel, or a recovery in Europe thanks to the Draghi Plan or the Juncker Plan, is no more than naivety. A political conformation like the German government, with Merkel's alliance with the Social Democratic Party, SPD, demonstrates how the system of domination is protected. The President of the Eurogroup, who is the Dutch Finance Minister, is living proof of how these neoliberal social democrats assume the role of Merkel's Prussian Cavalry. A new government in Portugal cannot count on the facilities of the European institutions; it has to count on its people and their allies in the popular left in Europe.

29. The anti-austerity government must submit a categorical commitment to initiate negotiations to repudiate the debt from the first day. If a proposal for cancellation of the debt is not accepted by the European authorities, the best answer would be the unilateral imposition of a moratorium on the payment of the debt, and negotiation with the various creditors of an exchange of debt for securities of a lower value and linked to future growth, and the control of movement of capital—a strategy that nowadays even the IMF accepts for countries under extreme conditions.

30. The anti-austerity government needs to have enough strength to impose a major fiscal change, creating the means for a reorganization of the productive system, including reindustrialization for employment, import substitution, energy and environmental reconversion and a focused investment on these lines. Once more, this economic policy attacks financial capital.

31. In this context, the new government should be prepared for all conflicts, including the pressure to force an exit from the Euro. In the book Dividadura (The dictatorship of the debt; 2012), Mariana Mortágua and I wrote that, politically, exit from the Euro is a very difficult path that would only be acceptable to the population "when there is strictly no other alternative, when they have exhausted all the alternatives, when survival requires it. There is only one condition in which exit from the Euro may become necessary for the Portuguese people, and that situation cannot be ruled out: if, due to a collapse of the European institutions and rules, the independence of Portugal was questioned and there was no other solution than to leave the European Union and, consequently, the Euro, to regain the power of decision-making. And yet it is necessary that the majority of the population commit itself in this respect, so that the strength of the popular movements and the defence of the interests of labour are reinforced". I continue to maintain this point of view, as she does.

32. I do not think that exit from the Euro will be made easy for Portugal. Nor should we expect kindness to support a departure of Portugal. We should not expect the German government to authorize an unconditional loan to promote the policies of a left-wing government that had to exit the Euro. Even if the German government was seeking to impose that exit as Wolfgang Schauble tried in relation to Greece, no funding is likely—rather it would seek to make such a choice a bad example. The hypothesis of a gentlemen's agreement, or a kind negotiation protecting the different interests at stake, seems politically unviable. Among the European leadership, there is no place for chivalry, just extremely authoritarian social interests.

33. An exit from the Euro conducted under the instructions of the interests of the German government or of a right-wing government would mean a class struggle with no quarter given against the working population, to transform and accelerate the process of capital accumulation for the exclusive benefit of a part of the oligarchy. What is more, this would not give any guarantee of the cancellation of the debt; on the contrary, in such a case, this option could be a way of accentuating the transfer of income from labour towards capital through austerity accelerating violent adjustment. The anti-austerity left that is confused over this hypothesis does not deserve to survive politically, because it would fall on the side of austerity Whoever argues for exit from the Euro without the cancellation of the debt will not succeed in resolving the democratic problem of Portugal.

34. In the battle against the debt, if a country under an ani-austerity government is forced to leave the Euro it should be alongside the people, mobilized to reject the threats of financial capital, and be willing to stand up for democracy. The effects of an exit from the Euro will run deep and can be justified only by a national emergency, administrated by a government to create a great social mobilization. This political question will always be essential, given the pressure and the difficulties involved in the management of this process. Only the democratic power of the people ensures the strength to take the necessary decisions in this context. Those who ignore this threat and high intensity risk are not prepared to fight for power.
35. Exit from the Euro, whose political difficulties I noted, is however the only alternative when there is no deep debt restructuring obtained by negotiation. In this case, it is the only way. This is for two reasons: firstly, because exit from the Euro restores a national currency, and therefore allows imposition of the conversion of all public debts in Euros to the new currency, subject to national legislation, devaluing this debt; secondly, it allows the control of capital and the management of a policy of devaluation, the two measures that favour the creation of investment and the revival of demand and employment.
36. So, whoever wants to prepare a daring and successful policy against these risks must submit a proposal taking into account all the scenarios and the best alternatives for each problem, including exit from the Euro to the devaluation of the new escudo. A study of the way to control the negative effects in the short and medium term of a possible exit from the Euro has to consider necessarily the following:

(a) Portugal runs the risk that the new currency, the escudo, would be for some months merely scriptural, so that internal transactions take place in foreign currency. Its circulation will tend to decrease and it will be dependent on a European Central Bank with which the country can enter into conflict, so a short-term issue of provisional notes would be necessary.
(b) Depositors will feel threatened and harmed and will react by withdrawing their bank deposits in Euros. Measures should be taken to generate confidence in the banking system, which will necessarily be under public control.
(c) The immediate impact of the increase in import prices following the devaluation of the escudo will only later be compensated in the trade balance by an increase in exports, which will depend on orders. Hence, there must be an emergency plan for reducing the impact of price increases in energy, transport and medicines.
(d) Interest rates will tend to rise, with effects on the distribution of national income to the detriment of debtors, while inflation will rise, which also has redistributive effects to the detriment of wages and pensions, which is why it will be necessary to take compensatory tax measures in the popular sectors.
(e) The legal redefinition of the value of the internal debt, in defence of debtors, and the effects of this redefinition on the balance sheets of the banks, will require a systemic resolution of the banks (which would already be necessary with the restructuring of the public debt).

(f) A study of the forms of social redistribution of the benefits that devaluation would give the export sector is needed, namely a new tax taking a part of that benefit to be used in investment.
(g) There would need to be an institutional restructuring, including a new definition of the legal functioning of the Bank of Portugal and the public bank, the CGD, as well as the administration of the financial system, which means having a new law for the resolution of the national bank as quickly as possible and appropriate intervention processes.

37. This study would also include the European political conditions for the decision of a left government: (a) Verification that there is the majority required for taking the possible decision of exit from the Euro, taking account the power of the President and the need for a parliamentary majority that in the long run will be able to overcome the latter's right of veto; (b) Defining the new model of exchange in a context of conflict with the European authorities and their possible hostility to the inclusion of Portugal in the European system of countries outside the Euro area; (c) Consideration that the state can legally claim the sovereign power to re-denominate its debt in local currency, but that companies indebted abroad do not have that legal power and, therefore, their balance sheets would be adversely affected; (d) The redefinition of relations with the European Union, in particular, to allow policies that protect industrialization, the creation of employment and the renationalisation of key strategic common goods for budget management.
38. There are answers, difficult as they are, to all these threats and problems, and Ferreira do Amaral and I worked together to propose some of them (Louçã and do Amaral 2013). None of these responses is a slogan. A slogan is useless for this purpose since it does not replace the detailed preparation of responses to economic and social problems. The slogan is a flag. It is legitimate to play politics with a flag. However, a flag is not a form of government. We cannot renounce the creation of a left government to search for answers to the problem of democratic Portugal, which is the debt. A winning strategy depends on a thorough job of preparing responses, taking account of the difficulties in carrying them out.
39. Realism is a condition of intelligence. All realistic responses require an economic policy such as Portugal needs: control of credit, public intervention in the financial system, mobilization of fiscal resources, and a strategy for employment. It is not realistic to accept the blackmail of the debt or to oppose it with solutions that do not stand up.

## 4 Conclusion

40. My conclusion is the following: the agenda that will create an anti-austerity majority is the fight against the debt. A new government can only win if it forms an alliance and this alliance requires clarity with respect to the cancellation of the debt. This government must be prepared to reject all the pressures of financial capital and

take all the necessary measures in this regard, including exit from the Euro if that is the only solution that remains. This preparation requires careful and detailed work, bringing together some of the best economists. This work is yet to be done. And it is better to start now.

41. The current government in Portugal, which results from an electoral defeat of the right, is not a left government with the commitment to restructure the debt. It is a government of a centre party, the Socialist Party with the conditional support of the left, in the context of commitments to the recovery of wages and pensions, an end to the privatization process and no rise in direct and indirect taxes on employment. These commitments allow social relief, a recovery of demand, and therefore benefit the living conditions of the majority of the population, and have received the support of broad sectors of the population. Yet, there are relevant differences concerning political choices, not only from a strategic perspective but also in some cases regarding short-term solutions. In the case of the decision to inject three billion Euros into the recovery of a small bank, Banif, which was sold (for 150 million euros) to Santander, the left parties opposed this decision of the government and voted against its law, with a correction of the budget for 2015. The relationship between the different parties will thus always depend on specific decisions. It remains to be seen if these decisions are confronted with the position of the Commission, which is important in the definition and application of the state budgets for 2016 and subsequent years. In any case, the opening of a new immediate solution implying a non-austerity policy is already a major change for Portugal.

42. Once again, will the euro survive the next financial crash, in the meantime favoured by the massive injection of liquidity in the financial markets and therefore the creation of a new bubble? That remains to be seen. But the economic implications of a prolonged period of austerity are already visible not only in the realm of social life in the peripheral countries of the European Union, but also and more significantly in the instability of the regimes of the central countries—including France and Italy, and even Germany or Austria, not to speak of Hungary and Poland. The strategy of capital accumulation through financial piracy, or extraction, leaves no room for the trivial expectation of a better life for the general population, and that has an immense democratic consequence. Therefore, the announcement of a prolonged stagnation and successive recessions, under the exhaustion of the effects of monetary policy, indicates the unsolved problem of the years to come.

In any case, discussing the present danger is the only door that can open upon an eventual solution, and that requires imagination, courage and non-conformism.

## References

Alesina A, Barbiero O, Favero C, Giavazzi F, Paradisi M (2015) Austerity in 2009-13. Econ Policy 30(83):385–437

Hansen A (1939) Economic progress and declining population growth. Am Econ Rev 29(1):1–15

Krugman P (2013) Bubbles, regulation, and secular stagnation. NY Times, blog, 25 September, available at: http://krugman.blogs.nytimes.com/2013/09/25/bubbles-regulation-and-secular-stagnation/?_r=0
Louçã F, do Amaral JF (2013) A Solução Novo Escudo. Lua de Papel, Lisbon
Louçã F, Mortágua M (2012) A Dividadura. Bertrand, Lisbon
Lucas R (2003) Macroeconomic priorities. Am Econ Rev 93(1):1–14
Summers L (2014) Reflections on the 'new secular stagnation hypothesis'. In: Teulings C, Baldwin R (eds) Secular stagnation: facts, causes and cures. CEPR Press, London, pp 27–38

# Part II
# A Monetary Union Relying on Fiscal Policy Coordination: Achievements, Shortcomings and Future Perspectives

# European Monetary Union: Political Motivation

**Luís Máximo dos Santos**

**Abstract** The article analyses the political motivation that governed the different stages of the European monetary integration process, and in particular the set of circumstances that made possible the agreement realised in the Maastricht Treaty, which led to the creation of the European Monetary Union. It examines how, later, the European ideal gradually lost its gloss until we reached the current deep crisis.

**JEL Classification** F33

## 1 Introductory Remarks

The creation of the European Monetary Union is one of the most daring acts of economic and political voluntarism ever conducted, regardless of the evaluation we make about its rationale and the results which it has led to.

History records many monetary unification processes. Countries like the United States, Switzerland, Italy or Germany went through monetary unification processes. And in the nineteenth century many sovereign nations tried to build monetary unions (Germano-Austrian Monetary Union, Scandinavian Monetary Union, and Latin Monetary Union, among others). Belgium and Luxembourg have long been living in monetary union within the framework of the economic union they created in 1921. Ireland and the United Kingdom have been under a regime of exchange rates union, which ended with the creation of the European Monetary System (EMS), in the late 1970s, since it allowed exchange rate fluctuation margins relative to the bilateral central exchange rates.

---

The present Chapter was written before the 'Brexit' decision in the referendum of 23 June 2016. Since June 2016 he is member of the Board of Directors of Banco de Portugal, the Portuguese central bank. The views expressed in the article are of his exclusive responsibility.

L. Máximo dos Santos
Faculty of Law, Centre for Research in European, Economic, Financial and Tax Law, University of Lisbon, Lisboa, Portugal
e-mail: luis.maximo@netcabo.pt



N. da Costa Cabral et al. (eds.), *The Euro and the Crisis*, Financial and Monetary Policy Studies 43, DOI 10.1007/978-3-319-45710-9_8

But, in its design, scope, complexity and worldwide consequences, the Economic and Monetary Union (EMU) built within the framework of the European Union is an unprecedented experience. Never before has such a large and diverse set of nations, both in their levels of economic and social development as well as their history and institutions, decided, freely and in peacetime, to live together in a monetary union.

The euro zone is now composed of 19 of the 28 European Union countries. Seven of the Member States[1] do not meet the requirements to enter the third stage of EMU and two (the United Kingdom and Denmark) enjoy an opt-out clause.[2]

This said, we would be almost tempted to say that the euro zone has been a huge success. In fact, the eleven founding member states that started it on 1 January 1999[3] (Germany, Austria, Belgium, Spain, Finland, France, Ireland, Italy, Luxembourg and Portugal) have in the meantime been joined by a further eight: Greece (2001), Slovenia (2007), Cyprus and Malta (2008), Slovakia (2009), Estonia (2011), Latvia (2014) and Lithuania (2015).

Analysed only from the point of view of its expansion, the euro zone has been successful. It has seen out its seventeenth year with eight more members than those who founded it. So far, not even at the height of the Greek crisis, has any state shown willingness to leave the euro zone. We should not be surprised that it is so, given that it is supposed that the commitment to participation in a monetary union tends to be irreversible.

There are undoubtedly many historical examples of monetary unions that came undone. But they were, as a rule, traumatic processes often associated with wars or very severe and prolonged crises that fragmented countries.

Article 50 of the EU Treaty provides for the possibility that any Member State withdraws from the European Union. The same article also applies to the States belonging to the monetary union. Thus, if a State which has the euro as currency decides to withdraw from the European Union it will also be deciding to leave the monetary union.

The treaties are silent on the possibility of a state leaving the monetary union while remaining in the European Union. This omission is understandable. The simple provision for the possible exit from the monetary union would seriously weaken the strength of the project making it clear that the commitment might not be definitive. The logic of the treaties is exactly the opposite: with the exception of the cases where there is an opt-out clause, there is a commitment from Member States to converge to meet the criteria for access to the third stage of EMU. There is a widespread perception—which is correct—that exit from the monetary union would have very high costs for any country daring to do so. Why, then, even after the peak of the euro crisis in 2010–2012, the feeling, still very strong, that the euro zone continues to be at risk?

---

[1]Bulgaria, Croatia, Hungary, Poland, Czech Republic, Romania and Sweden.

[2]Contained in Protocols n. 11 and 12, annexed to the European Union Treaty.

[3]The date since when a single monetary policy governed by the Central European Bank has been in existence. The material circulation of the euro, however, only took place on 1st January 2002.

For the permanence of this mistrust, we can point to innumerable economic reasons. First, the realisation that the fundamental flaws of the EMU project remain unsolved and there are no signs that they may be overcome, at least in the near future. In particular, the size and structure of the European Union budget expenditure has not changed, and because of its inadequacy, is incompatible with the requirements of a monetary union that guarantees balanced development prospects to all Member States.

We can also point to fears regarding the credibility of the euro zone due to the persistence of mediocre economic growth, despite all the arsenal of monetary policy measures that the European Central Bank (ECB) has resorted to and a context marked by the fall in the price of oil.

We can equally point to the serious imbalances that exist within the European Union, particularly between debtor countries and creditor countries. We may also allude to the persistence of major problems in the banking sector, the failure to overcome the Greek crisis or the asymmetric process of the creation of a banking union.

However, notwithstanding the relevance and importance of economic factors in the monetary union crisis, its real root has to be sought at another level. The creation of EMU was the most important structural reform carried out by the European Union. It undoubtedly impacted on everything in the economic order. But, by virtue of its institutional and political implications, the impact of EMU would necessarily go far beyond the economy, as actually happened. No wonder, therefore, that the reasons for the current EU crisis have to be sought in political factors that affect the core of the European integration project.

What is now at issue is the fact that, for different reasons, the attractiveness of the European project clearly has lost strength in almost all Member States, albeit to different degrees. The result of a set of circumstances, the national interests of Member States have become more difficult to harmonise and the respective peoples began to evaluate the EU very differently relative to, for example, the charmed period that marked the decade of the 90s and the early years of the twenty-first century.

## 2 From the Comfort of Bretton Woods to the Failure of the 70s

The period between the signing of the Treaty of Rome and the late 60s is characterized by the absence of initiatives leading to European monetary integration. The Bretton Woods Agreement ensured a monetary order that satisfied, in essence, the objectives of the Member States.

Monetary integration was not a priority. The challenges, in fact, were different then. Through the European Payments Union (1950) the hard bilateralism resulting from the post-war period had been overcome and, in 1958, thanks to the implementation of the European Monetary Agreement, signed in 1955, the convertibility of European currencies was achieved. European integration was focused then on the liberalization of trade, the creation of the Customs Union and the Common Agricultural Policy.

But the comfort provided by the order of Bretton Woods was to erode as the crisis of the international monetary system became increasingly more acute, culminating in its collapse in August 1971, with the famous announcement by President Richard Nixon "suspending" the convertibility of the US dollar into gold.

The devaluation of the French franc and the revaluation of the deutschmark in 1969, by very significant amounts, rang alarm bells. The effects of the international monetary disorder tumbled onto European integration putting into question some of its cornerstones.

The reaction could not have been faster and more spectacular: at a summit held in The Hague in December 1969, the Heads of State or Governments of the Member States agreed to the building in stages of an economic and monetary union, which should come into force in 1980. The project had as primary catalysts two reports prepared by Raymond Barre and later, in 1970, it was anchored to the report prepared by a committee chaired by Pierre Werner, Luxembourg's Prime Minister.

The first point to underline in this process is that behind it was, mostly, France. The creation of EMU was taken over by France as a strategic goal of the first order. Italy and the Benelux countries viewed the project favourably. Germany, on the other hand, accepted it somewhat unwillingly, given that it preferred a strategy that would previously ensure a convergence of economies.

The project was a resounding failure. The most visible result was the creation of the "currency snake" a concerted floating mechanism for the member currencies, with a margin of 2.25 %, in both directions, around the central rate fixed against the dollar. Within a few years, the "currency snake" was confined to the participation of the currencies of a small group of countries whose economies were closely linked to the German thus revealing the intra-European imbalances.

The incipiency of the project, the effects of the collapse of the Bretton Woods system and the oil crisis made the construction of EMU a distant dream. In the late 70s, the economies of the Member States diverged deeply, at least in terms of the indicators that most relate to exchange rate stability, in particular interest rates and the inflation rate. For many, the failure of the project was proof that EMU was an unrealisable goal.

## 3 From the European Monetary System to the Maastricht Treaty

On 13 March 1979, the European Monetary System (EMS) came into force, following the decisions of the European Council in July and December 1978, held in Bremen and Brussels, respectively.

Despite previous failures, France insisted again on the goal of creating a European monetary order. It saw its efforts rewarded in the late 70s with the creation of the EMS. In its genesis were two remarkable statesmen: Valéry Giscard d' Estaing, President of France, and Helmut Schmidt, Chancellor of the Federal Republic of Germany. The first wanted to move forward with the French policy of supporting greater European monetary integration. However, he was aware of the excessive ambition of the previous project, so it was important to start again, with more realistic initiatives. The second was a convinced pro-European. He recognized the importance of greater exchange rate stability for the successful journey of the European integration process but knew that there was strong opposition in Germany, especially the *Bundesbank*, to voluntarism in this respect.

The difficult negotiating process that led to the creation of the EMS shows, quite clearly, the strategies of the different Member States in relation to the issues of monetary integration and its contradictions. It is still symptomatic to see that the main factors that have marked this process were: (i) France's determination to make progress with the EMS, to which Germany eventually acquiesced, particularly due to the strong commitment of its political leadership; (ii) the concessions that had to be made to Italy and Ireland, granting them special conditions of participation in the EMS, namely enshrining "measures tending to strengthen the less prosperous economies" and an increased margin of fluctuation (only in the case of Italy) and (iii) the United Kingdom's refusal to join the exchange rate mechanism.

The creation of the EMS represented a new stage of European monetary integration. Technically it was much better designed than the "currency snake", from the outset due to the introduction of a novelty: the ECU (European Currency Unit). In the first years of operation, the EMS functioned in an unstable manner, with frequent changes in central rates, but would eventually establish itself, despite the enormous scepticism of many. Especially since 1983, it was clear that greater exchange rate stability and greater convergence of economic policies were being achieved, which led to a decline in inflation rates. Excellent EMS behaviour after1987 together with the consolidation of ECU as the European Community accounting unit and the strengthening of its use, including in the private sector, led to a general atmosphere of optimism and created room for bolder initiatives of monetary integration.

Supporters of the political and economic project of monetary union felt they could move forward. It is in this context that, following a decision of the Hanover European Council, in June 1988, the Delors Report was presented and approved in 1989; this was a fundamental document for the relaunch—this time successfully—of the plan to create an EMU. Thus began the journey that would lead to the Treaty of Maastricht.[4]

[4]The Single European Act, which entered into force on 1 July 1987 and brought about the first revision of the Treaty of Rome, did not have a relevant impact in the field of monetary integration, focusing on the objective of building the single market.

At least as far back as the 50s, with the works of Meade (1953), Scitovsky (1958) and Triffin (1957) the issues of integration and monetary unification merited the attention of scholars. However, it was mainly from the 60s, with the famous article by Mundell (1961), who presented the theory of optimal currency areas, that the economics literature on the issue of monetary unions gained an increasing audience and prominence, generating an unstoppable interest, also motivated by the study of the concrete case of the European Union.[5]

Therefore, it is safe to say that when the Maastricht Treaty was prepared and negotiated, the advantages and disadvantages of the creation of EMU, the risks it could generate and the necessary requirements for the project to be viable were all well known and clearly identified.

The common advantages associated with any monetary union (the elimination of the costs of calculation, transaction and especially of the exchange rate risk; the economy of foreign exchange reserves, since the union will require less reserves than the sum total of those of each State; the achievement of higher profits of *segniorage gains*) were added to those which resulted specifically from the process of European integration. EMU has been justified as an essential complement to the single market, a key instrument for the completion of the single capital market and also as a rationalization factor for the international monetary system itself by lending "money personality" to the international economic relations of a commercial giant. With a single currency, with international weight, excessive dependence on the dollar (which caused so many problems to the EMS) would be overcome, also giving rise to greater stability for the European Union.

On the other hand, monetary union was seen as the only feasible response to the "inconsistent triangle": it was not possible to ensure simultaneously, in a durable way, the objective of exchange rate stability, pursued by the EMS, of free capital movement, a pillar of the single market and the maintenance at national level of the definition of monetary policies.[6] Only monetary union would ensure the free movement of capital and exchange rate stability.

EMU critics argued that the only monetary unions that prevailed historically were those in which, previously or simultaneously, there was a political unification, a reality that did not exist in the European Union. They stressed that the viability of monetary union was dependent on fiscal union, which also did not exist. Moreover that the loss of autonomy in exchange rate policy and, to some extent, economic policies in general, would lead to costs asymmetrically distributed by countries given that not all were in the same position with regard to the degree of (in) effectiveness of exchange rate policies. Thus, the loss of a country's ability to manage its exchange rate would necessarily lead to the sacrifice of internal balance,

[5]The seminal work of Robert Mundell was developed by many other authors. We would highlight in particular: McKinon (1963), Kenen (1969), Ingram (1973), Magnifico (1973), and Corden (1972).

[6]Tommaso Padoa-Schioppa added to this inconsistency the goal of free trade and called it "inconsistent quantet".

generating higher levels of unemployment and/or inflation than those that would exist if the exchange rate instrument was maintained.

In the late 80s and beginning of the 90s a single set of events arose that opened a new era in European and world affairs. The fall of the Berlin Wall, German reunification and the disappearance of the Soviet Union, and consequent end of bloc politics, were not entirely unforeseeable events, but the speed, at which they occurred, it can be said, was surprising.

Thus a set of conditions came about that made possible the securing of the Maastricht Treaty and, above all, the creation of EMU. In history there is no evidence to the contrary, but there is a lot of data to sustain the view that without German reunification, the traditional opposition to EMU would hardly have disappeared, at least in such a speedy fashion. This opposition was not merely circumstantial, but anchored in the deep objectives of Germany, based on the value and the importance of the deutschmark, the instrument and greatest symbol of German success in the post-war period, which it did not wish to give up. EMU sealed a strategic compromise between France and Germany: reunification would be supported, but Germany would have to increase their connection to the Union by sharing a common currency.

Faced with an exceptional set of circumstances, the larger countries made their choices: France achieved one of the great enduring objectives of its European policy[7]—monetary union—through which it thought it would derive much benefit, Germany achieved what even a couple of years earlier seemed unthinkable—reunification—and the United Kingdom chose to remain outside the single currency, which was to be expected.

To understand the obvious imperfections of the architecture of the EMU—which in any case are not new to anyone—one must have in mind the difficulty of the Maastricht agreement. It was believed that they could be overcome in time as the project solidified.

When the Maastricht Treaty was signed in 1992, there were only 12 Member States, which means a much greater degree of cohesion than that which exists today. When the third stage of EMU was entered into, there were already 15 Member States, the result of the accession of Austria, Finland and Sweden in 1995. These States only failed to become members earlier due to considerations of a geopolitical order, linked to their neutral status, considerations that ceased to have meaning with the collapse of the Soviet Union and the end of bloc politics.

No one contemplated that the single currency might not include all the six founding members, despite the problems of Belgium and Italy in meeting the convergence criteria. Southern countries, like Portugal and Spain, wanted to get a central status and feared that, staying outside, at such a unique time, would prolong and aggravate their distance from a "hard core" of countries, to which Germany still had hope of restricting access to the single currency. Therefore, they set out to fulfil

[7]Even so, in the referendum of 20 September 1992 the "yes" vote to the Maastricht Treaty was given by a slim margin: 51.04 %, versus 48.96 % supporting "no".

the convergence criteria, facilitated by a context that was then one of strong growth. Similar considerations apply to explaining the participation of Ireland. The inclusion of Austria and Finland are perfectly natural in the light of economic and geopolitical criteria.

It is also important to note the favourable impact on the acceptance of EMU by lighter weight states, of the argument that participation in the euro, more than a real loss of sovereignty, merely represented a formal loss, since alignment with German monetary policy had already produced the actual loss of autonomy of monetary policy, which—it was said—could even be recovered by exercising shared sovereignty in the European institutions.

Greece acceded to the third stage of EMU in 2001, with an assessment of compliance with the convergence criteria that proved to be controversial. With it, all the countries of southern Europe were included in the euro before the eastward enlargement in 2004. The United Kingdom, Denmark and Sweden have chosen to stay out for strict political reasons, in the case of Denmark, determined by a negative referendum.

## 4 From the Euphoria of the 90s to the First Signs of the Crisis of European Integration

In the 90s, Germany seized the historic opportunity that faced it. Chancellor Helmut Kohl asserted himself over the fears of the *Bunsdesbank* firstly in the acceptance of a one to one rate of conversion of the mark of the Federal Republic of Germany with the mark of the German Democratic Republic and then in the acceptance of European Monetary Union. He showed determination with the will to do what was necessary to achieve the reunification of Germany.

It was a decade marked by a sense of Euro-optimism such as had not been seen in a long time. The euphoria caused by victory in the Cold War, a victory without bloodshed and, to some extent, without a peace treaty, a cultural environment marked by excessively linear interpretations of the meaning of Francis Fukuyama's idea of the "end of history" and vibrant economic growth, generated an unfavourable framework to anticipate the problems that were to come.

Several European countries outside the European Union splintered: Yugoslavia, in a dramatic way, resulting in six new States; Czechoslovakia, peacefully, creating the Czech Republic and Slovakia. Later and also violently, Serbia itself fragmented, with the Kosovan War.

The statement that Germany might be too big for Europe and too small for the world is attributed to Henry Kissinger. After the 90s, with German reunification and the division of several major countries, and, more recently in the twenty-first century, with the resumption of serious problems of national unity in Spain and the United Kingdom, one can say that Germany's size began to loom larger in the European context.

The outset of the euro zone went by without any major problems, including the physical replacement process of national currencies by the euro, which strengthened the integrationist dynamics. European integration, at least apparently, was strengthened not only by its deepening, with EMU, but also with the enlargement to the East, which led to the simultaneous accession of ten new Member States on 1 May 2004. Such enlargement, by virtue of its size and consequences, at all levels, has changed the nature of the Union, leading to a much more complex phase of the European integration process.

The first signs of crisis came, however, with the referenda in France and the Netherlands that by a large majority, and with a high turnout, resulted in rejection of the Constitutional Treaty, entitled "Treaty establishing a Constitution for Europe". On 29 May 2005, the French rejected the project with 55 % of the vote and, on 1 June, the Dutch did the same with an even higher percentage: 61.6 % of votes.

These results, in two founding countries, with marked European traditions, were a clear sign that something was going wrong. Were they merely the rejection of the excessively "confidential" method that presided over the drafting of the Treaty or did they reveal a deeper departure from the principles of European integration as they were being interpreted by national and European leaders?

Unfortunately, after the initial shock, and despite promises to the contrary, the meaning of these votes was quickly forgotten. Things went ahead, again through unworkable processes, on a path that led to the Treaty of Lisbon, which came into force on 1 December 2009, almost without being noticed, whilst attention was immersed in the consequences of the global financial crisis.

The deficiencies of the architecture of the EMU, the deepening of globalization, especially after China's accession to the World Trade Organization, which had very asymmetric impacts in the Union, and the persistence of a management model of the problems that has not proved up to the new challenges, have led to a climate of great disenchantment towards the European Union and political systems in general. Europeans began to lose hope. A strong sense of economic insecurity without adequate political representation in the pro-European currents began to set in.

Thus, even before the financial crisis, the growing weakening of the European ideal was already visible in most countries, that is to say the lack of political support for more integration. The eradication of policy by bureaucracy, the gulf separating the Eurocracy from the people, rule by unelected powers, led to questioning whether European integration, at least in its practice, might not be colliding with fundamental principles of democracy.

This is the main current threat to the process of European integration, which has been accentuated by events subsequent to the financial crisis.

## 5 The Post Global Financial Crisis

When in 2007–2008 the global financial crisis broke out, confidence in the European Union was already considerably shaken by the factors set out above. One of the legitimate expectations generated by European integration is that Member States would protect themselves from the global crisis better within it than they would be able to do isolated.

At first, the euro area weathered the impact of the financial crisis fairly well. But in 2010, with the announcement of the Greek crisis and—moreover—with the inadequate reaction to it, a period of extreme difficulties began, which only started to reverse itself in 2012, mainly because of the action of the ECB. It became apparent that the Union was not prepared to handle a crisis of this magnitude, which did not come as a surprise to those who knew the weaknesses of the construction of EMU. Even so, the enormous weakness of European integration was a shock.

There was an attempt to explain the problems of the southern countries exclusively in terms of their economic policy errors, which was only part of the truth and, probably, not the most important part, because these errors were the result of poor EMU architecture and that was, obviously, everyone's responsibility. With such a high degree of integration, is it possible to imagine that the responsibility for the problems stemmed exclusively from the States?

It was the entire model of integration, especially in the financial sphere, which issued erroneous stimuli to the States and the economic agents. It is important to remember, for example, that the European financial sector was a key player in the debt spiral in the decade before the crisis of 2008. Given higher quality risk management policies, surely the problem of excessive debt, public and private, would not have reached such dimensions.

On the other hand, we are convinced that if the ECB had done in 2010 what it started doing from 2012 the history of this period would have been quite different, and for the better.

It is a fact that the rescue programs avoided greater evils when they prevented the bankruptcy of supported countries, which would necessarily occur as a result of the unbearable rise in the cost of external financing or even its complete cessation. But would allowing sovereign default to happen even be an acceptable option after so many years of economic integration? The adjustment programs have left a very deep trace in economic and social costs for the countries that were subject to their abrupt application and, at the political level, undermined, lastingly, the cohesion of the Union.

The set of response measures to the crisis increases the strengthening of the instruments for budgetary integration, through changes in the Stability and Growth Pact by the "Two Pack" and "Six Pack" mechanisms, the strengthening of economic policy coordination by the rules known as the "European Semester", and the launch of the banking union. The beneficence of some of the practices that the banking union introduced is yet to be demonstrated. Furthermore, it has not yet been completed in terms of the central pillar of deposit security, which can be a source of distortion and of problems difficult to manage in this transition phase.

Part of this evolution was made by means of mechanisms external to the EU framework, that is, inter-governmental in nature, such as the Treaty on Stability, Coordination and Governance, better known as the "Budgetary Treaty".

None of these measures, however, solves the essential problem: as already mentioned, for the smooth functioning of EMU, that is, so that there are protective mechanisms against "asymmetric shock", we need a larger Union budget and one which fosters a redistributive effect between Member States.

All evolution after 2008 resulted in a serious deterioration of unfavorable factors to the integration that had been taking place. The European institutions receded and lost their initiative before the most powerful States. The weakening of some States—usually very important players, such as Italy or Spain—has greatly reduced their ability to influence the solutions adopted, not to mention the countries that were the subject of formal bailout programs such as Greece, Ireland and Portugal.

At critical moments, the decision making process showed a lack of democracy sometimes outside the rules of the Treaties, through the prevalence of the inter-governmental method, without a clear logic. Lack of transparency and in some cases the feeling of superficiality and absence of serious reflection were the main perceived result.

The outbreak of the financial crisis and, above all, the subsequent sovereign debt crisis, (a somewhat reductionist term to explain the reality of the facts), and the discussion concerning the allocation of responsibilities and the solutions to adopt, had the merit of bringing out into the open a new face of the Union and to make transparent new alignments within it, giving a clear sign that we had entered a new phase.

Many Member States made a strict and closed reading that they jointly interpreted as the "national interest", ignoring the perspective that the proper functioning of the Union, through ensuring internal harmony that only an overview can give, might perhaps be the best indicator to assess the degree of realization of the national interests of each of the Member States, at least in the medium and long term.

Unfortunately, the way they dealt with the sovereign debt crisis has left deep wounds, difficult to heal, and generated, in a totally unnecessary way, resentment among European peoples, such as had not been seen for a long time, awakened old ghosts, thus facilitating various types of demagogy. This was therefore a huge gift to all those who want the European project to fail, creating conditions for them to flourish easily.

But will the dynamics of disintegration prevail? Some signal that the size of the "dream", the idealistic view, moved camp: that it may reside today in those who oppose the political experience which resulted in the European Union. We cannot ignore that the political battle against the euro and European integration now has more arguments in its favor that at any other time. It is made in the name of appealing values such as the defense of democracy and political autonomy of the States.

The biggest mistake would be to demonize the anti-European positions instead of removing their arguments through reforms and a *praxis* that eliminates the undisputable deficiencies and corrects the huge mistakes that we have witnessed in the European Union. The Union needs the affirmation of a new spirit, which might revive the European ideal. It should not seek to assert itself by frightening its citizens with the consequences of its failure. To spread fear in an environment where, as a result of economic instability and terrorism, a feeling of insecurity already prevails, would be another mistake, totally counterproductive.

# 6 Final Considerations

One of the reasons that motivated the creation of European Monetary Union was, as we have seen, the desire to create a monetary identity in Europe, which would provide financial expression to the weight of the European Union in international trade and reduce the extreme dependence on the US dollar. Could this reason have disappeared? We think not. On the contrary, it gained even more ground due to the emergence of new powers like China.

The more we deepen the process of globalization, the more justified the process of monetary integration seems.

Let us imagine that the eurozone falls apart and we see the general return to national currencies. Would this be a positive scenario for economic growth in Europe? Even disregarding the inevitable transition costs, we can't see how, structurally, this would favor the strategic position of Europe in the world or of its different countries. It would be a movement contradictory to the trend of globalization, which we do not believe will regress in any significant manner.

The euro has not had problems externally. Its acceptance is a fact. Its expansion a reality. Moreover: for some powers its failure would also be a strategic setback, as it would be a setback in the perspective of achieving a multipolar world.

The main problem of the euro area occurs within the Union, that is, the inability that has existed to make EMU and all European policies ensure all States conditions for their respective economic development.

In another hand, the big problem we are facing now is that the reinforcement of the EMU requires measures that imply more political integration and in this moment there are no political conditions to adopt it. Europe has lost its *momentum* to reform itself and, consequently, we live in a contradictory situation: we know what should be done to make EMU sustainable but we cannot do it by absence of political conditions. Even the measures in the field of budgetary integration are very unpopular because they are perceived as diminishing the powers of the parliaments and thus a weakening of democracy.

To understand the historical moment we are going through in Europe, one cannot ignore that much of the malaise that exists in many countries is the result of the undigested clash with globalization. This is not always clear, appearing amalgamated with problems of European integration.

In a remarkable work, Rodirk (2011) maintains that in the current model of globalization, which he calls "hyperglobalisation", States are unable to achieve self-determination and thus democracy is suppressed. He states that you cannot have both hyperglobalisation, democracy and national self-determination simultaneously. As an alternative, he advocates a more limited "smart globalization", inspired by the vision of Bretton Woods revisited for a new order in the twenty-first century.

But it is also here that the European Union has not fulfilled its mission. Waivers to sovereignty that are inherent in European integration and, in particular, in EMU, only gain justification and acceptance if they result in a greater capacity to solve together what you could not do in isolation. And the results are not encouraging, even in the field of the promotion of peace.

If we take as a starting point the Schuman Declaration, the European integration process will have run for 70 years in 2020. EMU is still in its adolescence, with its 17 years. Historically, it is a very short time. It is the task of our time to decide if European integration and monetary union will be seen in the future as just another episode in the secular histories of the people who lived them or as a perennial and successful political experience of peace, democracy and prosperity.

## References

Corden WM (1972) Monetary integration. Princeton University Press, Princeton

Ingram JC (1973) The case for European monetary integration. Princeton University Press, Princeton

Kenen PB (1969) The theory of optimum currency areas: an ecletic view. In: Mundell RA, Swoboda AK (eds) Monetary problems in the international economy. University of Chicago Press, Chicago

Magnifico G (1973) European monetary unification. Macmillan, London

McKinon RI (1963) Optimum currency areas. Am Econ Rev LIII(4):717–725, Mundell R, Swoboda A (eds) (1969) Monetary problems of the international economy. University of Chicago Press, Chicago

Meade JE (1953) Problems of economic union. Allen & Unwin, London, and The balance of payments problems of a European free trade area. Econ J, 1957

Mundell RA (1961) A theory of optimum currency areas. Am Econ Rev XXI

Rodrik D (2011) The globalization paradox—why global markets, states and democracy can't coexist. Oxford University Press, Oxford

Scitovsky T (1958) Economic theory and western European integration. Unwin University Books, London

Triffin R (1957) Europe and the money muddle. Yale University Press, New Haven

# The Great Recession of 2012–2014: The Monetary Union Challenged by National Egoisms

**Pierre-Alain Muet**

**Abstract** Eight years after the outbreak of the financial crisis, while the United States have for several years emerged from recession, Europe, after a long recession whose only precedent is the 30s deflation, has barely recovered the level of GDP per capita that existed before the 2008 crisis.

The argument developed in this article is that this crisis is inherent to a monetary union which has failed to build the political institutions necessary for its functioning. Coordination through rules is not enough. Without an "economic government" able to set up a discretionary coordination of fiscal policy, the monetary union has been unable to implement a policy mix suitable for the whole euro area and let deflationary policies develop, pushing the whole of Europe into depression.

## 1 Introduction

"No one should be surprised that the economy of the euro zone is once more going in reverse. This is an entirely predictable outcome of the misguided policies that European leaders stubbornly insist on pursuing, despite all evidence that they are exactly the wrong medicine." This New York Times editorial from August 2014 perfectly sums up how history will remember the absurd policies implemented by European leaders from 2011 to 2014—calling here and there for structural reforms and supply-side policies while the whole continent sank into a slump in demand caused by the generalization of austerity policies whose magnitude was never fully assessed.

Eight years after the outbreak of the financial crisis, while the United States have for several years emerged from recession, Europe, after a long recession whose only precedent is the 30s deflation, has barely recovered the level of GDP per capita that existed before the 2008 crisis.

P.-A. Muet
Paris, France
e-mail: pam@pa-muet.com

 
N. da Costa Cabral et al. (eds.), *The Euro and the Crisis*, Financial and Monetary Policy Studies 43, DOI 10.1007/978-3-319-45710-9_9

How did that happen? How have European nations been able to pursue policies so at odds with the history of European integration? How the principle of solidarity—a foundation of the European Union—could be so absent from our national economic policies?

## 2 Europe: From Financial Crisis to Deflation

In its scale, its roots and its consequences the crisis, which erupted in 2008, is comparable to the crash of 1929. Both are the outcome of two major phases of globalization and financial deregulation that preceded them. Both are born from the uncontrolled excesses of finance and an explosion of inequalities that fed artificial growth based on profitability requirements incompatible with the real economy.

The constant pressure on wages resulting from these profitability requirements has profoundly deepened inequalities between stagnating low incomes and exploding high incomes, leading to a tremendous accumulation of wealth in the hands of a small minority. On the one hand, the indebtedness of poor households took the place of increasing wages to maintain growth in demand, fueling an artificial growth based on debt. On the other, drifting high incomes fueled senseless risk taking, maintained by the proliferation of financial innovations, which led to a surge in asset prices until everything collapsed when market expectations turned sour.

Unlike the 1929 crisis, governments were able to extinguish the financial fire and prevent bank defaults through a massive injection of public funds, transferring bank debts to the states. They also took stimulus measures in all countries in 2009 to avoid a massive collapse in demand. But, as in the 30s, the crisis originated in the United States produced its most disastrous effects in Europe by triggering a sovereign debt crisis at the heart of the euro zone.

Yet the euro zone was much less indebted than the US and Japan, and the countries at the heart of the storm were—with the exception of Greece—countries which had in fact reduced their debt and deficits in the years preceding the crisis. But the continent was the most vulnerable to speculative attacks due to a monetary union without financial solidarity. Sovereign debt crises are self-fulfilling prophecies in the sense that when a country is attacked, its debt interest rates rise sharply and may make it insolvent. This vicious cycle can only be stopped in two ways: the default of the state in question or loans from other member states. But since the ECB cannot directly buy a state's securities and no solidarity mechanism existed between the states' debts due to the "no-bailout" clause of the Maastricht Treaty, the default of a state, never truly considered by financial markets during the first 10 years of monetary union, became credible. And if it was possible for Greece, it could become so for others. As Paul Krugman summed up, in establishing doubts about their supposed solidarity, European leaders have transformed the Greek bailout into a generalized crisis in the euro zone. It took indeed more than two years for the establishment of a European Stability Mechanism (ESM) to put an end to the speculative crisis.

Unable for several years to take steps to curb speculative attacks affecting some of its members, corseted in budgetary rules and economic policy principles of another age, Europe has imposed upon itself a dose of austerity whose main impact has been a massive collapse in production and employment and the longest recession ever known in Europe since the Second World War.

The appropriate response to the crisis was a policy implementing real financial regulations through the separation of banking activities, and a strong, national and European action in favor of employment and investment to come out of recession. In a way, these were the policies set out by Roosevelt in the 30s and whose generalization after the Second World War contributed to the long postwar period of financial stability and prosperity.

But it meant leaving the neoliberal dogma that dominates the European continent and led to austerity policies that plunged Europe into depression. This reasoning was, in the space of a presidential campaign, carried out by the French President François Hollande. But having failed to influence European policies, France's economic policy eventually merged into the prevailing European dogma, reflecting the inability of our continent to think and even build a relevant macroeconomic policy at the right scale: that of the monetary Union.

## 3 National Egoisms, Recession and Deflation

Coming out of the 2009 recession, almost all European countries faced increased public deficits and rising debts, to which was added the chronic lack of competitiveness of half the Eurozone countries. In applying an economic policy cocktail of massive cuts in public spending and reduced labor costs, which can be effective when a only one country is doing so, but leads to disaster when all do the same, Europe sank into recession and deflation; a replica, 80 years later, of the deflationary policies of the 30s.

When one single country undertakes to reduce public spending, the recessive effect is partly offset by the growth of its partners, so that tax revenues are not reduced too much and the end result is indeed a lower public deficit. But when all do the same, especially in a situation where growth is limited by demand, the depressive effect is so high that revenue losses offset spending cuts and the deficit is not reduced, or only slightly. The main result is to accentuate the recession.

The same pattern happens with labor costs. A country can actually improve its competitiveness by lowering labor costs, but it improves its situation while complicating that of its partners. If everyone did the same thing in Europe, the result would be nullified in terms of intra-European competitiveness; there remains only a general decline in prices, that is to say deflation! As for its effect on Europe's competitiveness as a whole, it would have been possible without deflation (and that was made in 2014) by devaluating the Euro.

The result is that we miss the three targets we had fixed: unemployment rises, the public deficit is only slightly reduced, the impact on the external intra-European deficit is negligible, and as there is neither growth nor inflation, the debt ratio increases.

## 4 The Negation of Europe's Fundamental Values

It is little wonder that people are moving away from Europe and nationalisms rise everywhere. What happened in recent years on our continent is the very negation of what was the European construction. The constraints imposed on Greece by the Troika were as absurd as the reparations imposed on Germany with the Treaty of Versailles—which Keynes denounced at the time. The lesson had been learned by the Allies after World War II: instead of overwhelming the vanquished country, they reached out and it was instead a Europe of solidarity that emerged from the rubble of the war. A solidarity that went as far as to clear 60 % of the German debt at the London conference in February 1953 to allow West Germany to recover.

How can we accept that Europe, which for decades has managed to pull up all newly-joined countries, has done the exact opposite over the past three years? When Spain and Portugal joined the EU, many feared that wage competition would draw the wages of most developed countries down or generate strong relocations. This would probably have occurred if Europe had only been a large market. But fortunately there were solidarity mechanisms such as the structural funds that have encouraged the investment and modernization of new entrants so that convergence went upwards.

The hallmark of austerity budgetary policies or competitiveness by lower wage costs is to be non-cooperative, in that they will improve the situation of one country by damaging those of others. And it is the opposite for policies of demand stimulus or supply stimulation through innovation that also benefit partners by disseminating rising demand or innovation. Where cooperative policies generate an upward adjustment, non-cooperative policies engender a downward adjustment. One might think that after the deflation of the 30s, Europe would be terminally cured of non-cooperative policies. But the shortsightedness of the prevailing economic thought that has dominated Europe in the last decade has proved unfortunately boundless. And in the absence of a federal power worthy of the name—something the Barroso Commission never was—national egoisms have always prevailed over solidarity.

## 5 More Favorable Circumstances

When nations are unable to take control of their common destiny, a more favorable conjunction of stars can sometimes get us out of a recession. This is what fortunately happened with the oil price decline that loosened fiscal policy constraints and allowed broadly neutral policies across the EU in 2015. To this was added an appropriate policy of quantitative easing from the ECB, the depreciation of the euro and the investment plan of the new Commission, which, although still modest given the needs in investment and growth, reflects a more favorable change in the direction of European policies.

If we want to prevent a downward adjustment from happening again, we must outlaw non-cooperative policies and favor competitiveness policies through innovation that benefit all; establish minimum wages differentiated by countries to link social progress and productivity gains and develop solidarity mechanisms that are desperately needed in the monetary union. Finally, Europe must once again become an area of solidarity and not a large market making states compete against each other.

This is even more necessary now that a Europe of 28 predominantly consists today of small countries for which non-cooperative strategies in a large market are more effective than participation in cooperative projects.

Since 2012, the annual diagnosis of three institutes (OFCE, IMK, ECLM)[1] has regularly fed the reflections of some political groups in Parliament (in particular the Socialists and Democrats group). It showed, in 2012, the risk of recession emerging in the Union because of the generalization of austerity policies and highlighted in the following years the deflationary risk facing the euro area. This had little influence over national economic policies, including in the states of the Union where social democratic parties were in power alone, or in large coalitions.

The euro crisis has shown that a monetary union with 18 different public debts on which markets can freely speculate, 18 tax and benefit systems in competition with each other and no executive worthy of the name, it does not work.

As noted by Joseph Stiglitz in a speech in Paris: Europe's main structural problem « is the problem of the structure of the euro-zone, not the structure of individuals countries ... The euro was a political project, where there was not sufficient political will to create an economic framework that would enable it to work ».[2]

## 6 A "Euro-Treaty" for a "Euro-Government"

The euro crisis has revived the debate on the political integration of the euro. In Germany, the Glienieker Gruppe's contribution, "Towards a Euro Union", emphasized Stiglitz's argument: "Europe has structural problems that require structural solutions. Even though this is not a popular view at the moment, we are convinced

[1]Independent Annual Growth Survey (IAGS) published yearly by the OFCE (Observatoire français des conjonctures économiques), the IMK Institute of the Hans Boeckler Foundation and the ECLM (Economic Council of the Labour Movement) Institute.

[2]Joseph Sitglitz: Speech to the French national Assembly, Paris, January 13, 2015 http://www.alterecoplus.fr/tribunes-debats/comment-sortir-la-zone-euro-de-lorniere-201502051824-00000762.html

that the monetary union needs deeper integration. More particularly, it needs a sufficiently powerful European economic government".[3] A converging reflection was published in France by the authors of the "Manifesto for a political union of the Euro",[4] whose proposals are widely echoed in this article. The Brexit debate and the disintegration of solidarity within the union of 28 make even more urgent a political response from the nations committed to the monetary union.

The first condition for change is a specific budget for the euro zone of around ½ percentage point to 1 percentage point of GDP, financed by own resources and with a borrowing capacity to boost recovery and investment initiatives. Powered by a European tax applying a lower rate to the corporation tax base, it would help to achieve within the monetary union the common consolidated corporate tax base, an essential tool to fight against the aggressive tax planning of multinational groups. The cohesion of the euro zone could be strengthened by a common unemployment insurance system that would complement national systems to cushion economic shocks affecting member states.

The need to vote a tax and euro zone budget would justify the creation of a parliament of the euro zone which could draw on the proposal for a European chamber made by Joschka Fischer in 2000,[5] bringing together some of the national parliamentarians of the monetary union's member states. It is indeed based on national parliamentary sovereignty that the monetary union may advance, since no national parliament would agree to relinquish its power to vote taxes. This new architecture would eventually lead to a true bicameralism, ending the fiction that the Council of Ministers can act as a second chamber representing the states. To move in due time to the majority rule on tax and spending decisions that countries in the euro zone would choose to share, it is indeed essential that the chamber representing the states should include all national political forces and not only national finance ministers. The Inter-parliamentary conference on stability timidly paved the way for such a development, that a treaty specific to the euro zone could further develop.

In short, as shown repeatedly over 60 years of European construction, it is in responding to crises that Europe was built. The euro crisis and Brexit may be the opportunity for a new start if the nations that constitute the heart of Europe feel so incline.

[3]Glienicker Gruppe: "Towards a Euro Union", English version, original version published in German by Die Zeit, October 17 2013

[4]http://www.lemonde.fr/idees/article/2014/02/16/manifeste-pour-une-union-politique-de-l-euro_4366865_3232.html

[5]http://www.cvce.eu/obj/discours_de_joschka_fischer_sur_la_finalite_de_l_integration_europeenne_berlin_12_mai_2000-fr-4cd02fa7-d9days-4 cd2-91c9-2746a3297773.html

# The Fiscal Compact and the Excessive Deficit Procedure: Relics of Bygone Times?

**Ansgar Belke**

**Abstract** This paper takes a critical look at the Fiscal Compact as a key element of the future EU governance. It shows that the "Excessive Deficit Procedure (EDP)" is representing an Achilles heel of the fiscal pact. We put a finger in a wound that has been neglected up to now, probably because it has evaded daily politics analysis as a statistical-econometric issue: the "purposefully structured" data revisions in GDP and the government budget balance figures. The road to a sustainable "economic governance" of Europe can only work through fiscal federalism in conjunction with an incentive-compliant banking union. In that case, market-based interest rates provide a better incentive and sanction mechanism than the "Excessive Deficit Procedure" which is plagued by inherent manipulation leeway and political cycles but is decisive for the success of the Fiscal Compact. A further important omission of the Fiscal Compact is that it scarcely focuses on the relation between France's lack of budget consolidation and the country's shrinking international competitiveness—an economic relationship which is referred to based on the example of Greece.

## 1 Introduction

This paper deals with strategic, economic-conceptual and operationalization problems of the Fiscal Compact as a contract outside the EU framework.[1]

In the remainder of the paper we proceed as follows. In Sect. 2, the Fiscal Compact is classified as part of the Treaty on Stability, Coordination and Governance (TSCG). It is described institutionally closer in terms of its critical components such as the Excessive Deficit Procedure (EDP). We will also discuss in more detail whether the Fiscal Compact and the Six-pack represent complements or

[1]This contribution heavily relies, on Belke (2015).

A. Belke
CEPS, 1, Place du Congrès, 1000, Brussels, Belgium

Institute for the Study of Labor (IZA), Schaumburg-Lippe-Str. 5-9, 53113, Bonn, Germany
e-mail: ansgar.belke@uni-due.de; http://www.uni-due.de/makro

 
N. da Costa Cabral et al. (eds.), *The Euro and the Crisis*, Financial and Monetary Policy Studies 43, DOI 10.1007/978-3-319-45710-9_10

substitutes.[2] Section 3 provides a critical but innovative econometric statistical observation of the core of the Fiscal Compact, the EDP, considering the use of real-time data and possible opportunistic cycles in the revisions of budget-related data. Real-time data denote the macroeconomic data available to decision makers in the Fiscal Compact at the time of decision, but which may be revised ex post even several years later. Exactly these ex post revisions have created substantial *evasive leeway* for governments within the EDP, which runs counter the character of the Fiscal Compact and can even undermine it.[3] As econometric statistical issues are at stake here, this (operationalization) problem inherent in the EDP appears initially very abstract and chiselled. For the practical efficiency of the Fiscal Compact and its EDP these deficiencies are significant and politically relevant though. Upon closer inspection, they provoke even an intensive audit of the institutions involved in the Fiscal Compact. Unfortunately, these weaknesses of the enforcement of the Fiscal Compact are hardly known by the public and therefore we feel legitimized to let them represent the main focus of this paper.

The following sections then class the Fiscal Compact within a wider context. Here, we do not deal with a problem of operationalization, but with rather fundamental strategic and economic-conceptual problems of the Fiscal Compact.

Section 4 deals with various ways towards a sustainable economic governance of the Eurozone and the EU, of which the fiscal pact is (only) one possible option. We check whether the bundle fiscal pact in return for debt mutualisation through, for example, Euro Bonds (which has been targeted and partly already practiced in the EU) is inferior to a consistent fiscal federalism in conjunction with an incentive-compliant banking union. And we do this not just from an econometric-statistical point of view, but also from a strategic perspective (strategic problem of the Fiscal Compact). In Sect. 5 we briefly assess whether the risk of a repeated official sector involvement (OSI) is not due to the high government debt ratio, but to the lack of growth in the example of the program country Greece. The lack of export growth could then be much more important for the markets than just achieving a primary surplus of the government budget. In this case, it would be a problem that the Fiscal Compact with its focus on the second message considers these issues only inadequately, especially in application to non-programme countries such as France. The paper ends with a conclusion and a brief outlook.

---

[2]For an explanation of the Six-pack see http://ec.europa.eu/economy_finance/articles/governance/2012-03-14_six_pack_en.htm.

[3]De Castro et al. (2013, pp. 1955ff.), for instance, come up with a survey (dependent on the EU country considered) of systematic under-estimations of first announcements of the budget deficit as a share of GDP.

# 2 The Fiscal Compact as Part of the Treaty on Stability, Coordination and Governance (TSCG)

## *2.1 The Treaty on Stability, Coordination and Governance (TSCG)*

The "Treaty on Stability, Coordination and Governance (TSCG)" came into force on 1 January 2013—for those 16 countries that had fully ratified it before that date.[4] Ratification by at least 12 member states was needed. It is an intergovernmental agreement, but not EU law, i.e., a "contract outside the EU". It was signed by 25 EU member countries (all EU members except Britain and the Czech Republic). The TSCG will be binding only for all Eurozone countries, while the other contracting parties will be bound once they have adopted the euro, or even earlier if they seek to do it. They may choose rules that would fulfill them (ECB 2012). The fiscal part of TSCG is called "Fiscal Compact".

The TSCG requires the contracting parties to respect and ensure convergence to the country-specific medium-term objective (MTO). This target value is defined in the Stability and Gowth Pact (SGP)—with a lower limit for the structural budget deficit (i.e., excluding cyclical impacts and one-off measures) of 0.5 % of GDP (and 1.0 % of GDP for member countries with a debt-to-GDP ratio significantly below 60 % of GDP). Correction mechanisms are meant to ensure automatic action in the event of deviation from the MTO or the adjustment path towards the MTO, with exceptions for extraordinary circumstances. Compliance with those rules is monitored by independent institutions (ECB 2012).

These budget rules have to be implemented into national law through legislation with binding and permanent character, preferably constitutional.

The European Court can impose financial sanctions (0.1 % of GDP), if a country does not properly implement the new budget rules in national law and does not meet the rule of the ECJ that requires exactly this from him. In the case of euro-zone member countries sanctions on the ESM are channeled—probably the most effective and only "strong" regulation throughout the Fiscal Compact! For the other Member States the sanctions will run via the EU budget (ECB 2012).

Compliance with the rule to implement the MTO in national law is also monitored at the national level by independent institutions.

Other provisions are aimed at strengthening the implementation of the Stability and Growth Pact (SGP): a repeating of the budget rule in the Six-pack, a behavioral obligation to reproduce the reverse qualified majority voting (RQMV) among the

[4]See http://www.consilium.europa.eu/uedocs/cms_data/docs/pressdata/en/ecofin/134543.pdf. For subsequent ratifiers, it entered into force on the first day of the month following the deposit of ratification instruments.

Eurozone member countries when the EU Commission is considering that an excessive deficit exists (ECB 2012).[5]

Finally, it is often argued that the TSCG is setting milestones for enhanced surveillance and coordination of economic policies, including an ex ante coordination of debt issuance plans among the contracting parties and economic partnership programs for member countries of the EDP. The latter describe the structural reforms needed for an effective and durable correction of their excessive budget deficits in detail.

The TSCG also includes a section on economic governance of the Eurozone (for example, euro summit taking place at least twice a year, enhanced economic cooperation etc.).

## 2.2 *Fiscal Compact and Six-Pack: Complements or Substitutes?*

The Fiscal Compact, the fiscal part of TSCG, and the Six-pack run in parallel by nature. On the one hand, certain rules of the TSCG reflect concepts which have already existed in the Stability and Growth Pact (SGP) that has been reformed by the Six-pack—such as the "medium-term objectives (MTOs)", "significant deviation" and "exceptional circumstances" (EU Commission 2013).

On the other hand, some provisions of the TSCG turn out to be more stringent than the Six-pack. For example, the former states that at every stage of the EDP, the member countries of the Eurozone support the recommendations of the European Commission and the Council proposals if a member country of the Eurozone contravenes against the budget deficit criterion. However, this is only excluded if a qualified majority of them against it. In practice this means that in case of a breach a sort of reverse qualified majority voting (RQMV) is applied to all stages of the EDP, even if this is not provided in the Six-pack (EU Commission 2013).

In addition, the TSCG requires member countries to implement the country-specific MTOs into national binding law, preferably of a constitutional nature. What is more, the TSCG amplifies, according to prevailing opinion, the economic governance of Europe. Finally, the European Commission strongly supports the goal of pouring the main terms of TSCG as fast as possible in EU law. In the TSCG, a 5-year horizon is mentioned; but some schemes could be implemented without delay in secondary legislation.

Figure 1 below finally compares the corrective part of the strengthened Stability and Growth Pact with the Fiscal Compact and works out the crucial position and role of the Excessive Deficit Procedure.

---

[5]A formal modification of voting rules, however, would necessitate a change of the treaties.

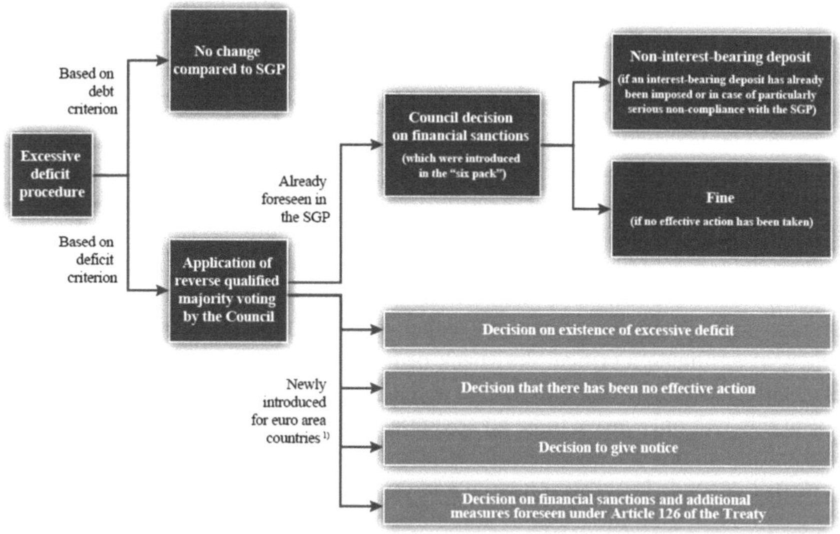


Source: ECB.
Notes: Under the reinforced SGP an excessive deficit procedure can be initiated on the basis of a breach of the deficit criterion and/or a breach of the debt criterion. The fiscal compact strengthens the decision-making procedure of the excessive deficit procedure following a breach of the deficit criterion by a euro area country, but not that in case of a breach of the debt criterion. In particular, the fiscal compact provides for the application of reverse qualified majority voting by the euro area countries on important steps in the excessive deficit procedure (marked in lighter blue), for which Article 126 of the Treaty demands qualified majority voting. This increases the automaticity of the excessive deficit procedure following a breach of the deficit criterion. If a Member State repeatedly fails to comply with a decision by the Council, the Council may apply additional measures under Article 126 of the Treaty. The Council may, for example, require the Member State concerned to publish additional information or to invite the European Investment Bank to reconsider its lending policy towards that Member State.
1) According to Article 7 TSCG, the contracting parties whose currency is the euro commit to supporting the proposals or recommendations submitted by the European Commission.

**Fig. 1** Comparison of the corrective part of the strengthened stability and growth pact with the fiscal compact. Source: ECB (2012, p. 91)

# 3 The "Excessive Deficit Procedure" (EDP): A Critical Examination

## *3.1 Background*

The Fiscal Compact leads to *greater degree of automaticity* provided in the corrective part of the SGP procedures applicable to breaches of the deficit criterion by a country of the euro area (ECB 2012). This concept harks back to a proposal by Daniel Gros in the 1990s (the "Gros" rule, see Gros 1997). Contracting parties whose currency is the euro commit themselves to support the proposals and recommendations of the Commission for Council decisions in the excessive deficit procedure, unless a qualified majority (without the Member State concerned) speaks out against such a decision (see Fig. 1 above).

The introduction of such a commitment by the euro area countries in important procedural steps such as the opening of an excessive deficit procedure, the decision about whether a Member State has adopted effective measures, as well as the introduction of possible further steps to correct an excessive deficit, enable a more automated process compared to the strengthened SGP. If the EU Commission, for example, concludes that in a country which has violated the deficit criterion an excessive deficit exists and then directs an official statement to the Member State concerned as well as a proposal to the Council, this proposal will be adopted—unless a qualified majority within the Council in other Member States of the euro area is voting against (ECB 2012).

Overall, the stronger automatism for countries that violate the deficit criterion introduced by the Fiscal Compact seems to be a step into the right direction, as it reduces the political discretion within the excessive deficit procedure and increases the likelihood of a stricter application of the rules and the imposition of financial sanctions. This will (if only partly because of the *non-application to the debt criterion*) eliminate a critical drawback of the corrective part of the SGP. This, in turn, shifts the incentives in favour of sound fiscal policies (ECB 2012).

But this will only prove to be an advantage if the "Excessive Deficit Procedure" really works in practice, because the effectiveness of the strengthened fiscal framework still depends heavily on a strict and consistent application of the rules by the EU Commission. So the Commission plays a crucial role when assessing whether an excessive deficit exists or a Member State has taken effective action for its correction. Another example in this regard: the EU Commission can give the Council a recommendation for the reduction or suspension of the new financial sanctions. This can either be conducted in case of an exceptional economic situation or at the request of the concerned Member State (ECB 2012).

Extensive reviews and assessments of the Fiscal Compact and its underlying assumptions[6] have already been made elsewhere.[7] Therefore, the question to be answered in the following is *whether the "Effective Deficit Procedure" has been implemented effectively*, which is important for the implementation in practice, but has so far been insufficiently examined.

## 3.2 Key Questions

The first key question in our context runs as follows: Is the quality of statistical data used for EDP purposes adequate? To answer this, we have to determine whether (a) the European Commission (Eurostat) provides adequate and effective guidance and support to the national authorities of the member countries to ensure the quality of statistical data for EDP purposes, (b) the national authorities of the member countries implement really all actions that are needed to ensure a high quality of

[6]Belke (2012a), for instance, illuminates the now-famous hypothesis of an "expansionary fiscal contraction", according to which above all public expenditure cuts raise economic growth via induced expectations of lower interest and tax rates prevailing in the future.

[7]See, for instance, ECB (2012) and Gros (2012). Permanent criticism of the EDP sparks off from the target "government budget balance", which only indicates the *change* in government debt but not its level.

transmitted data for the purpose of EDP statistics and (c) the European Commission (Eurostat) checks the quality of the data transmitted for EDP purposes statistical data effectively.

The second main question is: Are adequate analysis and adequate corrective and monitoring mechanisms implemented in the context of the EDP? The relevant sub-questions are: (a) Does the EU Commission (DG ECFIN) analyse current and predicted EDP data systematically enough and take appropriate actions on this basis?, (b) Do the Member States implement appropriate and effective corrective action in response to the "Council" recommendations and in the "notices" issued context of the EDP?, and (c) Does the EU Commission (DG ECFIN) perform an effective monitoring of the "corrective action" by the Member States prescribed by the EDP?

We will comment on some of these, publicly not yet adequately reflected, questions hereafter.

## 3.3 The "Excessive Deficit Procedure": Interim Results

Any track record of the "Excessive Deficit Procedure" would certainly not turn out well. The most important facets of this assessment are summarized below:

- *The process has not worked ex post.* The general government structural balance was most of the time lower than −0.5% of the potential GDP ceiling for most countries and the general government balance in about 50% of all cases under the −3 % deficit ceiling (Moghadam 2014). In practice, the EU fiscal framework and the SGP could not prevent the emergence of large fiscal imbalances in some Eurozone countries, while the accumulation of massive current account imbalances within the EU has been neglected. As long as the EDP represents a significant part of the Fiscal Compact, but depends crucially on the quality of the externally supplied data, there is the danger that things will stay like this—as demonstrated in the following.
- *Of all the data transmissions (in national responsibility), most "notifications" were related to deficits smaller than 3 %.*[8] In fact, this represents a significant bias and distortion which ECFIN should admit frankly. National instances regularly trot out higher growth and / or higher tax elasticities and / or higher income from governmental income-enhancing measures as actually realised ex post.
- Therefore *national authorities predict (and transmit) a budget (in reality even just a plan) for the next year, which is in almost all cases too optimistic.* But ECFIN has actually little scope to correct for this distortion.

[8]See http://epp.eurostat.ec.europa.eu/portal/page/portal/government_finance_statistics/excessive_deficit/edp_notification_tables.

- It is also worth looking at the detailed *pattern of data revisions*. They are in the majority of cases *directed upwards*, that is they later on reveal a higher deficit than originally transmitted.
- The *emphasis on cyclically-adjusted deficits after 2003 has not helped, because the economic and financial cycle are of different lengths* (Borio et al. 2013). The financial cycle has a stronger impact on the revenues of the government sector, but can neither be accurately measured nor even identified. Now for the details.

The inclusion of information on the financial cycle is important to improve the measurement of the potential output and the output gap (i.e., the difference between current and potential output). From a conceptual point of view it is too limited to equate potential output with non-inflationary output. The potential output is considered as sustainable. However, experience shows that the output may be located on an unsustainable path, even if inflation is low and stable—namely, if financial imbalances build themselves up. As long as the potential output is equated with the non-cyclical component of output fluctuations and financial market factors play a key role in explaining the cyclical part, ignoring these factors destroys valuable information. Within a simple and transparent framework Borio et al. (2013) show that the inclusion of information about the financial cycle is able to generate measures of potential output and the output gap, whose estimates are not only accurate, but also much more robust in real time. It can be shown as part of a policy application, that such "finance-neutral" output gaps produce reliable estimators for cyclically-adjusted balances. Hence, they can serve as a better guideline for EDP in the Fiscal Compact (Borio et al. 2013).[9]

- To illustrate the essence of the problem in more detail: Borio et al. (2013) use their output gap estimator to determine cyclically-adjusted government budget balances. This requires estimates of the elasticities of tax revenue and of government expenditure in relation to the output development. To this end, they employ OECD estimates (Girouard and André 2005). It should be stressed that they do not correct for the additional effects that asset price booms and other facets of financial market boom have on the budget balances—for example, through impacts on the structure of government revenues and expenditures. There is ample evidence that *asset price booms are "revenue-rich"* (Price and Dang 2011; Suárez 2010). What is more, these estimates do not consider the *additional expenditures incurred by the handling of the subsequent bust*, for example by actively strengthening the banking system. Thus, differences between the cycle-adjusted budget balances reflect only those that are determined by output gap estimates. They therefore *underestimate the true extent of the necessary adjustment.*

  The authors focus only on the real-time estimates which represent the relevant variables for the policy and the EDP. However, this real-time perspective has the

[9] A similar argument is of course valid vis-a-vis the usage of these improved output gaps as a target for monetary policy. For an application to the ECB see Belke (2014a).

disadvantage that for governments under the "Multilateral Surveillance" revisions of budget balances and the underlying estimates of gross domestic product are *subsequently* possible and rather attractive. GDP and budget balances estimates are initially *recorded too high* to avoid negative consequences such as sanctions, or *reported too low* to benefit from exemptions such as those that occur in circumstances that the member countries do not have to take the responsibility for (see next section).
- There is *no simple distinction between the private and public budget balance*: private imbalances may possibly end up as imbalances on the public sector balance sheet. This can happen through a direct "bailout" of the banking system (as in Ireland) or through the lost government revenue and the growing government spending caused by a deep and long-lasting decline in output (as in Spain).

From this perspective, the Maastricht Treaty's main focus on fiscal policy acted in a limiting way, with respect to the identification of risks as well as to the effectiveness of policy responses. To really enhance the growth prospects of the euro area and the EU, we need a process that monitors and enforces the already agreed structural reforms (for example, the "Service Directive") and advocates growth-enhancing reforms proactively. This would bring the European economy on a higher growth path, which in turn would also help to reduce the current high and sometimes even rising (!) debt levels which are partly due to the ultra-low interest rates (Moghadam 2014). The conclusion from this can only be: "Watch out, the Fiscal Compact will not work either".

## 3.4 *Real-Time Data and the "Excessive Deficit Procedure": Political-Economic Considerations*

Statistical revisions of government budget balances in Europe could be problematic, as the observance of multilateral surveillance rules is carried out *based on first releases* of relevant data. The problem of dependence on real-time data is to be set forth below with reference to three pieces of current research.

### 3.4.1 De Castro et al. (2013): Revisions of Fiscal Policy Data in Europe

Using a pool of real "vintage"[10] of data for 15 EU countries over the period 1995–2008, De Castro et al. (2013) are able to identify the following empirical patterns that would be well used for an audit of the EDP:

(i) Preliminary releases of fiscal data are distorted and are not efficient predictors of subsequent releases.

[10]In the case of GDP, it takes eight (!) halfyears until its final empirical realisation is fixed.

(ii) Such a systematic bias is a fundamental feature of the entire underlying samples.
(iii) Eurostat decisions explain a significant amount of distortion and provide evidence for "window dressing" practices.
(iv) The expected real GDP growth, political cycles and the severity of fiscal rules also contribute to the explanation of the temporal pattern revision.

*What are the factors that drive data revisions*? To investigate this issue, De Castro et al. (2013) arrange a comprehensive overview of revisions of the government balance figures and the GDP statistics from EDP notifications (collected from press releases).

Revisions of fiscal statistics can well be caused by imperfections in the process of data collection and incomplete information at the time of the first reporting. For example, data of the local administration are typically available only with some time lag. However, other factors mentioned below seem even more significant in the empirical results.

First, revisions of the data for the government budget deficit to GDP ratio are partly *due to revisions of macroeconomic aggregates* themselves, especially given the importance of nominal GDP as the denominator of the ratio.

Second, political-economic considerations suggest that governments have *incentives to hide budget deficits of the public sector*, especially if the macro-economic circumstances are bad, because unfavorable economic circumstances worsen the budget balance of the public sector per se, especially via the automatic stabilizers. In such a situation a government could bring itself to influence the National Statistical Institute to report a better than the actually observed budget deficit and to move part of the increase to future revisions, most likely into better economic times. Interestingly enough, all revisions by Eurostat in the sample of the study by De Castro et al. (2013), lead on average to lower government budget balances (i.e., in the direction of a higher budget deficit).

Third, *political budget cycles* could *affect the incentives of governments to report true fiscal data negatively*, particularly because of the high political cost of implementing an EDP procedure. In addition, a government could use information asymmetries and increase spending before an election and hide the resulting budget deficit. It is significant that this so-called political business cycle is mainly empirically confirmed in the area of fiscal policy. It works through incentives for "signaling" fiscal competence of the government (Persson and Tabellini 2000; Cimadomo 2011).

Fourth, the revision pattern of fiscal data could follow the relevance of *different fiscal rules*, insofar as they represent a permanent constraint on the national fiscal policies. In addition to their importance for ensuring fiscal discipline, such rules continue to also contribute to the reduction of uncertainty about future fiscal developments.

Reporting of fiscal data is a central element of the multilateral surveillance rules of the EU. The compliance with such rules is assessed using the initial data releases by EU Member States, in the framework of the so-called "Excessive Deficit

Procedure (EDP) Notifications", one of the foundations of the SGP. According to the SGP, deviations of the government budget balances from the reference value of −3 % of GDP in the base year ("not considered to be corrected over a given forecast horizon") result in the application of corrective actions. In this case, the country concerned is involved in a path of deficit reduction, which in turn must be approved by the Council of Ministers of the EU. Frequent and/or major revisions of fiscal data should raise concern about the reliability of official EDP statistics which is used in monitoring the SGP. Revisions of "fiscal data" may also imply that a country appears ex post as a no compliance case with the SGP while this was not the case at time of the initial reporting. This constellation was valid for Greece in the years 2000 to 2003 and 2007, Spain in 1997, Italy in 2001 and 2003, Austria in 2004, and Portugal in 2001 and 2004. This situation would have de facto *no consequences, since no corrective action procedure would be initiated, if the country concerned has broken the −3 % budget deficit limit EX POST just by the revision of past data—from the year $t + 2$ and beyond* (De Castro et al. 2013, p. 1188).[11]

Although the production and supply of "fiscal data" is falling in Europe in the responsibility of independent national statistical institutes and are subject to the control of the European Commission (Eurostat), some governments could have an incentive—from a political-economic perspective—to resort to practices creative accounting, so initially published figures are distorted (Kohen and Van de Noord 2005; Leal et al. 2008; and specifically for Greece Belke et al. 2014).

Moreover, frequent ex post executed data revisions imply structural breaks in the subsequent targeted and projected time paths over the medium term—in the context that the objectives and projections of the government are connected to a base year in which these goals and projections were produced. *If sizable fiscal data revisions become a stylized fact, no less than the credibility of governments is at stake.* In the cases where revisions have no clear recurring pattern, but still occur frequently, the comparison of successive paths of government objectives could become imprecise, and the reliability and consistency of fiscal policy choice could even be undermined over time (De Castro et al. 2013).

In the ideal case, however, revisions of the budget deficit figures in the public sector can be explained by updates of the underlying statistical sources and/or methodological improvements and changes of accounting standards (Mink and Rodríguez-Vives; Bier et al. 2004; McKenzie 2006). Since national statistical authorities have up to four years to provide final data on government budget balances, **inescapable margins of uncertainty** in relation to the early "Vintage" out of given numbers exist (De Castro et al. 2013).

[11]In case excessive deficits arise, Member States are required to, among others, comply with Council recommendations under Article 126(7) TFEU to take effective corrective actions by a deadline of 6 months (3 months if the situation is particularly serious) and ultimately to correct the excessive deficit by the end of the year following the identification. See Article 3.4 of Council Regulation (EC) No 1467/97.

### 3.4.2 Ley und Misch (2013): Macro-economic Monitoring in Real Time and Fiscal Policy

Ley and Misch (2013) develop a simple but comprehensive modeling framework to formalize the relationship between output data and revisions of fiscal policy. They apply the former to a current aggregate data set with final and real-time output data for 175 countries from the World Economic Outlook of the International Monetary Fund. For their estimations, they include a period of 17 years. Based on a simulation, the authors find that output data revisions significantly undermine the reliability of real-time estimates of total and structural budget deficits of the public sector and that this may lead to an unplanned and substantial accumulation of debt. They also show that there are significant differences between country income groups in that respect (Ley and Misch 2013).

The results of this study bear important policy implications. On the one hand, the authors warn not to take the real-time estimates of the structural budget balance for the purpose of fiscal surveillance at face value and show that the real-time estimates can well remove from the truth to a significant extent. On the other hand, they suggest that governments should consider in the context of the budgetary planning that they can miss their fiscal targets just because of output revisions. This in turn implies that governments should set goals that should include *safety margins to account for the fact that initial growth estimates have to be significantly revised.* The empirical results of Ley and Misch (2013) provide an orientation of how such safety margins can be based on past experience. The bottom line of these and other studies discussed in this paper are: in real time, the total and the structural budget balances should be rather considered as "known unknowns" than (in wishful thinking) as "known knowns" fiscal indicators. "What you do not know did you do not know may be sometimes more important what you did certainly know" (Ley and Misch 2013, p. 27).

### 3.4.3 Kempkes (2012): Cyclical Adjustment of Fiscal Rules and Real-Time Distortions for EU Countries

Most EU member states tend to assume fiscal rules, which relate to cyclically adjusted borrowing limits. Under the standard procedure for the cyclical adjustment a trend increase in public debt is prevented, if the real-time output gaps used to calculate the cyclical components compensate over time to a mean of zero. Kempkes investigates real-time output gaps estimated by the EU, the IMF and the OECD for the EU-15 countries and the sample period 1996 to 2011. Compared to the final estimates of the three international organizations he finds that real-time output gaps are negatively distorted in his support period. He observes these distortions (i) regardless of the exact data source, (ii) in all vintages of real-time data, and (iii) in principle for the whole country sample. In addition, the amount of distortion is considerable: on average in cyclical components determined in real time are biased downwards as a percentage of GDP by about 0.5 percentage points per year. Kempkes' results suggest therefore that fiscal rules ex post should include checks of unbiasedness of cyclical components which are used within the rule. Potential distortions would then reduce future borrowing limits or possibly even increase them.

### 3.4.4 The Bigger Picture: The Fiscal Compact, Fiscal Federalism and International Competitiveness

But how useful is it from a strategic and economic point of view to put the main focus on the budgetary adjustment in general and the fiscal pact in particular—not least in the countries which have just left their adjustment programme or are to leave it soon?

The emphasis on the enforcement of a fiscal union, including the Fiscal Compact as a crucial prerequisite of a debt mutualisation means that the debate became—at least in Germany—a question of "all or nothing": either a deeper political union ("Building Block 2" of the concept of "Genuine Economic and Monetary Union", European Council, 2012) or a "sinking into chaos" (Belke 2012a, b, c). This reduces the strategic options of the players—even Germany—to an unnecessarily high extent. This "all or nothing view" imposed above all by the Merkel government is also partially responsible for the rising tensions between the North and the South of the Eurozone, the so-called "North–south divide" (Belke 2013a, b), which may prevent the realisation of a "Genuine Monetary and Economic Union". But this paper argues in Sect. 4 that indeed an alternative option is available to this variant of a cooperative fiscal federalism which also contains bailouts and debt mutualisation besides the (at least suggested) "chains" of the Fiscal Compact: a competition-based fiscal federalism, similar to that which is practiced in countries such as the United States, Canada and Switzerland.

And doesn't this mainly fiscal focus prevent one from looking at the actually even more important restoration of international competitiveness? Especially as a growing international competitiveness avoid negative government budget balances and thus a sustainable reduction of public debt only made possible. This connection is followed by the example of Greece, which will be primarily subject to the fiscal pact after its exit of the adjustment program under Sect. 5.

## 4 Solutions of the Euro Crisis: Banking Union and Competition-Based Fiscal Federalism

After the Euro Summit decided in June 2012 to break the vicious circle between banks and sovereign states, it seemed as if the political leaders were finally ready to do something against the threat of the euro area break-up. But this optimism quickly disappeared in the wake of contradictory interpretations of the resolutions. Nevertheless, the heads of government have brought the problem to the point that is not adequately covered by the Fiscal Compact: weak banks and weak sovereigns are like two poor swimmers that are pulling each other under water (Belke 2014a, b, c, d; Belke and Gros 2016).

## *4.1 Two Irreconcilable Camps?*

Whom to save first? Representatives of the Southern position as Greece, Italy, Portugal and Spain, and since the appointment of Francois Hollande also France argue that we should start with the sovereign states, by throwing them the lifejacket in form of an issue of common debt. The richer countries would then vouch actually, at least for a part, of the debt of weaker (Belke 2013a, b).

Representatives of the position of the North, led by Germany, Austria, Finland and the Netherlands argue in favour of a prefixed rescue of the banks. This could be achieved through a stronger central bank supervision and the pooling of part of the losses in the banking sector, for example through a common fund for the settlement and restructuring of insolvent banks and a Europe-wide guarantee for bank deposits (Belke 2014a, b, c, d).

Both sides recognize the danger that the pooling of debt promotes risky behavior ("moral hazard") and could bring higher costs for creditor countries and have therefore agreed on the Fiscal Compact. The South believes that the panic that results in ever higher interest rate spreads and could thus drive the countries into insolvency, is the biggest threat to the Eurozone. At the same time the Southern Eurozone Member Countries fear the anger of their citizens about the recessionary consequences of "austerity" which is not least accelerated by the Fiscal Compact.

By contrast, the Northern euro area governments believe the main threat would be created by a too-quick removal of this beneficial pressure generated by market: the need for reforms would be weakened. At the same time in the north to high liability commitments of creditor nations provide discontent in the population (Belke 2014a, b, c, d).

Nevertheless, the positions of both sides are in some ways not so far apart (Belke 2013a, b). The North admits that a certain pooling of debt is necessary, if only to recapitalize the banks. The south again accepted that a pooling must be limited in order to prevent moral hazard.

## *4.2 The Contentious Issue "Debt Union"*

The main argument of the South is: since the 1970s, economists refer to a *budgetary union* (and the Fiscal Compact may be subsumed hereunder) as a *necessary condition for a viable monetary union*. Although the founders of the Eurozone threw this cautioning to the wind, it has in the meantime become clear that the Eurozone must now *decide between a budgetary union, expressed by the Fiscal Compact, or the surrender of the euro.*

The starting point of the argument of the South is simply the realization that the Eurozone governments are issuing debt paper in euros, but basically have no control over this currency. Countries outside the Eurozone, however, can guarantee the holders of government bonds that the amount of payable money at maturity is always available. The fact that the Eurozone governments are not able to give such a guarantee, exposes its bonds to increasing mistrust of financial markets. This may trigger liquidity crises, bringing the respective countries in significant arrears. This forces them directly into austerity programmes, which in turn lead right away to recession and cause the collapse of weaker banks (Belke 2013a, b).

The supporters of Southern position argue that pooling of sovereign debt is necessary in order to counteract this undesirable development. By this the weakest countries would be better protected in the union from the destructive panic attacks in the financial markets of a monetary union.

However, they recognize that those who benefit from the creditworthiness of the strong countries could exploit this by not reducing (or, as currently observed, even increasing) their debt and deficits. The second obstacle to such debt mutualisation is that the strongest countries would then be obliged to pay a higher interest rate for their own debt due to their joint liability. Therefore, the debt pooling must be designed so that these problems are out of the way (Belke 2013a, b).

## 4.3 Principles of a Debt Union

Temperate representatives of the southern position—apparently in accordance with the second Merkel government—have agreed that three principles should be followed. First, only a *partial pooling of debt* should be made—that is, national governments must remain solely responsible for a significant portion of the debt, so the incentive for debt and deficit reduction persists. Second, an *internal transfer mechanism between the countries involved* should ensure that the less creditworthy countries (at least partially) compensate the creditworthy ones. Thirdly, there must be a *strict control mechanism* which has to be a central element of debt pooling (without manipulation discretion in the underlying data. It is intended to which monitor the progress of national governments towards reasonable debt levels and is put into place through the subsequent Fiscal Pact (Belke 2014a, b, c, d; Belke and Gros, 2016).

But one important problem remains, independent on "common debt". According to the Northern view, the pooling of debt in the Eurozone would not tackle the core problems in the long run at the root, but could—by lowering (real) interest rates also for financially distressed countries—*prepare the ground for a possibly even greater crisis.* This is exactly what has happened in the early years of the euro. The lack of discipline in countries such as Greece and Portugal caused the development of asset bubbles in other Member States such as Spain and Ireland. Structural reforms have been postponed, while wages rose faster than productivity. The result was an enormous *loss of competitiveness on the periphery, which cannot be offset by the pooling of debt* (Belke 2013a, b), and as shown in the following section, hampered the functioning of the Fiscal Compact and the desired control of public deficits.

## 4.4 The "German" View: Fiscal Union Should Precede a Debt Union

The conditions within the Eurozone are so different that a political union should not work, at least not in the next few years. In the Northern perspective, one concludes that *the basis for eurobonds is extremely thin.*

The North argues that the introduction of eurobonds must be accompanied by close supervision of national fiscal and economic policies (Fiscal Compact). This, however, cannot be pushed through as long as the individual members of the Eurozone strive to preserve their sovereignty (Belke 2014a, b, c, d).

A direct intervention into the fiscal sovereignty of Member States would presuppose a functioning pan-European democratic legitimacy. But we are far away from that. Voters in Southern countries can still easily reject the strict regulations imposed by Brussels at any time, while the voters in Northern countries can well refuse to continue to pay for the South. And the one and the other may finally decide to leave the Eurozone (Belke 2013a, b).

The focus on the introduction of a fiscal union as a condition for the pooling of debt means that the debate has become an "all-or-nothing" question at least in Germany. As a financial union as between US states currently seem to be distant, *a pooling of debt*—whatever configuration—*is on this basis difficult to achieve.*

## 4.5 Learning from the USA, Canada and Switzerland?

However, there is an alternative to the cooperative fiscal federalism with its bailouts and the pooling of debt in connection with a Fiscal Compact: a fiscal federalism on the basis of competition, as is successfully practiced in the US, Canada and Switzerland (Belke 2013a, b).

These federal states have been able to largely avoid serious and permanent public debt of their local authorities. If sub-federal units are facing insolvency, there is *sufficient incentive for them*—even without a centralized fiscal policy coordination—*to initiate early corrective action.* This system is a compromise between the views of the South and the North of Europe.

In order to achieve this kind of federalism, it is necessary to *separate the fate of banks from the fate of sovereign states.* As was shown in Sect. 3, the EDP cannot adequately distinguish between the two categories bank debt and sovereign debt. What is needed is not primarily a fiscal union, but first and foremost a *banking union*. The latter should be based on four elements: a European Banking Supervisor endowed with far-reaching intervention power, reformed banking regulations with significantly higher capital requirements, a bank resolution fund and a European deposit guarantee scheme. Such kind of banking union should be better to accept for the north than the Europeanisation of fiscal policy as a whole (Belke 2014a, b, c, d; Belke and Gros 2016).

Of course, a central resolution authority would have to be equipped with the necessary resources to shut down large transnational banks. The money should partly financed by the banking sector—from a German perspective.

If the banking and debt crisis are once disentangled in this way, losses in the banking sector will no longer pose a threat to the solvency of solid sovereign states. Also neither euro bonds nor bailouts of sovereign states would then be required. The sovereign debt of some countries could be restructured and so move closer a long-term solution (Belke 2013a, b; Belke and Gros 2016).

Even with such a compromise, of course, were still some questions unanswered: What happens to the losses that European banks would suffer from a haircut to government debt? How deep must political integration steps be foster such a competition-based fiscal union? How much more political union would be desirable at all, if it is only for the preservation of a currency?

Nevertheless, the positions of the two European "camps" to Eurozone reforms are not as incompatible as they seem at first glance. A competition-based fiscal federalism could include the arguments and preferences of both sides and contribute to a more stable future of the Eurozone.

## 5 Fiscal Compact and the Beacon Greece: Central Importance of International Competitiveness

The euro crisis appears to be over, basically. Risk premia continue to fall across a broad front. And two of the three ESM programmes (GR, PT und IRL) are essentially concluded. Ireland and Portugal are now able again to refinance themselves on the markets and their economies appear to grow again.[12]

In contrast, Greece is still confronted with problems to fulfil the targets of its adjustment programme. Its economy is shrinking again and the government of the country finds itself in apperently endless negotiations about a new multilateral rescue package. Why? The problem can be summarised in one word: exports or, lack of export growth. Two figures demonstrate the dilemma of the country: the Greek government has achieved a primary surplus (public budget balance minus

[12]For the following see Gros et al. (2014).

interest payment on debt) in. And Greece exported less in 2013 than in 2012.[13] That the Greek government is for the first time since decades able to pay its expenditures with its own income, is indeed a milestone. But the second news (the lack of export growth) is the more relevant in the longer term (Gros et al. 2014; Belke und Gros 2014).

The European Parliament has just critically trialed the effectiveness of the Troika in the programme countries, especially Greece, with an eye on reporting standards, the democracy principle and transparency.[14] The core results of our study for the Committee on Economic and Monetary Affairs (ECON) of the European Parliament on the "State-of-play in implementing macro-economic adjustment programmes in the Euro-area" (Gros et al. 2014) for Greece can be summarised as follows. They lay open an economic-conceptual problem of the Fiscal Compact.

The *truly important target* for every country with a double-digit current account deficit which starts an adjustment programme must be *export growth.* Admittedly, the *stabilisation of the budget*, the main focus of the Fiscal Compact, *is also unavoidable.* The ultimate long-term goal must be to lead the economy back on a sustainable growth path. This is not possible without export growth and lower wages alone do not guarantee that this goal will be reached. The *stabilisation of the government budget will then follow swiftly* (Belke und Gros 2014).

What went wrong in Greece, was not the budget adjustment. On the contrary: the policy of expenditure cuts was possibly *too successful* (and painful). But it was the wrong "Going alone"-target (Belke et al. 2014). This, in turn, has unambiguous implications for the significance of the Fiscal Compact for countries not under the programme.

## 6 Conclusions and Outlook

Seen on the whole, thus, the fiscal concept is probably useful, at least in theory. After all, it forces the member countries to introduce more binding and increasingly effective national "fiscal frameworks" at home. Some governments, most probably the majority among them, would have done this anyway, under the pressure of the markets. But the new "contract beyond the EU" will probly make up for an only marginal difference (Gros 2012). The only true "enforcement" is a generally too little noted add-on to the "Treaty establishing the permanent bail-out fund, the European Stability Mechanism (ESM)". It says that only countries which are obeying tot he Fiscal Compact have the right for support by the ESM (Gros 2012).

[13]Siehe http://ec.europa.eu/economy_finance/eu/forecasts/2014_winter/el_en.pdf.

[14]See http://www.europarl.europa.eu/news/en/top-stories/content/20140110TST32314/html/Parliament-investigates-the-decisions-that-have-been-made.

The main danger is that the Fiscal Compact has been "oversold", i.e., beyond its intrinsic value. It *does not represent a step towards a fiscal or political union*. The national ratification processes as in Ireland and the implementation in financially distressed and low growth countries such as France have in fact stifled minds (and the media) and thus conveyed the impression of a high significance of the Fiscal Compact. However, already now—with the initial excitement gone and the national fiscal rules implemented—the TSCG appears to fall into oblivion. Its only remaining footprint will be future regular Euro summits, which usually contain conclusions such as "Member States commit to everything desirable (structural reforms, etc.)". And most probably these conclusions will become irrelevant as soon as the heads of governments return to their capitals and have disappeared again in their domestic realities (Gros 2012).

It was doubtful from the start whether the national parliaments would really swallow the loss of sovereignty induced by the Fiscal Compact. If the Fiscal Compact would really be credible, it should have led to a massive improvement of the rating of sovereign bonds in the euro area. In fact, the interest rates/yields became lower. But unfortunately, there is an easily solvable identification problem: it has been the ECB which has nearly completely decoupled government bond yields from ist fundamental drivers such as government debt and the absence of debt brakes through its ultra-expansionary and unconventional monetary policies. As the current discussion about the change of paradigm in Italy and, above all, in France shows (Handelsblatt 2014), the ECB's monetary policy is currently levering out the Fiscal Compact completely. This is because the ultra-low interest rates seduce the governments not to stick to the agreed ceilings of budget deficits and to incur ever more debt. The French budget deficit, for instance, was forecasted to amount to 3.4% in 2015 and "(i)n der Eurozone wächst die politische Neigung, sich damit abzufinden und Frankreich noch einmal eine Galgenfrist zu gewähren. Es wäre das dritte Mal" (Handelsblatt 2014, p. 4).[15] Admonitions by the EU Commission went unheard, probably because one calculated with a more lax new commission. A further important omission of the Fiscal Compact is that it scarcely focuses on the relation between France's lack of budget consolidation and the country's shrinking international competitiveness—an economic relationship which has been referred to in Sect. 5 based on the example of Greece.

To conclude, the debt brake is one central vertex within the Fiscal Compact. The second one is the accentuation of the excessive deficit punishment procedure. Such a procedure can, according to the EU treaty, be triggered if a country knocks off the 3% deficit ceiling. However, this never happened up to now in spite of numerous violations, because a qualified majority of the Euro Finance ministers had to approve it and this left much room for political deal-making.

As described in Sect. 2, the participants commit themselves through the Fiscal Compact to accept the recommendation of the EU Commission to initiate

[15]In English: "In the euro area, the political inclination is currently growing to settle with that and to grant France again a last respite. It would be the third time".

proceedings quasi-automatically—unless a qualified majority of the finance ministers votes against the recommendation. The inherent problem is that the Fiscal Compact conflicts with current EU law. This is because the new rules cannot be incorporated in the EU treaty due to the British resistance ("Treaty outside the EU"). This is a further reason why many analysts interpret the Fiscal Compact as a toothless tiger, as for instance Daniel Gros: "Dieser ganze Fiskalpakt kommt mir wie ein Sturm im Wasserglas vor. Dieser neue Fiskalpakt schreibt nur fest, was schon zehnmal vereinbart wurde, was schon im Stabilitätspakt steht. Deswegen wird dieser neue Schuldenpakt wohl nicht viel erreichen."[16]

We have shown in Sect. 3 that the "Excessive Deficit Procedure" represents the Achilles heel of the Fiscal Compact due to data-induced operationalisation problems. We have brought up a painful subject which has been treated only as an orphan before, probably because it, as a primarily statistical and econometric issue, evaded everyday politics: the "targeted design" of data revisions of the GDP and the government budget balance. Due to the high importance of the EDP for the sustainability of the Eurozone's governance there is an urgent need of an audit through an independent supranational institution such as, for instance, the European Court of Auditors.

The way towards a sustainable "Economic Governance" of the Eurozone and the EU can only lead via a consistent fiscal federalism combined with an incentive-compatible Banking Union (Sect. 4). Market-based interest rate would, under the new conditions—offer a much better incentive and sanction mechanism than the "Excessive Deficit Procedure" which is plagued by inherent manipulation leeway and political cycles but is decisive for the success of the Fiscal Compact. Note that even the German government is nowadays silent in view of the current violations of the SGP by big countries such as France and of the non-relevance of the Fiscal Compact.

Using the example of the programme country Greece we have shown that the menace of a repeated "official sector involvement (OSI)" is not due to the high debt as a proportion to GDP but to the lack of growth. As a consequence, an important insight is that the *absence of export growth* represents the *much more import message* for the markets than the achievement of a primary surplus in the government budget. The Fiscal Compact with its focus on the second message is taking these issues into account only to an insufficient extent, also for non-programme countries.

---

[16]See http://www.tagesschau.de/wirtschaft/fiskalpakt118.html. In English: "This fiscal compact appears to me as a storm in a teapot. This new fiscal compact only codifies what has been agreed upon already ten times or more, as for instance in the Stability and Growth Pact. For this reason the new debt pact will not achieve much."

## References

Belke A (2012) Euro debt: should the Eurozone's debt be mutualised? Economist debates. Paul de Grauwe vs. Ansgar Belke. The Economist Online

Belke A (2012a) The eurozone crisis as a tale of north and south: conjectures on the Merkel government view. Appl Econ Quart—Konjunkturpolitik 58(4):265–278

Belke A (2012b) Χρειάζεται νέο «κούρεμα» χρέους και αποπληθωρισμός—Ein noch größerer Schuldenschnitt wird unvermeidbar. Interview mit der *griechischen Tageszeitung Kefalaio*

Belke A (2013a) Towards a genuine economic and monetary union—comments on a roadmap. Polit Gov 1(1):48–65

Belke A (2013b) Focus: the eurozone crisis—a tale of north and south. Stateman's Yearbook Online

Belke A (2014) Lösungen für die Eurokrise—Bankenunion und auf Wettbewerb basierender Fiskalföderalismus. Journal Internationale Politik und Gesellschaft

Belke A (2014a) Monetary dialogue 2009-2014: looking backward, looking forward. Briefing paper prepared for presentation at the Committee on Economic and Monetary Affairs of the European Parliament for the quarterly dialogue with the President of the European Central Bank. March. Brussels

Belke A (2014b) State-of-play in implementing macroeconomic adjustment programmes in the Euro Area—the case of Greece. Interview mit der griechischen Tageszeitung Eleftherotypia. http://www.enet.gr/?i=news.el.politikh&id=345855

Belke A (2014c) More exports or ... Greater Haircut. Interview mit "capital.gr". http://www.capital.gr/NewsTheme.asp?id = 1962907

Belke A (2015) Der Fiskalpakt als Vertrag außerhalb des EU-Rahmens—Strategische, ökonomisch-konzeptionelle und Operationalisierungsprobleme. In: von Alemann U, Heidbreder EG, Hummel H, Dreyer D, Gödde A (eds) Ein soziales Europa ist möglich—Grundlage und Handlungsoptionen, Springer, Heidelberg, pp 285–309

Belke A, Gros D (2014) Bilanz makroökonomischer Anpassungsprogramme in der Eurozone—Sonderfall Griechenland? Ökonomenstimme

Belke A, Gros D (2016) On the shock absorbing properties of a banking union—Europe compared with the United States. Comp Econ Stud 58(3):359–386

Belke A, Gros D, Alcidi C, Coutinho L, Giovannini A (2014) State-of-play in implementing macroeconomic adjustment programmes in the Euro Area. Policy note. Directorate General for Internal Policies. Economic Governance Support Unit. European Parliament. Brussels, February

Bier W, Mink R, Rodríguez-Vives M (2004) Extended statistics for the support of the stability and growth pact. Hacienda Pública Española, Monografía, pp 35–63

Borio C, Disyatat P, Juselius M (2013) Rethinking potential output: embedding information about the financial cycle. BIS working papers 404

Cimadomo J (2011) Real-time data and fiscal policy analysis—a survey of the literature. ECB working paper series 1408

De Castro F, Perez JJ, Rodríguez-Vives M (2013) Fiscal data revisions in Europe. J Money Credit Bank 45:1187–1209

ECB (2012) Monthly Bulletin, May

European Commission (2012) Box I.5: Forecast errors and multiplier uncertainty. Autumn 2012 forecast. Eur Econ 7:41–43

European Commission (2013) Six-pack? Two-pack? Fiscal compact? A short guide to the new EU fiscal governance. European Commission, Brussels

European Council (2012) Towards a genuine economic and monetary union. Interim Report, European Council

Girouard N, André C (2005) Measuring cyclically-adjusted budget balances for OECD countries. OECD Economics Department working papers

Gros D (1997) Excessive deficits and debts. Centre for European Policy Studies (CEPS) working document 97
Gros D (2012) The treaty on stability, coordination and governance in the economic and monetary union (aka Fiscal Compact). Centre for European Policy Studies Commentaries
Gros D, Alcidi C, Belke A, Coutinho L, Giovannini A (2014) State-of-play in implementing macroeconomic adjustment programmes in the Euro Area. European Parliament
Handelsblatt (2014) Geld her! Das Ende der Enthaltsamkeit rückt näher: Frankreich, Spanien, Italien und Griechenland fordern eine Abkehr von der strikten Sparpolitik. Handelsblatt. 3. Juni. 1, 4f
Kempkes G (2012) Cyclical adjustment in fiscal rules: some evidence on real-time bias for EU-15 countries. Discussion Paper Deutsche Bundesbank 15
Kohen V, Van de Noord P (2005) Fiscal Gimmickry in Europe: one-off measures and creative accounting. OECD economics department working papers 417
Leal T, Pérez JJ, Mika Tujula M, Vidal JP (2008) Fiscal forecasting: lessons from the literature and challenges. Fisc Stud 29:347–386
Ley E, Misch F (2013) Real-time macro monitoring and fiscal policy. mimeo. 8 March. an earlier version has been published as world bank working paper 6303
McKenzie R (2006) Undertaking revisions and real-time data analysis using the OECD main economic indicators original release data and revisions database. OECD statistics working papers 2.
Moghadam R (2014) Maastricht and the crisis in Europe: where we've been and what we've learned. Remarks at the ECB/NBB conference on: "Progress through Crisis?". Wednesday, February 12
Persson T, Tabellini G (2000) Political economics: explaining economics policy. MIT Press, Cambridge
Price RW, Dang T-T (2011) Adjusting fiscal balances for asset price cycles. OECD economics department working papers 868
Suárez J (2010) The Spanish crisis: background and policy challenges. CEPR discussion papers 7909

# A Conceptual Framework for Reforms Versus Debt in the Context of a Fiscal Union Within the European Monetary Union

**Yannis M. Ioannides**

**Abstract** This paper emphasizes the importance of differences in population sizes in a model of a monetary union under alternative scenaria of monetary and fiscal policy coordination. It goes beyond Casella (The American Economic Review 82 (4):847–863, 1992) by allowing for coexistence of fiscal policy, national as well as union-wide, along with monetary policy. The paper also allows for inefficiencies in tax collection that serve as another difference across countries and for the possibility that tax and spending policy in the union are decided by means of different procedures. This is intended to explore the contrast between monetary policy outcomes determined by deliberations and voting in the ECB, given the fiscal policy stance, and national fiscal policy stance, given monetary policy. It examines what options this logic confers on smaller versus larger members of a currency union. It goes beyond both Casella (The American Economic Review 82 (4):847–863, 1992) and Ioannides (The Cyprus Bail-in: Policy Lessons from the Cyprus Economic Crisis. World Scientific Imperial College Press, 2016) in examining the impact of market reforms and of various types of technological progress and explores their consequences for the sustainability of national public debt.

## 1 Introduction

The Eurozone (EZ) is at a crossroads. The global financial crisis revealed the importance of the dearth of macro policy tools available to members of the European monetary union. This is in stark contrast to US. A critical issue is the limits to monetary policy tools in the absence of a fiscal union. This is the case for the Eurozone, in sharp contrast to the US fiscal union. The paper develops a stylized

This paper stems from the research effort that was conducted jointly with Christopher Pissarides, which led to our joint paper "Is the Greek Crisis One of Supply or Demand?" *Brookings Papers on Economic Activity*, Fall 2015. He is not responsible for the content of this paper.

Y.M. Ioannides
Department of Economics, Tufts University, Medford, MA 02155, USA
e-mail: yannis.ioannides@tufts.edu; http://sites.tufts.edu/yioannides/

 
N. da Costa Cabral et al. (eds.), *The Euro and the Crisis*, Financial and Monetary Policy Studies 43, DOI 10.1007/978-3-319-45710-9_11

model with two countries, differing in size, which accommodates autarky versus economic integration while allowing for a fiscal union within a monetary union. The model allows examination of broad policy options and advantages that adding a fiscal union confers on those available to a monetary union. Finally, the paper extends Ioannides (2016) by allowing for market reforms and technological change as well debt in addition to tax finance.

One of the most important considerations that confronts students of the design of European integration is heterogeneity of the constituent parts. Heterogeneity is expressed in many dimensions, such as political, cultural, economic and of course in terms of the population and economic size. Newer theories of comparative advantage, such as those associated with product differentiation that new trade theory and new economic geography have utilized, have emphasized that due to the advantages of agglomerations and path dependence advancing economic integration may make constituent states even more heterogeneous. As a consequence, suboptimalities in the currency area they make up may thus be further exacerbated.

This paper emphasizes the importance of differences in population sizes. Population size directly affects real economic outcomes. It also underlies perceptions of relative importance in international economic governance and thus state actions. Therefore, it affects notions of democratic legitimacy both within and across countries. In the EU, size is critically enshrined in numerous decision making structures, such as qualified majority rules. At the same time, EU member states are equally represented in the European Commission, which is made up of a single national from each member state. This is very similar to the US parliamentary structure, where states are equally represented in the US Senate but in proportion to their populations in the US House of Representatives.

This paper borrows Casella (1992)'s framework and examines a number of scenaria above and beyond hers. In particular, it allows for coexistence of fiscal policy, national as well as union-wide, along with monetary policy. The paper also allows (c.f. Sibert 1992) for inefficiencies in tax collection that serve as another difference across countries. It allows for the possibility that tax and spending policy in the union are decided by means of different procedures. This is intended to express the contrast between monetary policy outcomes determinant by deliberations and voting in the ECB, given the fiscal policy stance, and national fiscal policy stance, given monetary policy. What options does this logic confer on smaller versus larger members of a currency union? How a small country's fundamentals affects its bargaining power, especially over a full range of fiscal policy, like taxes on different aspects of activity is an important question. It goes beyond Casella (1992) and Ioannides (2016) in examining the impact of market reforms and of various types of technological progress and explores their consequences for the sustainability of debt.

## 2 International Equilibrium Ala Casella (1992)

Casella (1992) assumes that individuals value a composite good, which is produced by means of intermediate varieties, and a public good, which is financed publicly by means of seignorage. The indirect utility functions depend on the country's size and real money growth in each country. A non-cooperative game among governments yields that if the elasticity of substitution among intermediates exceeds 1, uncoordinated policies give inefficient allocations. That is, each government provides more of the public good than globally socially optimal, because it ignores the negative effects on the foreign country of withdrawing resources from private production. The smaller country always allocates a larger proportion of its endowment to the public good. With a monetary union, the exchange rate between two countries' currencies is set equal to 1 and inflation rates are equalized. Then, individual private consumption is equalized across the two countries. There is no international financial equilibrium to be cleared, and the monetary regime does not impose discipline in each country's policy.

Specifically, utility functions are defined as the sum of the logs of a Dixit-Stiglitz aggregate of consumption intermediates, $C_{ij}$, and of the public good, $\Gamma_j$,

$$U_j = (1-g)\ln\left(\sum_{i=1}^{n} c_{ij}^{\theta}\right)^{1/\theta} + g\ln\Gamma_j, \ ,j = A, B, 0 < \theta < 1, \tag{1}$$

where $n$ is the total number of intermediate varieties of the private good and $\Gamma_j$ is the public good, and $j = A, B$ denotes the two countries. The elasticity of substitution among varieties is given by $\frac{1}{1-\theta}$. If it approaches 1, the two economies that are otherwise identical except for size enjoy no advantage from trade. There are no spillovers across countries and no scope for international cooperation.

Individuals live for two periods: working when young, consuming when old, saving only in the form of money holdings. New money issued finances the public good. Money of the old plus new money equals money held by the young.

Intermediates are produced with IRS using labor:

$$\ell_i = \alpha + \beta x_i, \ i = 1, \ldots, n, \tag{2}$$

where $\ell_i$ is the labor required to produce $x_i$ units of variety $i$. The industry organizes as monopolistic competition, each variety is produced by one producer, entry is free and at the equilibrium each firm earns zero profits. The advantage of the Dixit–Stiglitz model is that the size of a country translates immediately into the number of goods produced domestically, with no counterbalancing effect on the terms of trade. If a change in the countries' relative endowments affects the terms of trade, national income depends on the overall solution of the general-equilibrium problem and is therefore much more difficult to analyze (Casella *op. cit.*, p. 851). At the free entry equilibrium, each variety is produced at the same quantity:

$$x_{ij} = \frac{\alpha\theta}{\beta(1-\theta)}. \tag{3}$$

The monopolistic competition price is given by $p_j = \frac{\beta}{\theta} w_j$, and is a markup on the marginal costs in the usual fashion. The corresponding labor requirement is $\frac{\alpha}{1-\theta}$. The public good is produced using labor $\ell_{\Gamma j}$ with CRS,

$$\Gamma_j = \ell_{\Gamma j},\ j = A, B.$$

The government pays for the public good by new money printing, $M_j$, tax revenue, or a combination of both. If country A's size is $2 - \sigma$, then the number of varieties produced is given by

$$n_A = (2 - \sigma - \Gamma_A)\frac{1-\theta}{\alpha}. \tag{4}$$

## 2.1 *Market Reforms Versus Technological Progress*

The above development is predicated on free entry by all producers of intermediates. What if the range of intermediate varieties is given, $\overline{n}_A$? Then, one could think of allowing for free entry in the intermediates industry as a type of market reform. If the range of intermediates is given, monopolistic pricing still leads to the same markup $p_j = \frac{\beta}{\theta} w_j$, but profits (losses) are earned (realized). Letting free entry determine the number of varieties generally improves welfare but causes losses (gains) to the varieties producing sector. If $\overline{n}_A < n_A$, then lifting of restrictions may be seen as a stylized market reform that brings about overall benefits.

Next we introduce technological progress in the production of intermediate varieties in the following manner. Let the total labor cost of producing $x_i$ of variety $i$ be defined as:

$$b(x_i) = \frac{1}{\xi_i}(\alpha + \beta x_i) w_i, \tag{5}$$

where $\xi_i = \overline{\xi}(1+\eta)^t$ is TFP-type of technological progress, with an exogenous growth rate $\eta$.

It is easy to see from (3) that at the free entry, each variety is produced at the same quantity, but since the labor cost of producing each variety, $\frac{\alpha}{\xi_i(1-\theta)}$, decreases more and more varieties are produced at equilibrium. Thus, welfare increases much more, relative to the consequences of market reform, as defined earlier.

The welfare impact of market reform, that is entry liberalization, is a function of $n_A - \overline{n}_A$, and thus has a *level effect*. The introduction of technological change in the form of TFP *growth*, increases welfare as a function of $(1 + \eta)^t$, thus implying a growth effect on social welfare.

The labor market is assumed to be Walrasian here. We could easily introduce a labor market with Pissarides-type frictions. Labor market reforms can take the form of reducing frictions as well as allowing various forms of active labor market policies.

## 2.2 Autarky

Under autarky, each individual consumes $C_{aut,\, A=\frac{1}{2-\sigma}\frac{\alpha\theta}{\beta(1-\theta)}}$ of each variety. The public good is financed by money creation:

$$\Gamma_A = \ell_{\Gamma_A} = m_A.$$

The range of varieties produced is given by:

$$n_A = (2 - \sigma - m_A)\frac{1-\theta}{\alpha}.$$

The corresponding value of the utility function is:

$$U_A = (1-g)\ln\left((2-\sigma-\Gamma_A)\frac{1-\theta}{\alpha}\left[\frac{1}{2-\sigma}\frac{\alpha\theta}{\beta(1-\theta)}\right]^{\theta}\right)^{1/\theta} + g\ln\Gamma_j. \quad (6)$$

Optimal policy is characterized by the optimal provision of the public good. The autarky solution is easy to obtain and given by:

$$\Gamma_{aut,A} = \frac{\theta g}{\theta g + 1 - g}(2-\sigma) = m_A.$$

The inflation rate follows from equilibrium in the money market. That is, from each individual's budget constraint, we have:

$$n_A c_{aut,A}\frac{\beta}{\theta}w_A = w_{A,-1}$$

And from money market equilibrium, we have:

$$(2-\sigma)w_A = (2-\sigma)w_{A,-1} + M_A.$$

It is trivial to show that these two conditions are consistent, which confirms Walras' law.

## 2.3 International Equilibrium with National Currencies

Under international equilibrium with national currencies, each variety is still produced at the same quantity at equilibrium, but traded in both countries. Each individual spends the same amount on each variety. The imported quantity is purchased with the currency of the country where it is produced. Thus the exchange rate, in units of A currency per unit of B

$$ep_B x_{iB} = p_A x_{iA}. \tag{7}$$

Therefore,

$$ew_B = w_A,\ ep_B = p_A.$$

The number of varieties produced are:

$$n_A = (2 - \sigma - \Gamma_A)\frac{1-\theta}{\alpha},\ n_B = (\sigma - \Gamma_B)\frac{1-\theta}{\alpha}. \tag{8}$$

Individuals work when young, receive their wages, $w_{A,} \; - 1, w_{B,} \; - 1$ in the form of money and consume when old. Thus, each variety in each country is consumed at:

$$c_A = \frac{w_{A,-1}}{p_A}\frac{1}{\eta_A + \eta_B}, c_B = \frac{w_{B,-1}}{p_B}\frac{1}{\eta_A + \eta_B}.$$

The market for each variety is at equilibrium if:

$$\frac{\alpha\theta}{\beta(1-\theta)} = (2 - \sigma)c_A + \sigma c_B.$$

Equilibrium in the foreign exchange market requires that total expenditure on A products by B must be equal to total expenditure on B products by A:

$$\sigma p_A n_A c_B = e(2 \; - \sigma)p_B n_B c_A.$$

This condition determines the exchange rate, if it is flexible, or constrains the countries' monetary policies, if it is fixed.

In each country, total money demanded by the young must equal total money supplied by the old plus newly created money. That is:

$$(2 \; - \sigma)w_A = (2 \; - \sigma)w_{A,-1} + M_A; \quad \sigma w_B = \sigma w_{B,-1} + M_B. \tag{9}$$

Dividing through by $w_A, w_B$, respectively, expressing real money growth by $m_A$, $m_B$, using the pricing condition and solving we have:

$$\frac{w_A}{w_{A,-1}} = \frac{2-\sigma}{2-\sigma-m_A}, \frac{w_B}{w_{B,-1}} = \frac{2-\sigma}{\sigma-m_B}. \tag{10}$$

If public good provision is financed by money creation only, we have: $\Gamma_A = m_A$, $\Gamma_B = m_B$. Solving for the consumption per person of each variety, we have:

$$c_A = \frac{\alpha\theta}{\beta(1-\theta)} \frac{2-\sigma-\Gamma_A}{(2-\sigma)(2-\Gamma_A-\Gamma_B)}); \; c_B = \frac{\alpha\theta}{\beta(1-\theta)} \frac{\sigma-\Gamma_B}{\sigma(2-\Gamma_A-\Gamma_B}. \tag{11}$$

The resulting indirect utility functions are:

$$U_A = K_A + \frac{(1-g)(1-\theta)}{\theta} \ln(2-m_A-\mathrm{m}_B) + (1-g)\ln(2-\sigma-m_A) + \mathrm{g}\ln m_A, \tag{12}$$

$$U_B = K_B + \frac{(1-g)(1-\theta)}{\theta} \ln(2-m_A-\mathrm{m}_B) + (1-g)\ln(\sigma-m_B) + \mathrm{g}\ln m_B, \tag{13}$$

where $K_A, K_B$ are functions of parameters (which notably include country sizes, 2 $-\sigma, \sigma$):

$$K_A = \frac{(1-g)(1-\theta)}{\theta} \ln\left[\frac{1-\theta}{\alpha}\right] + (1-g)\ln\left[\frac{\theta}{\beta(2-\sigma)}\right];$$

$$K_B = \frac{(1-g)(1-\theta)}{\theta} \ln\left[\frac{1-\theta}{\alpha}\right] + (1-g)\ln\left[\frac{\theta}{\beta\sigma}\right].$$

The spillovers associated with international equilibrium are clear. Money growth in A appears in country B's utility and vice versa. Higher money growth in A finances a greater quantity of the public good, benefitting A residents, but hurts B residents by withdrawing resources from the production of varieties. The equations expressing the first order conditions for country A's government with respect to $m_A$, taking $m_B$ as given, and for country B's government with respect to $m_B$, taking $m_A$ as given, the *reaction functions* for the two governments, are as follows:

$$\frac{(1-g)(1-\theta)}{\theta(2-m_A-m_B)} = \frac{g}{m_A} - \frac{1-g}{2-\sigma-m_A}; \quad \frac{(1-g)(1-\theta)}{\theta(2-m_A-m_B)} = \frac{g}{m_B} - \frac{1-g}{\sigma-m_B}. \tag{14}$$

Solving them simultaneously defines a Nash equilibrium in the two countries' *uncoordinated* monetary policy decisions.

Although the reaction functions cannot be solved in closed form, some results do follow. E.g., if $\theta < 1$, the elasticity of substitution is greater than one, then a government's setting its own monetary policy ignores the externality it generates for the other government. That is, each government supplies more of the public good than is socially optimal, since it ignores the negative effects on the foreigners of the associated withdrawing of resources from private production. Furthermore, it is possible to show that the *larger* of the two countries devotes a *smaller* share of its resources to the public good. This in turn implies that the larger country supplies a greater amount of the public good than the smaller one.

In sum, the public good is financed by money printing. Size matters because it affects the range of tradeable varieties. With national currencies, the exchange rate determined by international trade equilibrium: if flexible, it is determined by market clearing; if fixed, clearing establishes relationship between national monetary policies. With national currencies, total real consumption in each country depends on its labor endowment, not monetary policy. Money issues are like lump-sum taxes.

### 2.3.1 Market Reforms Versus Technological Progress Revisited

The results of this section may be reworked to allow for market reforms versus TFP-type technological progress. As we discussed, arbitrarily specifying a range of intermediates gives rise to profits, whereas allowing for free entry dissipates those profits, and allows a distinction between private losses and social gains from market reform. The impact of such a reform on international equilibrium with national currencies depend, of course, on the comparison between the fixed range against the equilibrium range of varieties. In this highly stylized setting, one can see that losses to those earning rents, prior to the liberalization, may be offset by gain to the economy as a whole.

Implementation of TFP-type reforms by both countries benefits them both in a symmetric fashion. If, however, only one country does, the consequences are quite dramatic. The condition for trade equilibrium, (7), must be modified. The logic of the model requires that all varieties be consumed by all individuals in both countries. Suppose that country $B$ only introduces TFP-type technological progress. Labor in that country becomes ever more productive, which improves the real exchange rate in its favor, reducing welfare for country $A$. The presence of TFP at a constant growth rate $\eta$ is incompatible with steady state. So, unless country $A$ also institutes reforms, steady state equilibrium is not possible.

### 2.3.2 Public Debt Finance

The model so far allows for individuals to be able to transfer purchasing power over time by means of money. In addition to $M_A, M_B$, [Eq. (9)] newly created money in each country, we may also allow for new debt borrowing (or repayment), $d = D - D_{-1}$. We may distinguish debt from money finance by means of adding frictions; more on this, later. The challenge is to link a country's ability to deal with repayment by means of introducing structural reforms Ioannides and Pissarides

(2015). It is easier to visualize this in the context of national currencies with a fiscal system; see Sects. 3.2 and 3.3 below.

## 2.4 Common Currency

With countries A and B sharing a common currency, the exchange rate is always equal to one, and the international financial equilibrium does not constrain monetary policy. Nominal wages are equalized across the two countries, and for monetary equilibrium, we have that:

$$(2-\sigma)w+\sigma w=2w=2w_{-1}+M_A+M_B. \tag{15}$$

Per capita consumption of each variety is the same across the two countries:

$$c_A=c_B=\frac{1}{2}\frac{\alpha\theta}{\beta(1-\theta)}.$$

The total number of varieties produced is $(2-m_A-m_B)\frac{1-\theta}{\alpha}$. The associated indirect utility functions for the two countries are:

$$U_A=K'_A+\frac{1-g}{\theta}\ln(2-m_A-m_B)+g\ln m_A, \tag{16}$$

$$U_B=K'_B+\frac{1-g}{\theta}\ln(2-m_A-m_B)+g\ln m_B, \tag{17}$$

where

$$K'_A\equiv K_A+(1-g)\ln\frac{2-\sigma}{2}, K'_B\equiv K_B+(1-g)\ln\frac{\sigma}{2},$$

Even though the two countries share a currency, they can still pursue uncoordinated money creation. If money creation aims at maximizing (16), respectively (17), and thus ignore the intercountry externality, expressed by $m_A$'s presence in the RHS of (16), respectively of (17), it would lead to too much inflation. These quantities can in fact be obtained in closed form. That is:

$$m_A=m_B=\frac{2g\theta}{2g\theta+1-g}. \tag{18}$$

Monetary policy, and the magnitude of the public good provided do not depend on country population sizes, but of course the constants $K'_A, K'_B$ in (16)–(17) do.

A common central bank ought to internalize this externality and instead pursue monetary policy with an objective of maximizing a weighted sum of countries' utilities:

$$\max_{m_A, m_B} : (2-\gamma)U_A(m_A, m_B) + \gamma U_B(m_A, m_B), \tag{19}$$

with a given set of weights $(2-\gamma, \gamma)$. The resulting optimal monetary policy is:

$$m_A = \min\left\{2-\sigma, (2-\gamma)\frac{g\theta}{1-g+g\theta}\right\}, \ m_B = \min\left\{\sigma, \gamma\frac{g\theta}{1-g+g\theta}\right\}. \tag{20}$$

If each country's welfare is assigned the same weight, $\gamma = 1$, then as one can see, by comparing (20) with (18), the coordinated monetary policy is less expansionary than the uncoordinated one. Uncoordinated monetary policy is excessively expansionary, a well known phenomenon that has been discussed by the literature; see Casella (1992, p. 856, fn. 4).

A strictly democratic setting—a person, a vote—would require that different countries' utilities be weighted by their respective population shares. That is, in (19), $\gamma = \sigma$. As a consequence, monetary policy would reflect relative population sizes. But, what other considerations are there in setting the relative weights? How do weights affect the attractiveness of different countries' joining the monetary union. Similarly, given that they are in a monetary union, how do weight setting deters them from leaving the union?

Casella (1992) proves that in her model, there exists a minimum $\overline{\sigma}$ such that for all $\sigma < \overline{\sigma}$ the small country will require a larger relative weight in aggregate welfare than its relative size. That is, $\forall \sigma, \sigma > \overline{\sigma}$ all cooperative equilibria, if they exist, will have $\gamma > \sigma$. This is concisely summarized in *ibid.*, Fig. 3A, which plots the minimum percentage weight $\gamma$, as function of the smaller country's relative size, for such a country to be in a currency union, and in *ibid.*, Fig. 3B, which plots the minimum percentage weight $\gamma$, as function of the smaller country's relative size, for such a country to coordinate monetary policy, when countries have their own national currencies. The intuition of this result is that when a country is very small, it must demand more than proportional weight in the cooperative agreement. If this were not the case, the control exercised by the larger economy would result in a very unbalanced solution of the externality problem: the small country would end up facing the costs of the coordination without reaping enough of the benefits. Casella emphasizes that since the small country's alternative is to revert to the Nash equilibrium, "this cannot be used as a threat by the large country to enforce cooperation."

# 3 International Equilibrium with Fiscal Systems

In view of the Fiscal Compact Treaty of 2012 European Union (2012), it is natural to explore the scope for fiscal coordination within a monetary union. Taking cues from Sibert (1992), I assume that each government finances its public good from tax revenue, which allows for country-specific inefficiency in tax collection, and from its share of seignorage. The model also allows for effects of differences in size between the two countries in the style of Casella (1992). As already indicated, both Casella and Sibert recognize that lump-sum taxation and money creation cannot coexist: the former would be completely offset by the latter. In developing the case fiscal coordination within a monetary union, it is important to allow for proportional taxation of labor income, wages. That together with inefficiency in tax collection allows for meaningful tradeoffs. Critical conceptual problems are present here, even in the autarky case, that is whether the central bank and the government act in an uncoordinated way, whereby the resulting Nash equilibria involves setting of monetary and fiscal policy. I formulate the autarkic case first in order to fix ideas and set notation.

## 3.1 Autarky with a Fiscal System

Under autarky, each individual in country $A$ consumes an equal amount, $c_{aut,A} = \frac{1}{2-\sigma}\frac{\alpha\theta}{\beta(1-\theta)}$, of each variety. The provision of the public good is financed by money creation and taxation. That is public spending is equal to $M_A + \kappa_A \tau_A w_A$ (and similarly for country B), where $\tau_A$ denotes the tax rate on wage income and $\kappa_A$ the fraction of nominal tax revenue which the government collects. Thus, in real terms, the budget constraint may be expressed as:

$$\Gamma_A = \ell_{\Gamma_A} = m_A + (2-\sigma)\kappa_A\tau_A.$$

The range of varieties produced is given by:

$$n_A = (2 - \sigma - m_A - (2-\sigma)\kappa_A\tau_A)\frac{1-\theta}{\alpha}.$$

The corresponding value of the utility function for country $A$ (and similarly for country $B$) is:

$$U_A = (1-g)\ln\left(\left((2-\sigma)(1-\tau_A) - m_A\right)\frac{1-\theta}{\alpha}\left[\frac{1}{2-\sigma}\frac{\alpha\theta}{\beta(1-\theta)}\right]^{\theta}\right)^{1/\theta}$$
$$+ g\ln[m_A + (2-\sigma)\kappa_A\tau_A]. \tag{21}$$

Optimal provision of the public good is the same as in the autarky case:

$$\Gamma_{aut,A} = \frac{\theta g}{\theta g + 1 - g}(2-\sigma),$$

and thus is independent of how it is financed. Following Sibert (1992), optimizing (21) with respect to $\tau_j$, given $\kappa_j \neq 0$, determines fiscal policy as distinct from monetary policy. Or else, only $(2-\sigma)\tau_j + m_j$ may be defined. The inflation rate follows from equilibrium in the money market. That is, from each individual's budget constraint, we have:

$$n_A c_{aut,A}\frac{\beta}{\theta}w_A = (1-\tau_A)w_{A,-1}.$$

And from money market equilibrium, we have:

$$(2-\sigma)(1-\tau_A)w_A = (2-\sigma)(1-\tau_A)w_{A,-1} + M_A.$$

Walras' law is again confirmed, provided that $\kappa_j = 0$, or else the adding up property is violated.

## 3.2 National Currencies with a Fiscal System

If $x_j$ is the tax rate on wages, then inefficiency in tax collection leaves a tax revenue of $\kappa_j\tau_j w_j$. Thus, the public good is financed by a combination of seignorage and tax revenue

$$\Gamma_A = \ell_{\Gamma A} = m_A + (2-\sigma)\kappa_A\tau_A,\ \Gamma_B = \ell_{\Gamma B} = m_B + \sigma\kappa_B\tau_B. \tag{22}$$

The range of varieties produced in each country satisfy:

$$n_A = (2 - \sigma - m_A - (2-\sigma)\kappa_A\tau_A)\frac{1-\theta}{\alpha},\ n_B = (\sigma - m_B - \sigma\kappa_B\tau_B)\frac{1-\theta}{\alpha}$$

From money market equilibrium we have:

$$(2-\sigma)(1-\tau_A)w_A = (2-\sigma)(1-\tau_A)w_{A,-1} + M_A,$$

from which we obtain an expression for wage inflation,

$$(1-\tau_A)\frac{w_{A,-1}}{w_A} = 1-\tau_A-\frac{m_A}{2-\sigma},$$

and similarly for country B. Using this condition with the budge constraints allows us to solve for consumption per person of each variety. That is:

$$(n_A+n_B)c_A\frac{\beta}{\theta}w_A = (1-\tau_A)W_{A,-1}.$$

Therefore, per capita consumption of varieties in the two countries are:

$$\begin{aligned} c_A &= \frac{\alpha\theta}{\beta(1-\theta)(2-\theta)}\frac{(2-\sigma)(1-\tau_A)-m_A}{(2-m_A-m_B-(2-\sigma)\kappa_A\tau_A-\sigma\kappa_B\tau_B)}; \\ c_B &= \frac{\alpha\theta}{\beta(1-\theta)\sigma}\frac{\sigma(1-\tau_B)-m_B}{(2-m_A-m_B-(2-\sigma)\kappa_A\tau_A-\sigma\kappa_B\tau_B)} \end{aligned} \tag{23}$$

The corresponding utility functions are:

$$\begin{aligned} U_A = K_A &+ \frac{(1-g)(1-\theta)}{\theta}\ln[2-m_A-m_B-(2-\sigma)\kappa_A\tau_A-\sigma\kappa_B\tau_B] \\ &+ (1-g)\ln[(2-\sigma)(1-\tau_A)-m_A] + g\ln(m_A+(2-\sigma)\kappa_A\tau_B), \end{aligned} \tag{24}$$

$$\begin{aligned} U_B = K_B &+ \frac{(1-g)(1-\theta)}{\theta}\ln[2-m_A-m_B-(2-\sigma)\kappa_A\tau_A-\sigma\kappa_B\tau_B] \\ &+ (1-g)\ln[\sigma(1-\tau_B)-m_A] + g\ln(m_B+\sigma\kappa_B\tau_B). \end{aligned} \tag{25}$$

### 3.2.1 National Currencies and Debt Finance

In view of the discussion in Sect. 2.3.2 above, we may augment Eq. (22) above to allow for public debt finance. In like manner to the inefficiency of taxation, let $\delta_A, \delta_B$ be the fraction of borrowing that may drawn upon by country *A*,*B*, respectively. That is, net borrowing $d_A = D_A - D_{A,-1}$ yields $\delta_A d_A$ available for spending, per person, and let $\rho_A, \rho_B$ denote the interest rates associated with the outstanding debt. Augmenting Eq. (22) by introducing debt yields:

$$\begin{aligned} \Gamma_A = \ell_{\Gamma A} = m_A + (2-\sigma)[\kappa_A\tau_A + \delta_A d_A - \rho_A D_{A,-1}], \Gamma_B = \ell_{\Gamma B} \\ = m_B + \sigma[\kappa_B\tau_B + \delta_B d_B - \rho D_{B,-1}]. \end{aligned} \tag{26}$$

The model continues to allow for individuals to transfer purchasing power over time by means of money. Revenue from issuing debt is distinguished from money finance and from tax finance by means of frictions, denoted by the parameters $\delta_A, \kappa_A$, respectively. The resulting modification of the model is rather trivial. Essentially, because taxes and debt revenue are lump-sum, the above formulas may be adapted easily.

The next step is to link a country's improved ability to deal with servicing and/or repayment of debt with introducing structural reforms with either level- or growth-effects. If all debt is domestic, the financing options to the government depend on the dynamic efficiency properties of the economy. In this overlapping generations economy, introduction of debt finance is welfare enhancing if the economy is dynamically inefficient.

If debt is international, that is one country borrows from the other country, then the terms

$$(2-\sigma)[\delta_A d_A - \rho_A D_{A,-1}] \text{ and } \sigma[\kappa_B \tau_B + \delta_B d_B - \rho D_{B,-1}]$$

are not independent from one another. For the same reason, international trade equilibrium requires that the debtor country has enough current account surplus to pay back the creditor country. With this refinement, the model could be developed fully for the case of debt finance with interest payments from the debtor to the creditor. We could take the previous debt level as given and we could envision alternative steady states associated with different current account regimes.

An important consequence of this is that productivity improvements in one country behoove the other to also implement them, or else it would be unable to meet its debt obligations. This is even more important in the case of productivity improvements of the growth- rather than of the level effect type.

## 3.3 Common Currency with a Fiscal System

We derive the counterpart for the case of common currency with national fiscal systems by working from condition for equilibrium in the money market. That is, the sum of the money holdings of the old generations plus money creation in the two economies equal to the sum of the money holding by young generations:

$$\begin{aligned}(2-\sigma)(1-\tau_A)w_A + \sigma(1-\tau_B)w_B = {} & (2-\sigma)(1-\tau_A)w_{A,-1} \\ & + \sigma(1-\tau_B)w_{B,-1} + M_A + M_B. \end{aligned} \quad (27)$$

Since nominal wages are equalized across the two countries, we may solve for $\frac{w_{A,-1}}{w_A}$ to get:

$$\frac{w_{A,-1}}{w_A} = \frac{2-(2-\sigma)\tau_A - \sigma\tau_B - m_A - m_B}{2-(2-\sigma)\tau_A - \sigma\tau_B}.$$

The total number of varieties is:

$$n_A + n_B = \frac{1-\theta}{\alpha}(2 - m_A - m_B - (2-\sigma)\kappa_A\tau_A - \sigma\kappa_B\tau_B).$$

$$c_A = (1-\tau_A)\frac{\alpha\theta}{\beta(1-\theta)} \times \frac{2-(2-\sigma)\tau_A - \sigma\tau_B - m_A - m_B}{\left(2 - m_A - m_B - (2-\sigma)\kappa_A\tau_A - \sigma\kappa_B\tau_B\right)\left(2-(2-\sigma)\tau_A - \sigma\tau_B\right)}, \quad (28)$$

$$c_B = (1-\tau_B)\frac{\alpha\theta}{\beta(1-\theta)} \times \frac{2-(2-\sigma)\tau_A - \sigma\tau_B - m_A - m_B}{\left(2 - m_A - m_B - (2-\sigma)\kappa_A\tau_A - \sigma\kappa_B\tau_B\right)\left(2-(2-\sigma)\tau_A - \sigma\tau_B\right)} \quad (29)$$

In the special case of no fiscal system, $\tau_A = \tau_B = 0$, we are back to $c_A = c_B = \frac{1}{2}\frac{\alpha\theta}{\beta(1-\theta)}$: all varieties are consumed in equal amounts.

The indirect utility functions are given by:

$$\begin{aligned} U_A = K_A^{'} + \frac{(1-g)}{\theta}&\ln(2 - m_A - m_B - (2-\sigma)\kappa_A\tau_A - \sigma\kappa_B\tau_B) \\ &+ g\ln(m_A + (2-\sigma)\kappa_A\tau_A) + (1-g)\ln(1-\tau_A) \\ &- (1-g)\ln(2-(2-\sigma)\tau_A - \sigma\tau_B); \\ U_B = K_B^{'} + \frac{(1-g)}{\theta}&\ln(2 - m_A - m_B - (2-\sigma)\kappa_A\tau_A - \sigma\kappa_B\tau_B) \\ &+ g\ln(m_B + \sigma\kappa_B\tau_B) + (1-g)\ln(1-\tau_B) \\ &- (1-g)\ln(2-(2-\sigma)\tau_A - \sigma\tau_B); \end{aligned}$$

National fiscal authorities would set tax policies so as to maximize $U_A$ with respect to $\tau_A$, and $U_B$ with respect to $\tau_B$, while taking monetary policy as given.

The objective the central bank for the monetary union seeks $(m_A, m_B)$ to maximize,

$$(2-\gamma)U_A + \gamma U_B,$$

now becomes:

$$K + 2\frac{1-g}{\theta}\ln(2 - m_A - m_B - (2-\sigma)\kappa_A\tau_A - \sigma\kappa_B\tau_B)$$
$$-2(1-g)\ln(2 - (2-\sigma)\tau_A - \sigma\tau_B)(2-\gamma)g\ln(m_A + (2-\sigma)\kappa_A\tau_A) + (2-\gamma)(1-g)$$
$$\times\ln(1-\tau_A) + \gamma g\ln(m_B + \sigma\kappa_B\tau_B) + \gamma(1-g)\ln(1-\tau_B).$$

From the first-order conditions for the union's central bank with respect to $(m_A, m_B)$, we have that the resources allocated to the public good in each country are given by:

$$\Gamma_A = m_A + (2-\sigma)\kappa_A\tau_A = (2-\gamma)\frac{g\theta}{1-g+g\theta},$$

$$\Gamma_B = m_B + \sigma\kappa_B\tau_B = \gamma\frac{g\theta}{1-g+g\theta}. \tag{30}$$

Notably, such an allocation to the public good provision coincides with the solution for optimal union-wide monetary policy with no fiscal system, which implies lower money growth in the monetary union in the presence of a fiscal system than in its absence. The national fiscal authority provide for some of the resources necessary for optimal provision of the public good.

Suppose that fiscal policy is under the control of national governments. Seeking $\tau_A$ (alternatively, $\tau_B$) to maximize $U_A$ (alternatively, $U_B$) leads to first-order conditions, which once the results above for optimum monetary policy have been used may be simplified as follows:

$$\frac{1}{2-\sigma}\frac{1}{1-\tau_A} - \frac{1}{2-(2-\sigma)\tau_A - \sigma\tau_B} = \frac{\kappa_A(1-g+g\theta)}{(1-g)\theta}\left[\frac{1}{2-\gamma} - \frac{1}{2}\right]; \tag{31}$$

$$\frac{1}{\sigma}\frac{1}{1-\tau_B} - \frac{1}{2-(2-\sigma)\tau_A - \sigma\tau_B} = \frac{\kappa_B(1-g+g\theta)}{(1-g)\theta}\left[\frac{1}{\gamma} - \frac{1}{2}\right]. \tag{32}$$

It is straightforward to establish conditions under which feasible optimum national tax rates exist. In view of the fact that Eq. (31–32) are quadratic functions, we note that in general there exist two sets of solutions. At any rate, the optimal tax rates of both countries are simultaneously determined.

Manipulation of Eq. (31–32) yields:

$$\frac{1}{2-\sigma}\frac{1}{1-\tau_A} - \frac{1}{\sigma}\frac{1}{1-\tau_B} = \frac{1-g+g\theta}{2(1-g)\theta}\left[\kappa_A\frac{\gamma}{2-\gamma} - \kappa_B\frac{2-\gamma}{\gamma}\right].$$

Numerous comparative dynamics results are possible. E.g., suppose that the fiscal systems of the two countries are equally efficient, $\kappa_A = \kappa_B$. Then the sign of the LHS above is positive (negative) if $\gamma < (>)1$, that is if country $B$ is given less weight in setting monetary policy for the monetary union. Also, suppose that country $B$ is also smaller, that is $\sigma < 1$. Then it follows that country $A$, the larger of the two, pays a higher tax rate. The condition above also implies that, other things being equal, the optimal tax rate of the country with a more efficient tax system would be higher. The above result allows us to explore what is implied for national optimal tax rates by the finding of Casella (1992), that the smaller country must be given more than proportional (to its population share) representation in order to voluntarily participate in a monetary union. Imposing the condition that $\gamma > \sigma$ constrains the relationship between the two respective taxes rates, country sizes and efficiencies of tax systems.

We conclude by emphasizing the fact that this simple theory shows that even though national fiscal authorities are entrusted with setting national fiscal policy, monetary union introduces profound interdependence which makes the country-specific optimal tax rates depend on the sizes of both countries as well as the efficiency of their tax systems. The result follows from a skeletal model, where countries differ only with respect to their sizes. Notably, the model does not allow for debt financing.

### 3.3.1 Common Currency, National Fiscal Systems and Debt Finance

In view of the discussion in Sect. 3.2.1 above, we may modify Eq. (27) above to allow for public debt finance, in addition to money and tax finance:

$$\begin{aligned}(2-\sigma)(1-\tau_A)w_A + \sigma(1-\tau_B)w_B = {} & (2-\sigma)(1-\tau_A)w_{A,-1} \\ & + \sigma(1-\tau_B)w_{B,-1} + M_A + M_B \\ & + \delta_A d_A + \delta_B d_B - \rho_A D_{A,-1} \\ & - \rho_B D_{B,-1}. \end{aligned} \tag{33}$$

Similarly, Eq. (30) must be suitably adapted to reflect the availability of resources from borrowing.

Regarding Eq. (33), if all debt is international and between the two countries in question, then $\rho_A = \rho_B$, and $D_{A,-1} + D_{B,-1} = 0$. While this simplifies (33), the condition for monetary equilibrium, it presumes that the debtor can run a trade surplus in order to be able to finance interest payments. This is sort of invisible in (33), but becomes relevant for the national budget constraints that ensure the finance of the national public goods. That is, Eq. (34) must be modified as follows:

$$\begin{aligned}\Gamma_A &= m_A + (2-\sigma)\left[\kappa_A\tau_A + \delta_A d_A - \rho_A D_{A,-1}\right], \\ \Gamma_B &= m_B + \sigma\left[\kappa_B\tau_B + \delta_B d_B - \rho_B D_{B,-1}\right]. \end{aligned} \tag{34}$$

This modification has major consequences for the equilibrium allocations and associated welfare.

In like manner to the inefficiency of taxation, let $\delta_A, \delta_B$ be the fraction of borrowing that may drawn upon by country *A*,*B*, respectively. That is, net borrowing $d_A = D_A - D_{A,-1}$ yields $\delta_A d_A$ available for spending, per person, and let $\rho_A, \rho_B$

denote the interest rates associated with the outstanding debt. Augmenting Eq. (22) by introducing yields:

$$\Gamma_A = \ell_{\Gamma A} = mA + (2 - \sigma)[\kappa_A \tau_A + \delta_A d_A - \rho_A D_{A,-1}],$$
$$\Gamma_B = \ell_{\Gamma B} = m_B + \sigma[\kappa_B \tau_B + \delta_B d_B - \rho D_{B,-1}]. \quad (35)$$

The model continues to allow for individuals to transfer purchasing power over time by means of money. Revenue from issuing debt is distinguished from money finance and from tax finance by means of frictions, denoted by the parameters $\delta_A, \kappa_A$, respectively. The resulting modification of the model is rather trivial. Essentially, because taxes and debt revenue are lump-sum, the above formulas may be adapted easily.

The challenge is to link a country's ability to deal with servicing and/or repayment of debt by means of introducing structural reforms with either level- or growth-effects. If all debt is domestic, the financing options to the government depend on the dynamic efficiency properties of the economy. As mentioned above, if the economy is dynamically inefficient, introducing debt finance is welfare-enhancing. If, on the other hand, one country borrows from the other country, then the terms

$$(2 - \sigma)\left[\delta_A d_A - \rho_A D_{A,-1}\right], \sigma\left[\kappa_B \tau_B + \delta_B d_B - \rho D_{B,-1}\right]$$

are not independent from one another. For the same reason, international trade equilibrium requires that the debtor country has enough trade surplus to pay the creditor country. With this refinement, the model could be developed fully for the case of debt finance with interest payments from the debtor to the creditor.

An important consequence of this is that productivity improvements in one country behoove the other to also implement them, or else it would be unable to meet its debt obligations. This is even more important in the case of productivity improvements of the growth- rather than of the level effect type.

## 4 Concluding Remarks

In numerous ways that have been documented widely, the EZ is made up of very diverse countries. In spite of such diversity, catastrophic wars among the core European countries, that have fought many vicious conflicts over the last few years, have been prevented. Given this political success, there ought to be vast scope for coming to terms with the international coordination that is necessary to carry out fiscal policy that operated along with monetary policy and is designed to optimize outcomes over the entire union. In addition to the conventional differences among countries that have been identified by the literature, this paper introduces two more: differences in the efficiency of fiscal systems and on the terms of sovereign borrowing.

The present model provides a simple deterministic framework for understanding the role of size in the interdependence of broad macroeconomic aggregates. The mechanism for setting country-specific fiscal policy is not independent from the conduct of monetary policy. The paper goes beyond (Ioannides 2016) in allowing for debt finance under the different scenaria of international equilibrium, that is, international economic integration with national currencies and with a common currency, both in the presence of national fiscal systems. It allows us to examine in detail the setting similar to where Greece and the EZ found themselves since 2010. That is, given economic integration with a currency union, how willing should the union be (in our case, the larger of the two countries) to negotiate with one of its members and prevent breakup of the monetary union. The central role of size in the model provides for a realistic setting in assessing this question and in much simpler terms than other approaches in the literature (c.f. Alvarez and Dixit 2014).

## References

Alvarez F, Dixit A (2014) A real options perspective on the future of the euro. J Monet Econ 61:78–109

Casella A (1992) Participation in a currency union. Am Econ Rev 82(4):847–863

European Union (2012) Consolidated versions of the treaty on European Union and the treaty on the functioning of the European Union. Off J Eur Union C326:55 October 26. https://www.ecb.europa.eu/ecb/legal/pdf/c 32620121026en.pdf

Ioannides YM (2016) Large versus small states in the eurozone, the democratic deficit, and future architecture. In: Michaelides A, Orphanides A (eds) The Cyprus Bail-in: policy lessons from the Cyprus economic crisis. World Scientific Imperial College Press, New Jersey

Ioannides YM, Pissarides CA (2015) Is the Greek crisis one of supply or demand? Brookings Papers on Economic Activity. Fall:349–373

Sibert A (1992) Government finance in a common currency area. J Int Money Financ 11 (6):567–578

# Sovereign Debt Restructuring in a Monetary Union: The Case of the Euro Area Member States

**Sérgio Gonçalves do Cabo**

**Abstract** "Sovereign debt restructuring" is often viewed as a *panacea*, a kind of miraculous solution for over-indebted Member States. In this article it is argued that in a monetary union characterized by a single monetary policy and financial market integration, public debt restructuring should be seen as the last option to avoid default by a euro area Member State, namely when there is a strong case for unsustainability of government debt in the medium to long term. Public debt sustainability goes hand in hand with the Maastricht fiscal criteria, EMU's Stability and Growth Pact and its revisions of 2005 and 2011, and with the EU Treaties, including the Fiscal Compact and the ESM Treaty. Restructuring public debt is at the antipodes of economic policy co-ordination and convergence of euro area Member States sharing a common currency. It represents a major failure of the decentralized economic governance system that underpins the single currency. Based on the exceptional nature of "public debt restructuring" and taking into account the foundations of European Economic and Monetary Union (EMU), this article analyses the legal conditions for public debt restructuring in the euro area, focusing also on its financial and economic consequences. It looks at both the institutional approach and the contractual approach for debt restructuring, setting aside unilateral debt relief as equivalent to redenomination to the former national currencies and to exiting the monetary union. Alternatives to government debt restructuring in the euro area are also flagged in the context of the ESM Treaty, seen as an *embryo* for a European Union Treasury and for EU joint issuance of public debt. References to the Banking Union in its triple dimension of a single rulebook and Single Supervisory Mechanism (SSM), Single Resolution Mechanism (SRM) and European Deposit Insurance Scheme (EDIS) and to the Eurosystem's Outright Monetary Transactions (OMT) in secondary sovereign bond markets are also made to reinforce the exceptional nature of sovereign debt restructuring in EMU.

**JEL Classification** K29 • K39

---

S.G. do Cabo
Law Faculty, European Community Law, University of Lisbon, Lisbon, Portugal
e-mail: sergio.cabo@netcabo.pt



N. da Costa Cabral et al. (eds.), *The Euro and the Crisis*, Financial and Monetary Policy Studies 43, DOI 10.1007/978-3-319-45710-9_12

# 1 Introduction

Together with (i) the irrevocable fixing of conversion rates between the euro and the currencies of the participating Member states [see Council Regulation (EC) 2866/98] and (ii) the conduct of monetary and foreign exchange policy in euro, one of the main elements of the *changeover scenario* approved in the Madrid summit of 15–16 December 1995 was that (iii) *all new tradable public debt will be issued by the participating Member States in euro since 1 January 1999*. The changeover scenario also foresaw that by 1 July 2002, at the latest, «*public debt denominated in the former national currencies will be redeemable only in the single currency*».

These decisions were further detailed in Council Regulation (EC) No. 974/98 of 3 May 1998 on the introduction of the euro (OJ L 139, 11.5.1998) where *redenomination* of both public and private debt was envisaged.[1] Indeed, article 8/4 of Council Regulation (EC) No. 974/98 foresaw that «*each participating Member State may take measures which may be necessary in order to redenominate in the euro unit outstanding debt issued by that Member State's general government, ..., denominated in its national currency unit and issued under its own law*». It also foresaw that «*if a Member State has taken such a measure, issuers may redenominate in the euro unit debt denominated in that Member State's national currency unit unless redenomination is expressly excluded by the terms of the contract*». This provision was applicable to debt issued by the general government of a Member State, as well as to bonds, money market instruments and other forms of tradeable debt issued by other debtors.

The changeover scenario and the said provisions of the Council Regulation on the introduction of the euro,[2] conceived *debt redenomination* as a means to promote the widespread use of the new currency and, in the absence of exchange rate risk, to foster *financial market integration*:

- With the introduction of the euro, both public and private issuers have redenominated their debts from the former national currencies to the euro;
- Those debts became due in euro, which is a currency common to the euro area Member States, that is managed by the Eurosystem, comprising the ECB and the national central banks of the now 19 euro area Member States,[3] whose primary objective is to maintain price stability. In other words, *public and private debt*

[1] According to recital 14 of Council Regulation (EC) No. 974/98 «*it is desirable to allow issuers of debt to redenominate outstanding debt in the euro unit; (...)* » and «*issuers should be enabled to redenominate outstanding debt if the debt is denominated in a national currency unit of a Member State which has redenominated part or all of the outstanding debt of its general government*».

[2] Still in force after several amendments, the last one introduced by Council Regulation No. 827/2014, of 23 July 2014, regarding the introduction of the euro in Lithuania (OJ L 228, 31.7.2014).

[3] Belgium, Germany, Ireland, Spain, France, Italy, Luxembourg, The Netherlands, Austria, Portugal and Finland (1999) Greece (2001) Slovenia (2007), Cyprus and Malta (2008), Slovakia (2009), Estonia (2011), Latvia (2014) and Lithuania (2015).

*became payable in a new currency, which is no longer controlled by a single Member State, but rather a currency common to a group of States* ("a currency without a State", as is frequently termed[4]) whose management is guided to achieve an inflationary target below, but close to, 2 % over the medium term[5];
- The issuance of national debt under a common currency means that participating Member States are issuing debt in a currency that they cannot control (a *foreign currency* as was pointed out by Christian Kopf[6] and Paul de Grauwe[7]). However, the issuance of national debt under a common currency was not accompanied by any form of *legal harmonization*, namely common terms and conditions, governing law and jurisdiction. In other words, currency redenomination of national debt was not followed by any change of the law governing the issuance nor by any attempt to harmonize the conditions of national debt issuance under a common currency (only "Collective Action Clauses" were introduced since January 2013[8]);
- Therefore, each participating Member State continued to issue its own debt as a national liability, according to its own laws and practices, since EU law kept economic and fiscal policies as a matter of *national competence*, although coordinated at EU level, and expressly provided for the non-liability of the Union or other Member States for the commitments of other Member States (see article 125/1 TFEU, comprising the so called *no-bailout clause*).

Having regard to the above and in order to fully understand the problem of public debt restructuring in a monetary union, one has to take into account, on the one hand, that the introduction of the euro was underpinned by a set of tools aiming at *economic and fiscal policy coordination for the euro area*, as set forth by the Maastricht Treaty (1991–1993) and, on the other hand, that *the introduction of the euro has spurred general market integration*[9] *and further financial market integration.*[10] As it is now well known, economic and fiscal policy coordination did not

---

[4]See Issing (2008).

[5]See European Central Bank (2011).

[6]See Kopf (2011).

[7]See De Grauwe (2011).

[8]See article 12/3 of the ESM Treaty: «Collective action clauses shall be included, as of 1 January 2013, in all new euro area government securities, with maturity above 1 year, in a way which ensures that their legal impact is identical».

[9]Inducing investment integration, increased trade in goods and services and in cross-border mobility of labor, bringing higher synchronization of business cycles among Member States as argued by Charles Wyplosz (2016, pp. 103–118).

[10]According to the first set of indicators of financial integration in the euro area published by the ECB in 30 September 2005 (European Central Bank 2005), although banking and equity markets were less integrated, *government bond markets were significantly integrated even before the start of EMU*. The indicators for the corporate bond market pointed to a high degree of integration and the unsecured money market has been fully integrated shortly after the introduction of the euro (see https://www.ecb.europa.eu/pub/pdf/other/indicatorsfinancialintegration200509en.pdf?006e28de34fde544bdbd77a82c66c291). Since then the work on financial integration has evolved

compensate for the *macroeconomic imbalances created by the single monetary policy in a context of general market integration* and *free movement of capitals*, and did not prevent the *credit boom* prompted by low interest rates and easy credit in countries used to higher inflation and higher interest rates.[11] In this context, it should be recalled that the sharing of a single currency required the fulfilment of a set of *convergence criteria* (see Protocol No 13 to the EU Treaties), but mainly it required the respect for certain basic rules and compliance with a set of *stability criteria*:

- Policy orientation towards a «*balanced economic growth and price stability*» (article 3/3 TEU) whereas both Member States and the Union institutions are bond to a *close coordination of national economic policies* (articles 2/2, 5 and 119/1 TFEU), being the definition and conduct of a single monetary policy a *Union exclusive competence* (article 3/1/c TFEU), and to comply with the principles of stable prices, sound public finances and monetary conditions (article 119/3 TFEU);
- General *prohibition of monetary financing* of Union institutions, central governments, regional, local or other public authorities, other bodies governed by public law, or public undertakings of Member States, including the prohibition of *direct purchases* of debt instruments issued by them from ECB or national central banks (article 123/1 TFEU)[12];
- *Prohibition of privileged access to financial institutions* by the European Union and its legal bodies, by the Member States, including Federal states, regional and local authorities and, in general, by public authorities, other bodies governed by public law or public undertakings (article 124 TFEU);
- "*No-bailout clause*",[13] meaning the non-liability of the Union or other Member States for the commitments of other Member States or the autonomy of the

---

and has resulted in the publication of a yearly report available at https://www.ecb.europa.eu/pub/pub/prud/html/index.en.html.

[11]See De Grauwe (2013).

[12]See the ECJ Decision in the *Pringle* Case (C-370/12) where is was stated «*that Article 123 TFEU is addressed specifically to the ECB and the central banks of the Member States*» and that «*the grant of financial assistance by one Member State or by a group of Member States to another Member State is therefore not covered by that prohibition*» (recital 125). It was further added «*that it is the ESM which grants financial assistance to an ESM Member*» and that «*even if the Member States are acting via the ESM, the Member States are not derogating from the prohibition laid down in Article 123 TFEU, since that article is not addressed to them*» (recital 126).

[13]See Pipkorn (1994, p. 275) and Smits (1997, pp. 77–78). See also the ECJ Decision in the *Pringle* Case (C-370/12) where is was stated that «*article 125 TFEU does not prohibit the granting of financial assistance by one or more Member States to a Member State which remains responsible for its commitments to its creditors provided that the conditions attached to such assistance are such as to prompt that Member State to implement a sound budgetary policy*» (recital 137); that «*the instruments for stability support of which the ESM may make use under Articles 14 to 18 of the ESM Treaty demonstrate that the ESM will not act as guarantor of the debts of the recipient Member State. The latter will remain responsible to its creditors for its financial commitments*» (recital 138). The ECJ concludes that «*The granting of financial assistance to an ESM Member in*

national budgetary policies (article 125/1 TFEU). Each Member State is thus responsible for its own financing and EMU does not foresee any financial or budgetary transfer mechanisms to the Member States other than the existing mechanisms resulting from the common policies supported by the Community budget (namely, common agricultural policy and cohesion policy)[14];

- *Avoidance of excessive government deficits* according to common accepted reference values of government deficit and debt to GDP, as set forth in the protocol on excessive deficit procedure (3 % for the ratio of the planned or actual government deficit to GDP at market prices and 60 % for the ratio of government debt to GDP at market prices) and in the Stability and Growth Pact (SGP), aimed at strengthening the surveillance of budgetary positions and the surveillance and

---

*the form of a credit line, in accordance with Article 14 of the ESM Treaty, or in the form of loans, in accordance with Articles 15 and 16 of the ESM Treaty, in no way implies that the ESM will assume the debts of the recipient Member State. On the contrary, such assistance amounts to the creation of a new debt, owed to the ESM by that recipient Member State, which remains responsible for its commitments to its creditors in respect of its existing debts. It should be observed in that regard that, under Article 13(6) of the ESM Treaty, any financial assistance granted on the basis of Articles 14 to 16 thereof must be repaid to the ESM by the recipient Member State and that, under Article 20(1) thereof, the amount to be repaid is to include an appropriate margin*» (recital 139).

[14]The clause of non-liability must not be confused with a prohibition of financial help or support, since its purpose is not to avoid financial aid to States which are in difficulties. Article 122 TFEU provides for the possibility—by way of exception and duly justified—of the European Union (and not the other Member States) to adopt "measures appropriate to the economic situation" or to "grant financial assistance" to a Member State. It was under this legal basis that Council Regulation (EU) No 407/2010 of 11 May 2010 establishing a European financial stabilization mechanism (OJ L 118, of 12.5.2010) was approved. This provision was later circumvented by the European Council Decision of 25 March 2011, amending Article 136 of the TFEU with regard to creating a stability mechanism for Member States whose currency is the euro (2011/199/EU), where it is assumed that *Article 122(2) of the TFEU will no longer be used in situations of risk to the financial stability of the euro area as a whole, as have been experienced in 2010* (see recital 4). Such situations would be dealt by creating a specific stability mechanism to be activated when "*indispensable to safeguard the stability of the euro area as a whole*". Such specific stability mechanism was created by an intergovernmental treaty establishing the European Stability Mechanism (ESM) signed by the euro area Member States on 2 February 2012. The ESM was inaugurated on 8 October 2012 upon ratification and has provided financial assistance to Spain for the recapitalization of its financial sector (the Financial Assistance was provided by the EFSF and then transferred to the ESM), and is providing financial assistance to Greece (Third Economic Adjustment Programme for Greece) and Cyprus.

Before this EU Council decision, financial assistance to Greece was provided via bilateral loans pooled by the European Commission (the so-called "Greek Loan Facility") for a total amount of 80 billion euros to be disbursed over the period May 2010 through June 2013 and through IMF support (30 billion euros) (First Economic Adjustment Programme for Greece) and financial assistance to Ireland, Portugal and Greece (Second Economic Adjustment Programme for Greece) was provided by the European Financial Stability Facility (EFSF), a *société anonyme* incorporated by the euro area Member States in Luxembourg, on 7 June 2010, with the purpose of providing financial support to euro-area Member States that lost access to financial markets.

On this issue see Louis (2010, pp. 975–986), Ruffert (2011, pp. 1777–1806) and De Gregorio Merino (2012, pp. 1613–1646).

coordination of economic policies (*preventive arm*)[15] and to speed up and clarify the implementation of the excessive deficit procedure (*corrective arm*).[16]

These basic rules and stability criteria are part of a *coordinated economic and fiscal policy framework* which is closely interlinked with the setting up of a *common monetary policy*, implemented as from 1 January 1999: a single central bank interest rate would be offered to the whole banking sector of the euro area through *open market operations*, within a single collateral framework and a single transfer mechanism (the TARGET payments system), where public and private debt instruments (denominated in euro) would be eligible as collateral for accessing central bank credit facilities.[17]

The implementation of the single monetary policy created uniform financing conditions throughout the euro area that ultimately lead to the already mentioned *macroeconomic imbalances*, which were exacerbated since the financial crisis of 2007–2008, that forced sovereigns to rescue their "national financial systems", originating the European sovereign debt crisis of 2010–2011, that started in Greece (although caused by revelation of the budget deficit figures for 2009 and not by the financial system) and later evolved to Ireland (here the financial system was at the centre of the budget deficit), Portugal (here a mixture of expansionary budgetary policies, political and financial crises explain the request for financial assistance), Spain (where financial assistance was limited to stabilizing the financial sector) and Cyprus (not mentioning Latvia, at the time a non-euro area Member State, Hungary and Romania, that benefited from EU balance-of-payments assistance[18]).

## 2 Sovereign Debt Restructuring in the Euro Area: What Does It Mean?

It is against this background of general (and financial) market integration and macroeconomic policy coordination that the problem of sovereign debt restructuring as to be posed in an economic and monetary union (EMU), particularly when foreign government bonds rated AAA to AA—or any domestic government bond are considered to be risk-free assets *weighted 0 % under Basel III liquidity requirements* (sovereign debt is weighted at 20 % for countries rated below AA) and play a key role as *collateral* for central bank funding.

[15]Council Regulation (EC) No 1466/97.

[16]Council Regulation (EC) No 1467/97.

[17]The Eurosystem's regular open market operations consist of 1-week liquidity-providing operations (main refinancing operations, or MROs) as well as 3-month liquidity-providing operations (longer-term refinancing operations, or LTROs).

[18]See http://ec.europa.eu/economy_finance/assistance_eu_ms/index_en.htm.

As such, the first question to be asked is *what is meant by sovereign debt restructuring*? In answering this question one has to ponder that sovereign debt restructuring may be seen lato sensu and stricto sensu.

Lato sensu, sovereign debt restructuring may comprise a set of tools used for *government debt management*, such as exchange offers, buybacks and early redemptions, currency and interest rate swaps and other financial operations, made with the general objective of *lowering the costs of servicing the public debt* and fine tune debt maturities, allowing for a more even distribution over the years and avoiding excessive concentration of repayments.[19]

Stricto sensu sovereign debt restructuring involves an element of *debt relief for borrowers combined with losses for lenders*: lengthening the maturities of the old debt with lower interest rates, shifting contractual payments into the future, reducing the nominal value of the old instruments, among other solutions, providing an amendment to the agreed contractual terms and conditions of issuance that *fundamentally change the economic and financial situation of the lenders*, shifting the burden of adjustment from the borrower to the lender that has to assume some losses, implying an *haircut* to the net present value of its assets.

Therefore, the criteria that may be used to distinguish debt restructuring in ample or in strict sense lies in the presence of an element of debt relief combined with losses for lenders. If debt rescheduling or 'reprofiling' implies debt relief for the borrower and losses for lenders, because maturities of the old debt have been lengthened, involving lower interest rates, or a debt *moratoria* had been agreed or unilaterally imposed, or there is a reduction in the face (nominal) value of the bonds/bills, there is a debt restructuring stricto sensu. In other words, when lenders have to assume *losses on public debt* they hold there is a fundamental shift from debt management operations to debt restructuring.

Accordingly, 'reprofiling' of public debt through a change of maturities, interest rates or even governing law and currency (reprofiling with debt redenomination and change of governing law) or an exchange of outstanding sovereign debt instruments, such as loans, bonds or bills, for new debt instruments (also with debt redenomination and change of governing law) accompanied by losses for lenders would qualify as sovereign debt restructuring operations stricto sensu.

However, when debt rescheduling or reprofiling implies debt relief for the borrower but *no losses for lenders*, one can assume that the operation resembles a debt management measure, i.e. a debt restructuring in ample sense.

If a participating Member State ceases to have market access and replaces privately-held public debt by official sector debt, as it is the case under EU/IMF financial assistance programmes, there is no debt restructuring stricto sensu, but one can assume that such restructuring took place lato sensu, since there was a *change in the debt ownership composition*, replacing private sector investors by the public sector. Such change, as mentioned by the ECJ in the *Pringle* Case (C-370/12) means that the granting of financial assistance by one or more Member States to

[19]On this issue see Wolswijk and de Haan (2005).

another Member State (as was the case in the first economic adjustment programme for Greece) or the granting of financial assistance to an ESM Member in the form of a credit line (as was the case of the Economic Adjustment Programme for Cyprus), «*amounts to the creation of a new debt, owed to the ESM by that recipient Member State, which remains responsible for its commitments to its creditors in respect of its existing debts*» (see recital 139). That is particularly the case for Portugal, as can be seen from Fig. 1, taken from the May 2016 monthly bulletin of the Portuguese Agency for Public Debt Management (IGCP).[20]

From December 2010 to April 2016 there is a significant reduction in market instruments financing [OT/Portuguese Government Bonds (PGB)] and an increase in financial assistance financing (EU-IMF) although the share of PGB held by non-residents, excluding central banks (which account in February 2016 for 21 % of the total stock of Portuguese public debt), has been relatively constant, increasing to 47 % in March 2015, but being higher than the stock held by nationals, excluding the Portuguese central bank. In April 2016, 30 % of the debt stock was composed by the official sector against 0 % in December 2010.

## 3 Sovereign Debt Restructuring Stricto Sensu: Can It Take Place in the Euro Area? If Yes, How?

The Second Economic Adjustment Programme for Greece, approved on 14 March 2012, was preceded by a Eurogroup statement of 20 June 2011, later endorsed by the EU council of 24 June 2011, where it was decided that additional funding for Greece would also be provided by the private sector. Private sector involvement (PSI) was then designed «*to improve the sustainability of Greece's debt in the form of informal and voluntary roll-overs of existing Greek debt at maturity for a substantial reduction of the required year-by-year funding within the programme, while avoiding a selective default for Greece*» (see Eurogroup statement of 20 June 2011). Negotiations were undertaken with the Institute of International Finance (IIF) and lead to an amendment of the Greek debt law via "*the Greek Bondholder act*" (Law No. 4050/2012) and to an exchange offer addressed to the holders of certain "Designated Securities" to exchange each 1000 euros face amount for 315 euros aggregate face amount of 20 individual series of new Greek government bonds (governed by English law), 315 euros notional amount of GDP-linked Securities and 150 euros aggregate face amount of PSI Payment Notes (75 euros face amount of 1-year EFSF bonds and 75 euros face amount of 2-year EFSF bonds). Out of a total of 205.6 billion euros in bonds eligible for the exchange offer, approximately 197 billion euros, or 95.7 % have been exchanged involving a haircut calculated at between 53.5 and 77.1 %.[21]

---

[20] Available at http://www.igcp.pt/gca/?id=107

[21] See Kenadjian (2013, pp. 125 ss) and Chiotellis (2014, pp. 105 ss).

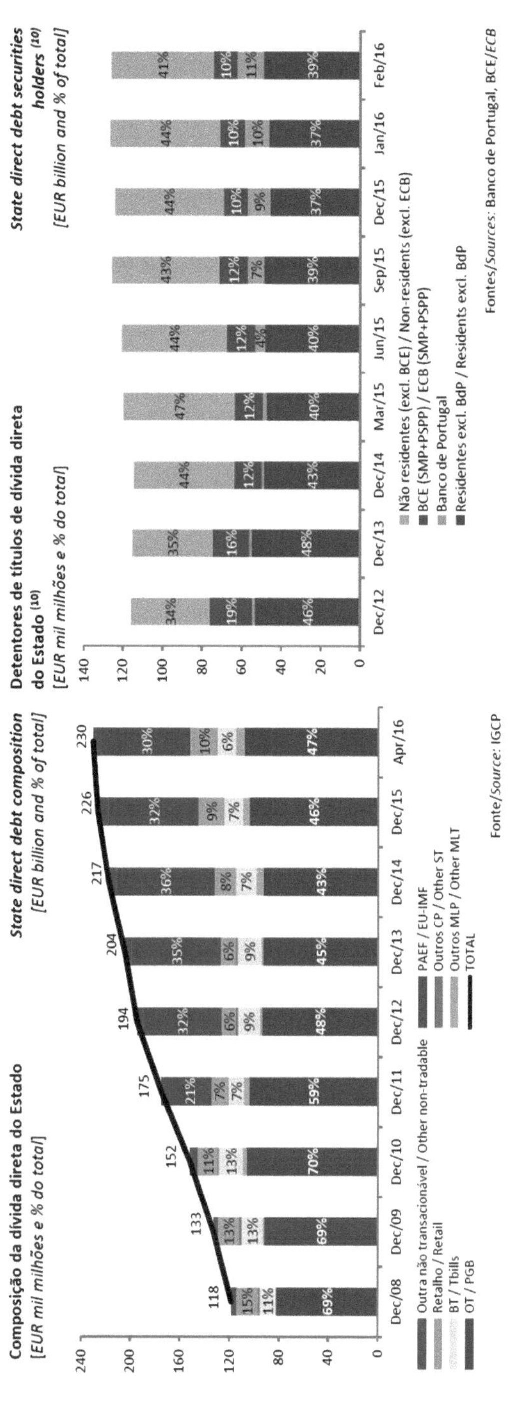


**Fig. 1** Portuguese debt composition

This arrangement was earlier qualified by the Heads of State or Government of the Euro Area and EU Institutions as an "*exceptional and unique solution*"[22] but that does not curtail the question of dealing with further restructuring operations of sovereign debt in the euro area or setting up insolvency proceedings for defaulting sovereigns in the euro area.[23]

The question was recently revived in the road up to the third economic adjustment program for Greece, when the Euro Summit of 12 July 2015 stressed that «*nominal haircuts on the debt cannot be undertaken*» and that «*the Greek authorities reiterate their unequivocal commitment to honour their financial obligations to all their creditors fully and in a timely manner*».[24]

Being so, can a second round of debt restructuring take place in the euro area, namely in the case of Greece?

Recital 12 of the ESM Treaty foresees that, by way of exception, "*adequate and proportionate form of private sector involvement shall be considered*" in accordance with IMF practice.

Looking at the most recent Eurogroup statements on Greece (of 9 and 25 May 2016[25]) it has been reconfirmed that "*nominal haircuts are excluded, and that all measures taken will be in line with existing EU law and the ESM and EFSF legal frameworks*" leading to the conclusion that sovereign debt restructuring stricto sensu, involving the private sector, will not be undertaken.[26]

---

[22]See the statement by Head of State or Government of the Euro Area and EU Institutions of 21 July 2011 where it was mentioned that "*Greece requires an exceptional and unique solution*" and that "*all other euro countries solemnly reaffirm their inflexible determination to honour fully their own individual sovereign signature and all their commitments to sustainable fiscal conditions and structural reforms. The euro area Heads of State or Government fully support this determination as the credibility of all their sovereign signatures is a decisive element for ensuring financial stability in the euro area as a whole.*"

[23]See on this topic Sáinz de Vicuña (2014, p. 192, 2013, pp. 15–24). The author supports the view that "*a statutory system for sovereign debt workouts can be built upon the already-existing institutional set-up with a Court of Justice, an independent Commission, a powerful ESM as possible financier of fiscal consolidation, and the expert advice of the ECB (...)*" but considers that such an initiative must be kept on hold during the current financial crises since it might be counterproductive at this juncture (see first work quoted, pages 191–192).

[24]See http://www.consilium.europa.eu/en/press/press-releases/2015/07/12-euro-summit-statement-greece/

[25]Available at http://www.consilium.europa.eu/en/press/press-releases/2016/05/09-eg-statement-greece/ and at http://www.consilium.europa.eu/en/press/press-releases/2016/05/24-eurogroup-statement-greece/

[26]According to Reuters the current holdings of Greek debt by private investors amounts to 38.7 billion euros following the debt swap of 2012. There are 15 billion euros in short-term Treasury bills hold by Greek banks and the remaining stock is held by the official sector (see http://www.reuters.com/article/us-eurozone-greece-debt-factbox-idUSKCN0P80XW20150628). Therefore it makes little sense to involve the private sector in further debt restructuring operations. On this topic see the comments of Gros (2016), referring that "*today Greece has only a few private-sector obligations*" and that "*Eurozone governments are the ones offering large amounts of funding*".

However, the debt sustainability analysis (DSA) carried out on 10 July 2015 pointed «*to serious concerns regarding the sustainability of Greece's public debt*» and «*to debt-mitigating measures that would be granted based on appropriate conditionality*».[27] Such measures are referred to in the above mentioned Eurogroup statements on Greece (of 9 and 25 May 2016) ranging, for the short-term, from smoothening the EFSF repayment profile, to reduced interest rate risk and waiving the step-up interest rate margin related to the debt buy-back tranche of the second Greek programme for the year 2017. Other measures producing debt relief are foreseen in the medium to long term, subject to a positive assessment on programme implementation. This means that *a specific form of official sector debt restructuration is under way*, and that EFSF loans will be reprofiled thus raising the question of losses to the other Member States. The aforementioned Eurogroup statements on Greece refers to the «*exceptionally high burden of some member States*» but it is still unknown how Greece's debt relief would materialize.

Having regard to the above, it seems fair to conclude that sovereign debt restructuring stricto sensu can take place in the euro area in two ways: (i) official sector restructuring in a somehow concealed manner, that excludes, for Greece, further measures that could affect the private sector; (ii) private sector involvement for other programme countries, by way of exception, in accordance with IMF practice (see recital 12 of the ESM Treaty). Both ways are highly problematic: official sector involvement (OSI) resembles a financial transfer between countries or to one country and private sector involvement (PSI) hampers future access to market finance. After all the financial assistance programmes should create the necessary conditions for countries do regain access to market finance, and PSI could hinder such objective. Therefore, the door seems to be open, namely in the case of Greece, for public debt restructuring within the inner circle of the ESM and EFSF legal frameworks, without affecting (at least directly) the markets for sovereign debt bonds. This means that, inasmuch as the ESM and EFSF finance have replaced market finance, there are special forms of debt relief provided under such mechanisms that should not be confounded with the classical situations of unilateral debt relief by default or repudiation, or with the use of contractual or institutional solutions for a defaulting sovereign. Thus, the question is: how do these classical solutions apply in the euro area?

It is submitted that besides official sector finance provided by the ESM and inner circle official sector restructuring within the ESM framework, currently, only contractual solutions can be applied in the euro area, thus excluding unilateral debt relief and (for the time being) any kind of institutional or statutory debt restructuring mechanisms.

(A) *Unilateral debt relief*

Regarding unilateral debt relief by means of repudiation, default or redenomination of national debt from the euro to the former national currencies

[27] See http://ec.europa.eu/economy_finance/assistance_eu_ms/greek_loan_facility/pdf/debt_sustainability_analysis_en.pdf

or to a newly established national currency, it should be noted that (i) the issuance of euro denominated debt by the participating Member States is largely governed by domestic law[28] and that (ii) the EU Treaty kept fiscal policies under national powers, providing for the non-liability of the Union or other Member States for the financial commitments of other Member States. Therefore, being a matter of *national competences*, unilateral debt relief cannot be totally excluded. However, public debt restructuring by a euro area Member State, on a *unilateral basis* and without creditor's consent, would hamper financial market integration so deeply, that its legal and economic impact would be equivalent to redenomination to the former national currencies and to exiting the monetary union. In this sense it could be argued that unilateral debt relief would run counter the basic principles of EU Law, being contrary to the general principle of market integration.[29] In economic terms, cross-border financial contagion and spillovers to other over-indebted sovereigns would lead to fragmentation and to renationalization of domestic financial markets, putting at risk the whole framework of the single currency.[30]

More bluntly, unilateral debt relief, imposing losses to all holders of Government Bonds and Bills (including other Member States, banks, central banks, insurance companies, pension funds and other institutional investors) would have a large economic and financial impact, tantamount to redenomination and exiting the monetary union.[31] Therefore, the question of sovereign debt restructuring is not restricted to the issuer, it rather encompasses the whole group of States involved in the single currency (affecting also the internal market) and thus, has to be solved within the institutional setup of EMU. This means that *any solution decided on a unilateral basis would be tantamount to redenomination and exiting the monetary union or the EU as such* and would have to be considered an infringement of the basic principles of EU Law, namely the general principle of market integration.

(B) *Contractual approach*

The use of Collective Action Clauses ("CACs") in government bonds is a relatively new phenomenon. The idea originated in G-10 group report of May 1996 in the wake of a fundamental shift in government finance, from syndicated bank lending to direct market finance.[32] Traditionally international bank lending to sovereigns took the form of loan agreements and debt restructuring was negotiated by bank advisory committees, known as the London Club. More recently, the role of commercial banks in State lending has changed and banks became broker-dealers passing the sovereign default risk to large

[28]See Moody's Investors Service (2012).

[29]This seems to be the opinion of Antonio Sáinz de Vicuña (2014, pp. 182–183).

[30]See Gros (2014, pp. 195–204).

[31]The magnitude of such impact and spillover effects can be deduced from Lojsch et al. (2011).

[32]See "Group of Ten—The resolution of sovereign liquidity crises", available at http://www.bis.org/publ/gten03.htm. See also Kopf (2013, pp. 153–157).

groups of bondholders, insurance companies, pension funds, investment funds, asset managers et al. The inclusion in sovereign debt instruments of contractual provisions that facilitate consultation and cooperation between debtors and their private creditors, thereby providing adequate contractual conditions for co-ordination among an amalgamate of creditors was seen desirable in the event of crisis.

In 2002, with the Argentinian debt crisis, the IMF recommended the use of CAC for all international sovereign issuers and the idea was adopted in 2003 by the Ecofin Council.[33] It was in the wake of the sovereign debt crisis in Europe that in its statement of 28 November 2010, the Eurogroup identified that standardized and identical Collective Action Clauses ("CACs") should be included, in such a way as to preserve market liquidity, in the terms and conditions of all new euro area government bonds. As requested by the European Council on 25 March 2011, the detailed legal arrangements for including CACs in euro area government securities were finalized by the Economic and Financial Committee (EFC) by 18 November 2011.[34]

In accordance with paragraph 3 of Article 12 of the modified version of The Treaty establishing the European Stability Mechanism (ESM)—endorsed on 2nd February 2012 by the euro area Member States—it has become mandatory on such Member States to include the Model Collective Action Clauses (CACs) in all new euro area government securities with maturity above 1 year issued on or after 1st January 2013, in a way which ensures that their legal impact is identical.

CACs allow for a proposed modification of euro area government securities to be made binding on all holders of the affected securities if approved by holders of the requisite principal amount of the affected securities, thus facilitating the agreement of private-sector creditors to a possible modification of euro area government debt securities that contain such standardized CAC.[35]

(C) *Institutional approach*

There are several drawbacks to this contractual approach, namely the fact that such clauses have to be tested against the governing law of the securities issued and could be overturned by legislative action of the sovereign.[36] For this reason and also to avoid the political management of debt restructuring operations, several authors claim for a statutory procedure, modelled, to a certain extent, in the insolvency procedures governed by private law.[37] Such proposals have not

[33]See Sáinz de Vicuña (2014, p. 187) and Kenadjian (2013, pp. 117–118).

[34]See http://europa.eu/efc/sub_committee/cac/cac_2012/index_en.htm

[35]There is a large number of legal studies on this subject matter. We refer to Bauer et al. (2013) and to Billington (2014, pp. 399–416).

[36]See Sáinz de Vicuña (2014, p. 188–190) and Audit (2014, pp. 218–220).

[37]See, inter alia, the Bruegel proposal, Bruegel (2011) and Paulus (2013, pp. 181–205), suggesting the creation of a Sovereign Debt Tribunal; Sáinz de Vicuña (2014, pp. 191–192) and Olivares-Caminal (2014, pp. 333–358).

been endorsed so far, but their adoption cannot be ruled out, since there are several advantages in treating private sector involvement in sovereign debt restructuring trough an appropriate set of institutions, under pre-defined legal procedures. Among others, equal treatment of creditors, avoidance of conflicting interests, legal certainty and transparency, application of legal rules and principles and international jurisdiction seem to favor an institutional approach.

However, it should be noted that this statutory approach is mainly addressed to sort out the situation of the private creditors (domestic or foreign) and that, as suggested under the IMF Sovereign Debt Restructuring Mechanism (SDRM), a more encompassing solution should be sought, including also the official sector.[38]

## 4 How to Avoid the Risk of Further Sovereign Debt Restructuring Operations in the Euro Area: Is the New Economic Governance Framework up to the Job?

In the wake of the sovereign debt crisis a number of significant actions were put in place *reinforcing the economic governance of the euro area* in order to prevent the accumulation of fiscal and macroeconomic imbalances and, most of all, in order to avoid the emergence of future sovereign debt crisis:

- The SGP has been strengthened by Regulation (EU) No 1175/2011 of the European Parliament and of the Council and by Council Regulation (EU) No 1177/2011;
- Regulation (EU) No 1173/2011 of the European Parliament and of the Council of 16 November 2011 on the effective enforcement of budgetary surveillance in the euro area added a system of effective, preventive and gradual enforcement mechanisms in the form of the *imposition of sanctions on Member States whose currency is the euro*;
- In order to ensure closer coordination of economic policies and sustained convergence of the economic performance of Member States, the *European Semester* has become the framework for economic policy coordination[39] and surveillance to prevent and correct macroeconomic imbalances under

[38] Available at https://www.imf.org/External/np/pdr/sdrm/2002/081402.pdf. See also Krueger (2002) and Olivares-Caminal (2014, pp. 334–344).

[39] The *European Semester* includes the formulation, and the surveillance of the implementation, of the broad guidelines of the economic policies of the Member States and of the Union (*broad economic policy guidelines*); the formulation, and the examination of the implementation of the *employment guidelines*; the submission and assessment of Member States' stability or convergence programmes; the submission and assessment of Member States' national reform programmes supporting the Union's strategy for growth and jobs, established in line with the broad economic guidelines, with the employment guidelines and with the general guidance to

Regulation (EU) No 1176/2011 of the European Parliament and of the Council of 16 November 2011 (on the prevention and correction of macroeconomic imbalances) has been strengthened by Regulation (EU) No 1174/2011 of the European Parliament and of the Council of 16 November 2011 (on enforcement measures to correct excessive macroeconomic imbalances in the euro area), establishing interest-bearing deposits in case of non-compliance with the recommendations to take corrective action[40];

- Council directive 2011/85/EU of 8 November 2011 on requirements for budgetary frameworks of the Member States, provided for the adoption of a medium-term budgetary framework and a fiscal planning horizon of at least 3 years;
- Regulation (EU) No 473/2013 of the European Parliament and of the Council of 21 May 2013, on common provisions for *monitoring and assessing draft budgetary plans and ensuring the correction of excessive deficit of the Member States in the euro area*, complements the European Semester with a common budgetary timeline, as well as the procedure for the prevention and correction of excessive macroeconomic imbalances, the multilateral surveillance system of budgetary policies, the procedure for correcting a Member State's excessive deficit, therefore assuring consistency between budgetary policies and measures and reforms taken in the context of the procedure for prevention and correction of excessive macroeconomic imbalances;
- Regulation (EU) No 472/2013 of the European Parliament and of the Council of 21 May 2013 on the strengthening of economic and budgetary surveillance of Member States in the euro area experiencing or threatened with serious difficulties with respect to their financial stability or to the sustainability of their public finances, leading to potential adverse spill-over effects on other Member States in the euro area, foresees that a Member State may be subject to *enhanced surveillance* and regulates the terms for receiving *financial assistance* and *post-programme surveillance*;
- A permanent financial assistance mechanism, subject to strict conditionality, was established by the euro area Member States upon amendment to Article 136 of the TFEU and an intergovernmental treaty, establishing the European Stability Mechanism (ESM), was signed on 2 February 2012 and entered into force on 8 October 2012. The ESM purpose is to provide financial support to euro area the countries following a European financial assistance programme when their regular access to market financing is impaired or is at risk of being impaired. Besides its paid in capital of 80,221.2 million euros and capital calls up to 701,935.3 million euros, the ESM issues debt and is entitled to enter into financial or other agreements or arrangements with ESM Members, financial

Member States issued by the Commission (*the annual growth survey*) and the European Council at the beginning of the *annual cycle of surveillance*.

[40]Such deposits are converted into an annual fine in the case of continued non-compliance with the recommendation to address excessive macroeconomic imbalances within the same imbalances procedure.

institutions or other third parties in order to secure funds to finance loans and other forms of financial assistance to euro area Member States.

- The Fiscal Compact (Treaty on Stability, Coordination and Governance in the Economic and Monetary Union), signed on 2 March 2012 by all Member States of the European Union (EU), except the Czech Republic and the United Kingdom, expanded the "balanced budget rule" to all "Contracting Parties" in accumulation with their obligations under EU law, targeting a structural deficit not exceeding a country-specific Medium-Term budgetary Objective (MTO) which at most can be set to 0.5 % of GDP for states with a deb-to-GDP ratio exceeding 60 % or at most 1.0 % of GDP for states with debt levels within the 60 % limit (article 3/1). In addition, a "debt brake rule" has been introduced for Member States whose government debt-to-GDP ratio exceeds the 60 % reference level in the latest recorded fiscal year (article 4) and a mechanism for "debt issuance coordination" has been set forth (article 6);

The EU economic governance framework has been further developed with the setting up of an independent advisory European Fiscal Board (Commission Decision of 21.10.2015, OJ L 282, 28.10.2015, p. 37)[41] as foreseen in the "Five Presidents' Report: Completing Europe's Economic and Monetary Union" of 22 June 2015, and steps are being taken towards a peculiar form of *Fiscal Union*, albeit the *prospective stabilisation function* is defined in a negative fashion, since «*it should not lead to permanent transfers between countries or to transfers in one direction only*», it should «*not be conceived as a way to equalise incomes between Member States*» and «*it should neither undermine the incentives for sound fiscal policy-making at the national level, nor the incentives to address national structural weaknesses*» (see Five Presidents' Report, p. 17).[42] In a positive definition, the *prospective stabilisation function* is intended to prevent moral hazard, being tied to compliance with the broad EU governance framework and with the procedures for the coordination of economic policies.

The "Five Presidents' Report" tries to strike a balance between "more joint decision-making on fiscal policy" and recognition of national competences in the fields of taxation and allocation of budgetary expenditures, since these "are matters of national preferences and political choices". In other words, the current institutional framework, still based on the conferral principle where competences and legitimacy lie at Member State level poses strong limits to joint-decision making in areas where revenue and expenditure policy are at stake. The "Report" hints at this problem and finds itself under a *dilemma*: on the one hand, it recognizes that whilst

[41] The European Fiscal Board is supposed to perform its tasks independently and to prepare its opinions autonomously from any national or European institution. The Board has been set up to provide the Commission with an evaluation of the implementation of the Union fiscal framework and to contribute to a more informed discussion of the overall implications of budgetary policies at euro area and national level in order to achieve an appropriate fiscal stance for the euro area.

[42] It is also mentioned that such stabilisation function should not be an instrument for crisis management since that is a task assigned to the European Stability Mechanism (ESM).

"the euro area evolves towards a genuine EMU, some decisions will increasingly need to be made collectively", like having "a future euro area treasury", on the other hand, there is a problem of "ensuring democratic accountability and legitimacy".

This later problem is not limited to the concept of Fiscal Union, it encompasses the whole area of economic governance, since sharing a common currency requires an effective system of co-ordination of national economic policies (and economic convergence of euro area Member States) which has proven very difficult to attain when the core decisions of economic, social and budgetary nature are taken at national level, based on national legitimacy and on national preferences.

So, in order to answer the question, is the new economic governance framework capable of avoiding the risk of further sovereign debt restructuring operations in the euro area, the answer cannot be a simple yes or no. It has improved effectiveness of economic policy coordination in the euro area and created financial mechanisms to avoid default by a Member State on its debt, therefore assuring the financial stability of the euro area. However, it is doubtful that enforcement mechanisms in the form of the imposition of sanctions would function as deterrent given the problem of national preferences, democratic accountability and legitimacy. The risks of political bargaining at both European and national level and the amplifying effect of sanctions in financial markets, triggering the need for a financial rescue might, in the very end, bring the decision-makers to the conclusion that sanctions could be counter-productive, leading to undesirable results.

To sum up, the risk of further sovereign debt restructuring operations in the euro area has not been totally removed by the new economic governance framework.

However, more than the new economic governance framework, the setting up of a Banking Union in its triple dimension of a single rulebook and Single Supervisory Mechanism (SSM),[43] Single Resolution Mechanism (SRM)[44] and European Deposit Insurance Scheme (EDIS)[45] designed at breaking the so called "deadly embrace" between the sovereigns and banks, together with the announcement of the Eurosystem's Outright Monetary Transactions (OMT) in secondary sovereign bond

[43]See Capital requirements regulation and directive—CRR/CRD IV (Regulation (EU) No 575/2013 on prudential requirements for credit institutions and investment firms (CRR) and Directive 2013/36/EU on access to the activity of credit institutions and the prudential supervision of credit institutions and investment firms (CRD IV)—and Council Regulation (EU) No 1024/2013 conferring specific tasks on the European Central Bank concerning policies relating to the prudential supervision of credit institutions.

[44]See the Bank Recovery and Resolution Directive (BRRD) (Directive 2014/59/EU) and Regulation (EU) No 806/2014 establishing uniform rules and a uniform procedure for the resolution of credit institutions and certain investment firms in the framework of a Single Resolution Mechanism (SRM) and a Single Resolution Fund (SRF). See also the Agreement on the transfer and mutualisation of contributions to the Single Resolution Fund (IGA) signed by all EU Member States, except Sweden and the United Kingdom, on 21 May 2014.

[45]See COM(2015) 586 final—Proposal for a Regulation amending Regulation (EU) 806/2014 in order to establish a European Deposit Insurance Scheme.

markets,[46] have reduced further the risk of further sovereign debt restructuring operations in the euro area.

## 5 Is Sovereign-Debt Restructuring Still Necessary: Debt Sustainability Analysis and Access to Market Finance

Being this the case, the real question behind sovereign debt restructuring (stricto sensu) in the euro area, be it via OSI or via PSI, which has not been totally solved by the new economic governance framework, lies in the problem of debt sustainability. Debt Sustainability Analysis (DSA) is carried over by the EU Commission in the framework of the SGP preventive arm when assessing stability programmes and convergence programmes [articles 5.1, 2nd par. and 9.1, 2nd par. of Council Regulation (EC) No 1466/97, as amended by Regulation (EU) No 1175/2011]. DSA is also conducted by the EU Commission in the context of the Macroeconomic Imbalance Procedure (MIP) and by the IMF.[47]

According to article 13.1 (b) of the ESM Treaty, DSA is also conducted by the EU Commission, in liaison with the ECB and, when appropriate and possible, with the IMF, if a ESM Member requests for the financial assistance. DSA analysis is also performed for countries receiving financial assistance and subject to post-programme surveillance according to the *enhanced surveillance* framework set forth in Regulation (EU) No 472/2013.

Looking to the particular case of Portugal, the EU Commission analysis contained in the 26 May 2016 Assessment of the 2016 Stability Programme for Portugal,[48] in the Post-Program Surveillance Report of April 2016[49] and in the MIP Commission Staff Working Document of 26 February 2016[50] point to low risk in the short term but to medium term vulnerabilities due to sensitivity to macro-economic and financial-market shocks.[51]

---

[46]See the ECJ judgement of 16 June 2015, Case C-62/14, Gauweiler et al., where the OMT programme was deemed compatible with articles 119, 123(1), 127(1) (2) TFEU and articles 17–24 of the ESCB Statute.

[47]See https://www.imf.org/external/pubs/ft/dsa/index.htm

[48]See http://ec.europa.eu/economy_finance/economic_governance/sgp/convergence/index_en.htm

[49]See http://ec.europa.eu/economy_finance/publications/eeip/ip022_en.htm

[50]See http://ec.europa.eu/economy_finance/economic_governance/macroeconomic_imbalance_procedure/mip_reports/index_en.htm

[51]«**Risks for Portugal's capacity to service its debt to the European Financial Stability Mechanism (EFSM) and European Financial Stability Fund (EFSF) remain low in the short-term.** (...). In the medium to long-term, debt servicing risks will remain contained if Portugal shows greater resolve in fiscal consolidation and growth enhancing structural reforms. The debt sustainability analysis shows that following a moderate decline in the short term, the public debt-to GDP ratio stabilises in the medium-term at a high level and is vulnerable to macro-economic and financial-market shocks. Borrowing conditions for Portugal remain favourable, driven largely by European and global factors. However, financial markets have recently become

This assessment contrasts with the case of Greece, where in the framework of the third Economic Adjustment Program the debt sustainability analysis (DSA) carried out on 10 July 2015 pointed «*to serious concerns regarding the sustainability of Greece's public debt*» and «*to debt-mitigating measures that would be granted based on appropriate conditionality*».[52]

Given the characteristics of EMU, based on a single monetary policy and financial market integration, and taking into account the general principle of market integration, restructuring the public debt of a euro area Member State, via OSI or PSI, has to be seen as the last option to avoid default, namely when there is a strong case for unsustainability of government debt in the medium to long term. "Sovereign debt restructuring" is not a *panacea* and as deep economic and financial consequences, as can be seen in the case of Greece whose market access has been lost, depending on ESM financing. DSA is thus a key indicator to assess the evolution of the debt-to GDP ratio and to evaluate the risks and policies to follow in order to avoid debt restructuring.

## 6 Alternatives to Government Debt Restructuring in the Euro Area: The ESM Treaty as an Embryo for a European Union Treasury and for EU Joint Issuance of Public Debt

To conclude, there is one last question linked to the problem of sovereign debt restructuring in EMU: is the ESM Treaty an *embryo* for a European Union Treasury and for EU joint issuance of public debt? In our view the answer is positive.

If one looks back to May 2010 and to the solutions found to overcome the Greek debt crisis, first based on bilateral loans pooled by the EU Commission (the so-called "Greek Loan Facility"—GLF) for a total amount of 80 billion euros[53, 54] where the shares of participating Member States in the total loan were calculated using the adjusted ECB paid capital key, and later based on the European Financial Stability Facility (EFSF), incorporated by the euro area Member States on 7 June 2010 as a temporary crisis resolution mechanism, whose funding would come from taping the bond markets or from other financing arrangements, backed by

more volatile, making financing the high levels of sovereign debt more of a challenge for the government» (quotation taken from the Post-Program Surveillance Report of April 2016, p. 6).

[52]See http://ec.europa.eu/economy_finance/assistance_eu_ms/greek_loan_facility/pdf/debt_sustainability_analysis_en.pdf

[53]This amount was reduced by 2.7 billion euros, because Slovakia did not to participate in the GLF whilst Ireland and Portugal stepped down as they requested financial assistance as well.

[54]The financial assistance agreed by euro-area Member States was part of a joint package, with the IMF committing an additional 30 billion euros under a stand-by arrangement (SBA).

irrevocable and unconditional guarantees of the euro-area Member States,[55] proportionate to the ECB Capital subscription key, it seems clear that, even though for a special purpose (to provide financial assistance to euro area Member States without access to financial markets), a preliminary form joint issuance of public debt was on the making. It is clear from the EFSF Framework agreement[56] that there is no joint liability of the Guarantors and that each Guarantor is only liable for its commitments as set forth in annexes 1 and 2 [see article 2 (3) (6) of the EFSF Framework agreement]. However, the whole exercise of having other euro area Member States stepping in when another euro area Member State experiences financial difficulties and requests financial support represents the creation of a European financial backstop facility for the euro area that resembles a European Union Treasury.

The institution of the ESM as a permanent financial backstop facility for the euro area reinforces this function, although for a "limited purpose": the granting of financial assistance under strict conditionality to the benefit of ESM Members affected by severe financing problems, if indispensable to safeguard the financial stability of the euro area as a whole and of its Member States (see article 3 of the ESM Treaty).

There are four features of the EFSF/ESM framework that may expand its "limited purpose" as financial backstop:

- The first one is the transformation of a temporary mechanism (the EFSF) into a new "international financial institution" (see article 1.1 of the ESM Treaty). Although the ESM Treaty conceives such transformation as a means to avoid financial contagion and reaffirms that the first line of defence against confidence crises affecting the stability of the euro area lies in the "strict observance" of the "economic governance rules of the European Union" and on "sound and robust management of public finances" (see recitals 4 and 5 of the ESM Treaty) the sheer fact that such institution is created on a permanent basis might lead to changes in its purposes in accordance to the evolution of EMU[57];
- The second one is related to the modalities of financial assistance provided for in articles 14–18 of the ESM Treaty [(i) ESM precautionary financial assistance; (ii) Financial assistance for the re-capitalisation of financial institutions of an ESM Member; (iii) ESM loans to Members; (iv) Primary market support

[55]Greece, Ireland and Portugal have become "Stepping-Out Guarantors" upon their request for financial support from the EFSF. The aggregate of the active Guarantee Commitments for the Guarantors which are not Stepping-Out Guarantors was 726,000.00 million euros.

[56]Available at http://www.efsf.europa.eu/about/legal-documents/index.htm

[57]As suggested by Bénassy-Quéré (2016) "*In the medium term, the ESM could be turned into a fully-fledged treasury that would manage a crisis fund (the ESM itself) and possibly other funds (unemployment insurance, investment, refugees…)*". See also the proposal made by de Grauwe and Ji (2016) of using the ESM as a "stabilization fund" to finance Member States deficits during recessions (buying "national government bonds and issue an equivalent amount of ESM-bonds (Eurobonds) backed by the participating member countries") and sell government bonds during booms ("buy back the ESM-bonds and sell the national bonds into the bond markets") and the suggestion of Micossi et al. (2016) that the ESM could be used as a backstop to the proposed European Deposit Insurance Scheme (EDIS).

facility; (v) Secondary market support facility]. These modalities of financial assistance may be reviewed by the ESM Board of Governors as foreseen in article 19 of the ESM Treaty;
- The third one has to do with EFSF/ESM funding. By taping the bond markets EFSF/ESM actually create a sort of *intermediation finance* to Member States banned from market access (adding operational costs and margin—see article 20 of the ESM Treaty). Such intermediation is accompanied by a macroeconomic adjustment programme that should allow Member States to regain market access (the problem lies in the failure of the adjustment program and in the transformation of intermediation financing into *principal financing*);
- That brings us to the last feature of the EFSF/ESM framework that may expand its "limited purpose" as financial backstop: EFSF/ESM bonds are backed by guarantees, paid capital and further capital calls upon Member States, which resemble a form of joint issuance of public debt.[58]

Taken together, these features might pave the way to the creation of a European Union Treasury (as mentioned in the Five Presidents' Report, but not necessarily addressing the ESM) since the ESM is a permanent backstop facility that may evolve to other forms of financial support to euro area Member States, as can be seen from the third economic adjustment program for Greece. In this sense the ESM can also be seen as an alternative to government debt restructuring in the euro area.

## 7 Final Remarks

To sum up, the new economic governance framework, including the ESM, Banking Union in its triple dimension and central bank intervention via the OMT programme, make it less probable for government debt restructuring operations in the euro area, although such operations, be it via OSI or PSI, would not follow any standardised procedures, but would take place in a rather ad hoc or contractual fashion.

## References

Audit M (2014) A debt restructuring mechanism for European sovereigns: an emerging idea. In: Paulus CG (ed) A debt restructuring mechanism for european sovereigns. C. H. Beck, Hart, Nomos, München, pp 218–220

Bauer K-A, Cahn A, Kenadjian PS (eds) (2013) Collective action clauses and the restructuring of sovereign debt. De Gruyter, Berlin

[58]On this subject-matter is important to look at the EU/EFSF/ESM presentations to investors, available at http://ec.europa.eu/economy_finance/eu_borrower/documents/eu_investor_presentation_en.pdf and http://www.esm.europa.eu/investors/index.htm, respectively.

Bénassy-Quéré A (2016) Fixing a sovereignless currency. Available at http://voxeu.org/article/fixing-sovereignless-currency
Billington D (2014) European collective action clauses. In: Lastra RM, Bucheit L (eds) Sovereign debt management. Oxford University Press, Oxford, pp 399–416
Bruegel (2011) A European mechanism for sovereign debt crisis resolution: a proposal. available at http://bruegel.org/2010/11/a-european-mechanism-for-sovereign-debt-crisis-resolution-a-proposal/
Chiotellis AP (2014) Sovereign debt restructuring and the internal legal framework: the Greek experience. In: Paulus CG (ed) A debt restructuring mechanism for sovereigns—do we need a legal procedure. C. H. Beck, Hart, Nomos, München, p 105 ss
De Grauwe P (2011) The governance of a fragile eurozone. CEPS Working Document No. 346, May 2011. Available at https://www.ceps.eu/publications/governance-fragile-eurozone
De Grauwe P (2013) Design failures in the eurozone—can they be fixed? Economic Papers 491, Apr 2013
De Grauwe P, Ji Y (2016) Flexibility versus stability a difficult trade-off in the eurozone. CEPS Working Document No. 422, Apr 2016
De Gregorio Merino A (2012) Legal developments in the economic and monetary union during the debt crisis: the mechanism of financial assistance. CMLR 49, pp 1613–1646
European Central Bank (2005) Financial integration in the euro area. https://www.ecb.europa.eu/pub/pdf/other/indicatorsfinancialintegration200509en.pdf?006e28de34fde544bdbd77a82c66c291.
European Central Bank (2011) The monetary policy of the ECB, 3rd edn. European Central Bank, Frankfurt
Gros D (2014) Restructuring in a monetary union—economic aspects. In: Lastra RM, Buchheit LC (eds) Sovereign debt management. Oxford University Press, Oxford, pp 195–204
Gros D (2016) IMF go home. Project Syndicate, 8 Jun 2016
Group of Ten—The resolution of sovereign liquidity crises. Available at http://www.bis.org/publ/gten03.htm
Issing O (2008) The euro: a currency without a state. CFS Working Paper No. 2008/51. http://nbn-resolving.de/urn:nbn:de:hebis:30-62303
Kenadjian PS (2013) The aggregation clause in euro area government securities: game changer or flavour of the month? Background and the Greek experience. In: Kenadjian PS, Cahn A, Bauer K-A (eds) Collective action clauses and the restructuring of sovereign debt. De Gruyter, Berlin, p 125 ss
Kopf C (2011) Restoring financial stability in the euro area. CEPS Policy Brief No. 237, 15 Mar 2011. Available at https://www.ceps.eu/publications/restoring-financial-stability-euro-area
Kopf C (2013) Sovereign debt restructuring: lessons from history. In: Kenadjian PS, Cahn A, Bauer K-A (eds) Collective action clauses and the restructuring of sovereign debt. De Gruyter, Berlin, pp 153–157
Krueger AO (2002) A new approach to sovereign debt restructuring. IMF, Washington, DC
Lojsch DH, Rodríguez-Vives M, Slavík M (2011) The size and composition of government debt in the euro area. ECB Occasional Paper Series No. 132, Oct 2011
Louis JV (2010) Guest editorial: the no-bailout clause and rescue packages. CMLR 47, pp 975–986
Micossi S, Bruzzone G, Cassella M (2016) Fine-tuning the use of bail-in to promote a stronger EU financial system. CEPS Special Report No. 136, Apr 2016
Moody's Investors Service (2012) Unilateral action threatened by Greece is also available to other sovereigns. 6 Feb 2012
Olivares-Caminal R (2014) Statutory sovereign debt resolution mechanisms. In: Lastra RM, Bucheit L (eds) Sovereign debt management. Oxford University Press, Oxford, pp 333–358
Paulus CG (2013) A resolvency proceeding for defaulting sovereigns. In: Kenadjian PS, Cahn A, Bauer K-A (eds) Collective action clauses and the restructuring of sovereign debt. De Gruyter, Berlin, pp 181–205

Pipkorn J (1994) Legal arrangements in the treaty of Maastricht for the effectiveness of the economic and monetary union. CMLR 31, p 275
Ruffert M (2011) The European debt crisis and European Union law. CMLR 48, pp 1777–1806
Sáinz de Vicuña A (2013) Identical collective action clauses for different legal systems: a european model. In: Kenadjian PS, Cahn A, Bauer K-A (eds) Collective action clauses and the restructuring of sovereign debt. De Gruyter, Berlin, pp 15–24
Sáinz de Vicuña A (2014) Restructuring in a monetary union—legal aspects. In: Lastra RM, Buchheit LC (eds) Sovereign debt management. Oxford University Press, Oxford, p 192
Smits R (1997) The European central bank. Kluwer, The Hague, pp 77–78
Wolswijk G, de Haan J (2005) Government debt management in the euro area—recent theoretical developments and changes in practices. European Central Bank Occasional Paper Series No. 25, Mar 2005
Wyplosz C (2016) The common currency: more complicated than it seems. In: Badinger H, Nitsch V (eds) The Routledge handbook of the economics of European integration. Routledge, Basingstoke, pp 103–118

## *Court Cases*

ECJ judgement of 27 November 2012, Case C-370/12, *Thomas Pringle v. Government of Ireland*
ECJ judgement of 16 June 2015, Case C-62/14, *Peter Gauweiler and Others v. Deutscher Bundestag*

# Part III
# New Perspectives for Macroeconomic Stabilizers in the European Union

# The Crisis Management of the ECB

**Fritz Breuss**

**Abstract** A succession of crises—the global financial and economic crisis (GFC) in 2008, the Great Recession of 2009 and the following Euro crisis—forced the economic policy to action. After the fiscal policy has used up its ammunition in the fight against the effects of the 2009 recession, monetary policy remained the only expansive player in the political arena. The European Central Bank (ECB) responded—like the other major central banks in the world—first with a zero interest rate policy, then by "quantitative easing". However, the ECB acted in comparison with the Fed with some delay.

In the evaluation of the crisis management of the ECB must clearly state that it has missed its own inflation target of 2 %. However, it has been successful in reducing the high government bond yields after the famous "Whatever it takes" speech by ECB President Draghi in July 2012 and the subsequent announcement of the OMT (outright monetary transactions) programme.

Whether the quantitative easing program by the ECB in the years 2015/2017 with a view to achieving the primary objective, namely an inflation rate of 2 % will be successful is an open question. Simulations with the Global Economic Model of Oxford Economics indicate that the quantitative easing policy will achieve the inflation target but with a great delay. The impact on the real economy will not be as large as QE experiments in the USA. Other unintended effects—such as the formation of bubbles on the stock markets—are greater than the intended effects.

**JEL Classification** E32 • E44 • E52 • F15 • C52

F. Breuss
WU Vienna University of Economics and Business and Austrian Institute of Economic Research, Vienna, Austria
e-mail: Fritz.Breuss@wu.ac.at; Fritz.Breuss@wifo.ac.at



N. da Costa Cabral et al. (eds.), *The Euro and the Crisis*, Financial and Monetary Policy Studies 43, DOI 10.1007/978-3-319-45710-9_13

# 1 Different Rapid Responses to the Crises

A succession of crises—the global financial and economic crisis (GFC) in 2008, the Great Recession of 2009 and the following Euro crisis—forced the economic policy to action. After the fiscal policy—due to the accumulation of unsustainable high debt—had shot its "Keynesian" powder in the fight against the negative impact of the recession in 2009 (see European Commission 2009; OECD 2009a, b; Breuss et al. 2009), monetary policy remained the only expansive player in the political arena. The US Fed reacted probably fastest compared to the other dominant central banks of the world. Shortly after the collapse of Lehman Brothers in September 2008 it reduced the benchmark interest rate (federal funds rate) to near zero, and started with the use of unconventional measures, such as "quantitative easing"(QE). Since the expansionary monetary policy was accompanied by a stimulating fiscal policy, the US economy recovered faster and more sustainable from the Great Recession than Europe. Not least thanks to the then Fed Chairman Ben Bernanke (2015), who had studied thoroughly the Great Depression, this time the Fed responded quickly and more correctly than in the Great Depression in the thirties. Generally, in contrast, however, to the "Great Depression" in the 1930s the policy reaction of the industrial countries was much better and more appropriate in the present crisis (see Eichengreen 2015; Baldwin and Giavazzi 2015; BIS 2015; Breuss 2016).

The European Central Bank (ECB) also responded to the crises with conventional (zero interest rate policy) and unconventional measures (QE), but with a significant delay to the US Fed. in September 2014 the ECB set its base interest rate (main refinancing operation rate) to near zero and a QE program was launched in March 2015. In the euro zone, monetary policy was expansionary, but the fiscal policy after the euro crisis starting in 2010 (also due to the tightening of the fiscal rules: Sixpack; fiscal pact, etc.) switched to austerity. Therefore, the recovery from the Great recession was only short-lived and culminated already back into a "double dip" recession in 2011–2013. The lack of economic policy coordination was the main reason while the economy of the euro zone, unlike the US still barely reached pre-crisis levels of real GDP.

The present analysis of ECB's crisis management and its evaluation focuses primarily on its ability to reach its self-defined goal. In contrast to the Fed, which has two objectives (price stability and full employment), the EU Treaty (TFEU, Article 127) assigns the ECB only one primary goal: "The primary objective of (monetary policy) the European System of Central Banks (hereinafter referred to as 'the ESCB') shall be to maintain price stability. Without prejudice to the objective of price stability, the ESCB shall support the general economic policies in the Union (secondary objective) with a view to contributing to the achievement of the objectives of the Union as laid down in Article 3 of the Treaty on European Union."

## 2 Is the ECB a "Crisis Winner"?

The primary objective of the ECB—as part of the European System of Central Banks—is to maintain price stability (Article 127, TFEU). For this purpose, it lays down and executes a monetary policy, uniform for the whole euro area. In the wake of various crises and the reform of the governance of Economic and Monetary Union (EMU—tightening of fiscal policy coordination; Banking Union) the ECB has accrued more and more tasks. Therefore, one could call the ECB a "crisis winner". Her dominant role results from the fact that due to the crises she acts more and more as a "multitasker":

1. Common monetary policy: The diverse crises have amplified the already existing heterogeneity of the euro area (no "European business cycle") and lead to split of the euro zone economy in a more or less prosperous core (or north) and a debt-driven periphery (the South). This constellation makes the main task of the ECB, namely the implementation of a single monetary policy for the euro area increasingly difficult.
2. Banking Supervision: Since November 2014, the ECB within the framework of the first stage of the European Banking Union (Single supervisory mechanism—SSM; see ECB 2014b; Breuss et al. 2015) monitors the largest banks in the euro area.
3. Troika: As part of the rescue operations in the euro zone, the ECB is part of the Troika (together with the European Commission and the IMF). The ESM Treaty mentions the ECB several times as an important partner (e.g. "... the Commission, in liaison with the ECB...") when negotiating, with the ESM Member States concerned, a memorandum of understanding (an "MoU") (see Article 13) for the so-called programme countries (earlier, Cyprus, Greece, Ireland, Portugal and Spain; now Greece is the remaining country within a bail-out programme of the euro area).

This "multi-tasking" the ECB is widely criticized because it could jeopardize the actual main task, the implementation of the single monetary policy in complete independence (Article 282, TFEU). In particular, with the banking supervision and especially through participation in the Troika, there is the risk of interference in the fiscal policies of the Member States of the euro zone. Some observers (e.g. the German Council of Economic Experts 2012) suspected that with this multitasking role the ECB could come into conflict with its competence for monetary policy according to the EU Treaty.

# 3 Successes and Failures of the ECB

## 3.1 *"Whatever It Takes"*

The ECB scored a great success in bringing down government bond yields which got out of control since the outbreak of the Euro crisis in 2010. In particular, the yields of government bonds of the peripheral countries—especially those of Greece, but also Ireland, Portugal and Spain—jumped up considerably. After the famous "Whatever-it-takes" speech by ECB President Mario Draghi in London in July 2012 and the subsequent announcement of the OMT program[1] the spreads of yields on euro government bonds got significantly smaller.

After the start of EMU, the financial markets cultivated the so-called "no bail-out illusion", meaning that buyers of government bonds from euro zone countries believed that the default risk of all countries belonging to the euro zone would be practically equal—namely zero. Only after the outbreak of the euro crisis, triggered by implausible budget figures in Greece in late 2009, the financial markets (and ratings agencies) realized the differences of country risks and began to rate the default risk realistically. Initially this led to an overshooting and the spreads in yields rose sharply. Those of peripheral countries scored strongly upwards (most in Greece), while the core countries—particularly in Germany—even declined. The Draghi speech plus the OMT announcement ended this spook and resulted in a nearly realistic assessment of the risks of sovereign defaults by member states of the euro zone.

## 3.2 *ECB Lost Control Over Inflation*

In contrast to the success of a successful announcement policy of the ECB (OMT program) the ECB failed in the field of its main task, namely the maintenance of price stability according to its own definition.

Since 2003, the ECB has achieved the self-defined objective of achieving an annual inflation rate of the Harmonized Index of Consumer Prices (HICP) of "below but close to 2 %" in the medium term. Since 1999—according to Eurostat—the inflation rate was 1.81 %. In the period before the crisis

[1]The OMT program (Outright Monetary Transactions) was strictly tied to reform conditions and was designed essentially only for the program euro-zone countries (Greece, Ireland, Portugal and Spain; see ECB 2012). However, no program countries has made use of the OMT program. Nevertheless, OMT has been the subject of a major dispute (complaint: the ECB is pursuing "Public Finance"), first raised before the German Constitutional Court and (after request for a preliminary ruling) subsequently was decided by the European Court of Justice. On 16 June 2015, the ECJ ruled in Case C-62/14 Gauweiler and others that the OMT program is compatible with EU law. Now the Federal Constitutional Court (Bundesverfassungsgericht) had to make a final decision.

(1999–2008) the average annual inflation rate was 2.18 %. Before the start of EMU (1991–1998), the inflation rate was 2.62 %.

Since the Great Recession of 2009, however, the ECB has lost control of its self-imposed inflation target. On average, between 2009 and 2015 the rate of inflation was only 1.26 % with negative (deflation) phases 2009, 2015 and early in 2016.

Hidden behind the average rate of inflation of the euro area (February 2016 −0.3 %, March 2016 −0.1 %) there are large spreads between the Member States. Out of the 19 Euro area countries, in February 2016 still 11 member states exhibited a deflation and eight a slight inflation. The deepest deflation rates were in Cyprus (−2.2 %), Spain (−1 %) and Slovenia (−0.9 %). Austria and Malta observed the highest inflation rates with each 1 %.

## 3.3 *The Wrong Inflation Target?*

The ECB seems to have not only lost control of the inflation target, it also aims at the wrong inflation index. The definition of price stability (2 %) of the ECB aims to headline inflation of the HICP. However, it cannot control all components of total inflation, in particular the energy, commodity and food prices. These are set on the international commodities markets and thus are beyond the control of the ECB.

It would therefore make more sense if the ECB would only target core inflation (HICP excluding energy and food prices) as its price stability objective. Especially in times of strong fluctuations in the energy and commodities markets as 2008 (boom) and 2014/2015 (trough), core inflation would be closer to the self-imposed goal of price stability (see Fig. 1). The core inflation rate rose since the start of ECB's QE gradually: from 0.6 % in March 2015 to around 1.0 % in 1Q2016. Although one can see in this inflation increase the traces of the unconventional intervention of the ECB, it is still too early to call this development a great success of the QE program of the ECB.

## 3.4 *Target Range Rather than Point Target*

The ECB could save the spasmodic attempt to achieve an inflation rate of just under 2 %, if she returned to the original (valid until 2003) inflation target, namely below 2 %. That would—as practiced by the Swiss National Bank—correspond a target range rather than a point target (see Fuster 2016).

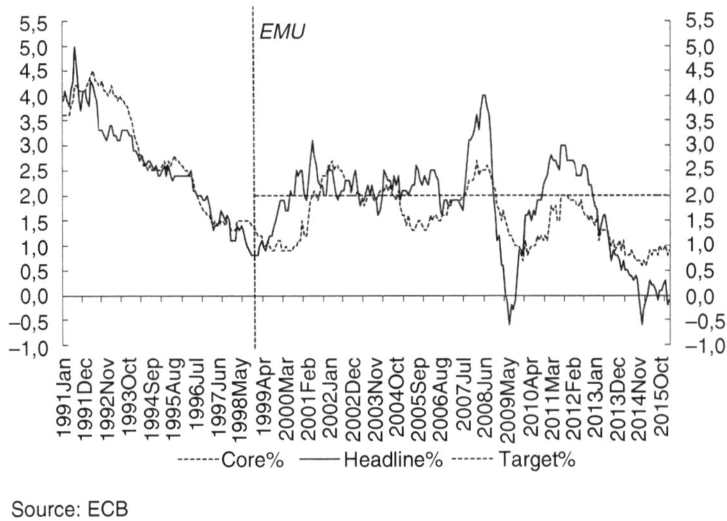


**Fig. 1** Euro area inflation rates—core and headline inflation (Annual percentage changes). Source: ECB

# 4 Lessons from the Great Depression

The collapse of Lehman Brothers on 15 September 2008—in stark contrast to the misbehavior of monetary policy during the Great Depression of the thirties—gave the central banks of the major industrialized countries the signal, to intervene expansionary without limits. Initially this was done with conventional and after they were exhausted with unconventional means.

## *4.1 From Conventional . . .*

When the subprime crisis of 2007 took its course, US Fed—even before the collapse of Lehman Brothers—responded with a reduction in its main interest rate (Federal Funds Rate—FFR). Starting from 5.25 % in 3Q2007 the Fed decreased the FFR steadily to 0–0.25 % in December 2008. The ECB responded only after a delay to the crisis.[2] In July 2008, she even increased its main policy rate for main refinancing operations (MRO) from 4 to 4.25 %. Only after the Lehman Brothers crash she began to reduce her interest rates gradually until the most recent monetary decision on March 2016 when the ECB decreased the MRO rate of the Eurosystem by five basis points to 0.00 % and, hence reached really the zero bound

[2]Since the inception of EMU in 1999, the ECB reacted always with a lag to the interest rate decisions of the Fed (see Breuss 2002).

of conventional monetary policy. The interest rate on the marginal lending facility has been decreased by five basis points to 0.25 %. The interest rate on the deposit facility was decreased by ten basis points to an "penalty rate" of −0.40 %.

Other major central banks (the Bank of England—BoE) reacted more quickly. The Bank of Japan (BoJ)—even before the GFC in 2008 and the Great Recession of 2009—tried (unsuccessfully so far) to fight deflation,

The near zero interest rate policy (or a policy at the zero lower bound—ZLB) of the national banks of the Western world in the last post-crises years one could also interpret as an inadvertent entry into Islamic banking. Its most important element is the prohibition of interest, also known as "riba".

## *4.2 . . . to Unconventional Measures*

Once the interest rates of the main central banks reached the zero level, they switched from conventional to unconventional measures (according to the ECB to nonstandard measures). The US Fed responded not only with conventional measures (interest rate cuts), but also with unconventional measures (especially QE) shortly after the collapse of Lehman Brothers. This was followed by the BoE, and much later, by the ECB (for an overview of monetary policy in the crisis, see Table 1).

Although Japan and the United States practiced the QE policy even before the crisis, only the Great Recession 2009 forced them to a strong expansion. The Fed and the BoE increased their QE programs up to 20 % and 25 % of GDP. The ECB only reached a level of 13 % of GDP. The BoJ—with the start of "Abenomics"—launched since 2013 a massive expansion of the QE program, which could be increased up to the end of 2017 to 90 % of GDP.

### 4.2.1 Intended and Unintended Impact of QE

As the monetary policy at the zero lower bound (ZLB) has become ineffective, practically all major central banks of the industrial world are applying unconventional measures (QE). As part of the QE policy the Central Banks buy private and government bonds. This increases the total assets of the Central Bank and the monetary base.[3] The QE policy has intended and unintended side effects.

QE intends to avoid deflation and should help to rise inflation (in the euro zone near to 2 %). Important is also to improve the transmission, i.e., the transmission of monetary easing into the banking sector: interest rates should decline, credit

[3]A short-cut version of QE would be "Helicopter money", firstly proposed by Milton Friedman (1969), where money is directly (not in the case of QE via bank lending) is transferred to consumers.

**Table 1** Monetary policy in the crisis—unconventional measures

| ECB | Fed | BoJ |
|---|---|---|
| 2008—Fixe-rate full allotment—FRFA | 2008—Term-Auction Facility—TAF; Term Securities Lending Facility—TSLF<br>2008/12—FFR down to 0–0.25 % | 2008—Securities Lending Facility—expansion |
| 2008/2009/2011—Long-term Refinancing Operations (6m, 1Y, 3Y)—LTRO | 2008—Primary Dealer Credit Facility—PDCF<br>Forward guidance | 2008—Outright purchases JGBs |
| 2009/2011/2014—Covered Bonds Purchase Programme (s)—CBPP<br>2010—Securities Markets Programme—SMP | 2008—Asset-Backed CP MMMF Liquidity Facility—AMLF (and MMIFF) | 2008—CP repo operations—expansion; Outright purchases CP |
| 2012—Outright Monetary Transactions (announcement)—OMT | 2008—Commercial Paper Funding Facility—CPFF | 2008—Special Funds-Supplying Operations to Facilitate Corp. Financing |
| 2013—Forward guidance<br>2013/11—MRO rate down to 0.25 % | 2009—Term Asset-Backed Securities Loan Facility (ABS CMBS)—TALF | 2009—Outright purchases Corporate Bonds |
| 2014—Targeted Long-term Refinancing Operations—TLTROs | 2009—Liquidity to credit markets—consumer, small businesses CMBS—TALF | 2010—Asset Purchase Programme—APP |
| 2014—ABS and Covered Bond Purchase Programme—ABSPP, CBPP | 2008/2010/2012—Large-scale Asset Purchases—QE1, QE2, QE3—LSAP | 2012—Loan Support Programme |
| 2015—Expanded Asset Purchase Programme—APP—QE: 3/2015 to 3/2017: 60 billion euros per months ("QE" = PSPP) | 2008/2011/2012/2013/2014 QE4—"tapering"<br>Forward guidance (qualitative and quantitative)<br>2015/12—phase-out of ultra-expansionary policy (FFR increases to 0.25–0.5 % | 2013—Quantitative and Qualitative Monetary Easing<br>(70 trillion Yen a year) under "Abenomics"<br>2014—Expansion of QE (80 trillion Yen a year) |
| 3/2016—ECB expands APP to 80 billion euros per month<br>MRO rate set to 0 %<br>New TLTRO II, maturity 4 years | | |

*ABCP* High-quality Asset-Backed Securities, *ABS* Asset-Backed Securities, *ABSPP* Asset-Backed Securities Purchase Programme, *AMLF* Asset-Backed Commercial Paper (CP) Money Market Mutual Fund Liquidity Facility, *APP* Asset Purchase Programme, *CBPP* Covered Bond Purchase Programme, *CMBS* Commercial Mortgage-Backed Securities, *FFR* Federal Funds Rate, *JGB* Japanese Government Bonds, *LSAP* Large-Scale Asset Purchases, *MMIFF* Money Market Investor Funding Facility, *MMMF* Money Market Mutual Funds, *MRO* Main Refinancing Operations, *PSPP* Public Sector Purchasing Programme, *SMP* Securities Markets Programme, *TALF* Term Asset-Backed Securities Loan Facility
Source: Constancio (2015a)

lending should increase. This should ultimately lead to a stimulation of the economy through greater investment, consumption and employment.

Unintended are the formation of bubbles on the stock markets, the distortion of prices in the financial markets (especially in the bond market), the deterioration of income distribution (debtor—private and state—win, savers lose[4]) and ultimately QE raises the European law questions whether the ECB does not engage in prohibited state financing.

### 4.2.2 Forward Guidance

In 2008, when the GFC began to evolve the Fed was the first central bank to introduce "forward guidance".[5] Forward guidance about the Federal Reserve's target for the federal funds rate should be a clear communication about the timing of its policy stance. The Fed has two objectives: maximum employment and two percent inflation.

Since December 2008, the Federal Reserve's target for the federal funds rate has been between 0 and 0.25 %. Through "forward guidance," the Federal Open Market Committee (FOMC) provides an indication to households, businesses, and investors about the stance of monetary policy expected to prevail in the future. By providing information about how long the Committee expects to keep the target for the federal funds rate exceptionally low, the forward guidance language can put downward pressure on longer-term interest rates and thereby lower the cost of credit for households and businesses and also help improve broader financial conditions.

Whereas the turnaround in conventional (interest rate) monetary policy announced in December 2015 was a successful example of good "forward guidance", the previous ad hoc announcement of "tapering" the QE programme (e.g. the scaling down of monthly bond purchases from before US$80 billion to 65 billion) by the former Fed Chairman Ben Bernanke in June 2013 was badly prepared. In January 2014 this winding down of monetary (QE) stimulus was implemented. The 2013–2014 Fed announcement relating to tapering of asset purchases had considerable reactions on the financial markets, in particular on the exchange rates, government bond yields, and stock prices for 21 emerging markets (see Mishra et al. 2014).[6]

---

[4]Zero interest rates lead on the one hand—via "financial repression" (see Reinhard and Sbrancia 2011; Reinhard et al. 2011)—to a creeping loss of savers (they earn returns below the rate of inflation) and on the other hand it can help to liquidate government debts, but it might also lead to large renewed expansions in debt.

[5]See: http://www.federalreserve.gov/faqs/money_19277.htm

[6]The impact of Fed's "tapering" (wind down the QE programme) and increase of its interest target rates will not only be restricted to the USA. During low-interest rate policy in the U.S. and Europe financial capital looked for more profitable investments in developing or BRICS countries. After the announcement and implementation of U.S. "tapering" of QE capital is flowing back into the industrial world causing problems in some of the developing or BRICS countries (incl. Turkey and

Since July 2013 the Governing Council of the European Central Bank (ECB) has been providing forward guidance on the future path of the ECB's policy interest rates conditional on the outlook for price stability (see ECB 2014a). Overall, the ECB's forward guidance is aimed at clarifying the Governing Council's assessment of the inflation outlook in the Euro area and its monetary policy strategy based on that assessment. The evidence suggests that forward guidance has so far served the ECB's intentions well by providing greater clarity on the Governing Council's conditional monetary policy orientation.

### *4.3 Transatlantic Divergence in Monetary Policy*

The crisis management of the ECB so far always lagged behind that of the Fed. This constellation can also be expected for the near future. While the ECB lowered its expansionary monetary policy in December 2015 and again in March 2016 by the reduction of her policy rates, the Fed already launched their phase-out of the ultra-expansionary monetary policy. On 16 December 2015 Janet Louise Yellen, since 1 February 2014 the new Chair of the Board of Governors of the Federal Reserve System (Fed) announced the turnaround of US monetary policy by increasing the Federal Funds Rate with a bandwidth of 0–0.25 % up to 0.25–0.50 %.

This first step towards normalization leads to a transatlantic divergence of monetary policy of the USA and the Euro Zone with unforeseeable consequences (weakening of the Euro; international capital flows towards USA).

## 5 Panel Estimation of Monetary Policy in the Crisis

The central banks of four countries are experiencing QE (in a broad sense) since the crisis of 2009, namely, Japan, the USA, UK and the Eurozone. In the following we estimated with a panel econometric approach the impact of QE in the four countries over the period 1Q2009–4Q2016. The database is the Global Economics Database of Oxford Economics.

According to the intended and unintended impact postulated in Sect. 4.2.1 we test which effects had the standard measure (interest rate cuts) and non-standard measures (QE programmes) on the major macroeconomic variables (GDP, long-term interest rates, credit expansion, inflation and on the stock market prices). The estimation results of Table 2 are the following:

---

Argentina; see NZZ 2014). Also in general, changes in Fed's target interest rates influence the rates on other national banks around the globe (see NZZ 2015).

**Table 2** Monetary policy in the crisis—impact on GDP, interest rates, credits, inflation and stock market prices (1Q2009–4Q2016)

| | Con-stant | Rcb | QE | LPR | D(U) | GDP | R2 |
|---|---|---|---|---|---|---|---|
| GDP1 | 0.96** | −1.87** | 0.03** | | | | 0.13 |
| GDP2 | −0.18 | −0.77** | 0.05** | 1.02** | | | 0.75 |
| GDP3 | 1.22** | −0.20** (R) | 0.01** | 0.91** | −0.55** D(D) | | 0.76 |
| Interest rate | 1.98** | 1.81** | −0.03** | | | | 0.78 |
| Credit1 | −1.57** | **1.17** | 0.09** | | | | 0.14 |
| Credit2 | −1.93** | −0.14 | 0.10** | | | 0.31** | 0.28 |
| Inflation1 | 0.41** | **1.27**** | 0.02** | | | | 0.32 |
| Inflation2 | 0.28 | **1.75**** | 0.02** | | −0.69 | | 0.06 |
| SMP1 | 5.79 | −10.60** | 0.21** | | | | 0.23 |
| SMP2 | 1.64 | −2.51 | 0.06 | | | 4.33** | 0.32 |

Bold = sign not in conformity with theory

Dependent variables: GDP = real GDP (% changes); Interest rate (R) = long-term interest rates (10-years government bond yields), Credit = loans to non-financial corporations (% change); Inflation = HICP inflation rate (%); SMP = stock market price index (% changes)

Explaining variables: QE = quantitative easing in % of GDP; Rcb = central bank's target interest rate (%); LPR = Labour productivity (% change); U = unemployment rate (%); D(U) = absolute change of the unemployment rate; D(D) = absolute change of the debt to GDP ratio; GDP = lagged by 2 quarters in explaining Credit2

Panel estimation with fixed country effects: four countries (Eurozone, Japan, UK, USA); period: 1Q2009–4Q2016; in the equation Credit2, real GDP enters with a lag of 2 quarters

**Statistically significant at 95 % and 99 % levels

GDP2 = Verdoorn's law; GDP3 = expanded GDP equation with monetary and fiscal policy explanations; Inflation2 = Phillips curve

Data source: Oxford Economics: Global Economics Database; own estimates with EViews 8

Standard policy: Interest rate policy of the four central banks do not yield clear-cut results. This may be due to the fact, that relative early after the GFC central bank's target interest rates were reduced to a zero-level bound (ZLB). Therefore, over the whole period, the influence of interest rate policy can hardly be measured. In the case of influencing real GDP, the interest rate, credit demand and stock market prices, the estimated coefficients reflect the correct theoretically expected sign. In some cases, the sign is not correct (in one version of the credit equation and in both inflation equations) and in both credit equation the coefficient is not significantly different from zero.

Non-standard policy: QE had in all cases the correct sign and (with the exception of one stock market equation) a significant influence. A 10 % increase of QE has increased real GDP only between 0.1 and 0.5 %—depending on the type of the estimated GDP equation (i.e. the QE multiplier is between 0.01 and 0.05), long-term interest rates (bond yields) came down by 0.3 %, credits expanded by 0.9–1.0 %, inflation increased by 0.2 %, and stock market prices were stimulated by around 2 %.

# 6 DSGE Model Evaluations of QE

There is already a considerable literature evaluating the QE policy of central banks, primarily in the case of the USA,[7] but also in the UK and Japan. Most studies use Dynamic Stochastic General Equilibrium (DSGE) models, others apply econometric time series techniques.

## 6.1 USA

A prototype DSGE model to analyse QE policy by the US Fed is those of Gertler and Karadi (2013), based on earlier work by Gertler and Karadi (2011) and Gertler and Kiyotaki (2011). Shortly after the meltdown of the shadow banking system that followed the Lehman failure in September 2008, the Federal Reserve initiated what is now known as QE1, followed by QE2 and QE3. The new policy measures have been large-scale asset purchases (LSAPs), known more generally as quantitative easing (QE).

In their DSGE model, Gertler and Karadi (2013) interpret LSAPs as reflecting central bank intermediation. If private intermediaries are constrained in their ability to borrow, LSAPs can matter. The net benefits from LSAPs can be positive even if the central bank is less efficient than the private sector in intermediating the assets. These net benefits are likely to be increasing in a financial crisis, since in this instance limits to private arbitrage are likely to be unusually tight.

Under different scenarios the authors come to the conclusion expected from QE policy: GDP, inflation and asset prices goes up as expected, the yields on long-term bonds go down.[8] Gertler and Karadi (2013) find a QE multiplier of around 0.4, i.e. government bond purchase of 2.5 % of GDP leads (in the ZLB scenario) to a short-term real GDP increase of 1.0 %. Under the scenario with flexible interest rates (Taylor rule), the QE multiplier is only 0.1 (which comes near to our panel estimation in Table 2).

As a rare exception, Song (2014)—with a DSGE model with financial frictions and labour market search—analyses the impact of the US LASP programme on the labour market. Among the policy objectives, unemployment rate is a crucial target to the US Fed. The bond purchasing (QE) policy has stronger effects on labour market and the security purchase policy creates more volatility to the unemployment rate. Both policies have effective short-run effect yet ineffective even

[7] A short history of US's unconventional monetary policy since the Great Recession in 2009 can be found in Williamson (2015a, b).

[8] These results are in line with time-series estimates of Gambacorta et al. (2011). Christensen and Rudebusch (2012) find a negative effect of the Federal Reserve's first LSAP program and the Bank of England's QE program of between 50 and 100 basis points on 10-year government bond yields.

negative long-run effect. Also, timing effects of asset purchase policy reactions are different.

## 6.2 UK

There are many empirical studies on the macroeconomic impact of British QE done by LSAP. Joyce and Spaltro (2014) show that during the first round of British QE the increase in the growth of the credit action was relatively small, though QE was statistically significant for bank lending dynamics.

Weale and Wieladek (2015) examine the impact of large scale asset purchase announcements of government bonds on real GDP and the CPI in the United Kingdom and the United States with a Bayesian VAR, estimated on monthly data from 2009M3 to 2014M5. The results suggest that an asset purchase announcement of 1 % of GDP leads to a statistically significant rise of 0.58 % (0.25 %) and 0.62 % (0.32 %) rise in real GDP and CPI for the US (UK). In the US, this policy is transmitted through the portfolio balance channel and a reduction in household uncertainty. In the UK, the policy seems to be mainly transmitted through the impact on investors' risk appetite and household uncertainty. Their results are more in favour of QE then previous ones based on the similar methodology (see Baumeister and Benati 2013).

Butt et al. (2014) by studying the bank lending channel (BLC), found that the QE of the Bank of England did not boost bank lending. But it is consistent with other studies which show that QE boosted aggregate demand and inflation. UK policymakers did not rely on QE to boost bank lending and the evidence lends support to the use of other policies, rather than QE, to attempt to improve the supply of credit. Schuder (2014) stipulates that generally effects of expansionary monetary policy during economic crises are ambiguous.

Practically all DSGE models [for an overview, see Caglar et al. (2011)] apply small open closed economy models. An exception is Pietrzak (2015). He evaluates QE programmes of the Bank of England with a small open economy DSGE (SOE) model [in an extension of the model by Gertler and Karadi (2013)]. He demonstrates that QE policy in a closed economy model delivers much higher effects on real GDP, inflation and bond yields than in a SOE model with spillovers from and to other countries.[9] The QE multiplier in a closed model is 0.6, in a SOE model 0.3. A QE impulse of 14 % of GDP leads to an increase in real GDP in the first case of 9 %, in the second case of only 4 %.[10]

[9]For an econometric analysis of spill overs from monetary policies (interest rate and QE) in Europe and the USA to Mexico, see Morais et al. (2015).

[10]Falagiarda (2013), estimates the macroeconomic effects of QE with a DSGE approach for the US and the UK. His findings indicate that large asset purchases of QE2 in the US had a peak effect on long-term rates in annualized terms of around −63 basis points, on the level of real GDP of 0.92 %, and on inflation of 0.37 percentage points. In the UK, the preferred model specification suggests

### 6.3 The Euro Area

The hitherto QE literature was primarily concentrated on countries with a longer tradition in this kind of unconventional monetary policy, in the USA and in the UK. As the ECB is lagging behind this tradition the respective economic literature is not very much developed. Dedola et al. (2013), based on work by Gertler and Karadi (2011, 2013) develop a two-country DSGE model in order to study the spill overs to others countries of QE programmes executed in one country (Euro area) and the effects of international policy coordination. Due to the international transmission of the monetary policy in one country to others this implies that, under some circumstances, international coordination of unconventional policies may be especially important. On the other hand, gains from cooperation should not be expected to be much larger for unconventional policies than for more standard policies.

## 7 A New Evaluation of ECB's QE Since 2015

Because of considerable limitation so DSGE model simulations, we evaluate the most recent QE policy of the ECB with the Global Economic Model of Oxford Economics. Most DSGE models evaluating QE policies are one-country models, mostly closed economy models. As Dedola et al. (2013) have shown, international spillovers have to be taken into account. Furthermore, there are differences in the impact of QE in closed and SOE models as Pietrzak (2015) has demonstrated. In the case of the Euro area with a heterogenous set of member states, it would be necessary to evaluate the impact of ECB's QE not only for the average of the Euro area but for each Member State separately. The DSGE model technique, however, reaches very fast its limits with the three-country case (see Breuss and Fornero 2009). Whatever DSGE model type one take, it seems as if the macroeconomic impact of QE is overestimated.

### 7.1 ECB's QE Program 2015–2017

On 22 January 2015, the Governing Council decided that asset purchases—the program initiated on 4 September 2014—should be expanded to include a secondary markets public sector asset purchase program (hereinafter the "PSPP"; see ECB 2015). Under the PSPP the NCBs, in proportions reflecting their respective shares in the ECB's capital key, and the ECB may purchase outright eligible marketable debt

that the first phase of the APF programme had a peak effect on long-term rates of −69 basis points, on the level of real GDP of 1.25 %, and on inflation of 0.49 percentage points.

securities from eligible counterparties on the secondary markets. This decision was taken as part of the single monetary policy in view of a number of factors that have materially increased the downside risk to the medium-term outlook on price developments, thus jeopardising the achievement of the ECB's primary objective of maintaining price stability. The ECB does not call its Expanded Asset Purchase Programme (APP) explicitly a quantitative easing (QE) program.[11] It consists of three components:

(a) the third covered purchase program (CBPP3),
(b) the asset-backed securities purchase program (ABSPP), and
(c) the public sector purchase program (PSPP).

As of March 2015, in terms of the size of the PSPP, the ABSPP and the CBPP3, the liquidity provided to the market by the combined monthly purchases was initially planned to amount to 60 billion euros.[12] The ECB (2015) intended to carry out the purchases until the end of September 2016 (from March 2015 to September 2016 totalling 1140 billion euros).[13]

On 3 December 2015 the ECB decided to extend the asset purchase programme (APP). The monthly purchases of 60 billion euros under the APP are now intended to run until the end of March 2017 (totalling 1500 billion euros), or beyond, if necessary.

On 10 March 2016 the ECB decided to extend further the asset purchase programme (APP). The monthly purchases under the asset purchase programme have been expanded to 80 billion euros starting in April. This increases the total amount of ECB's QE program from March 2015 to March 2017 to 1740 billion euros.

To ensure the continued smooth implementation of the asset purchases, on March 2016 the ECB also decided to increase the issuer and issue share limits for the purchases of securities issued by eligible international organisations and multilateral development banks from 33 to 50 %. Further, the ECB decided to include investment-grade euro-denominated bonds issued by non-bank corporations established in the euro area in the list of assets that are eligible for regular purchases under a new corporate sector purchase programme.

---

[11]Constancio (2015b) calls only the PSPP a so-called QE programme. For a detailed description of ECB's QE program, see Claeys et al. (2015).

[12]ECB's documentation of the ongoing purchases under the Expanded Asset Purchase Programme (APP), See: https://www.ecb.europa.eu/mopo/implement/omt/html/index.en.html

[13]Cœuré (2015) discusses the concerns about the potential scarcity of bonds in the Euro area over the lifetime of the programme. Indeed, the European Commission forecasts that the aggregate euro area public budget deficit will fall to −2.2 % in 2015 and −1.9 % in 2016. As a result, the net issuance (defined as new debt minus redemptions) of medium- and long-term securities by the euro area debt management offices (DMOs) in 2015 was expected to be around 200 billion euros.

## 7.2 Macro Model Simulations of ECB's QE

As an alternative approach to the usually applied DSGE models we use the Global Economic Model of Oxford Economics to analyse the impact of ECB's QE programme over the years 2015 and 2017.[14] This is a fully integrated global economic model where the individual country models (of 47 countries and some aggregates, like the Euro Zone) are fully lined through global assumptions about trade, exchange rates, competitiveness, capital markets, interest rates, commodity prices and internationally traded goods and services. The rest of the world economy is covered in six trading blocs so that global GDP and trade are fully modelled.

In particular, we are interested in the impact of ECB's QE programme on the Euro area and its Member States as well as on spill overs to third countries. A specific feature of the Oxford model is that it not only models standard ECB monetary policy (the reaction on interest rate changes as of the Main Refinancing Operation rate) but also deals with non-standard instruments, like QE for the ECB and major industrial countries. QE feeds directly into the long-term interest rate and the credit conditions of private banks and hence, leading to impulses for investment and consumption and lastly to GDP.

### 7.2.1 Model Assumptions

We simulate the concrete QE programme of the ECB, announced in January 2015 and implemented in March 2015 plus the extensions announced on 3 December 2015 and on 16 March 2016. The size of PSPP amounts to monthly purchases of government bonds of 60 billion euros from March 2016 to March 2016. From April 2016 to March 2017 we consider the extension to 80 billion euros monthly puchases. The programme runs until March 2017 and totals then 1740 billion euros. As the Oxford model is a quarterly model we implement this programme as follows: Stating with 1Q2015 we input into the model 60 billion euros, then from 2Q2015 to 1Q2016 in each quarter 18 billion euros. From 2Q2016 to 1Q2017 we input 240 billion euros in each quarter which over nine quarters cumulates to the respective amount of 1740 billion euros. The relative size of the QE programme starts with 0.6 % in 1Q2015 and increases to 2.2 % in 1Q2017. The inputs for the QE simulations run until 1Q2017, the simulation results are presented until 4Q2020 in order to see what happens if the ECB stops its QE policy.

[14]See: http://www.oxfordeconomics.com/forecasts-and-models/countries/scenario-analysis-and-modeling/global-economic-model/overview

### 7.2.2 Model Results

Generally, our impact results are modest compared to other exercises with DSGE models for the USA. The novelty of our approach is that we are able to quantify the effects not only for the aggregate of the Euro area but also for the individual Member States. Furthermore, we are able to study the spill overs to third countries.

1. The intended impact of ECB's QE on macroeconomic variables
   As discussed earlier, QE policy can have intended effects, but may also lead to unintended impacts. In Fig. 2 we have depicted the intended impact on real GDP, interest rates, loans and inflation. As in reality, the QE policy does not transmit into the intended effects immediately. In contrast to simulations with DSGE models (e.g. Gertler and Karadi 2013) the QE stimulus does not have an immediate impact on the macro economy, rather it takes time. In our simulation ECB's QE program reaches the peak impact on real GDP only in 1Q2017 with a cumulative increase of 0.17 %. In the scenario with ZLB (the MRO of the ECB is kept constant at zero level throughout the simulation period) the GDP effect would be—similar to similations by Gertler and Karadi (2013)—somewhat higher, by 0.03 % There is, however an immediate impact on long-term interest rates (yield of government bonds). They go down immediately by 0.10 % but jump back after the run out of the QE program. The impact on loans to non-financial institutions continuously increase—even after the run out of the QE program—and will reach a cumulative increase of nearly 0.20 % in 2020. The major target, however, the increase of inflation, firstly takes time to be realized and, secondly will exhibit its expected impact only in the long-run; due to the QE impulse, inflation will only increase cumulatively by 0.30 % in 2020.

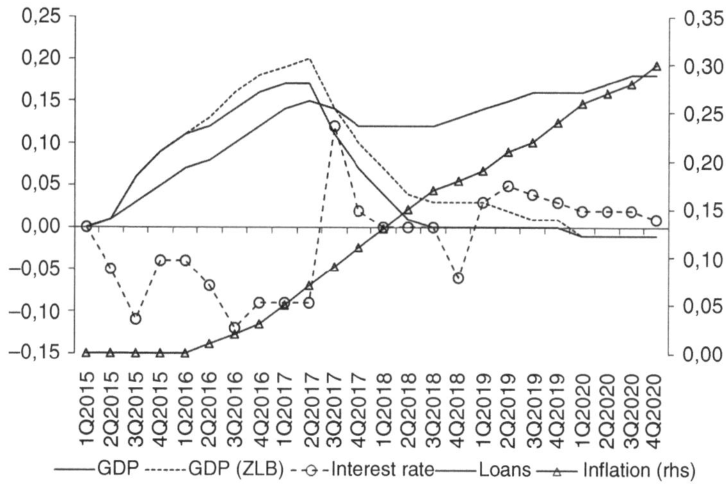


**Fig. 2** ECB's QE: Intended macroeconomic impact in the Eurozone (Cumulative deviations from baseline in %). Inflation is depicted on the right scale. Source: Simulations with the Oxford Economic World model

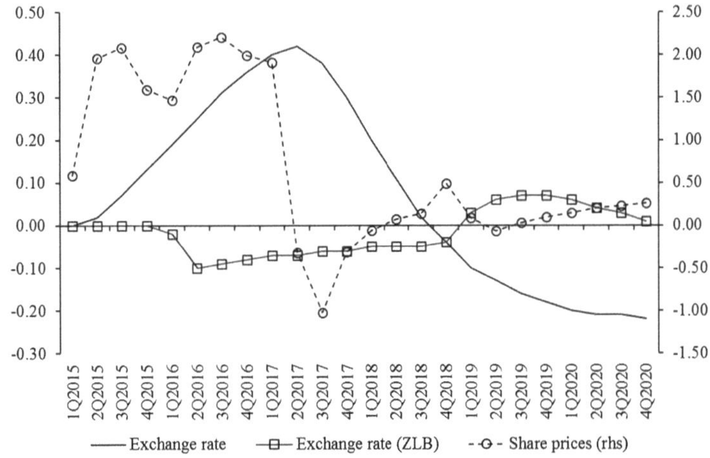


Shares prices are depicted on the right scale.

Source: Simulations with the Oxford Economic World model.

**Fig. 3** ECB's QE: Unintended macroeconomic impact in the Eurozone (Cumulative deviations from baseline in %). Shares prices are depicted on the right scale. Source: Simulations with the Oxford Economic World model

2. The unintended impact of ECB's QE on macroeconomic variables
   QE will probably also have an unintended impact on e.g. the exchange rate and share prices. Share prices are influenced immediately by around 0.4 % and collapse after the end of the QE program (see Fig. 3). One might expect that the monetary stimulation by QE would lead to ad depreciation of the Euro vis à vis the US dollar. In our simulations this effect is only true in the ZLB scenario. In the scenario with flexible interest rates (where the endogenous adjustment is executed via a Taylor rule) ECB's QE policy even leads to an appreciation of the Euro (see Fig. 3).
3. Spillovers to other Euro area and third countries
   The advantage of the Oxford World Model is that it allows not only to study the effects of QE policy in the country where it is executed but also to study the spillovers to other countries. In the case of ECB's QE the impact is not only interesting for the average of the Eurozone but also for its member states. In the following simulations we depict only the results for the flexible interest rate scenario for some selected Eurozone member states.
   In the large Eurozone countries, Germany and France the impact of ECB's QE on real GDP is more or less in line with the Eurozone average (see Fig. 4). However, a small core country, Austria may expect much weaker GDP effects than the Eurozone average.

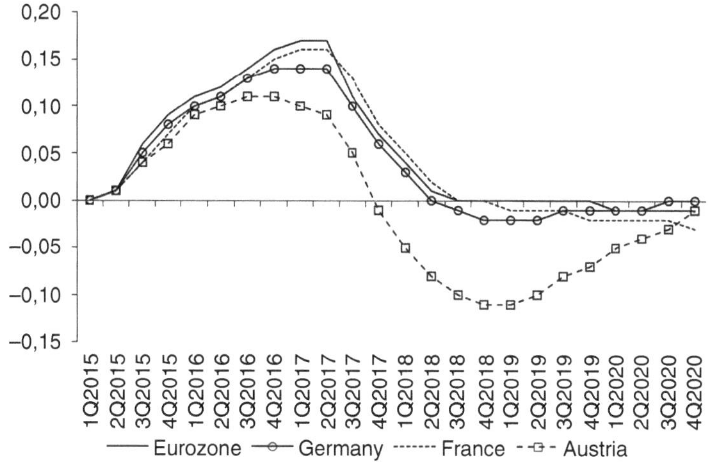


**Fig. 4** ECB's QE: Impact on real GDP in the core countries of the Eurozone (Cumulative deviations from baseline in %). Flexible interest rate scenario. Source: Simulations with the Oxford Economic World model

As it is probably intended by the ECB its QE policy is more effective in the periphery countries of the Eurozone (see Fig. 5). In particular, the additional impulse to the GDP of Greece and Spain is above average of the Eurozone.

The spillovers to third countries are much weaker than those within the Eurozone. ECB's QE will have only a slight positive GDP effect in the UK (in the peak of 1Q2017 of 0.06 %), whereas the USA GDP is only marginally influenced by ECB's QE (0.01 %).

4. QE multipliers in comparison

The actual development since the start of ECB's QE in March 2015 indicates that the intended impact on the Eurozone economy did not yet occur. Inflation is still subdued, real GDP growth in the Eurozone is weak, only some signs of hope are the slight increase in bank lending to private households and non-financial corporations (see ECB 2016). It seems therefore that the QE multiplier on real GDP (i.e. the impact of a 1 % of GDP increase in QE on the growth rate of real GDP) is much weaker (and has a long lag) than simulated with DSGE models. As reported earlier—in DSGE models—the QE multiplier on real GDP is in the range of 0.1–0.4 for the USA and 0.2–0.6 for the UK.

In our simulations with the Oxford World model the QE multiplier on real GDP is 0.08 (in the flexible interest rate scenario) and 0.09 (in the ZLB scenario). These moderate multipliers are closer but somewhat higher than the estimated multipliers for the period 2009–2016 in Table 2. They range from 0.01 to 0.05.

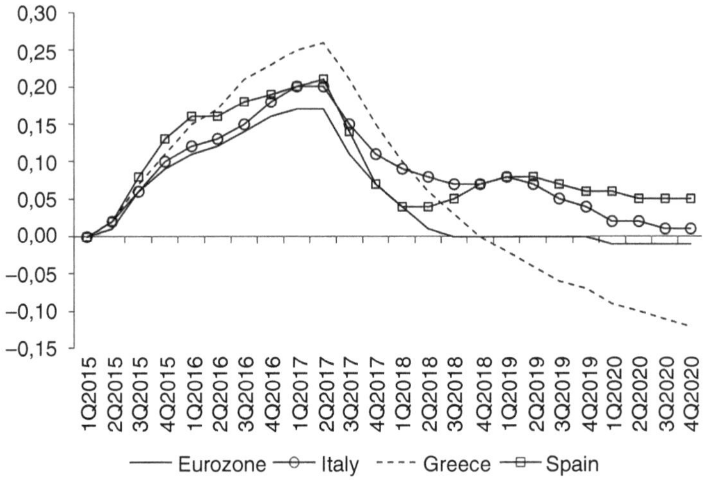


**Fig. 5** ECB's QE: Impact on real GDP in the periphery countries of the Eurozone (Cumulative deviations from baseline in %). Flexible interest rate scenario. Source: Simulations with the Oxford Economic World model

# 8 Conclusions

All major central banks of the industrial world have responded to the global financial and economic crisis (GFC) in 2008 and the Great Recession of 2009 with a very expansionary monetary policy. These are the lessons of the Great Depression of the thirties, when the Federal Reserve slammed on the brakes and caused a prolongation of the crisis. The ECB responded to the crisis with an expansionary monetary policy—though delayed compared to the US Fed. The ECB gained considerable power in the crises (GFC and Euro crisis since 2010). Therefore, one could describe the ECB even as a "crisis winner". It gathered—in addition to the core task of monetary policy—more and more tasks. By taking over the banking supervision as part of the European banking union and by participating in the rescue operations (in the Troika) in the peripheral (program) countries of the Euro area, the ECB became the "multitasker".

A preliminary assessment of the crisis management of the ECB leads to the conclusion that she was successful in lowering the yields on government bonds in the peripheral countries of the Euro area in particular due to its announcement policy (Draghi's famous "whatever it takes" speech and the OMT announcement). However, in recent years she failed to reach her real goal, to maintain price stability—at least in the self-chosen definition of an inflation rate of 2 %. She would have an easier life if she would only target core inflation and secondly when she would say goodbye to the point target (inflation at 2 %) and instead—would try to reach a target range (0–2 %)—as she did before 2003.

After the exhaustion of the traditional monetary policy instruments (driving down interest rates to its zero lower bound) during the crises, major central banks in the world—first the BoJ, the Fed and the BoE—and more recently the ECB—started with unconventional or non-standard measures (especially QE). While the QE policy in Japan miserably failed it seemed to have worked in the US and UK. Recently, the ECB also embarked to a specific QE policy. Our econometric analysis and model simulations show that ECB's QE policy could work properly, however only with a considerable delay and most likely not to the desired extent.

## References


Baldwin R, Giavazzi F (eds) (2015) The Eurozone crisis: a consensus view of the causes and a few possible remedies. A VoxEU.org eBook, CEPR Press, London

Baumeister Ch, Benati L (2013) Unconventional monetary policy and the great recession: estimating the macroeconomic effects of a spread compression at the zero lower bound. Int J Cent Bank 9(2):165–212

Bernanke BS (2015) The courage to act: a memoir if a crisis and its aftermath. W. W. Norton, New York

BIS (2015) 85th annual report, 1 April 2014–31 March 2015. Bank for International Settlements, Basel, 28 Jun 2015

Breuss F (2002) Was ECB's monetary policy optimal? Atl Econ J 30(3):298–319

Breuss F (2016) The crisis in retrospect: causes, effects and policy responses. In: Badinger H, Nitsch V (eds) Routledge handbook of the economics of European integration. Routledge, London, pp 331–350

Breuss F, Fornero JA (2009) An estimated DSGE model of Austria, the Euro Area and the U.S.: some welfare implications of EMU. FIW Working Paper No. 34, Aug 2009

Breuss F, Kaniovski S, Schratzenstaller M (2009) Macro-economic effects of the fiscal stimulus measures in Austria. Aust Econ Q 4/2009 (Volume 14):205–216

Breuss F, Roeger W, In't Veld J (2015) The stabilising properties of a European Banking Union in case of financial shocks in the Euro Area. European Economy, Economic Papers No. 550, Brussels, Jun 2015

Butt N, Churm R, McMahon M, Morotz A (2014) QE and the bank lending channel in the United Kingdom. Bank of England, Working Paper No. 511, Sept 2014

Caglar E, Chadha JS, Meaning J, Warren J, Waters A (2011) Non-conventional monetary policies: QE and the DSGE literature. Discussion Papers KDPE 1110, University of Kent School of Economics, Jan 2011

Christensen JHE, Rudebusch GD (2012) The response of interest rates to U.S. and U.K. quantitative easing. Working Paper Series Nr. 2012-06, Federal Reserve Bank of San Francisco, May 2012

Claeys G, Leandro A, Mandra A (2015) European central bank quantitative easing: the detailed manual. Bruegel Policy Contribution, Issue 2015/2, Mar 2015

Cœuré B (2015) Embarking on public sector asset purchases. Speech by the member of the executive board of the ECB at second international conference on sovereign bond markets, Frankfurt, 10 Mar 2015

Constancio V (2015a) 2015 US monetary policy forum panel discussion on central banking with large balance sheets. Vice-President European Central Bank, New York, 27 Feb 2015

Constancio V (2015b) Assessing the new phase of unconventional monetary policy at the ECB. Panel remarks prepared by Vice-President of the ECB, at the Annual Congress of the European Economic Association University of Mannheim, 25 Aug 2015

Dedola L, Karadi P, Lombardo G (2013) Global implications of national unconventional policies. J Monet Econ 60(1):66–85

ECB (2012) Technical features of outright monetary transactions. ECB Press Release, Frankfurt, 6 Sept 2012. https://www.ecb.europa.eu/press/pr/date/2012/html/pr120906_1.en.html
ECB (2014a) The ECB's forward guidance. Monthly Bulletin, Apr 2014, p 65–73
ECB (2014b) Guide to banking supervision. Frankfurt, Sept 2014
ECB (2015) Decision (EU) 2015/774 of the European Central Bank of 4 March 2015 on a secondary markets public sector asset purchase programme (ECB/2015/10). Official Journal of the European Union L 121/20, 14.5.2015
ECB (2016) Monetary developments in the euro area: February 2016. Press Release, 29 Mar 2016
Eichengreen JB (2015) Hall of mirrors: the great depression, the great recession, and the uses—and Misuses—of History. Oxford University Press, New York
European Commission (2009) The EU's response to support the real economy during the economic crisis: an overview of member states' recovery measures. Occasional Papers 511. European Economy, Brussels, Jul 2009
Falagiarda M (2013) Evaluation quantitative easing: a DSGE approach. Department of Economics, University of Bologna, Sept 2013. http://mpra.ub.uni-muenchen.de/49457/
Friedman M (1969) The optimum quantity of money. Macmillan, London
Fuster T (2016) Zwei ist die neue Null: Warum Zentralbanken einen Unterschied machen zwischen Preisstabilität und stabilen Preisen. Neue Zürcher Zeitung, 11. Januar 2016, S. 25 (Fuster T Geldpolitik—Zielband statt Punktziel. Reflexe- Kommentare zum Wirtschaftsgeschehen, NZZ, 11.1.2016, S. 34).
Gambacorta L, Hoffman B, Peersman G (2011) The effectiveness of unconventional monetary policy at the zero lower bound: a cross-country analysis. Mimeo
German Council of Economic Experts (Sachverständigenrat zur Begutachtung der gesamtwirtschaftlichen Entwicklung) (2012) Stable architecture for Europe—need for action in Germany. Annual Report 2012/13, Nov 2012
Gertler M, Karadi P (2011) A model of unconventional monetary policy. J Monet Econ 58 (1):17–34
Gertler M, Karadi P (2013) QE 1 vs. 2 vs. 3...: a framework for analyzing large-scale asset purchases as a monetary policy tool. Int J Cent Bank 9(S1):5–53
Gertler M, Kiyotaki N (2011) Financial intermediation and credit policy in business cycle analysis. In: Friedman B, Woodford M (eds) Handbook of monetary economics. Elsevier, New York
Joyce M, Spaltro M (2014) Quantitative easing and bank lending: a panel data approach. Bank of England, London
Mishra P, Moriyam K, N'Diaye P, Nguyen L (2014) Impact of fed tapering announcements on emerging markets. IMF Working Paper, MCM and SPR WP/14/109, Washington, DC, Jun 2014
Morais B, Peydro J-L, Claudia Ruiz C (2015) The international bank lending channel of monetary policy rates and QE: credit supply, reach-for-yield, and real effects. International Finance Discussion Papers No. 1137, Board of Governors of the Federal Reserve System, Jul 2015
NZZ (2014) Das Fed am Pranger. Neue Zürcher Zeitung 4. Feb 2014, p. 23
NZZ (2015) Der lange Arm des Fed: Warum Amerikas Leitsätze auch die Zinsen anderer Länder beeinflussen. Neue Zürcher Zeitung 14. Sept 2015, p. 23
OECD (2009a) Fiscal packages across OECD countries: overview and country details. OECD, Paris
OECD (2009b) Policy Responses to the Economic Crisis: Investing in Innovation for Long-term Growth. OECD, Paris
Pietrzak M (2015) Evaluation of unconventional monetary policy in a small open economy. Paper presented at the 8th FIW research conference "international economics", Vienna, 3–4 Dec 2015
Reinhard CM, Kirkegaard J, Sbrnacia MB (2011) Financial repression redux. Financ Dev 48(2)
Reinhart CM, Sbrnacia MB (2011) The liquidation of government debt. NBER Working Paper Series 169893, Mar 2011

Schuder S (2014) Expansive monetary policy in a portfolio model with endogenous asset supply. Econ Model 41:239–252
Song X (2014) QE and unemployment: a financial Friction DSGE Model with LSAPs and labor market search. Unpublished paper, North Carolina State University, Apr 6, 2014
Weale M, Wieladek T (2015) What are the macroeconomic effects of asset purchases? CEPR Discussion Papers No. 10495, Mar 2015
Williamson SD (2015a) Current federal reserve policy under the lens of economic history: a review essay. Working Paper Series No. 2015-015A, Federal Reserve Bank of St. Louis, Jul 2015
Williamson SD (2015b) Monetary policy normalization in the United States. Fed Reserve Bank St Louis Rev Second Q 97(2):87–108

# The Unconventional Monetary Policy of the ECB and the International Economic and Financial Crisis: Effectiveness Versus Exhaustion

**António Mendonça**

**Abstract** On 10 March 2016 the ECB took the historic decision to reduce the interest rate on the main refinancing operations of the Euro system by five basis points to 0 %. In line with this, it reduced the rate on the marginal lending facility to 0.25 % (previously 0.3 %) and the rate on permanent deposit facility by ten basis points, to −0.4 %. This opened a new phase of unconventional monetary policy use.

In this essay we will discuss the issue of the effectiveness versus the exhaustion of monetary policy followed by the ECB in response to the Eurozone effects of global economic and financial crisis.

We firstly discuss the nature and justifications for the use of unconventional policy measures in the context of the crisis developments. We concentrate, in particular, on two central issues to understand the limits of monetary policy effectiveness, the so-called liquidity trap and the endogeneity versus exogeneity issue of money creation.

Secondly, we provide some additional considerations on the relationship between the decreasing effectiveness of monetary policy and the increasing use of unconventional measures, seeking also to understand the differences between the stances of the ECB and the US Fed.

Finally, we discuss the contradictions between the fiscal and monetary policies stances as a booster factor in exhausting the effect of the monetary policy, and conclude by affirming the absolute need to reform the Euro system.

**JEL Classification** E52 • E58 • E61

A. Mendonça
Lisbon School of Economics & Management, Universidade de Lisboa, Lisbon, Portugal
e-mail: amend@iseg.ulisboa.pt



N. da Costa Cabral et al. (eds.), *The Euro and the Crisis*, Financial and Monetary Policy Studies 43, DOI 10.1007/978-3-319-45710-9_14

## 1 Introduction: The "Zero Lower Bound"

On 10 March 2016, the ECB took the historic decision to reduce the interest rate on the main refinancing operations of the Euro system by five basis points to 0 %, with effect from the 16th of the same month. In line with this, it reduced the rate on the marginal lending facility to 0.25 % (previously 0.3 %) and the rate on the permanent deposit facility by ten basis points, to −0.4 %.

Simultaneously, and writing a comprehensive package of unconventional monetary policy measures, another four key decisions were taken: (i) to expand the monthly purchases under the asset purchase plan from 60 billion to 80 billion, with a time horizon until March 2017 or, if necessary, until the Governing Council considers that the objective of inflation rates below but close to 2 % over the medium term, is assured; (ii) to increase from 33 to 50 %, the share limits for issue and issuer as part of the acquisition of securities issued by international organizations and eligible multilateral development banks; (iii) to include, in the list of assets eligible for regular purchases under a new corporate purchase sector programme, the euro-denominated bonds with investment grade issued by euro-area based non-bank corporations; (iv) from June 2016, to launch a new series of four targeted longer-term refinancing operations (TLTRO II), each with a maturity of 4 years, with the particularity that the borrowing conditions applied to these operations can be as low as the rate on the deposit facility existing at the start of the operation, in the case of banks exceeding a reference value in the net credit provided to the economy.

Rounding out the picture, it reaffirmed its medium-term commitment to the guidelines adopted for monetary policy, stating the hope that the ECB main interest rates remain at current or lower levels for an extended period of time and beyond the horizon for the acquisition of net assets (Draghi 2016b). This was a stance reaffirmed and strengthened a few days later by Peter Praet (2016), an executive board member of the ECB, in an interview in which he claimed that the lower physical limit of interest rates had not yet been reached and that if new adverse shocks caused deterioration of the economic outlook or if the financial conditions did not fit as expected and it was necessary to stimulate the economy and the raising of the inflation rate, further reductions would continue to be part of the toolbox available to the ECB.

The basis of this set of decisions, impressive on all titles, was the analysis made by the ECB of the economic and monetary conditions outlook, indicating the deteriorating of growth prospects and the persistence of deflation risks, justifying the monetary stimulus measures adopted.

## 1.1 From the Negative Deposit Facility Rate to the Zero Main Refinancing Operation Rate

From a historical perspective, the 10th March decision can be seen as a culmination of a process of reducing interest rates and of adoption of unconventional monetary policy measures that developed from the Governing meeting of 5 June 2014, when the deposit facility rate became negative, for the first time, with a reduction of 10 bps to −0.10 %, in parallel with a reduction of 10 bps on the main refinancing operations rate to 0.15 %, and a reduction of 35 basis points on the marginal lending facility rate to 0.40 %. At the same meeting, with the express purpose of supporting lending to households and non-financial corporations, the first targeted longer-term refinancing operations (TLTRO I) were decided, with 4-year maturities, until September 2018, along with other credit stimulus measures, following a less optimistic analysis of the economic and monetary conditions in the euro zone, regarding economic growth and inflation dynamics. The economic forecasts were then revised downwards, not only for the year 2014 but also for the subsequent years, 2015 and 2016.

From this meeting, the process developed that would lead to the setting of the main lending rate at 0 %. At the meeting of 4 September of this same year, the Council fixed the rates at 0.05 % (main refinancing operations), 0.30 % (marginal lending facility) and −0.20 % (permanent deposit facility), with effect from the 10th of the same month. And after more than a year of apparent stability, the ECB backed a move on interest rates, but only at the level of the permanent deposit facility. At the meeting of 3 December 2015, a further decline of ten basis points on this rate was decided, to −0.30 %, against the expectations of economic agents that had anticipated a general reduction of all the main rates, which would only be actually implemented in March 2016.

Notwithstanding the decisions having fallen short of expectations, the Council meeting of 3 December was important from several perspectives, prefiguring the broader decisions that would be adopted in March 2016. In fact, the 60 billion euro assets purchase programme (APP), adopted on 22 January 2015, was extended until the end of March 2017, or beyond that period if necessary; the asset purchase programme in the public sector was extended to debt instruments issued by regional and local governments; and finally the Council decided to continue the policy of full allotment for fixed-rate refinancing operations, also as deemed necessary by the ECB and at least until 2017.

In any event, the December decisions made clear all the contradictions that had marked the process of the European response to the crisis. On the one hand, the measures adopted reflected a recognition of the risks inherent to the development of the economic situation and the awareness of the high probability that additional, wider and deeper measures, might be necessary. On the other hand, falling short of expectations, they reflected the fear of the potential reaction of most countries that have most opposed the monetary policy followed by the ECB, in particular Germany. At the Council meeting of 21 January 2016, these contradictions were still present when deciding to keep interest rates at the levels of December. We could also see a more optimistic stance when the Council asserted that the unconventional measures adopted since June 2014 were producing results that translated into real improvements for the real economy, more credit and better financing conditions, as well as in increasing the resilience of the Eurozone against global economic shocks. However, at the same time, it was recognized that, at the beginning of the year, downside risks had once again increased due to the increased uncertainty regarding the growth of emerging economies, the volatility in the financial markets and raw materials and furthermore geopolitical risks. And with coherence in the contradiction, the Council recognized the need to analyse and possibly to reconsider the monetary policy stance at the next meeting in March, as a result of new economic forecasts (not available at the meeting in January, but already foreseeable), already including the year 2018, which would in fact happen. All these contradictions were clearly present in Draghi's statement (2016a).

## 1.2 The Decisions of the 10 March 2016 ECB Governing Council Meeting

Thus the decisions of the March 2016 Council were not surprising. The economic forecasts were revised downwards, as was anticipated, including the annual inflation rate moving into negative territory (−0.2 % in February, compared with 0.3 % in January), were the support required for the adoption of broader measures of monetary and credit easing that translated into further falls in interest rates, especially the fixing of the main refinancing rate at the 0 % level, on the extension of the asset purchase programme and, above all, on the reassurance that further falls in interest rates had not been excluded from the tool box available, of note being the establishing of the main refinancing rate at 0 %, if deemed necessary—a profession of faith in the maintenance of the potential of the monetary policy but, at the same time, recognizing the limits of its effectiveness, when emphasizing the need for fiscal policy to assume its responsibilities in supporting economic recovery and for countries to adopt more friendly growth policies (Draghi 2016b).

Looking at the ECB's decisions in retrospect, particularly those involving the so-called unconventional monetary policy phase, one cannot help question the actual impact of the measures adopted. On the one hand, it is unquestionable that they helped to stabilize the economic situation and the maintenance of financing conditions for the economy or, at least, to prevent them from continuing to deteriorate. In general, the measures were being taken to address the observed or anticipated deterioration in the economic and financial conditions. However, on the other hand, notwithstanding the prevalence of certain shorter or longer periods of apparent stability, a tendency towards reducing the main interest rates had in fact been produced, until the current negative levels. This was a tendency that had developed from the outbreak of the 2008 crisis, that is not unique to the euro area, and that shows more a reaction to the ongoing dynamic—one running behind events—than an effective capacity for reversing it in a sustainable manner.

In short, and without wanting to definitely challenge the assessment made by the ECB that its (conventional and unconventional) intervention would have contributed to the economic and financial stability of the euro zone, all the facts seems to indicate that this intervention has above all, had a suppressing effect and not a sustained dynamics-reversal effect, falling into a process of progressive exhaustion of the effectiveness of monetary policy which is evident through the use of systematic and reactive interest rates cuts and the adoption of increasingly less conventional measures, pushing the frontier of its own statutes beyond all limits. An extreme and hardly sustainable situation, that the ECB is fully aware and implicitly recognizes in all its interventions, which have been increasingly incisive, particularly following the Governing Council meeting of March, when it insisted that the monetary policy that has been followed focuses on maintaining price stability in the medium term, and that its accommodative stance has provided support for economic activity but, at the same time, insisting that fiscal policy will have to be called upon to play its role—an indirect reminder to the other leaders of the euro zone (Fig. 1).

In this essay, we will discuss the issue of effectiveness versus exhaustion of the monetary policy followed by the ECB in response to the effects of the global economic and financial crisis on the Eurozone.

In point 2, the nature and justifications for the use of unconventional policy measures in the context of the development of the crisis will be discussed,

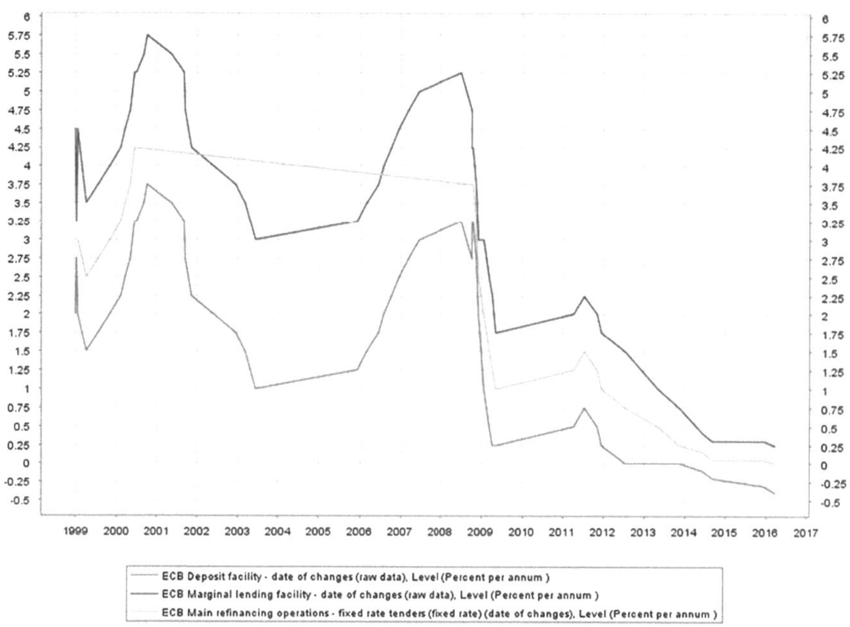


**Fig. 1** Evolution of the main ECB interest rates. Source (all series): European Central Bank (ECB)

concentrating, in particular, on two central issues to understand the limits of monetary policy effectiveness, namely the so-called liquidity trap and endogeneity versus exogeneity concerning money creation.

In Sect. 3, I will make some additional considerations regarding the relationship between the decreasing effectiveness of monetary policy and the increasing use of unconventional measures, seeking to also understand the differences between the ECB's and the US Fed's stances. Finally, in Sect. 4, I will present some concluding remarks.

# 2 The Economic and Financial Crisis and Unconventional Monetary Policy

According to the Treaty on the Functioning of the EU, the main objective of the European System of Central Banks (ESCB), which includes the ECB, is to maintain price stability. Without prejudice to this primary objective, the ESCB supports the economic policies of the Union, taking into account the fulfilling of the objectives of this Union as defined in Article 3 of the Treaty on European Union. Of note among these objectives is point 3 of the Article which sets out growth and economic principles, based on price stability. The goal of full employment is also mentioned but at a secondary level and subordinated to the fulfilment of the main objective. The role of the ESCB in this context is to define and implement the monetary policy of the Union, through short-term interest rates management, thus influencing the development of economic conditions in order to ensure mid-term price stability in the euro area. Price stability is defined in terms of the annual increase in the Harmonised Index of Consumer Prices (HIPC), at a rate close but below 2 % over the medium term. As monetary policy instruments, the ECB uses open market operations, designed to manage liquidity in the banking system and signal the stance of monetary policy, standing facilities, designed to provide or absorb liquidity in the overnight market, and reserve requirements, designed to maintain stabilization of interest rates in the money market and to create or enlarge a structural liquidity shortage.

## *2.1 The Unconventional Monetary Policy: First Phase (September 2008–June 2014). Direct Liquidity Injection in the Market*

Following the third quarter of 2008, after the outbreak of the international economic and financial crisis, the ECB decided to introduce a set of additional monetary policy measures, completely unprecedented with regard to their nature, scope and magnitude, which were designated as "unconventional measures". As early as August 2007, when the signs of the global crisis were already visible, the ECB decided to intervene, like its major partners, through the use of strong liquidity injections in an attempt to limit the effects on the functioning of the banking and financing system. Since then, the ECB has continued using these and other unconventional measures, given that it was its normal or conventional practice until then, widening the range of instruments that it started to use against the context in which the international economic and financial crisis developed and the way it manifested in the Eurozone. A new era of ECB intervention was opened, with all of its titles unprecedented and which, through evolving in stages, has extended to the present.

With the introduction of this new type of measures, the ECB widened the range of intervention possibilities in managing the crisis, expanding the toolbox available to deal with the operational needs of the monetary and financial system. However, simultaneously, it pushed the limits of its own field of intervention, statutorily established in the treaties of the Union, in particular concerning the financing of states and public institutions, and approaching the traditional intervention of central banks as lenders of last resort.

This evolution of the ECB as regards the conduct of monetary policy in the context of the European crisis has led to a number of serious divergences between European leaders, which have deepened since then, with the Bundesbank and the German government being their main opponents. A situation that has led the main heads of the ECB to refine the theoretical argument and the practical justification in which to frame the progressive adoption of less and less "conventional" measures, especially that of the Vice-President, Vítor Constâncio, who has had the most active role in this respect [see in particular, Constâncio (2011, 2013, 2015a, b, 2016)].

The main argument for unconventional monetary policy is the idea that the conventional monetary policy transmission mechanism ceased to function properly, as a result of the dysfunctions produced in the financial markets, and proved itself unable to contain the deflationary pressures that followed the crisis and, consequently, failed to properly secure the objective of price stability—an inflation rate below but close to 2 %.

The monetary policy transmission mechanism is the process through which monetary policy decisions are transmitted to the economy and, ultimately, to the prices level, the main target of the ECB's intervention (see ECB website, monetary policy). The scheme of this process can be schematically summarized by the diagram below (Fig. 2).

This process can be disturbed by several factors that are not controllable by monetary policy, namely variation in risk premiums, changes in bank capital that affect their credit conditions, changes in the economic environment and in the global economy, changes in fiscal policy or changes in commodity prices. These are called shocks outside the control of the central bank.

At the same time, even in normal conditions, the transmission mechanism is characterized by operating dynamics that are somewhat lengthy, variable and uncertain, particularly in contexts where shocks outside central bank control become dominant. This has been the case with the recent economic and financial

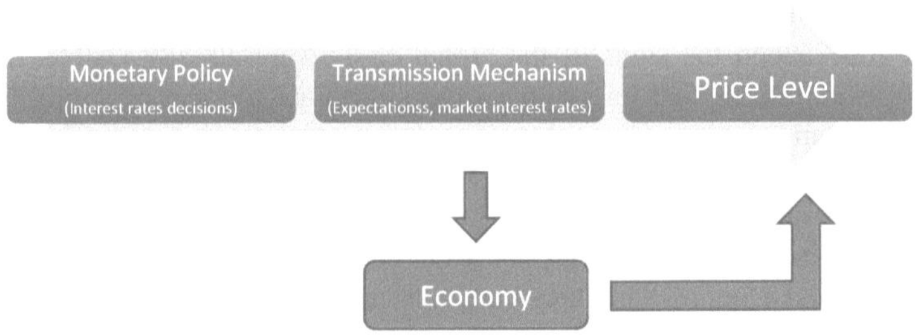


**Fig. 2** The monetary policy transmission mechanism ("normal" functioning)

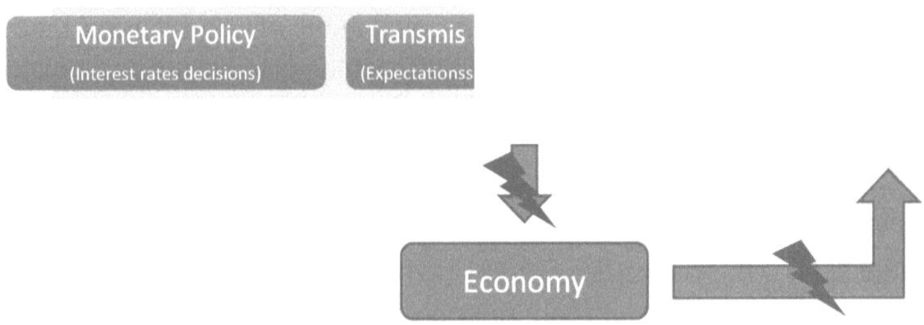


**Fig. 3** The monetary policy transmission mechanism (malfunctioning)

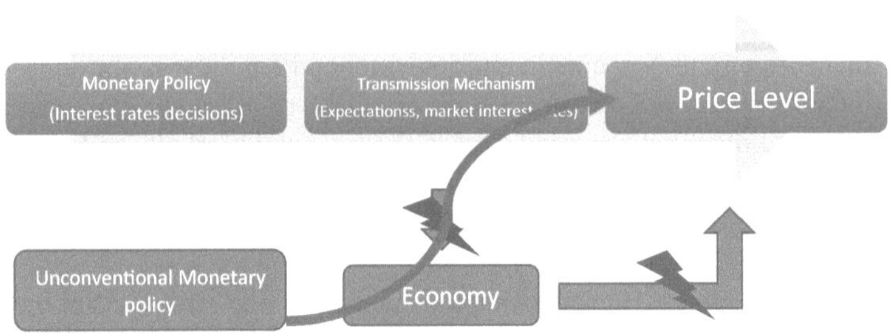


**Fig. 4** The "by-pass" of unconventional monetary policy

crisis, making monetary policy uncertain in its effects or, in extreme cases, completely ineffective.

In this extreme situation, there has been a malfunction of the mechanism transmitting central bank decisions to the economy that has distorted or even prevented the arrival of the effects, at least in the desired way, to the ultimate goal of the ECB, which is the level of prices. This malfunction justifies the adoption of exceptional measures, designated "unconventional", creating a sort of "bypass" between monetary policy and the level of prices, avoiding the constraints of normal financing channels (Figs. 3 and 4, below).

According to the official justification of the ECB, the basis of the adoption of unconventional monetary policy was the malfunctioning of some segments of the financial markets that have prevented normal financing of the economy, thus disturbing the operating of the transmission mechanism (Fig. 3). Direct supply of liquidity to the market by the ECB seeks to prevent the collapse of important financial institutions, with the central bank assuming the role of lender of last resort in a liquidity crisis context.

A second justification for the introduction of unconventional monetary policy has to do with the nature and scope of the measures. In addition, this domain introduces the so-called "separation principle" (Constâncio 2011).

According to this principle, there is a clear separation between the purposes of conventional and unconventional measures. Unconventional measures are complementary to the former in having clearly defined and temporally limited objectives. They are intended to ensure that disruptions in financial markets do not prevent the conventional policy from doing its job by influencing prices through interest rates. In addition, they should be used as long as the malfunctioning of the monetary policy transmission mechanism is evident and withdrawn as soon as this feature is recovered.

In this sense, and also according to the heads of the ECB, non-standard measures are distinct from the "quantitative easing" that is used by the Fed or the BoE, because they are not intended as a substitute for conventional interest rate policy in the context of "zero lower bound" or as a way to manage the "trade-off" between inflation volatility in the short run and price stability in the long run. Rather, unconventional measures are designed to ensure that the conventional measures are effective in all timeframes.

They work thus as a support mechanism to the conventional policy in a period of exception when disruptions in the normal financing channels of the financial system and of the economy as a whole manifest. They are no longer necessary when the situation normalizes and conventional monetary policy regains its effectiveness, and must therefore be removed. This is what automatically occurs in many situations, where financing operations have a defined time horizon and are not an object of explicit renewal.

## *2.2 Unconventional Monetary Policy: Second Phase (June 2014–March 2016). Approaching the Role of "Lender of Last Resort"*

Despite the statement regarding the exceptional and temporary character of unconventional measures, the reality is that they are here to stay and eventually become as "normal" as conventional measures being adopted regularly, in a form expected by economic agents and with increasing diversity. As a result of the persistent disturbance of the monetary policy transmission mechanism, of accentuation of deflationary trends and of the evolution of the actual economic and financial crisis, successive new "unconventional" measures were used, namely, liquidity provided at fixed rates, full liquidity allotment, extension of maturities for loans granted by the ECB, including those granted for very long terms, widened eligibility conditions for collateral, direct purchases of government bonds and mortgage bonds, decreased requirements for minimum reserves, in a continuous process growing in scale, the creativity of which tending to accelerate.

In June and September 2014 more unconventional measures were introduced, considered of a new class: two programs of assets purchased from the private sector—an Asset Backed Securities Purchase Program (ABSPP) and a Covered Bond Purchase Program (the third) (CBPP3), adopted in order to allow selective intervention in the markets with decisive influence on the financing of the non-financial sector; and a new series of Targeted Long-term Refinancing Operations (up to 4 years) (TLTROs), to improve bank lending to the non-financial private sector in the euro area. According to officials of the ECB, the measures marked a new phase in the development of unconventional monetary policy. A stage where the ECB clearly stated the willingness to actively expand the size of its balance sheet up to the levels needed to ease the monetary policy stance, in a situation where interest rates reached their lowest level.

These new measures represent a qualitative leap over previous measures in that they no longer intend only to overcome the dysfunctions of the transmission mechanism. They want to directly influence the economy through specific channels overtaking this transmission mechanism in its role. We reached a stage where the ECB no longer trusts in the ability of the banking system to use well the liquidity facilities that are provided, by injecting more money into the economy through lending operations, creating direct channels of monetary transmission (Fig. 4).

At the same time, the ECB aimed to create better conditions for the banking system itself to be able to make a correction of their balance sheets without this translating into a narrowing of credit for the economy.

It meant, in fact, a new attitude of the ECB involving a closer approach more of a "quantitative easing" stance, followed by the Fed and other central banks, in line with the role of "lender of last resort". A formally rejected stance, or at least not assumed up to here.

At the same time, these new measures also meant the ECB's commitment to the maintenance of low interest rates, in an extended time horizon, even beyond the achievement of economic recovery. A situation of inflation rate "overshooting" is even accepted, in the context of economic growth that is intended to encourage the use of these and other measures of an unconventional character.

## *2.3 Unconventional Monetary Policy: Third Phase (March 2016 - ...). The Liquidity Trap*

This new phase of unconventional monetary policy was opened following the decisions of the Governing Council meeting of March 10, 2016.

The "zero lower bound" is fully reached with the setting of the interest rate on the main refinancing operations at 0 %. However, the most significant fact is the acceptance of the possibility of financing the economy at rates as low as the rate applicable to the permanent facility deposit existing at the operation start date—that is, at negative rates. This possibility is foreseen under the new target long-term refinancing operations (TLTRO II) in the case of banks exceeding a reference value of net credit provided to the economy.

With this decision, a new stage of intervention is opened. A real Pandora's Box from which no one truly knows what can result, despite all the declarations that monetary policy will continue to be able to use the interest rate instrument. The next step, with it still being necessary to reduce interest rates, can only be the setting of the main refinancing rate in negative territory. Which can only be considered as a denial of monetary policy theory, not to mention its actual practice.

The important question in this situation is this: will the unconventional monetary policy work? Despite all the positive reassurances on this issue, the reality is that the use of increasingly radical unconventional measures may only show otherwise. That is, unconventional monetary is entering a progressive exhaustion process in its ability to influence the economy in the desired direction, as a drug addict who requires increasingly stronger doses to address the symptoms of a disease, as the body will be used to the substance and the disease does not stop spreading.

This is an image that can be applied to the so-called liquidity trap, a situation where, according to many opinions, the global economy, and European economy in particular, find themselves in.

### 2.3.1 The Liquidity Trap

The analysis of the liquidity trap can be used as a reference for understanding the ongoing economic situation in Europe and also, with the necessary adaptations, the current situation of the global economy [see, among others, Krugman (2012) and Temin and Vines (2014)].

We are faced with significantly lower investment levels compared to pre-crisis levels. Furthermore, at the same time, interest rates have reached negative levels, if we refer to the banking system's relations with the ECB, with obvious effects over the non-financial sector.

The traditional IS/LM model, despite the simplifying assumptions that underpin it, can be a useful analytical framework for understanding what is happening to monetary policy, both in its conventional and unconventional components.

As it is known, the IS curve (Investment/Saving) is constructed from three relationships: the investment demand function; changes on aggregate demand as a result of changes on investment decisions when the interest rate varies; and the relationship between different levels of interest rate and output and the equality between savings and investment. On the other hand, the derivation of the curve satisfies the following propositions: an increase in the interest rate causes a reduction in investment demand, which in turn is reflected in an output reduction.

The IS curve represents, therefore, the combinations of interest rate and output levels that ensure the equilibrium condition in the market of goods and services. That is, total demand D, given the income level $Y$ and the cost of credit $i$, equals the total supply $Y$, $(D\ (Y, i) = Y)$, always bearing in mind the equality between investment and saving. Its slope is, therefore, negative, in the space of the interest rate and output dynamics.

In turn, the LM curve (Liquidity Preference, Money Supply) is derived from the following relationships: the relationship between output and money demand; the relationship between money demand and interest rate; and the relation between the money market equilibrium (money demand and money supply balance) and the different levels of the real interest rate. The derivation of the LM curve conforms to the following propositions: an increase in output generates an increase in money demand which, in turn, generates an increase in the interest rate.

The LM curve represents, then, the different combinations of interest rate and level of output that ensure equilibrium in the money market. That is, the balance between money demand and money supply, $M^d\ (Y, i) = M/P$, given the nominal supply of money $M$ and the price level $P$. The slope of the LM curve is therefore positive in the space of the interest rate and output dynamics.

In "normal" conditions, simultaneous equilibrium in the market of goods and services and the money market produces a positive interest rate ($i_1$) and a certain level of real output ($Y_1$). The equilibrium point is located graphically in the first quadrant, with movements to the left and to the right being conceivable for both

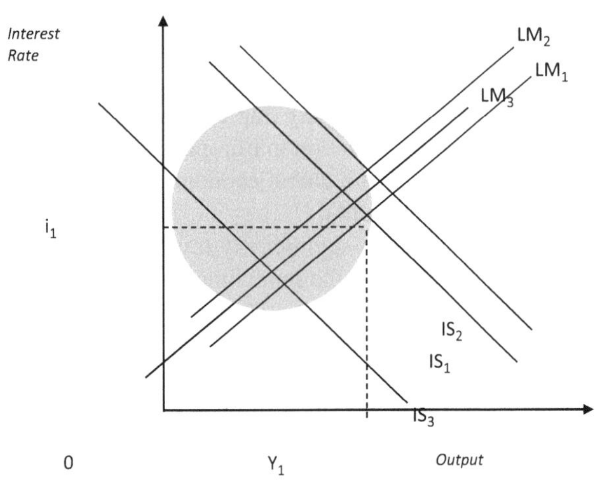


**Fig. 5** "Normal" simultaneous equilibria in both the markets for goods and services (IS) and money (LM)

**Fig. 6** "Abnormal" simultaneous equilibrium

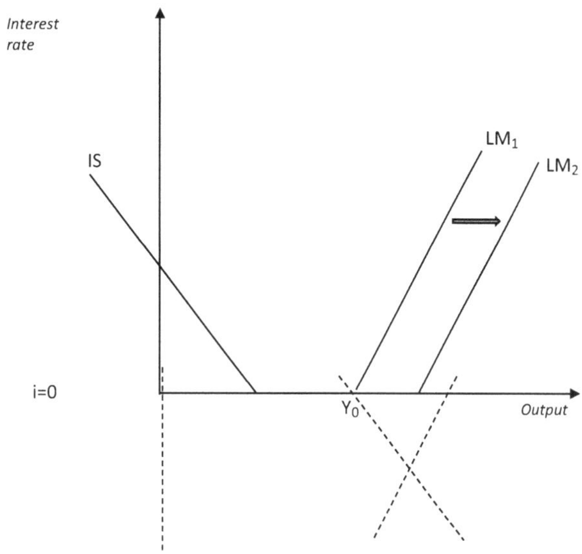


curves, ensuring the conditions for monetary and fiscal policies effectiveness and different combinations of simultaneous equilibrium in both markets, represented by the different intersections of IS/LM curves within the shaded circle of Fig. 5, below:

Consider, however, the case where the intersection of the IS/LM curves does not match in the first quadrant, but in the fourth quadrant. That is, a situation where theoretically the intersection occurs in an area of negative levels of interest rates for different output levels.

This can occur in a context where the IS curve has a strong shift to the left as a result of contractionary fiscal policies as happened in Europe following the so-called sovereign debt crisis in Europe, where concerns with containment of deficits and public debt led to a widespread decline in public spending.

In such a situation, represented in Fig. 6 below, equilibrium output is given by $Y_0$ and the interest rate is equal to 0. An increase in the money supply moves the LM curve to the right, ($LM_1 \rightarrow LM_2$) but has no effect on the interest rate that, at least theoretically, cannot go down more. This means that investment can no longer be stimulated in this way. Monetary policy becomes ineffective.

By contrast, fiscal policy, through public spending or by tax reduction, can shift the IS curve to the right stimulating, in this way, the output level. Fiscal policy acquires an additional effectiveness to the extent that, given the loss of effectiveness of monetary policy, it becomes the only way to increase output.

It can also be seen, regarding the effectiveness of monetary and fiscal policy, that the LM curve can be modified only through the action of two factors: changes in the money supply and changes in autonomous money demand. The IS curve, in turn, is influenced by five factors: autonomous consumption spending, investment spending, government consumption, net exports and the level of taxes. This means that in a situation of monetary policy blocking, the IS curve can be shifted to the right,

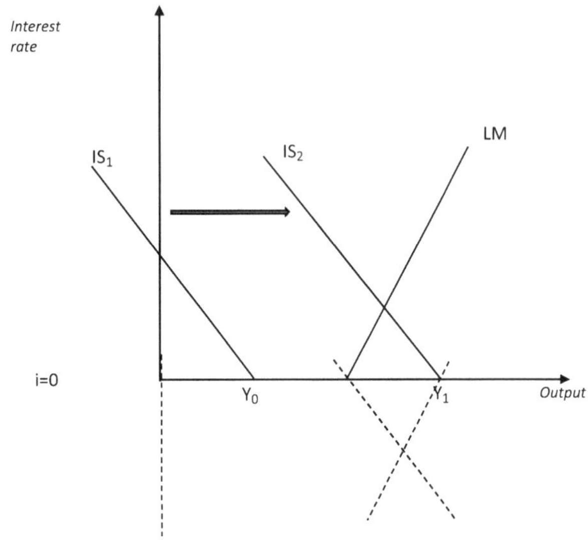


**Fig. 7** The role of fiscal policy

through the influence that fiscal policy directly or indirectly has on the economy through the operation of these channels.

The analysis using the IS/LM model can also explain the relationship between the two macroeconomic policies. Fiscal policy works through the economic relationship represented in the IS curve. In turn, monetary policy works through the relationship translated by the LM curve. However, as can be seen in Fig. 5, the LM curve only affects the economy when it intersects the IS curve with a positive interest rate. In a situation where the intersection between the two curves, theoretically, only operates in a negative interest rate zone, monetary policy become completely ineffective and the economy falls down in the liquid trap.

Moreover, we come to the crux of the matter. Can monetary policy back to play a role in this situation?

No longer working through its normal channels, monetary policy may act indirectly facilitating the operation of fiscal policy to move the IS curve to the right ($IS_1 \rightarrow IS_2$) (Fig. 7). This can be done through the accommodation of any public deficits, that result from the use of expansionary fiscal policy, through direct funding from the central bank.

Which, to a certain, it is already being carried out by the ECB and other central banks.

### 2.3.2 Endogeneity of Money Supply Hypothesis

Another important issue for understanding the current situation relates to the discussion of the process of monetary creation by the economic system.

In the framework of the IS/LM model, the construction of the LM curve is associated with the hypothesis of exogenous money supply. That is, it is assumed that money supply is controlled by the central bank, being independent from the demand that results from the activity of economic agent.

Underlying this idea is the theory of the money multiplier, which introduces the separation between the Monetary Base—composed of currency in circulation and the required reserves held by the Central Bank—and the money supply itself, which is the money, created by the banks in their relations with economic agents. The money multiplier mechanism works between these, which is supposed to convey the changes in the monetary base, the central bank's responsibility, to the money supply, as represented in the movements in the LM curve.

This exogeneity of money supply, as described here, has always been controversial in economic theory. Moreover, the current situation involving the intervention of the ECB, in particular with its evident inability to influence the economy, with the desired strength, through its conventional and unconventional liquidity injections, has raised more doubts about this exogeneity hypothesis, giving strength to the opposite hypothesis of money supply endogeneity. That is, unlike the exogenous money supply hypothesis, banks first provide liquidity to the economy through the credit they grant and only then do they turn to the central bank for refinancing to establish the reserves needed to cover the deposits that they manage through lending. Therefore, the route is not from the central bank to the economy, but from the economy to the central bank.

According to the endogeneity hypothesis, the central bank can only accommodate the money created by commercial banks in their relations with economic agents, and had no ability to determine any quantitative goals for money supply. This is, incidentally, one of the arguments most frequently used by the heads of the ECB to justify the adoption of unconventional measures, as a means to undo the

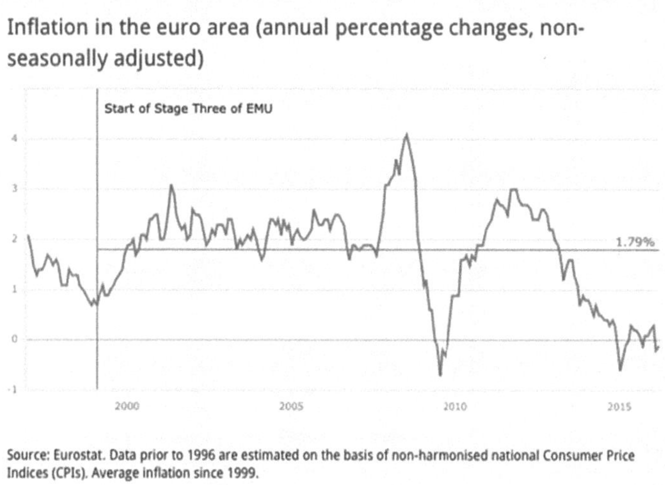


**Graph 1** Inflation in the euro area

tensions in the banking system funding. Instead of causing an uncontrolled expansion of the money supply (M3) generating inflation, the expansion of the ECB balance sheet has served above all to prevent its further decline (Graph 1). According to the proponents of unconventional monetary policy, in the absence of unconventional measures the growth of money supply would have fallen much more. In all probability, it would have reached the levels seen in the crisis of the 1930s, with all the known consequences for levels of economic activity and unemployment.

The endogeneity hypothesis of money supply is very important and allows us to understand a number of difficulties that monetary policy is facing today.

Recalling the relation of the monetary base with lending by commercial banks, we can describe the following sequence Fig. 8:

Obviously, the demand for credit depends on the state of the economy and the level of confidence in the future by economic agents.

The fact that money supply can be considered endogenously determined means that the LM curve is horizontal for a given interest rate, the financing being elastic at this interest rate. The IS curve to the right ($IS_1 \rightarrow IS_2$) ceases to have any influence in determining the interest rate. This situation is shown in Fig. 9, below.

As is easily understandable, when the economy reaches a situation of this nature, it means that monetary policy ceases to have any role in determining the level of economic activity. If the central bank expands the reserves in a voluntary manner, trying to get economic results by expanding the money supply, it can only generate

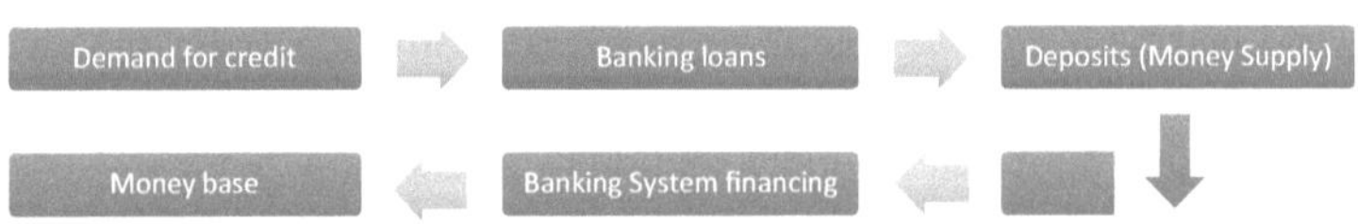


**Fig. 8** Money creation sequence

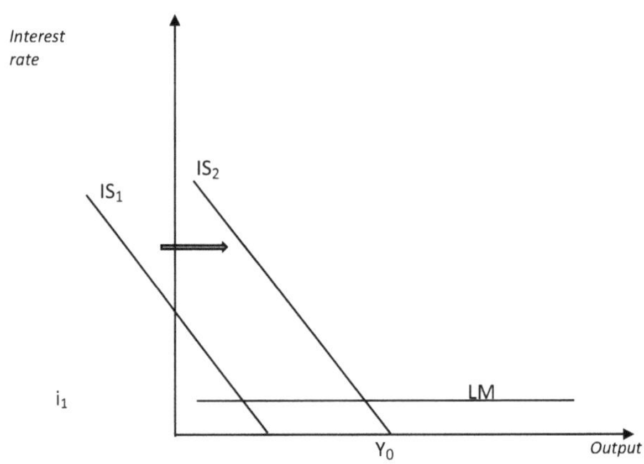


**Fig. 9** Endogeneity of money supply

excess reserves by commercial banks pushing interest rates down. No increase in money supply is effectively produced.

By contrast, fiscal policy obtains full importance.

Somehow, this is what is currently happening in the Eurozone and other economic zones with the central banks expanding the reserves of the banking system beyond all limits through "quantitative easing", without having been able, at least until now, to expand the demand for funds by the non-financial sector as necessary to significantly influence the level of aggregate demand, as would be their intention.

## 3 Conventional Monetary Policy Versus Unconventional Monetary Policy: Additional Considerations

Graph 2 shows the evolution of the reference interest rates, homologous monthly inflation rate and the homologous quarterly change in real GDP.

The three stages of the response of the unconventional monetary policy to the crisis are represented by the vertical lines slicing the horizontal axis in September 2008, June 2014 and Mars 2016. One can clearly see that the unconventional monetary policy has progressively lost the ability to deal with the worsening of the general economic conditions.

Firstly, the graph displays the difficulty in fulfilling the fundamental goal concerning the inflation rate, 'below but close to 2 %'. Regardless of the successive decrease in the interest rates since October 2008 together with the three intakes of

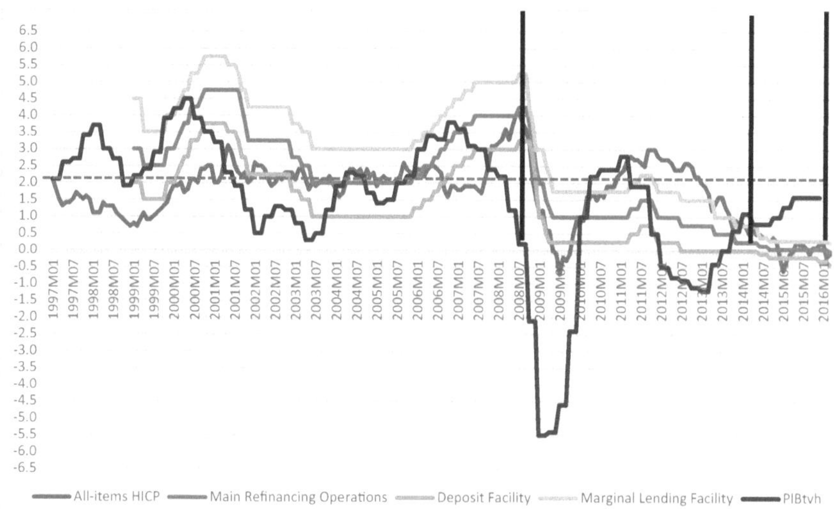


**Graph 2** Interest rates, GDP and inflation in the Eurozone

unconventional measures, in reality, it has not been possible to invert the deflationary tendencies, that accompany the low growth tendencies of GDP, in a sustainable manner.

The inversion witnessed in 2010 until mid-2011 was temporary and was most likely related to the extension of the 'more Keynesian' effects, i.e. more fiscal, measures taken in the heat of the crisis in 2009, than with monetary policies (conventional or unconventional), that have, in this first stage, a more accommodative character of the general fiscal policies of sustention of demand. Still, one must refer, even if in a negative manner, to the concern with the recovery of an inflationary path occurring in this period, which culminated with the decision to raise the main interest rates in April and later in July 2011, from 1 % to 1.25 % and to 1.5 %, respectively, when the GDP dynamics were already signalling a recession, in 2012 and 2013, thus favouring a new decrease in inflation and increasing the need for extra measures for monetary easing.

This decision of the ECB is yet another display of all the incoherence and lack of strategic meaning within the European economic policies to solve the crisis. The decision makers in the ECB were probably aware of the dangers related to the increase of in interest rates but the general political environment, highly influenced by the German position and its transmission within the European Commission, is likely to have favoured the adoption of a measure that would reveal itself to be counterproductive, given the general tendencies of the European and international economies, and would, in the end, not have avoided the relapse of the European economy observed next, if not having directly contributed to it.

This new recession is precisely the reason behind the adoption of new and broader unconventional measures of monetary policy, which have come along with a new decrease in interest rates, up to the current negative level. The second phase of this unconventional monetary policy occurred in June 2014, when the deposit facility rate was fixed at −0.1 %. The third phase took place in March 2016, when the main refinancing rate was fixed at 0 %.

It is clear that the deflation/lack of economic dynamism binomial marks the evolution of the unconventional monetary policy, from the simple quantitative increase in the supply of liquidity to the banking system, visible in the first phase, to a change in the quality of the positioning of the ECB concerning assets eligible as collateral for funding, the length of the programmes and the acceptance of negative interest rates.

However, the effectiveness of the measures successively adopted in order to reach the desired goals is not evident. Quite on the contrary, what the graph suggests is that there has been a progressive loss of effectiveness, which has translated into the need to apply ever more heterodox measures, from the point of view of the dominant theoretical monetary policy references, and be far more elastic concerning the interpretation of the legal and institutional framework of the ECB's intervention.

If the desired effectiveness had been reached and the transmission mechanism had been recovered through its functioning, the use of increasingly less conventional measures and the adoption of negative interest rates would not have been

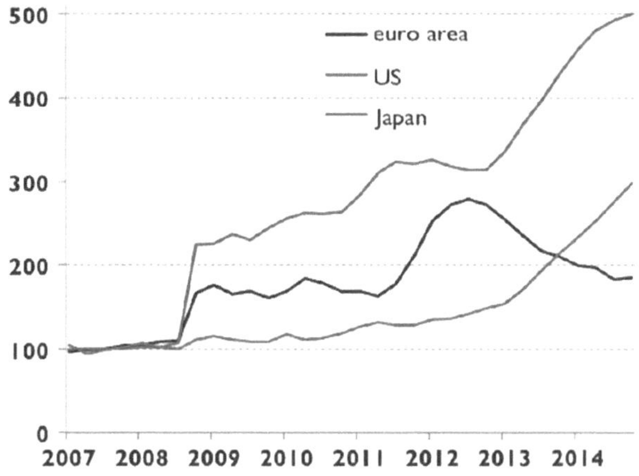


**Fig. 10** Central banks' balance sheets. Sources: ECB, Federal Reserve Board, Bank of Japan and ECB staff calculations. Constâncio (2015a)

justified. Given that this was not achieved, one witnessed a complete breakdown of the so-called conventional monetary policy and a clear display of the construction errors in the architecture of the Euro System.

## *3.1 ECB Versus Fed: A Brief Comparison*

In order to make a proper analysis, it might at this point be interesting to compare the use of unconventional monetary policy by the ECB with that of the Fed (Tuckwell and Mendonça 2016).

In both Central Banks, the impact of these policies is visible in the enlargement of the banks themselves, although the Fed appears to be more coherent than the ECB (see Figs. 10 and 11, below). In fact, whereas in the former there has been a continuous increasing trend since the first signs of the crisis in 2007 until today, in the latter there was an increasing trend until 2012, which became negative from then onwards. The Fed's stimulus to the economy using unconventional measures has been quantitatively more significant than the ECB's. The Fed has also a greater component of assets related with the issuing of public debt than the ECB, thus reflecting its 'lender of last resort' nature.

What is more, the Fed opted for a clear 'quantitative easing' since the beginning, with the goal of increasing the price of assets, thus reducing the yields, which led to a greater economic stimulus. On the other hand, the ECB cared more about supplying liquidity to the banking system, without a stated purpose of expanding the assets on its balance sheet, given that these measures were accompanied by parallel operations of monetary sterilization. Following this line of reasoning, the operations conducted by the ECB are closer to what can be considered 'credit easing', since their goal was not to directly inject liquidity in the economy, as the

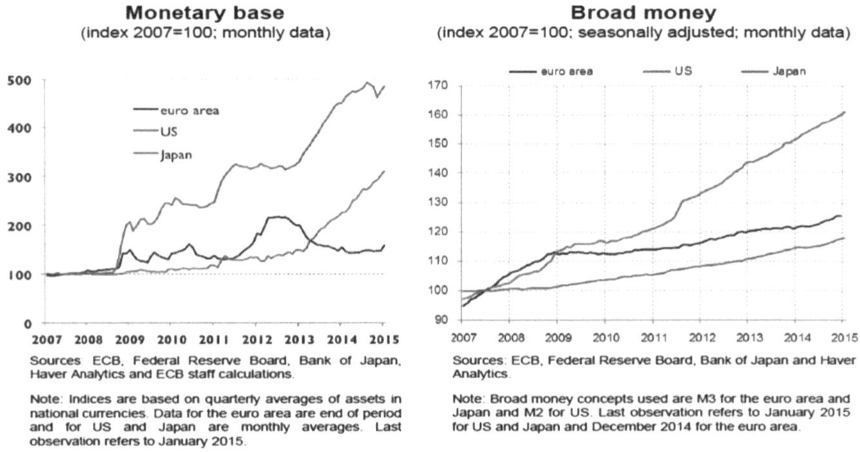


**Fig. 11** Monetary base and broad money. Source: Constâncio (2015a, b)

Fed's operations did, given that this was seen as the most expeditious way of stimulating the economy.

The differences between these two central banks' performances reflect, first of all, their different financial structures and the different conventional intervention frameworks. The ECB works on a financial structure based on the banking system, which implied approaching the crisis through the expansion route and the improvement in the financing conditions of the banking system. Indeed, the supply of liquidity to the banking system had a significant impact on the ECB's balance sheet. As a counterpart, the Fed operates under a financial structure essentially based on the market, which is reflected in their adoption of unconventional policies. The Fed has always adopted a posture of directly injected liquidity into the economy through the markets.

Some authors claim that the Fed was more original and creative in dealing with the financial crisis (Lenza et al. 2010; Cecioni et al. 2011). But it is also true that the ECB has been able to extend the usage of its traditional instruments, beyond limits that were not imaginable before the crisis, thus avoiding a more direct use of 'quantitative easing', at least until the second phase of what is being called here unconventional monetary policy was reached.

In fact, the legal constraints affecting the ECB's intervention, as opposed to those of the Fed, led the ECB leaders to build a true theory justifying unconventional monetary policy, where conventional policies are still present, as previously discussed. All measures are justified in order to assure the functioning of the monetary policy transmission mechanism. If this was not the case, according to Articles 123, 124 and 125 of the Treaty of the Functioning of the European Union, it could already be in contravention of these, with the possibility of being accused of acting as a 'Lender of Last Resort'. This can be seen in the SMP programme, aimed at purchasing sovereign debt from the peripheral countries, in the LTRO operations,

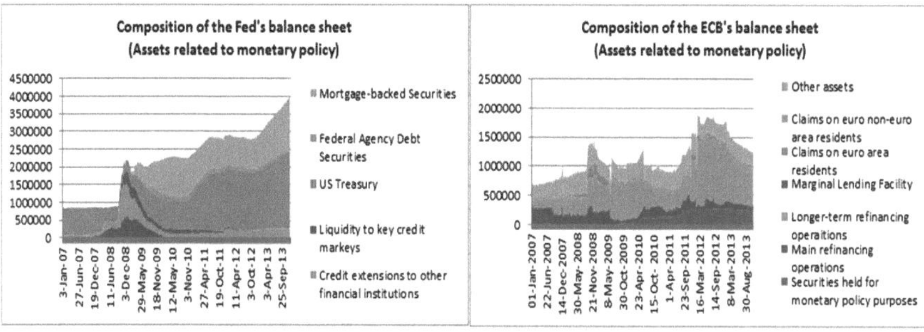


**Fig. 12** Composition of the Fed's and the BCE's balance sheets (2007–2013). Source of data: Federal Reserve Bank of Cleveland (2014) and European Central Bank (2014), in Tuckwell and Mendonça (2016). Note: The values are in millionsof dollars (Fed) millions of euros (ECB)

related to the Italian and French sovereign debts, or even in the Troika programmes, for the cases of Greece, Ireland and Portugal, and more recently in the TLTRO programmes [see, among others, De Grauwe (2011) and Buiter and Rahbari (2012)]. It is worth noting the controversy regarding the use of the 'Outright Monetary Transactions', considered as contrary to Article 123 and to European Union law itself by the Federal Constitutional Court of Germany (Bundesverfassungsgericht 2014). Finally, one must mention the developments regarding the evolution of collateral, progressively enlarged so as to include the debt instruments issued by the States affected by the sovereign debt crisis, including those issued by local and regional governments.

As for the Fed, the most extreme unconventional measures do not contradict any provision of the Federal Reserve Act. Similarly, the monetary policy legal does not establish any restriction, qualitative or quantitative, regarding the purchase of public debt bonds by the Fed (see Fig. 12).

## 4 Concluding Remarks

There is little left over to use regarding the "tool box" available by the ECB. And as regards what is left, only with a large degree of "elasticity" of interpretation will it fit within what the ECB is supposed to be able to do under the European Treaty and its own statutes.

An additional problem has to do with coordination of monetary policy with fiscal policy in the euro area. The former, increasingly oriented in an expansionary direction and the latter continuingly tied to a contractionary view of response to the crisis, particularly with regard to the countries most affected by its effects, more indebted and, therefore, more dramatically dependent on a stimulus demand to be able to get out of economic anaemia in which they find themselves.

There is, therefore, somewhat of a manifestation of an economic schizophrenia, which can be verified at the level of institutions with more responsibility in the conduct of international economic policies, particularly with regard to the ECB and the IMF.

In all its last interventions, following the Governing Council meetings of the ECB, Mario Draghi has urged governments to use fiscal policies that promote growth. Even in the last press conference, to present the decisions of ECB Governing Council Meeting of 10 March, Draghi (2016a) stated that "Fiscal policies should support economic recovery . . .", at the same time as affirming that ". . . while remaining in compliance with the fiscal rules of the European Union", to add at the end "at the same time, all countries should strive for a more growth-friendly composition of fiscal policies".

Discounting the aforementioned schizophrenia, evident in the contradictory statements between the call to use fiscal policy and the appeal for "compliance" with the rules of the Stability and Growth Pact, the ECB president's concern with the continued refusal of the use of fiscal policy in the euro area is clear, particularly by countries with economic surplus, with Germany at the head. But also, jointly by the EU and the euro area member states, as an instrument to streamline economic activity via aggregate demand stimulus. A situation that, if it continues, could accelerate even further the exhaustion process of monetary policy, both in its conventional and unconventional versions.

It is this awareness that justifies the growing concern of the ECB to build a theoretical and empirical justification for the need to promote public investment. There is a clear orientation of economic studies in this direction, which also meet the need to provide institutional support to the fragile Juncker Plan, "A new start for Europe", presented to the European Parliament on 15 July 2014, following his election as the new President of the European Commission.

In this regard the recent study published in the *ECB Economic Bulletin*, Issue 2/2016, "Public Investment in Europe" (ECB 2016) should be mentioned, which recognizes the sharp drop in public investment in Europe, since the crisis, and states that "An Increase in public investment has positive demand effects and can contribute to the economy's potential output by increasing the stock of public capital" (ECB 2016, p. 13). Considering the monetary policy followed by the ECB, the study recognizes that ". . . an increase in public investment will have the strongest short-term demand effects, including in terms of spill overs to other countries, with an anticipated accommodative monetary policy", and that " this finding strengthens the case for increasing public investment in the current low-inflation environment". Still following the study, it concludes that ". . . a debt or revenue financed increase in productive public investment implies significantly larger short-term output gains compared with an increase in investment financed by cutting other public expenditure". Conclusions which, however, do not seem to have been suitably taken into account regarding the general direction of economic policies pursued by the EU and the euro area, leading to the inconsistency and schizophrenia already mentioned.

Also at the level of the IMF, there is a recognition of the importance of relaunching public investment on a comprehensive and coordinated scale, although this had not been exempt from criticism of incoherence and schizophrenia as manifested with particular sharpness in assistance programs in which the IMF participated as a member of the Troikas. Even before the ECB, the IMF, through the statements of its leading figure, Christine Lagarde, and also through the statements of its most senior economists, such as Oliver Blanchard, drew attention to the effects of the austerity policies implemented across the board and without taking into account the specific situations of regions and countries, recognizing the negative impact on growth and employment and, more than that, for the persistence at the world economy level, of a general trend towards economic stagnation. In this regard, it is important to read the *World Economic Outlook*, April 2016 (IMF 2016), significantly entitled "Too slow for too long", where growth-oriented policies receive clear support from the analysis made of the general economic conditions and the factors that led to them. And, finally, the most recent paper published on the IMF Journal, *Finance & Development*, by Ostry et al. (2016), where the authors clear conclude, after a cross-countries analysis of the policies that have been adopted in response to the crisis, that instead of delivering growth, some neo-liberal policies have increased inequality, in turn jeopardizing durable expansion.

This re-orientation of IMF concerns began to become evident in the *WEO* of October 2014 where, in the third chapter it significantly raises the issue, "Is it time for an infrastructure push? The macroeconomic effects of public investment.", to give the answer "This chapter finds that increased public infrastructure investment raises output in both the short and long term, particularly during periods of economic slack and when investment effectiveness is high. This suggests that in countries with infrastructure needs, the time is right for an infrastructure push: borrowing costs are low and demand is weak in advanced economies, and there are infrastructure bottlenecks in many emerging market and developing economies. Debt-financed projects could have large output effects without increasing the debt-to-GDP ratio, if clearly identified infrastructure needs are met through efficient investment."

The OECD seems to be going in a similar direction when emphasising, in its *Interim Economic Outlook,* of February 16, 2016, following the recognition of the weak economic growth, that "A strong collective policy response is urgent. Global macroeconomic policy, comprising monetary, fiscal and structural actions, must become more supportive of demand and resource allocation. Experience to date suggests that reliance on monetary policy alone has been insufficient to deliver satisfactory growth, so that greater use of fiscal and structural levers is required".

Seen retrospectively, the monetary policy response of the ECB to the development of the crisis seems to be more a reaction to developments than an effective response to the economic problems. Although there has been an improvement, compared to the times of the former President Jean-Claude Trichet, someone who showed himself to be completely out the historical and economic period Europe and the global economy has been passing through, the reality is that the current team responsible failed to act in advance, intervening mainly in extreme situations to prevent disaster.

However, if this intervention has proved crucial to prevent further worsening of the problems, it is also true that it has contributed to the accumulation of tensions that threaten to explode cyclically pushing the economy to situations at the limit. It is precisely this dynamic of the accumulation of tensions that has increasingly driven ECB intervention toward the unconventional measures.

However, these unconventional measures have not found, until now, the necessary support in terms of fiscal and budgetary policies, which continue to manifest a resistance to meet the real needs of the economy. Instead, as these policies continue to focus on issues of fiscal balance and public debt, they have acted in the opposite way, demanding more and more from monetary policy that, by its very nature, is limited in its capacity to deal with all the problems that manifest in the economy.

It is, precisely, this contradiction between the stances of fiscal and monetary policies that has boosted the effect of exhaustion of monetary policy that has been discussed in this essay.

When called upon to use less and less conventional instruments, monetary policy that is supposed to be followed by the ECB reveals its weak institutional architecture and its inconsistent theoretical framework. While not being completely negative, in that it has enabled pragmatism in response to the crisis, it has pushed monetary policy towards a boundary zone where it has begun to deny itself, when it accepted within its toolbox the use of negative interest rates.

To conclude, we will say that what is at stake in how Europe and the Eurozone in particular have reacted to the crisis, is the euro system itself.

Designed to provide a joint response of the monetary zone to the problems of international adjustment it has not internally found a suitable complement to the correction of asymmetries between countries that, as opposed to the starting assumptions, have ended up accentuating these, denying the verification of the optimistic endogeneity hypothesis for the monetary area.

Within this perspective, ideas that point to a solution of a "more Europe" kind to address the problems do not seem to make sense. This solution runs the risk of accentuating the removal of decisions from the concrete realities of countries, strengthening theoretical approaches to the detriment of diversified analyses and the power of distant bureaucracies to the detriment of the ability to intervene of those agents subject to the direct scrutiny of citizens. Which, ultimately, can lead to the denial of the very concept of economic and monetary integration applied to the reality of Europe and the Eurozone.

A general review of the euro system is x, justified in order to adjust it to the current dynamics of the different European economies and to their joint participation in the global economy. Furthermore, the immediate recovery of all rights of citizenship for fiscal policy is also justified in order to curb the monetary policy exhaustion process and enable it to bring back the economy to a sustained area reversing the stagnation tendencies that affect it.

# Bibliography


Buiter WH, Rahbari E (2012) The ECB as lender of last resort for sovereigns in the Euro area. Centre for Economic Policy Research, London

Bundesverfassungsgericht (2014) Press release No. 9/2014 of 7 February 2014

Cecioni M, Ferrero G, Sechi A (2011) Unconventional monetary policy in theory and in practice [Online]. Banca d'Italia, n.l

Constâncio V (2011) Challenges to monetary policy in 2012. ECB, 8 Dec 2011

Constâncio V (2013) The global financial crisis—5 years on. Intervention at the China-Europe Economists Symposium, Beijing, 12 Jan 2013, ECB

Constâncio V (2015a) Slides of the presentation for the panel discussion "Central banks with large balance sheets" at the U.S. Monetary Forum in New York City, 27 Feb 2015, ECB

Constâncio V (2015b) Assessing the new phase of unconventional monetary policy. Panel remarks at the Annual Congress of the European Economic Association, University of Mannheim, 25 Aug 2015, ECB

Constâncio V (2016) In defence of monetary policy. Opinion piece. ECB, 11 Mar 2016

De Grauwe P (2011) The European central bank: lender of last resort in the government bond markets. CESifo, Leuven

Draghi M (2016a) Introductory statement to the press conference. ECB, 21 Jan 2016

Draghi M (2016b) Introductory statement to the press conference. ECB, 10 Mar 2016

European Central Bank (2014) Statistical data warehouse [Database]. http://sdw.ecb.europa.eu/. Accessed Aug 2014

ECB (2016) Public investment in Europe. Economic Bulletin, Issue 2

Federal Reserve Bank of Cleveland (2014) Credit easing policy tools [Database]. http://www.clevelandfed.org/research/data/credit_easing/index.cfm. Accessed Aug 2014

International Monetary Fund (2014) World economic outlook: legacies, clouds, uncertainties. Oct 2014

International Monetary Fund (2016) World economic outlook: too slow for too long. Apr 2016

Krugman P (2012) End this depression now. W. W. Norton, New York

Lenza M, Pill H, Reichlin L (2010) Monetary policy in exceptional times. ECB

OECD (2016) Interim economic outlook. 16 Feb 2016

Ostry JD, Loungani P, Furcery D (2016) Finance & Development. Jun 2016

Praet P (2016) Interview with La Republica. ECB, 19 Mar 2016

Temin P, Vines D (2014) Keynes—useful economics for the world economy. MIT Press, Cambridge

Tuckwell C, Mendonça A (2016) The global crisis and unconventional monetary policy: ECB versus Fed. Working Paper CESA/CSG 141/2016. ISEG, Lisbon

# The Eurozone's Private and Governmental Shock Absorbers: Current Setup and Future Prospects

**Nazaré de Costa Cabral**

**Abstract** In this chapter, the author analyses the two main types of shock absorbers—private and governmental shock absorbers—that have been proposed after the 2007–2008 financial crisis, even though in some cases their theoretical origins are not new. As for private shock absorbers that imply the reinforcement of 'market forces' within the E(M)U, the author indicates certain measures that intend either to ensure the completion of the internal market or to address sectorial market fragmentation, as it is the case of the creation of the Banking Union. As for governmental shock absorbers, the author then distinguishes between macro stabilizing measures that can be implemented outside the EU's budget (e.g. the creation of a new 'Debt Agency' or the institution of a new 'European unemployment insurance scheme') and those measures that can be adopted through the EU's budget. In this latter case, within the current set of (tax) revenues and expenditures, the EU budget might evolve to embrace some stabilization properties, even if significant changes in the design of tax assignment criteria and of funds allocation rules should be required.

**JEL Classification** E52 • E63 • F45 • H72

N. de Costa Cabral
Center for European, Economic, Financial and Tax (CIDEEFF), Lisbon University, Lisbon, Portugal

Faculdade de Direito da Universidade de Lisboa, Lisbon Law School, Lisbon University, Lisbon, Portugal

Alameda da Universidade, 1649-014 Lisbon, Portugal
e-mail: nazarecabral@fd.ulisboa.pt



N. de Costa Cabral et al. (eds.), *The Euro and the Crisis*, Financial and Monetary Policy Studies 43, DOI 10.1007/978-3-319-45710-9_15

# 1 Introduction

In the aftermath of the 2007–2008 financial crisis several proposals, concerning both monetary and fiscal policies, have been made to cope with its negative effects on E(M)U's countries and on the Eurozone as a whole. The financial crisis has in fact transformed itself into a much more profound crisis—a severe economic and sovereign debt crisis and ultimately a monetary crisis that has put the Euro in question. The Euro crisis has, on the other hand, exacerbated deeper insufficiencies involving the conception of the Eurozone's construction and this fundamental fragility is mostly due to the lack of a political union or at least of more integrated and democratic governance institutions. In fact, as noticed by McNamara (2015), the Eurozone, unlike other currency areas, is not an 'embedded' area, and this occurs precisely because it is not politically sustained.[1] Therefore, the fragility of the Eurozone framework is not only due to the fact that the area does not fulfil the optimum conditions presented by the Optimum Currency Areas (OCA) theory[2], but mostly because it is still a territory of 'one currency and multiple political authorities'. This insufficiency also explains why is it so difficult to implement a complete budgetary union in the area that could substitute incomplete factors mobility, and through which a system of fiscal transfers could be implemented providing for fiscal adjustments in the event of asymmetric shocks (see on this issue von Hagen 1998, pp. 5–6). Differently, the conception of macroeconomic shock absorbers intends either to improve 'market forces' within the E(M)U's territory or to be an alternative path to the conception of a (complete) budgetary union. In this latter case, the approach relies on the acknowledgment that a budgetary union is bound to deeper political integration, and this is a complex and difficult process for which basic conditions have not yet been gathered (and probably never will be). Despite being less ambitious than the conception of a budgetary union, these 'alternative' shock absorbers, if well designed and implemented, can be quite effective in the response to (regional) macroeconomic imbalances.

Departing from the two broad and standard categories of shock absorbers—private and governmental shock absorbers—the objective of this chapter is therefore to examine their types, main characteristics and future perspectives. To do this, it will be taken into account that some of the shock absorbers are directly conceived to address cyclical shocks—in this case, they should be qualified as 'visible' and 'direct' stabilization mechanisms—whereas others have, in contrast, stabilizing

[1]Recall that the idea of 'embeddedness' is driven from the *Opus Magnum* of Karl Polanyi, *The Great Transformation,* where he claims that, within capitalist economies, markets are strongly embedded mostly because they are political institutions and submitted to political control (McNamara 2015, p. 25).

[2]Starting from the seminal article of Mundell (1961), the main conditions for an optimum currency area are, on the one hand, the mobility of factors of production including labour and, on the other hand, price and wage flexibility. As a result, when facing an adjustment problem, these two conditions are mechanisms that can grant automatic equilibrium to the participating economies. Furthermore, the similitude or symmetry of economic structures between countries belonging to the same currency area may also work out as a condition to reach the optimum.

effects in an 'indirect' and 'invisible' way. The latter are in fact designed to pursue other economic goals than stabilization (and only indirectly do they provide for this macroeconomic effect). Furthermore, some of these other economic goals can be of a structural nature, in the sense that they are related either to the completion of the internal market, or to the convergence between the economic structures of the E(M)U's member countries. Hence, when distinguishing between private and governmental shock absorbers it will be shown below that the former usually produce stabilization effects in an indirect way, while the latter can be visible or invisible stabilization mechanisms.

## 2 Private Shock Absorbers: Main Features, Taxonomy and Future Prospects

Private shock absorbers can be defined as measures that, while aiming to promote the completion of the internal market and the reduction of the rigidities of the market, and to address sectorial fragmentation of markets, can also work out as macroeconomic stabilization devices. In this sense, they are made to enhance market conditions, in fact OCA conditions (flexibility of prices and wages and mobility of factors) that ultimately may guarantee a smooth functioning of the monetary union—and indirectly perform as a shock absorber. The crisis has made it evident that these elements were not working sufficiently, with there being important functional hurdles in the Eurozone, reason for which an immediate response was provided in 2011 with the institution of the Macroeconomic Imbalance Procedure (as one of the new elements introduced by the '*Six Pack*').[3] The main purpose of this new Procedure is precisely to prevent macroeconomic imbalances in non-fiscal areas such as private leverage or unit labour costs (Bénassy-Quéré 2015, p. 77), either by preventing the regional concentration of credit risks or by ensuring wage flexibility in each of the Eurozone members.

Two main categories of measures (considering their direct goal) that can act as private shock absorbers can be thus distinguished.

### *2.1 Measures Aiming to Promote the Completion of the Internal Market and/or to Reduce Market Rigidities*

The internal market, a precondition of the monetary union, was implemented in the EU (with the Single European Act of 1987) to ensure a free market environment,

[3]Regulation (EU) No 1174/2011 of the European Parliament and of the Council of 16 November 2011 on enforcement measures to correct excessive macroeconomic imbalances in the euro area.

sound competition rules, and freedom of movement of goods, services and workers. Since the inception of the EMU, and as mentioned again by Enderlein et al. (2012, p. 28), "deeper market integration was expected to improve the functioning of the euro area, and the latter was expected to trigger more trade integration". However, during the first years of the EMU the enhancement of the Single Market did not occur. For that reason, and following the Monti Report of 2010, the Commission presented in 2011 the '*Single Market Act*' *Communication*, identifying the major areas in which improvements should be made: in the first place, the single market for services enhancement, notably through the full implementation of the Service Directive and the removal of obstacles to their mobility; in the second place, labour mobility, by suppressing policy-induced factors that hamper the mobility of workers in Europe (*Ibidem*, pp. 28–29).

Despite the attempts, mobility of factors, and notably the mobility of workers, is an objective very difficult to attain in a territory with the *sui generis* nature of the EU. In fact, the presence of economic, historical, cultural and institutional constraints severely impairs the prospects of achieving complete mobility. Alternatively, other sorts of measures have been claimed now, in order to reduce labour market rigidities: E(M)U's countries (notably the countries assisted after the crisis) were urged to adopt reforms in the labour markets and the ultimate purpose of these reforms was to increase wage flexibility. Being, in fact, another optimum condition in the light of the OCA theory, labour market reforms should however not be considered a panacea deprived of shortcomings. In fact, flexibility implies wage cuts, fewer unemployment benefits, lower minimum wages and easier firing (De Grauwe 2015, p. 101). The conventional menu, of a neoclassical type, of structural reforms leading to nominal devaluations implies, on the other hand, deflationary/contractionary effects that can be counterproductive in times of crisis (Pesenti 2015, p. 160).[4] For all these reasons, the flexibility movement is not free of criticism. Furthermore, labour market conditions along with social security systems remain very different amongst E(M)U members and there does not seem to exist conditions, at least in the near future, for harmonisation in these social areas. Because of all this, labour will remain weakly mobile in the E(M)U and labour markets will preserve their *natural* rigidity.

## 2.2 Measures Aiming to Address Sectorial Markets Fragmentation

This is the case with the Banking Union (BU) launched in 2013, seeking to "*sever the doom loop between sovereign and banking crises*, notably by directly

[4]As an alternative approach, the Author suggests that to foster European adjustment, structural reforms should target obstacles to the entry of firms, start-up costs, and the incentives for product differentiation, and not to achieve a narrow objective of cost-competitiveness but to expand the net array of tradable varieties of goods and services (*Idem*, p. 160).

recapitalizing failing banks, which in turn required to transfer supervision to the European Central Bank (ECB) through the new Single Supervisory Mechanism (SSM), and by establishing a resolution system that would eradicate bankers' moral hazard by making shareholders and creditors responsible for losses (bail-in)" (Micossi 2015, pp. 139–140).[5] As mentioned, on the other hand by Schoenmaker (2015, p. 2), the sovereign-bank loop works in two ways. Firstly, banks carry large amounts of bonds of their own government on their balance sheet. A deterioration of a government's credit standing would automatically worsen solvency of that country's banks. Secondly, a worsening of a country's banking system could worsen the government's budget because of a potential government financed bank bailout. The BU is expected thus to work out as an effective private risk sharing mechanism via capital markets (*Ibidem*, p. 140), capable of limiting the effects of financial fragmentation and idiosyncratic risk premiums that the Euro crisis has clearly revealed.

In fact, the crisis has highlighted two effects that only apparently may be considered paradoxical. First effect, and as a consequence of the free capital movements (in itself an essential element of the EMU) is the existence of large cross-border financial flows between financial institutions of the Eurozone, the strong interdependency of financial markets within the area and because of this the existence of the specific risk of contagion in situations of distress. Second effect, and as mentioned by Breuss et al. (2015, p. 3), the financial markets (notably the capital markets) in the EMU are not fully integrated and thus only provide limited risk sharing across countries. Adverse financial shocks (e.g. mortgage loan losses in countries like Ireland and Spain) therefore have effects, which are largely confined to countries from which they originate, or—it could be added—countries that exhibit country-specific risks due to their fundamentals deterioration (see Caceres et al. 2011, p. 397), as was the case with Greece and Portugal. Financial interdependency did not create fully financial integration, in the sense that country-specific risks were not eliminated or reduced by the existence of risk sharing mechanisms indirectly provided by the financial markets. The creation of the E(M)U had brought the conviction that risk premiums should disappear within the area as markets believed the Maastricht Treaty promises of 'no devaluation', 'no default' and 'low inflation forever for all' (Baldwin and Giavazzi 2015, p. 22). The crisis has shown, on the contrary, that this was not the case because investors (lato sensu) started to negatively discriminate against sovereigns that presented poor fundamentals, exacerbating a 'flight to quality' effect that ultimately led to high

[5]Notice that besides the SSM and the Single Resolution Mechanism (SRM), the BU also includes harmonization (not centralization) of the national deposit insurance schemes. The key pieces of legislation concerning the BU are: EU Regulation No 1424/2013, which confers upon the ECB the task of prudential supervision of credit institutions; EU Resolution No 806/2014, which establishes the Single Resolution Mechanism (SRM), a Single Resolution Board (SRB) and a Single Resolution Fund (SRF); EU Directive 2014/59 (Bank Recovery and Resolution Directive—BRRD); EU Directive 2014/49, which harmonizes the key features of national deposit guarantee schemes (see Xafa 2015, p. 6). On this issue, see also Véron (2015, pp. 9–13).

divergences in the Eurozone for the 10-year government bond yields.[6] The crisis thus once again exhibited risk premiums and the idiosyncratic nature of sovereign risks.

It is a fact, on the other hand, that the BU was expected to help to overcome these sectorial markets (the financial markets) fragmentation and that it was presented by the Four E(M)U Presidents, in the 2012 Report, as a fundamental measure in the course of the process of reform of the monetary union.[7] Despite this, the BU has already been criticised due to its shortcomings as a risk-sharing mechanism.[8] Véron (2015) stresses that if it is true that the BU (notably when creating a SRM) intended to shift from bail-out to bail-in and thus to reduce moral hazard, there are still banking nationalisms that imply government bail-outs to national banks—at least until the complete implementation of the SRF (which is expected to happen only by 2024). But most of all, the BU is incomplete, because within the last of its branches—the harmonization of national deposit insurances—fragile steps were taken. And notice that harmonization does not mean centralization. Hence, completing the banking union should imply moving the deposit insurance functions to the euro-area (see Schoenmaker 2015). Some authors, such as Gros (2015), go even further and argue that with a full banking union that includes precisely a supranational deposit insurance, "*a fiscal backup would become unnecessary,* since emerging bank losses would be taken up by the deposit insurance system at the federal level, as in the US Federal Deposit Insurance system" (Micossi 2015, p. 140).[9] Finally, it should also be noticed that the European BU may not even become a truly 'private' banking union, unlike what happens in the US. In fact, the way the US effectively responded to the subprime crisis that hit certain American states in contrast to the poor response given in the Eurozone to shocks verified in some countries such as Ireland and Spain is due to the fact that in the US there is a complete BU (implying the aforementioned centralization of the deposit insurance scheme),

[6]Recall that this divergence was only interrupted from July 2012 onwards, after the speech then made by ECB President Mario Draghi, when he claimed that the ECB would do "whatever it takes" to keep the Eurozone together (see again Baldwin and Giavazzi *Idem*, p. 48).

[7]The Report was entitled *Towards a Genuine Economic and Monetary Union.*

[8]Others stress that the stabilizing properties of the BU are only complete when considering the intervention of the European Stabilization Mechanism (ESM) direct recapitalization instrument created in 2014 for the euro area financial institutions. This is a backstop mechanism that allows the ESM to recapitalise a systemic and viable financial institution (systemically relevant credit institution) hence acting as a 'last resort' device (see Breuss et al. *Idem*, p. 7).

[9]Notice, however, that if national deposit insurance should involve some fiscal burden sharing (at the federal level), then the banking union should imply the notion of budgetary union or at least the idea of a fiscal backstop. On this issue, see Wolff (2012, pp. 5–6). The Author mentions that despite the autonomy of the Federal Deposit Insurance Corporation (FDIC) the US Treasury stands behind providing for credibility in times of crisis. If a similar solution were to be adopted in the EU, then "one could view a euro-area budget as the backbone for such a common fiscal backstop for a new European resolution authority and fund. Such a fiscal backstop ultimately means that the federal level has the ability to borrow on the market" (*Idem*, p. 6), restoring confidence in situations of crisis.

but also because there is a 'private' BU, or a truly integrated banking market (Belke and Gros 2015, p. 11). In fact, bank owners in the US are not only 'national' owners but also 'foreign' owners (owners from other American states different from those hit by negative shocks, e.g. the case in Nevada or Florida) and this helped to smoothe the effects of the same shocks by distributing them over the whole territory of the US. That is, the US BU was able to trigger an effective private sharing risk mechanism between all its members. Unlike the US, the predominance in some Eurozone countries of domestic capital vis-à-vis the banking institutions (e.g. Spain), explains the concentration of risks within a country and the need for government bail out of its national banks. Furthermore, market mechanisms to absorb losses in sub-prime or non-conforming mortgages were developed in the US, through insurance and securitization (*Ibidem*, p. 12). Differently in the Eurozone, risk-sharing mechanisms provided either by institutions, backed up by the central government (as in the case of the FDIC) or by the private sector (large banks and sub-prime securitization) did not fully operate, which explains the bailing out response and in some cases the subsequent deterioration in fiscal outlook (e.g. soaring public debt levels).

Notice on the other hand, that the non-complete integration of banking markets is a consequence of the non-integration of the capital markets in general terms. Usually it is mentioned that euro area members' financial systems are heavily 'bank-centred' and stock and bond markets provide a relatively modest share of the financing to the private sector in most countries (see again Belke and Gros 2015, p. 143). If this is true, also true appears to be this peculiar inconsistency: even though the main financing channel is debt through the banking system, the banking market—as an important landscape and expression of the capital markets—is not in itself completely and soundly integrated (and not being clear, for the time being, if the BU will contribute to a sound integration of the banking market). Important consequences arise from this inconsistency, and the Euro crisis has highlighted them: the Eurozone once again reveals itself to be a *non*-Optimum Currency Area (as integration of capital markets should be a consequence of full capital mobility and yet it is not) that lacks adequate responses for asymmetric shocks[10] and that also prevents normal financing channels to households, firms and governments, ultimately impairing investment in the *real* economy. Ultimately, the incompleteness regarding financial market integration explains the launching of the *Green Paper Building a Capital Markets Union* by the European Commission, in 2015,

[10]Explaining in which way equity and bond markets work as a private insurance mechanism in case of asymmetric shocks, see De Grauwe (2014, pp. 18–19). Asdrubali et al. (1996) have empirically validated this idea for the US case. Recall that according to the results then presented (and that seem to maintain appropriateness), part of the shocks to gross state product (39 %) were absorbed by capital markets, while federal government smoothing was only on 13 % and credit markets smoothing of 23 % (with 6 % remaining of non-smoothed shocks). Hoffmann and Sørensen in a similar vein (2012) claim that from the three existing risk-sharing channels—the fiscal insurance, the credit markets and the capital markets channels—the most effective is the latter.

where alternatives to bank lending were suggested, notably through the development of equity or bond markets (e.g. improving access to finance, including to risk capital notably for SMEs, or the development of a more integrated European covered bond market for investment promotion).

# 3 Governmental Shock Absorbers: Main Features, Taxonomy and Future Prospects

It is a fact that private insurance elements that can be found for example in the Single Market enhancement or in the Banking Union can be quite effective and partially offset the lack of governmental shock absorbers. But for the time being their scope is limited and they will not be able to prevent or solve all types of shocks in the EU or in the Eurozone.

Government shock absorbers are thus central government insurance mechanisms (lato sensu) able to cope with asymmetric shocks that hit some economies, and ultimately to ensure macroeconomic stabilization effects. Notice that these mechanisms are expected to work in the E(M)U's current context, which is the context of an incomplete budgetary union. This occurs first of all due to the small dimension of the EU's budget (approx. 1 % of the EU's GDP) and to the fact that the existing set of taxes and expenditures in this budget is not able to fulfil the usual tasks taxes and expenditures are supposed to in a central budget, notably regional and personal redistributive tasks. Because of this, the EU's budget does not possess the conditions to provide for stabilization effects, at least in an invisible and indirect manner. Recall that the invisible action of a central budget is due either to general inter-regional redistributive mechanisms (e.g. grants coping with horizontal fiscal gap) or to inter-individual redistributive instruments (e.g. personal taxes and social benefits) provided by the same budget (see MacDougall et al. 1977). In fact, both personal income tax and social security benefits, as instruments of economic redistribution, also act as 'invisible' mechanisms able to correct regional macroeconomic imbalances: high incomes go with high tax payments and low incomes go with high revenues from the central government (*Idem,* p. 13).[11] Since there does not seem to be, in the next years, sufficient economic and political conditions to increase the EU's budget, stabilization instruments should be mostly *direct and visible stabilization mechanisms,* and not as much invisible stabilization ones (see Bajo-Rubio and Díaz-Roldan 2001, p. 7). This reason also helps to explain (even though it is not the only reason, as mentioned below) the fact that most of these instruments are provided by specific Funds (e.g. cyclical-type transfers) outside the

[11]Furthermore, as mentioned by von Hagen and Wyplosz (2008), even though redistributive transfers were not designed explicitly for that purpose, they can be considered insurance mechanisms against asymmetric cyclical shocks, since regions in a more favourable cyclical position than the federation on average pay transfers to regions in a less favourable position. This has the consequence of dampening the relative boom in the former and the relative recession in the latter.

EU's budget. Furthermore, it should be noted that these direct shock absorbers tend to exhibit actual characteristics of insurance devices, such as the need to address moral hazard—thus they can be effectively qualified as insurance mechanisms (stricto sensu).[12,13] Notwithstanding this, even though most prominent research and proposals—notably made after the financial crisis—rely on these direct insurance devices, an alternative path for future progress can also be anticipated: the enhancement of the EU's budget elements, both on the tax and expenditure sides. In this case, *some* stabilization properties can be indirectly achieved through an increase in public goods provision or the enhancement of the existing redistributive instruments (e.g. Structural Funds).

In view of this, I will therefore disentangle two broad categories of governmental shock absorbers and then for each of them consider sub-categories according to selected criteria. In this taxonomical exercise, after-crisis literature will be mostly considered, because unlike previous literature it acknowledges the incomplete nature of the E(M)U's budgetary union and is thus focused on providing for visible insurance mechanisms. On the contrary, previous contributions on this matter (the last quarter of the twentieth century) still assumed a fully federal model—in line with the *Mac Dougall Report*—in which actual spending and revenues were shifted to the euro-area level (Pisani-Ferry et al. 2013, p. 4) and which could, for that reason, have other economic goals than stabilization.[14]

---

[12]As referred to by Enderlein et al. (2013, p. 32), macroeconomic insurance can exhibit ex ante and ex post moral hazard: ex ante, countries have an incentive to reduce their own resilience to asymmetric shocks by disabling their own automatic stabilizers, triggering larger output gap deviations and thus relying on larger transfer payments from the central fund; ex post, countries could generate the funds they owe or use the funds they receive in a way that does not maximize the effectiveness of the scheme towards more business cycle convergence (they could use the funds where fiscal multipliers are not the highest but more desirable in political terms).

[13]Gros (2014) claims that the institution of a shock absorber within the Eurozone should take into account 'economics of insurance'—not only to prevent moral hazard behaviour but also to ensure that the mechanism is effective when *effectively* needed. In his opinion, the Eurozone does not need a system that offsets all shocks by some small fraction, but a system protecting against shocks that could be potentially catastrophic. A system of fiscal insurance with a fixed deductible would therefore be preferable to a fiscal shock absorber that offsets a certain percentage of all fiscal shocks. Notice that the idea of a deductible is first and foremost explained by the need to address moral hazard. But there are other alternatives to the 'deductible model'. One option relies on the integration of the new insurance device within the SGP framework that might imply either fiscal discipline enhancement as a condition (ex ante) to be eligible for funding if and whenever needed or a penalty (ex post) for countries that had circumvented SGP rules—e.g. overstating potential GDP in order to reduce its payment to the Fund (see on this issue von Hagen and Wyplosz 2008, p. 17).

[14]For this reason, Von Hagen (1998) when listing and classifying several proposals for shock absorbers, considered not only their specific insurance role, but also and first and foremost their general redistributive role. Amongst seminal contributions on this issue see, on the one hand, Sala-i-Martin and Sachs (1991), Von Hagen (1992, 1998), Goodhart and Smith (1993)—all using regression analysis to compute the contribution of fiscal variables, taxes and transfers, to the GDP—and, on the other hand, Pisani-Ferry et al. (1993), using a simulation exercise. See also Wyplosz and Pisani-Ferry (1990).

### 3.1 Visible Shock Absorbers Outside the EU's Budget

Following the classification that I have suggested elsewhere (Cabral 2016), visible shock absorbers can be grouped according to three main approaches:

*Cyclical Budget Approach* This approach refers to the creation of a government insurance-type mechanism financed and provided for by a specific Fund with respect to each country's position regarding the business cycle. Additionally, and also to address moral hazard issues (as mentioned below) the design of the insurance device can integrate or interact with the Stability and Growth Pact (SGP) framework—and in this case it would be meant to complete it—because the SGP also relies on the net budget balance of the business cycle effects (Wolff 2012, p. 8). One proposal of this kind (others will be mentioned below) is the *automatic transfer scheme,* a system of financial support based on the business cycle proposed by Wolff (2012) and Pisani-Ferry et al. (2013).

*Debt Pooling Approach* This approach is founded on the Eurobonds model[15] and permits Member states to borrow from a special Debt Agency or Fund even in situations of stress. For this reason and also due to the conditionality principle that involves access to financing, these proposals present similarities with the existing European Stability Mechanism (ESM) and in some cases they are effectively interlinked with the ESM framework. One proposal of this type—amongst others examined below—is the *guaranteed bonds quota* produced by Pisani-Ferry et al. (2013).

*Narrow Automatic Stabilizers Approach* I call this a narrow approach because it considers only one part of the automatic stabilizers that would also include, in a complete budgetary union, corporate and personal taxes, and other types of transfers as well. Furthermore, within this approach, automatic stabilizers can even be implemented outside the EU's budget (even though this is not strictly necessary), because they can be provided either by the Member States' budgets or through specific Funds created for that purpose. Finally, also notice that regarding narrow automatic stabilizers, their main and direct focus is to address economic shocks (and not to work as standard redistributive instruments). As mentioned below, this approach is fundamentally consistent with the proposal of the creation of a *European unemployment scheme* (EUBS)—the origins of which can be found in the report by Marjolin et al. (1975) and that was recently developed, notably by Dullien (2013), by Beblavý and Maselli (2014) and Beblavý et al. (2015).

[15]An initial version of this model was the 'Blue Bond proposal' made by Delpla and von Weizäker (2010): EU countries should pool up to 60 % of GDP of their national debt as senior debt, thereby reducing borrowing costs. On the contrary, red debt (beyond that percentage) would be issued as national and junior debt, claiming an enhancement of fiscal discipline as a way to prevent an interest rate premium.

Departing from these three approaches (in fact qualification criteria), Table 1 below presents the taxonomy and main features of several proposals made in the last years (namely after the crisis) concerning shock absorbers. As for the main characteristics of these proposed mechanisms, five topics will be considered (in each of the Table's columns). Firstly, *functional assumptions* of the insurance mechanism, e.g. type of shock (asymmetric or symmetric, temporary or permanent) and the shock indicator (e.g. change in the unemployment rate, output gap) (see Bajo-Rubio and Díaz-Roldan 2001). Secondly, in which way the proposed schemes fulfil *conceptual properties* usually assigned to insurance mechanisms, notably the following: the scheme must operate with simplicity and be automatic; it must avoid moral hazard; it must avoid wide coverage and guarantee budget neutrality so that regions not hit by the shock should contribute relatively more and only the regions affected should receive transfers; the whole amount collected should always be distributed, avoiding deficits and superavits of the mechanism (Bajo-Rubio and Díaz-Roldan 2001). Thirdly, the *existing link (if it exists) between these insurance instruments and the SGP framework*, considering on the other hand that this link can be of two types (or both): (1) *functional-type link*, in the sense that the insurance instrument is able to cope with moral hazard problems, notably through fiscal discipline enhancement (enclosed in the SGP rules)[16]; (2) *structural-type link*, in the sense that these insurance instruments are encapsulated in the SGP framework and act as an extension of the latter—and this would imply an alteration in the design of the SGP itself.[17] Fourthly, the *way these instruments articulate with national stabilization devices*, investigating in which way the former can work as a complement of the latter. Finally, whether the *geographical scope* of these insurance mechanisms is the EU or the Eurozone. As shown by Table 1, most of these shock absorbers are restricted to the Eurozone (and this is precisely the other reason explaining why these mechanisms can act outside the EU's budget), and this happens because we are dealing with prospects for a smooth functioning of the

[16]As mentioned by Schelkle (2005), the idea would be to complement the disciplinarian view present in the SGP with an insurance device, and yet controlling moral hazard.

[17]In this case, the SGP should be directly linked to the insurance mechanism. Hence, in good times, countries with budget surpluses would have to contribute to the Fund that would then work as a buffer to be used in case of economic downturn. In these circumstances, countries would also be allowed to run deficits (cyclically-motivated deficits) but only under condition of having accomplished SGP's and Fiscal Compact's rules, e.g. structural balance. In fact, past and current structural balance (the compliance of the 'medium term objective' settled by the SGP and the Fiscal Compact) should be a condition not only to run deficits but also to benefit from financial support in the event of adverse shock. Moreover, notice that this structural type-link should furthermore require technical arrangements in order to adapt the new financial scheme to the SGP framework, notably vis-á-vis the calculation of the GDP potential and output gaps (see on this computation Mourre et al. 2014).

**Table 1** Proposals for visible shock absorbers and their respective main features

| Approaches/ name of the proposed insurance instrument/ author and date | Stabilization formula and estimation method/ Description | Conceptual properties | Coping with moral hazard/articulation with the SGP framework | Articulation with national stabilization devices | Geographical scope |
|---|---|---|---|---|---|
| *Cyclical budget approach* | | | | | |
| – *Fiscal insurance system* (von Hagen and Wyplosz 2008): the purpose would be to insure the tax revenues of participating governments against transitory asymmetric shocks | – Assuming that tax revenues are proportional do GDP ($T_{it} = \alpha Y_{it}$), this can be achieved by tying payments to the deviation between actual (*Y*) and potential GDP (*Y**) $t_{it} = \lambda\alpha\big((Y_{it} - Y^*_{it}) - \beta\,(Y_t - Y^*_t)\big)$ where λ is the degree of insurance chosen by government and β is the weight of country *i* in euro-area potential GDP | – The mechanism is able to disentangle transitory shocks from permanent ones<br>– The shock indicator is the deviation from the potential output | – A moral hazard problem arises when the government overstates its *Y** in order to reduce its payment into the system. One way to address this would be to delegate these computations to an independent institution, e.g. the European Commission. An alternative would be to modify the transfer formula in order to assure balance over time, as follows $t_{it} = \lambda\alpha\big((Y_{it} - Y^*_{it}) - \beta\,(Y_t - Y^*_t)\big) - \sum_{j=0}^{t-N}(1+r_t)^{N+j}t_{it-N-j}$ The latter term is the penalty term, since in the event of cheating it reduces transfers received in period t by a part of the accumulated transfers in the past | – Not addressed | – Euro area |
| – *Cyclical shock insurance scheme*—CSI (Enderlein et al. 2013): the idea is to reduce the difference | – Country's annual transfers are calculated by the formula: $T_i = \alpha\,\big((Y_{Ez} - Y^*_{EZ})/Y^*_{EZ} - (y_i - y^*_i)/y^*_i\big) \times y^*_i$ The convergence variable α denotes the share of the difference between a member country and euro area output gap to be offset. In the baseline scenario, α = 0.5, which resulted in an average | – The shock indicator is the output gap, notably the difference of the gap of a euro area member | – To deal with ex-ante moral hazard, the introduction of a common rulebook for domestic stabilization is proposed<br>– To deal with ex-post moral hazard, the introduction of earmarking transfers is suggested and their advantages to both contributors and recipient sides are | – It is mentioned that the scheme should not prevent national stabilizers from | – Euro area |

| | | | | | |
|---|---|---|---|---|---|
| between individual member states' business cycle positions and that of the euro area (EZ) as a whole to achieve higher levels of business cycle convergence | reduction in the standard deviation of 40 %<br>– Simulation exercise using real time data (data set of 17,000 individual output gaps for euro area countries, covering the period 1981–2014). Assumptions: CSI payments affect only actual GDP ($Y$) and not potential GDP ($Y^*$); payments are based on this year's GDP net transfers for this given year; a total fiscal multiplier of 1.2 is assumed | relative to the euro area average output gap | discussed. Earmarking can have advantages mostly in the latter case, as it implies allocating funds to expenditure increase or to tax cuts where multipliers are higher (e.g. social security contributions and unemployment benefits) | operating; on the contrary, there must be an incentive (through earmarking) that funds are used in expenditures and or taxes where national multipliers are higher | |
| – *European Stabilisation Fund*—ESF (Delbecque 2013): insurance-type absorption mechanism to increase resilience of member states to economic shocks. | – When the projected real GDP growth forecast is below the estimated long-term real GDP growth, euro area members would benefit from a disbursement from an EMU fund (ESF). When the growth forecast is above the long-term real growth, they would make a contribution to the ESF. The formula for the net contribution is: $d = \alpha(Y^e - Y^*)$<br>where $d$ is the net contribution expressed as a percentage of the GDP, $Y^e$ is the projected real GDP growth rate and $Y^*$ is the projected long-term real GDP growth rate.<br>– Simulation exercise, assuming $\alpha = 0.5$, and that $Y^*$ is the average potential real GDP growth rate observed in 1999–2013 | – The shock indicator is the difference between real GDP growth estimates and the projected long-term real GDP growth rate<br>– ESF assets/debt would fluctuate in a narrow band around zero, since ESF would reduce its debt and accumulate reserves during times of economic boom and would use | – The ESF works on a temporary basis (only to cushion short-term cyclical fluctuations rather than promoting economic convergence), hence low economic growth would also reduce long-term real economic growth and thus the level of potential disbursements from the ESF<br>– Accepting, within the ESF, the development of a framework that would modulate transfers from the ESF to on-going compliance with mutually agreed commitments. | – Not addressed | – Euro area |

(continued)

**Table 1** (continued)

| Approaches/ name of the proposed insurance instrument/ author and date | Stabilization formula and estimation method/ Description | Conceptual properties | Coping with moral hazard/articulation with the SGP framework | Articulation with national stabilization devices | Geographical scope |
|---|---|---|---|---|---|
| | | its reserves or issue bonds (to borrow) in periods of recession | | | |
| *Debt pooling approach* | | | | | |
| – *European Debt Agency—EDA* (Enderlein et al. 2013): this Agency would issue its own bonds hence creating a liquid market of Eurobonds | – The EDA would be jointly guaranteed by all Eurozone members: in normal times all members would issue a pre-defined share of their debt (e.g. 10 % of their GDP) through the EDA<br>– In case of distress, the EDA would allow that country to increase its EDA share to the next level, a strictly limited amount<br>– Countries in economic difficulties could increase their debt issue through the EDA to up to 20 % of their GDP without strict conditions. However, requests for further increases would be negotiated and subject to strict conditionality | – Temporary shocks<br>– Non-specified indicator | – Increasing conditionality (depending upon increasing financing levels) could ultimately imply the loss of budgetary sovereignty by the assisted country | – Not directly addressed | – Euro area |
| *Narrow automatic stabilizers approach* | | | | | |
| – *European unemployment scheme I (EUBS I)* (Dullien 2013): this is a 'genuine EUBS', since | – Fiscal simulation, under the following assumptions: replacement payment is 50 % of the insured wage; over the cycle, contributions to the scheme cover all pay-outs; unemployment benefits are paid for 12 months; the macroeconomic multiplier of the unemployment benefits is 1 | – EUBS addresses both asymmetric and (temporary) symmetric shocks<br>– In the | – Ex post moral hazard is addressed in the sense that this is a scheme aiming to finance expenditures exhibiting high fiscal multipliers (only unemployment)<br>– The temporary nature of the EUBS benefits and caps on the amount might also limit moral hazard. | – The EUBS may top-up whenever national unemployment benefits are of a lesser | – Euro area |

| | | | | | |
|---|---|---|---|---|---|
| eligible unemployed would directly receive individual benefits from a European unemployment insurance, financed by contributions based on the sum of the wages of covered workers (payroll taxes) | | simulation, the pickup rate is a function of the increase in short-term unemployment (e.g. 7 % more) in the recent past (e.g. 12 months)<br>– In order to ensure equilibrium the scheme can run surpluses in good times and deficits in recessions | | amount, but not prevent the payment of higher benefits from the national scheme | |
| – *EUBS II* (Beblavý and Maselli 2014; Beblavý et al. 2015): not only the genuine EUBS, but also the 'equivalent' EUBS is admitted (financial transfers occur only from and to member states) | – Simulation exercise; from the four possible sources of finance (payroll tax, corporate tax, debt, and a contribution as a percentage of a country's GDP), the authors tend to prefer the latter | – The shock indicator is the unemployment rate<br>– Temporary shocks.<br>– Claw back mechanisms ensure equilibrium between contributions and payments in the long run | – To address moral hazard two mechanisms are proposed:<br>(i) The introduction of a *trigger*. In every period—e.g. a year—if the indicator (the unemployment rate) exceeds a certain threshold, transfers are made towards a particular country;<br>(ii) *Experience rating* or *claw-back mechanism*: contributions are increased in the event of poor past unemployment performance | – The EUBS may top-up whenever national unemployment benefits are of a lesser amount, but not prevent the payment of higher benefits from the national scheme | – EU |

Eurozone as a monetary union by the creation of government insurance mechanisms able to address macroeconomic shocks.[18]

## 3.2 *Invisible Shock Absorbers Through the EU's Budget*

Despite the fact that the EU's budget does not have a sufficient dimension to provide for invisible macroeconomic stabilization, one can expect that it might evolve to embrace *some* stabilization properties within its current set of revenues and transfers or at least maintaining its current design as a sectorial and targeted budget. Therefore, when examining future prospects for the EU's budget development, two cases should be considered: (1) firstly, to split the revenue side from the expenditure side and investigate, for each of them, separately, whether they will be able to provide for macroeconomic stabilization; (2) secondly, to consider the joint action as stabilizers of certain revenues allocated to certain expenditures (e.g. stabilization appropriations or funds within the EU budget financed by certain of its revenues).

Having in mind these two cases, I will start by the former, considering first the *(tax) revenue side*. The current 'own resources system' that exists in the EU was not conceived to produce any kind of stabilization effect—and this is due not only to its small size but also to the fact that their own resources (agricultural levies, customs duties, value-added tax -VAT and GNP-based own resource) are not cyclically sensitive, at least as much as national taxes (e.g. personal income and corporate taxes and social security contributions) tend to be. Unlike national taxes that pursue overall and indistinctive goals (e.g. inter-individual redistribution through tax progressivity), tax resources assigned to the EU's budget are 'one-purpose', which means that they are conceived to be targeted at sectorial areas (e.g. the Common Agricultural Policy and Regional Policies), also being capped by the expenditure levels settled by the Multiannual Financial Framework. Departing from this current framework, the point is to identify whether certain of the EU's own resources could be used to provide for certain stabilization effects and if so what should be done (either to increase the amount of these revenues or to rethink their nature and assignment conditions to the EU's budget). Amongst the two possible candidates, VAT and GNP own resource, the latter seems to be preferable, mostly because it has evolved to become the main financing source of the EU's budget. Moreover, as referred to by Schratzenstaller (2014), the evolution that took place at the end of the 1990s shifting the bulk of financing from VAT-based towards GNI-based resources was explained by the need to widen the financial scope of

[18] The main exception in this stance can be found in Beblavý et al. (2015, p. 17), concerning the introduction of the EUBS. In their study they include all EU member countries, and this is mostly because if the purpose of the scheme is to ensure countries against asymmetric shocks, then a larger pool of countries is better than a smaller one.

the EU budget and the need to ease the financial burden for the economically weaker member states. In fact, while contributions on the basis of VAT have a potential regressive effect, the contributions linked to GNI better reflect a country's economic capacity. On the other hand, as mentioned by Dullien and Shwarzer (2009, p. 163), VAT along with other indirect taxes is the least sensitive source of revenue in cyclical terms, as consumption is relatively smooth over the business cycle.[19,20] Even though for these reasons GNP own resource can be seen as a possible candidate to work out as a stabilization instrument (by itself or allocated to stabilization-type expenditures) some changes in its design will be required. Notably the following technical features should be discussed—firstly, the substitution/completion of the GNP as an assignment base for/by another tax assignment base that would more accurately translate cyclical movements or variations in the output gap (this would at the same time entail a stronger link with the SPG framework and the methodology used to compute the structural balance); secondly, that the assignment rate would become an individual, country-based, and also a constant, non-changeable, flat rate (non dependent on VAT collection or expenditure needs) that would permit tax sharing mechanisms to properly work out and that would allow the (positive or negative) cyclical movements to be translated each year into a (higher or lower) contribution by each country—countries more affected by negative shocks would contribute less.

Considering now the *expenditure side,* I should recall, in the first place, that the idea to use the existing expenditures within the EU's budget for stabilization purposes is not new. In the Mac Dougall et al. (1977) and Padoa-Schioppa Reports (1987) this idea was already mentioned. In the former Report an alternative approach to the 'top down approach' (a complete budgetary union based on a 'fully-federal model') was proposed. This approach, entitled a 'bottom up approach', examined the specific functions of the public sector in the supply of given goods or services in areas such as agriculture, education, health, etc., and how the provision of these goods might imply the pursue of broader objectives of redistribution and stabilization (MacDougall et al. 1977, pp. 23 and 43). What should now be highlighted is the fact that public goods provision may instrumentally be used for some kind of macroeconomic stabilization. On this stance, recall that the EU's (budget) regional policy (e.g. Structural Funds)—an inter-regional redistributive instrument by nature—has a targeted nature relying on conditional and earmarked grants for the provision of certain types of public goods or goods exhibiting high positive externalities (human capital and training, R&D, communications, transportation, etc.). The fact is that regional policy which has mostly

[19]This helps to explain, for example, why in the measurement of the output gap and of the cyclically-adjusted balance budget it is assumed that indirect taxes have a unitary elasticity with respect to output gap, clearly below the elasticity estimated to direct taxes and social security contributions. On this issue see Mourre et al. (2014).

[20]A different opinion is expressed by von Hagen and Wyplosz (2008, pp. 14–15) stressing that VAT is closer to demand shocks than income and payroll taxes and that the former reacts faster to cyclical movements in the economy than the latter.

been conceived as a redistributive instrument aiming to promote long-term convergence between regions in the EU (see Shankar and Shah 2009) can also play, as mentioned in the Report by Padoa-Schioppa (1987), an important role in macroeconomic stabilization by helping regions that experience short-term economic imbalances. This would imply certain changes in the design or in the functioning of these conditional grants, such as those referred to by Beblavý et al. (2015, p. 10): subsidizing the interest rate paid on loans taken on by the private sector from the European Investment Bank or other credit institutions, or using existing Structural Funds for regions in economic difficulty. The *Investment Plan for Europe*, launched by President Juncker in 2015, intending to promote EU investment for the next years on a massive scale in areas such as infrastructures and communications is also justified by the acknowledgment that these three dimensions—public goods provision, inter-regional distribution and macroeconomic stabilization—can be interlinked. When considering this stance, the proposal made by Drèze and Durré (2013) for the creation of a new public investment programme in areas of social housing, renewable energy and transportation should also be mentioned, since these investments should be applied to countries facing economic distress (due to their high multiplier effects). This proposal is interesting because it can be considered a first step in the use of existing regional funds (or other funds specially conceived for public goods provision) to directly address macroeconomic shocks.

Finally, as for the abovementioned second case, it should be examined whether certain specific types of revenues within the EU's budget could be allocated to certain types of expenditures, notably those with higher multiplier effects—ultimately leading to the creation of specific stabilization appropriations (or funds) within the EU budget. Von Hagen and Wyplosz (2008, p. 14) anticipated a model of this sort when they proposed the creation of a *common euro-area tax fund*, to which member countries would annually pay a fixed proportion of their revenues and that would pay out transfers to governments on a fixed (per capita) basis. Payments into the fund would then vary with the evolution of the tax base over time, while payments out of the fund would not allow any cyclical movements—thus countries with temporarily high tax bases would pay more, and countries with lower tax rates would pay less than they receive.

## 4 Final Remarks

In this chapter, the main proposals concerning the institution of macroeconomic shocks absorbers in the E(M)U were presented and the respective features and implementation conditions were highlighted. All these proposals tend to be more realistic and pragmatic than the fully-federal model, because they accept the current EU's budget status quo and present an alternative view within the existing possibilities and needs. Addressing these shocks can be carried out either by the improvement of 'market forces' within the E(M)U's territory or with narrow scope government insurance instruments. The assessment of the specific features of each mechanism (either private or governmental) allows one to conclude that some of these instruments are more feasible than others, some fit better in the current E(M)U scenario, some are more demanding than others. But they are all second best solutions, the effectiveness of which as macro stabilizers is not, for the time being, guaranteed. However, in my opinion their stabilization capabilities will not be the only or even the main argument to grant them success. Considering the current political scenario that prevails in the E(M)U, the acceptance of these instruments will most likely depend on moderation and conservatism, which implies balancing three types of antagonistic objectives: firstly, a sufficient dosage of solidarity yet avoiding moral hazard (creating proper incentives for fiscal discipline enhancement and thus reinforcing the SGP framework); secondly, a sufficient measure of risk sharing yet creating confidence that national macro stabilizers can do more and better; thirdly, a certain degree of fiscal backstop and centralization yet relying on the increase of (decentralized) market mechanisms within the E(M)U territory. This is a fact: at least the Market is strongly 'embedded' (as Karl Polanyi would say); the E(M)U is not.

## References

Asdrubali P et al (1996) Channels of interstate risk sharing: United States 1963–1990. Q J Econ 111(4):1081–1110

Bajo-Rubio O, Díaz-Roldan C (2001) Insurance mechanisms against asymmetric shocks in a monetary union: an application to the European Monetary Union. Available at: http://sites.uclouvain.be/econ/DP/REL/2003013.pdf

Baldwin R, Giavazzi F (2015) Introduction. In: Baldwin R, Giavazzi F (eds) The Eurozone crisis—a consensus view of the causes and a few possible solutions. A VoxEU.org Book, CEPR Press, London, pp 18–60

Beblavý M, Maselli I (2014) An unemployment insurance scheme for the Euro area: a simulation exercise of two options. CEPS Special Report No 98. CEPS, Brussels

Beblavý M et al (2015) A European unemployment benefit scheme: the rationale and the challenges ahead.CEPS. European Commission, Brussels

Belke A, Gros D (2015) Banking Union as a shock absorber. Ruhr Economic Papers 548

Bénassy-Quéré A (2015) Maastricht flaws and remedies. In: Baldwin R, Giavazzi F (eds) The Eurozone crisis—a consensus view of the causes and a few possible solutions. A VoxEU.org Book, CEPR Press, London, pp 71–83

Breuss F et al (2015) The stabilizing properties of a European Banking Union in case of financial shocks in the Euro Area. European Economy, Economic Papers 550. European Commission, Brussels

Cabral N d C (2016) Which budgetary union for the E(M)U? J Common Mark Stud 54(6): 1280–1295

Caceres C et al (2011) From financial crisis to sovereign risk. In: Kolb RE (ed) Sovereign debt—from safety from default, Kolb series in finance. Wiley, Hoboken, NJ, pp 393–400

De Grauwe P (2014) Economics of monetary union, 10th edn. Oxford University Press, Oxford

De Grauwe P (2015) Design failures of the Eurozone. In: Baldwin R, Giavazzi F (eds) The Eurozone crisis—a consensus view of the causes and a few possible solutions. A VoxEU.org Book, CEPR Press, London, pp 99–108

Delbecque B (2013) Proposal for a stabilization fund for the EMU. CEPS Working Document No. 385
Delpla J, von Weizsäcker J (2010) The blue bond proposal. Bruegel Policy Brief
Drèze JH, Durré A (2013) Fiscal integration and growth simulation in Europa. Discussion Paper 2013/13. Center for Operations Research and Econometrics, Louvain-La-Neuve
Dullien S (2013) A Euro-area wide unemployment insurance as an automatic stabilizer: who benefits and who pays? Social Europe. European Commission, Brussels
Dullien S, Shwarzer D (2009) Bringing macroeconomics into the EU budget: why and how? J Common Mark Stud 47(1):153–174
Enderlein H et al (2012) Completing the Euro: a road map towards fiscal union in Europe. Report of 'The Tommaso Padoa-Shioppa Group'. Notre Europe, Brussels
Enderlein H et al (2013) Blueprint for a cyclical shock insurance in the Euro area. Notre Europe, Brussels
Goodhart CAE, Smith S (1993) Stabilization. European economy—reports and studies, No. 5, pp 417–455, Brussels
Gros D (2014) A fiscal shock absorber for the Eurozone? Lessons from the economics of insurance. Available at: http://voxeu.org/article/ez-fiscal-shock-absorber-lessons-insurance-economics
Gros D (2015) The Eurozone crisis and foreign debt. In: Baldwin R, Giavazzi F (eds) The Eurozone crisis—a consensus view of the causes and a few possible solutions. A VoxEU.org Book, CEPR Press, London, pp 121–128
Hoffmann M, Sørensen BE (2012) Don't expect too much from EZ fiscal union—and complete the unfinished integration of European capital markets! Available at: http://voxeu.org/article/hedging-macroeconomic-risk-eurozone-fiscal-union-versus-capital-markets
MacDougall D et al (1977) Report of the study group on the role of public finance in European integration. Volume I: general report. Commission of the European Communities, Brussels
Marjolin R et al (1975) Report of the study group "Economic and Monetary Union 1980". Commission of the European Communities, Brussels
McNamara KR (2015) The forgotten problem of embeddedness: history lessons for the Euro. In: Matthijs M, Blyth M (eds) The Future of the Euro. Oxford University Press, New York, pp 21–43
Micossi S (2015) What future for the Eurozone? In: Baldwin R, Giavazzi F (eds) The Eurozone crisis—a consensus view of the causes and a few possible solutions. A VoxEU.org Book, CEPR Press, London, pp 134–151
Mourre G et al (2014) Adjusting the budget balance for the business cycle: the EU methodology. European Economy, Economic Papers 536. European Commission, Brussels
Mundell RA (1961) A theory of optimum currency areas. Am Econ Rev 51(4):657–665
Padoa-Schioppa T (1987) Efficiency, stability and equity: a strategy for the evolution of the economic system of the European community. Oxford University Press, Oxford
Pesenti P (2015) Structural reforms and monetary policy revisited. In: Baldwin R, Giavazzi F (eds) The Eurozone crisis—a consensus view of the causes and a few possible solutions. A VoxEU.org Book, CEPR Press, London, pp 153–162
Pisani-Ferry J et al (1993) Stabilization properties of budgetary systems: a simulation analysis. European Economy, Brussels
Pisani-Ferry J et al (2013) Options for a Euro-area fiscal capacity. Bruegel Policy Contribution 2013/01
Sala-i-Martin X, Sachs J (1991) Fiscal federalism and optimum currency areas: evidence for Europe from the United States. National Bureau of Economic Research Working Paper, Cambridge, MA
Schelkle W (2005) The political economy of fiscal policy coordination in EMU: from disciplinarian device to insurance arrangement. J Common Mark Stud 43(2):371–391
Schoenmaker D (2015) Firmer foundations for a stronger European Banking Union. Bruegel Working Paper 2015/13

Schratzenstaller M (2014) Reform options for the EU's system of own resources. Revue de l' OFCE 1/2014(132):327–355. http://ec.europa.eu/budget/mff/hlgor/library/selected-readings/06-DOC-COMM-ReformOption-Schratzenstaller-2014.pdf

Shankar R, Shah A (2009) Lessons from European Union policies for regional development. Policy Research Working Paper 4977. The World Bank, Washington, DC

Véron N (2015) Europe's radical banking union, Bruegel essay and lectures series. Bruegel, Brussels

Von Hagen J (1992) Fiscal arrangements in a monetary union: evidence from the US. In: Fair D, De Boissieu C (eds) Fiscal policy, taxation and the financial system in an increasingly integrated Europe. Kluwer, Dordrecht, pp 337–359

Von Hagen J (1998) Fiscal policy and intra-national risk-sharing. Working Paper B 13, 1998. Centre for European Integration Studies, Bonn

Von Hagen J, Wyplosz C (2008) EMU's decentralized system of fiscal policy. European Economy, Economic Papers 306. European Commission, Brussels

Wolff GB (2012) A budget for Europe's monetary union. Bruegel Policy Contribution 2012/22

Wyplosz C, Pisani-Ferry J (1990) Les implications budgétaires de l' union monétaire. Observations et diagnostics économiques: revue de l'OFCE 33:155–173

Xafa M (2015) European Banking Union, three years on. CIGI Papers No. 73. Center for International Governance Innovation, Ontario

# The European Banking Union and the Economic and Monetary Union: The Puzzle Is Yet to Be Completed

**Nuno Cunha Rodrigues and José Renato Gonçalves**

**Abstract** Given the various shortcomings of the current European monetary unification project, especially as shown by the international financial crisis which began in 2007–2008, various measures for its respective solution were successively proposed and implemented, including the establishment of a European banking union, which seemed not only necessary and urgent but also inadequate and unsatisfactory, in order to make the European Economic and Monetary Union solid and safe. Given all these reasons, "the puzzle is yet to be completed."

**JEL Classification** E42 • F15 • F33 • F41

## 1 An Inadequate and Incomplete European Monetary Union and the Aim of the Banking Union

After the Cold War era, in 1992, when Fukuyama contended that history was over because the winners were indisputable, the 12 members of the European Economic Community (EEC) signed a Treaty in the city of Maastricht with the clear goal of increasing economic and political integration and forming an "economic and monetary union", as well as a "political union". With the latter broad objective of

---

*[Summary: 1—An inadequate and incomplete European monetary union and the aim of the banking union; 2—The financial crisis, the European democratic deficit and the need to reform the Euro area; 3—The continuing fragmentary European financial system and the urgency to establish a banking union to recover the Economic and Monetary Union; 4—The insufficiencies of the European banking union; 5—Towards a more perfect banking union?]*

N.C. Rodrigues (✉) • J.R. Gonçalves
University of Lisbon School of Law, Lisbon, Portugal
e-mail: nunorodrigues@fd.ulisboa.pt; rgoncalves@fd.ulisboa.pt



N. de Costa Cabral et al. (eds.), *The Euro and the Crisis*, Financial and Monetary Policy Studies 43, DOI 10.1007/978-3-319-45710-9_16

political unity having been discarded, the new single currency was finally fully established on 1 January 1999.[1]

The proposal and justification for a single currency were not new. The fundamentals for the European Monetary Union had been laid down by Mundell (1961), McKinnon (1963) and Kenen (1969) with the theory of optimum currency areas (OCA), which served as the analytical framework for successive debates on the validity and sustainability of monetary unification. Mundell was an advocate for the Euro, even if various authors have used his theory to oppose the European monetary union project and to question its chances of success. In the dispute between "economists" and "monetarists" throughout the history of European monetary unification, from the Werner Plan to the Maastricht Treaty, Mundell supported the "monetarists" view: the fixing of exchange rates and the adoption of a common currency would assure sufficient convergence of the economies joining the union, especially inflation and interest rates.[2]

According to the optimistic scenario regarding the long-term prospects for monetary integration, endorsed and promoted by the European Commission and its experts, currency unification would be recognised over time as being advantageous for all regions and countries involved, and, in this sense, monetary union among European Union member States could be considered as "inevitable".[3]

[1]The determination to establish a single currency in the European Economic Community (EEC) had rearisen in the late 1980s in the context of revitalizing European economic and political integration. In 1988, a committee chaired by Jacques Delors, then president of the European Commission, was set up to propose steps for creating an economic and monetary union. The ensuing report laid the foundations for such a union, resulting in the adoption of the 1992 Maastricht Treaty. The main provision of the Maastricht Treaty, which came into effect on 1 January 1999, was to implement the new single currency, the Euro, but not immediately for all member States, as this depended on the convergence criteria that needed to be met before the countries were allowed to join (11 countries out of 12 on 1 January 1999, 19 countries out of 28 since 1 January 2015). See Fukuyama (1992, esp. 287–) and Gonçalves (2010a).

[2]In his famous article of 1961, Mundell raised an innovative question—on what economic criteria could the decision by various regions of the world to adopt a common currency be based—and responded with a cost-benefit analysis: the benefits of adopting a single currency include a reduction of the transaction costs generated by the existence of various currencies and a gain in the liquidity of the currency attributable, mainly to the expansion of its area of transactions, from which the financial markets would also benefit. The potential disadvantages would come from the elimination of the exchange rate between participants (it would no longer be possible to let the exchange rate absorb shocks asymmetrically, affecting the various regions or countries of the union). The analysis highlighted the criteria that monetary union must meet: absence of frequent and large-scale asymmetrical shocks, mobility in the factors of production, export diversification and a degree of economic openness. For an open and diversified economy, the benefits of joining a monetary union in terms of gains in liquidity and financial stability can offset the additional adjustment costs that could result from joining the union. See especially Mundell (1961, 1963) and Kenen (1969).

[3]According to the optimistic view, the relationship between the degree of economic integration and the occurrence of asymmetric shocks determines whether or not progress towards integration leads to economic convergence. In a cost-benefit analysis, as trade integration increases, the degree of symmetry between the participating countries increases, becoming more alike and facing fewer asymmetric shocks. See European Commission (1990).

In contrast, the pessimistic outlook regards economic integration as leading to less symmetry between regions and countries. According to this perspective, subscribed to by Krugman, although present European monetary union may not be an OCA, it could become one afterwards, since more integration leads to more specialisation and, as a result, to less symmetry and more asymmetric shocks. Then, the benefits of a monetary union would increase with the degree of integration: despite the decline in symmetry, more integration could result in an optimal currency area. But the net gains of a monetary union cannot increase strongly enough in line with the level of integration. In these circumstances, the costs of declining symmetry would outdo the benefits provided by a monetary union.[4]

In the context of an OCA, when prices and wages are flexible within and among countries with a single currency, the adjustment following economic shocks will be less associated with unemployment in one country and inflation in another, diminishing the need for exchange rate adjustments. Furthermore, high factor market integration within the countries with a single currency will reduce the need to change real factor prices and nominal exchange rate in response to disturbances. Trade theory has long established that the mobility of factors enhances efficiency and welfare, even if the mobility of factors is limited, especially in the short run, and thus eases adjustment to lasting shocks.[5]

However, in the real world, as well as in the European Union countries sharing a common currency, there are and do persist many political, juridical, economic, social and cultural differences and concerns, "impossible" or very difficult to overcome in the short, medium, and even in the long run, undermining the prediction of strong or complete factor market integration as a result. We can also

[4]Hence, in the long run, the prospects for a monetary union, including all European Union member Sates, will be bad; but, as Paul de Grauwe notes, that conjecture leads to an anomaly, because it implies that a lowering of trade integration can bring the EU into an optimal currency area. Thus, if the EU countries were to go back and disband, monetary union would become attractive. From the discussion of the Krugman model, authors such as De Grauwe have concluded that even if integration causes more asymmetric shocks, this may lead to increasing net gains for a monetary union for all member States. See de Grauwe (2014, pp. 70)and Krugman (1993).

[5]In the 1960s, literature on OCA theory identified various criteria from the debate on the merits of fixed against flexible exchange rate regimes, namely price and wage flexibility, mobility of product factors including labour, financial market integration, the degree of economic openness, diversification in production and consumption, similarities of inflation rates, fiscal integration and ultimately political unification. For instance, the higher the degree of economic openness, the higher the probability of changes in international prices of tradables being transmitted to the domestic cost of living, which would reduce the potential for money illusion by wage earners, as noted by McKinnon (1963). Then, the nominal exchange rate would be less useful as an adjustment instrument. Moreover, economic openness needs to be assessed along different dimensions, including the share of tradable versus non-tradable goods and services, the marginal propensity to import and the degree of openness vis-à-vis the countries with which it will share a single currency. Moreover, high diversification in production and consumption dilutes the possible impact of shocks specific to a particular sector, providing protection against a variety of disturbances, as pointed out by Kenen (1969). Furthermore, external imbalances could arise from persistent divergences in domestic inflation rates, derived from economic policies, structural developments in labour market or social preferences, including inflation aversion. See Dellas and Tavlas (2009) and Mongelli (2008).

imagine, of course, one or more countries with a common and critical objective, such as financial credibility, eventually but only temporarily prevailing over other burdensome political, economic or social difficulties.[6]

A major characteristic of the Maastricht Treaty was the constraints it put on fiscal policy and, under the provisions of the Excessive Deficit Procedure (EDP), the favourable result of member States in avoiding "excessive deficits" during the transition period to the last phase of Economic and Monetary Union (EMU), one of the four criteria controlling entrance to the single currency. After monetary union began, on 1 January 1999, the adherent States were unconditionally required to avoid excessive public deficits.[7]

The rationale for those criteria and procedures was that member States participating in the monetary union must be constrained from overborrowing to avoid destabilising the common currency and the monetary union on the whole. When excessive public deficits cause a debt crisis, the European Central Bank (ECB) and or other "central authorities" would come under pressure to bail out the imperilled government.[8]

Yet, if limits on the national right to borrow were crucial to ensuring the stability of the monetary union, one would expect such restrictions to prevail in most single currencies. Actually, fiscal limits are the exception rather than the rule in past and existing monetary unions—although the latest are few, and, until the Eurozone, most were comprised of low-income developing countries. This illustration could be expanded to federal States, since a typical federation has a common currency and devolves substantial fiscal responsibilities to subnational governments, resembling, in that context, a standard monetary union.

Another main prerequisite of OCA was and is financial market integration, which can decrease the requirement for exchange rate adjustments. An intense degree of financial integration would diminish disparities in long-term interest rates, easing the financing of external imbalances and promoting an efficient allocation of resources.

---

[6]According to Chari, Dovis and Kehoe, symmetric countries gain credibility when joining a monetary union only when the shocks affecting credibility are not highly correlated; they propose an amended optimal currency area criterion which is considered more relevant than the classic one. See Chari et al. (2013) and Dellas and Tavlas (2009).

[7]As stated by the Treaty of the European Community (TEC, now Treaty on the Functioning of the European Union—TFEU, after the revision of the Treaty of the European Union signed in Maastricht), a State has an "excessive deficit" when this is so declared by the European Council following a report by the European Commission and an evaluation by the Monetary Committee and the Excessive Deficit Procedure (EDP) starts when a country's deficit and general government debts respectively exceed 3 % and 60 % of GDP. Nevertheless, the EDP allows the Commission and the Council to consider the broader fiscal situation of member States.

[8]As von Hagen and Eichengreen noted, the bailout could be ex ante, in which case the European Central Bank (ECB) would keep interest rates low to lighten the debt-service burden, or ex post, in which case the ECB would monetise the government's debt. Or through both means, particularly in acute and persistent government debt crises. Either way, non-restricted fiscal policies could cause inflationary pressures that the ECB would find difficult to combat. The opposite situation could happen: extreme fiscal constraints could generate deflationary stress difficult to resist by the ECB, as last years' ECB monetary policy experience demonstrated. See Hagen and Eichengreen (1996).

Nevertheless, the international integration of financial markets cannot substitute a long-term adjustment when this is necessary. It can only smooth the process, even if temporary financial flows cause a postponement of real adjustment and render it more difficult at a later point. Mundell (1973) explained that countries sharing a single currency could mitigate the effects of asymmetric shocks by diversifying their income sources. This can operate through ex ante and ex post income insurance: when a country's residents hold claims to dividends, interests and rental revenue from other countries or regions, there can be smoothing of temporary and permanent shocks (ex ante adjustment), as well as when they buy and sell assets and borrow and lend on international credit markets, in response to income fluctuations (ex post adjustment).[9]

Then, similarity of shocks is not a strict prerequisite for sharing a single currency if all members of the currency area have been financially integrated and have held claims on each other's output. McKinnon and other authors speak of a "Mundell 1" in contrast to a "Mundell 2" positive and normative approach to EMU and the latter has important implications for the debate on monetary integration. In fact, a new currency could be shared by countries subject to asymmetric shocks as long as they "insure" one another through private financial markets. This explains the emphasis, in subsequent literature, on the need to strengthen financial integration.

Early OCA theory was gradually abandoned after the recognition of diverse weaknesses and limitations. Properties difficult to measure and to evaluate coherently—the problems of "inconclusiveness" and "inconsistency" (Tavlas 1994)—justified the conclusion of the "One Market, One Money" report, by Emerson et al., that "there is no ready-to-use theory for assessing the costs and benefits of economic and monetary union". Even if that OCA theory provided important early insights, afterwards it offered only a narrow and outdated analytical framework in which to define which countries should share a single currency. In the second half of the 1990s, several authors started raising the issue of the endogenous effects of monetary integration, that is, whether sharing a single currency may set in motion forces bringing countries more closely together.[10]

---

[9]In his second main contribution to an OCA, Robert Mundell discussed the role of financial integration in the form of cross-country asset holding, for international risk-sharing: Mundell (1973), McKinnon (2004, p. 689), Mongelli (2008, p. 2) and Dellas and Tavlas (2009).

[10]There are other weaknesses and limitations of OCA. Most studies are applied to sovereign countries but OCAs may not correspond to national frontiers, due to non-homogeneities within countries (US States, German Länder, Spanish *comunidades*, Italian regions); the discussion by many authors of the benefits and costs from sharing a single currency was "incomplete at best and quite vague and hazy at worst" (Mongelli 2008); early studies could not have predicted the growing importance of services in post-industrialised economies—they are more diversified, diffused and fragmented, therefore more similar across Europe than the manufacturing sectors; nor predicted the pervasive role of institutions inhibiting product and market flexibility and mobility; and last, but most likely not the least, the erosion of the conceptual framework of the OCA, based on the belief that monetary policy is an effective policy instrument which could help carry out business cycle stabilisation, facilitating the adjustment of relative wages and prices after some shocks with a less costly response than tolerating some unemployment through austerity policies. Buiter (1999) calls the argument that monetary and fiscal policy could successfully

By studying the effects of several past monetary unions, Rose and Frankel showed that monetary integration leads to a very significant deepening of reciprocal trade. Even Euro area countries, which were not an OCA before, may turn into one. Participating countries of the EMU, no matter what their motivation is, may satisfy OCA properties ex post, even if they do not ex ante. Hence, the borders of one currency union can enlarge after its creation with the consecutive expansion of trade integration and income correlation among participant economies, which has been called the "endogeneity of OCA".[11]

With a monetary union some transaction costs disappear or decrease, directly and indirectly, information costs decline and price transparency grows, reducing market segmentation and fostering competition. Then, a single currency is more efficient than multiple currencies in performing the roles of medium of exchange and unit of account.

A single currency among partner countries is seen as a "much more serious and durable commitment" than those market-based forces, because it rules out future competitive devaluations, stimulates foreign investment and the building of long-term links, and could endorse forms of political integration, promoting reciprocal trade, economic and financial integration and fostering business cycle synchronisation among the monetary area, which will help to achieve progress in OCA aspects. Some authors apply concepts similar to the "endogeneity of OCA" in other domains than trade: the endogeneity of financial integration or of diverse insurance schemes offered by capital markets, the endogeneity of product and labour market flexibility, or the endogeneity of labour market institutions.[12]

A common line in those sources of OCA endogeneity is the removal of diverse national "borders" among participant countries in a monetary union, firstly intended to expel domestic monies but also contributing to the narrowing of many differences and distances, consequently a change in the incentive structure of economic agents, and finally regarding the prospect of constructing and completing an European financial and banking union.

In the last 60 years, OCA theory has witnessed various ups and downs, but, in fact, it had limited direct influence in the plans for, and the accomplishment of, European

manipulate aggregate demand to offset private sector shocks the "fine-tuning fallacy". The rational expectations revolution, the monetarist critique and literature on the inflation bias postulating the long-run ineffectiveness of monetary policy helped change this perception. See Dellas and Tavlas (2009), Mongelli (2008, pp. 4–6), and Buiter (1999, p. 181).

[11]After the launching of the European Economic and Monetary Union and the Euro, the weaknesses and limitations of the OCA theory were gradually addressed and tested with the use of new advancements in economics and econometrics, in order to study, for instance, the transmission of shocks, output synchronisation, financial flows, etc. Over and beyond its many weaknesses and limitations, as Mongelli notes, the OCA theory has merits as an organising device and as a catalyst for analysis: "without the OCA theory there may not have been such a systemic scrutiny of so many economic features, which are after all the building bricks of monetary unions; going back to the analogy of EMU with a laboratory, this OCA patient has survived but it has been radically transformed over recent decades". See Mongelli (2008, pp. 7–9) and Frankel and Rose (1998).

[12]See Dellas and Tavlas (2009), Mongelli (2008, pp. 7–9), Grawe and Mongelli (2005), Blanchard and Wolfers (2000), and Gonçalves (2010b, pp. 289–320).

economic and monetary integration in the 1990s. Be that as may, its basic pioneering intuitions were remarkably strong and it seems incontestable that we continue to discuss and test OCA criteria, nowadays especially concerning the properties of the future Eurozone as a more complete and satisfactory banking union.

## 2 The Financial Crisis, the European Democratic Deficit and the Need to Reform the Euro Area

The financial market integration goal—the prerequisite of OCA that could decrease the need for adjustments among the European countries with a single currency—failed completely.

Since mid-2007, and specially after the Lehman shock of September 2008, European banking supervisors and policy-makers have been in constant crisis management mode,[13] exacerbated by the growing unwillingness of private investors to lend to States in the Eurozone periphery, first to Greece and later to Ireland, Portugal and others.[14]

The financial crisis of 2007–2008 derived, to a large extent, from a failure of governments in North America and Europe to appropriately supervise and respond to financial systemic risk, lacking more prudent credit policies and practices. The following vicious cycle between weak sovereigns and national banking credit conditions has revealed not only a crisis of the Eurozone periphery but also a failure of the Eurozone as a whole, in particular of its centre and its main actors and mechanisms, to act promptly and adequately.[15]

Another downfall emerged from the democratic deficit and from the "executive deficit" of the European institutions, a systemic problem of inadequate incentives and institutions rather than an individual leadership problem. Those two deficits

---

[13]At the debate of the public bail-out of IKB, a medium-sized lender, on 29 July 2007, Jochen Sanio, German banking supervisor, warned of "the worst banking crisis since 1931", in "Germany rescues subprime lender", *Financial Times*, 2 August 2007.

[14]Banking weaknesses and sovereign credit dynamics have been connected in a perverse country by country feedback loop, involving excessive implicit and explicit government guarantees on banks and high domestic biases in bank portfolios of European Union sovereign debt, as in Greece (94 %), Spain (90 %), Portugal (79 %) or Italy (78 %), in 2011. The result was national fiscal and banking problems feeding each other, which is incompatible with a sustainable monetary union. Eventually, on 29 June 2012, the leaders of the Eurozone countries made an unprecedented commitment when they, on 29 June 2012, issued a statement starting with the words "We affirm that it is imperative to break the vicious circle between banks and sovereigns". They officially acknowledged their intention to break the "doom loop" of mutually reinforcing deterioration of credit conditions hampering weaker member States and banks based in their territory. See Véron (2012).

[15]Some authors, such as Nicolas Véron, have discussed whether the policy errors of the Commission were or are less damaging than the absence of decisions: "Challenges of Europe's fourfold Union", hearing before the U. S. Senate on "The future of the Eurozone: Outlook and lessons" (1 August 2012). See Véron (2012).

feed each other, as Véron (2012) observes: "the lack of democratic legitimacy contributes to the paralysis of executive decision-making; and Europe's inability to solve its collective problems deepens citizens' distrust of its institutions".

With the EU expansion of powers into areas directly affecting national sovereignty, concerns have increased over its deepening "democratic deficit". The crisis of the European Monetary Union and of the sovereign debt exacerbated these concerns because most policy responses have privileged technocratic solutions over parliamentary scrutiny or democratic accountability.[16]

A common criticism after the Euro crisis has been that it was underestimated how the failure lo link monetary union to greater political union constituted a basic weakness of the project. It was claimed that measures to address the sovereign debt crisis troubling certain member States have been both ineffective and illegitimate, aggravating the existing democratic deficit. Furthermore, that these have implied the imposition of austerity programmes by creditor States on debtor States, through policies approved and implemented outside the established EU and national democratic decision-making procedures.

The huge European crisis caused substantial social problems across the Union, particularly in southern member States—12 % of the European labour force without a job and youth unemployment (regarding 16–24 years old) reaching unprecedented levels (24.4 % or 3.58 million under 25 years old were unemployed across the EU, over 50 % in Greece and Spain). Consequently, it has been more and more argued that social justice requires and also justifies a further level of solidarity among the member States to confront the vast problems, which would only be attainable and legitimate in a political union with an unquestionable democratic mandate.[17]

It is evidently decisive to go beyond the relatively sterile and counter-productive characterisation of frequent debates about the EU in which all pro-Europeans advocate more political union and those who want more political differentiation argue for the collapse and disintegration of the EU and are accused of seeking a

---

[16]According to Richard Bellamy, "the crisis has thereby also contributed to rising public disillusionment with established political systems at all levels" and, "historically, economic downturns may always have affected public confidence", asking if the Eurozone crisis is eroding trust in the Union in an unprecedented manner and, in that case, if political union is the source of the problem or its solution. See Bellamy (2012, 3 ss).

[17]The views are diverse about the appropriate answer to this enormous problem. Some consider that greater political unity within the EU is both a practical necessity and a moral obligation if the Euro-crisis is to be managed in a way that respects the conditions of justice and democracy, although they differ on the equilibrium between those two principles. Others fear that such a move risks combining the financial with a political crisis, because not only are the economic disparities among the States in the Eurozone difficult to deal with efficiently, but also the political cultures and identifications for European citizens are similarly too contrasting to accommodate an effective common democratic system. Just as those who advocate greater political unity would not deny the diversity of the EU and, in many aspects (as with its different languages), would celebrate it, those who emphasise the political and economic aspects of this diversity would not deny the need for cooperation to solve common problems or that mutual recognition implies a degree of social solidarity. See Bellamy (2012, 3 ss).

return to a Europe of separate and suspicious States. As Bellamy notes, this is a debate about different visions of how the EU can best be organised in a democratic and socially just way that reflects the interdependence of European citizens and the differences among European peoples.[18]

According to the Treaties, the European Parliament does not have effective control over monetary and financial policies and decisions. As pointed out by the Federal Constitutional Court of Germany, the European Parliament cannot act "in such a way that a decision on political direction taken by the European electorate could have a politically decisive effect", which means a "structural democratic deficit".[19]

On the other hand, the European Council is not accountable to any other institution at the European level. The heads of State and or heads of government ensure accountability to their national parliaments and, consequently, to their citizens and electorate, but the European Council as an institution is not accountable to any other EU institution (e. g., the Parliament). Identical doubts regarding legitimacy can be formulated for the summit meetings of the Eurozone as well as other key intergovernmental formations in this domain such as the ECOFIN Council and Eurogroup.[20]

As a central banker, the ECB is in a different institutional position, less dependent—or 'completely independent', in accordance with the European Treaties [21]—than other policy-makers, on the subject of democratic accountability mechanisms, in order to legitimise its policies and actions. At the EU level, the ECB has been more active than other institutions and exercised its authority forcefully, certainly because it is, in fact, less prejudiced by the weakness of democratic representation.

[18]"In European politics as in domestic politics two profound disagreements over policy need not imply that one side is more committed to co-existence within a common political framework than the other—separatism being by and large the exception rather than the rule—merely that both sides have different views of how that framework should be structured and run so as to best support the interests of its members". See Bellamy (2012, 3 ss).

[19]Federal Constitutional Court of Germany, Press release No. 72-2009, "Act approving the Treaty of Lisbon compatible with the Basic Law; accompanying law unconstitutional to the extent that legislative bodies have not been accorded sufficient rights of participation".

[20]The European Commission has a stronger accountability to the European Parliament, but in other domains, including competition policy, with frequent and important connections to this subject, in which the Commission can decide in favour or against concrete proposals for acquisition or capitalisation of financial institutions. See Véron (2012).

[21]The Independence of the ECB is laid down in the institutional framework for the single monetary policy, in the Treaty and in the Statute with the purpose of maintaining price stability. Neither the ECB nor the national central banks, nor any member of their decision-making bodies, are allowed to seek or take instructions from EU institutions, from any government of a member State or from any other body or agency. According to article 130 of the Treaty, EU institutions, bodies, offices and agencies and the national governments of the member States must respect the principle and not seek to influence the members of the decision-making organs of the ECB.

However, as the ECB should not act beyond the limits of its legal mandate, its ability to fill the EU's 'executive deficit' is inevitably bounded.[22]

As such, the appropriate solution for the persistent European financial and monetary crisis should answer those institutional deficits, of democratic representation and empowerment and of executive decision-making capability. And the main executive functions in need of strengthening are financial sector oversight, government financing and structural reforms.

Indeed, it was clearly necessary and urgent for the European Union to build a banking union, a fiscal union, and a competitiveness union.

Last but not least, all those developments require a revised institutional framework which grants democratic accountability, a central pillar of current European integration, which addresses the concerns of many governmental and non-governmental bodies and organisations—including the aforementioned 2009 ruling of the German federal constitutional court.[23]

## 3 The Continuing Fragmentary European Financial System and the Urgency to Establish a Banking Union to Recover the Economic and Monetary Union

The banking union has appeared therefore as an attempt to respond to a central problem encountered in many Member States within the context of cross-financial crises resulting from contagion between Member States by a financial system characterised by the fact that the European Central Bank (ECB) cannot act as LOLR—lender of last resort for the national Governments and the consequent reality of national banking being the lender of last resort for the States.[24,25]

---

[22]N. Véron notes that an early call for stronger European executive policy-making capacity in the context of the Eurozone crisis came from the then-president of the ECB, Jean-Claude Trichet, in his speech "Building Europe, building institutions", upon receiving the 2011 Charlemagne Prize in Aachen, 12 June 2011. See Véron (2012).

[23]This institutional transformation should not yet be called "political union", in proper or definitive terms, as some propose (Véron), although "it would entail the recognition of a political space at the European level and not only in individual member States". Certainly, this would be a new step or steps towards economic and inevitably political integration, but not necessarily or probably the 'last' and 'decisive' step or degree of international economic and politic integration, concluding in a complete political union, with the fading of the national member States...

[24]Cf. Article 123, paragraph 1 of the TFEU and Article 21, paragraph 1 of the Protocol on the Statutes of the European System of Central Banks and of the European Central Bank. This prohibition does not, however, prevent the ECB from intervening in the secondary markets, in particular under the provisions of the so-called OMT programme.

[25]Banks in Spain, Italy, Portugal and Ireland now hold more than 700 billion of domestic sovereign debt on their books while in 2007 this was around half that amount. See Geeroms and Karbownik (2014, p. 3).

In fact, the economies of a well-functioning Monetary Union supposedly benefit from a single interest rate, reflecting the monetary policy stance of the common central bank which must benefit, in an artificial way, particularly the periphery countries of Europe (such as Greece, Ireland, Portugal, Spain and Italy, as well as Cyprus and Slovenia).[26]

Nevertheless, the Euro-crisis revealed the fundamental problem of the "vicious circle" or "doomed loop" between sovereigns and banks.

The "contagion effect" that has been noted as a result of the crisis, between the banking sector and sovereign debt, has caused a crisis in the functioning of the Economic and Monetary Union.

This "contagion effect" led to the fragmentation of the existing financial system in the various Member States, exposing the fragility of certain banking systems—also motivated in part by the need to comply with the new Basel III rules—leading to loss of confidence by depositors, the deterioration of the financing conditions of States and individuals—since investors started adopting a different view on the fiscal and competitiveness position of each member of the currency union.

In the absence of a European fiscal backstop, only national governments could rescue their banks which therefore sets in motion a "vicious circle" or "doomed loop" between banks and sovereigns: weak banks are more likely to add to public debt problems and countries with a high or even unsustainable public debt are considered too weak to support their banks, leading to weak banks that are distrusted by other banks and which lose access to cheap funding via the interbank market.

In 2011, Paul de Grauwe (2011) outlined the reason why capital flow reversal provoked such an important asymmetric shock in the Eurozone. He shows that a member state, due to the very fact of joining the monetary union and giving up control of its own currency and monetary policy, becomes more vulnerable to capital flow reversals and speculation against its sovereign debt compared to countries that keep their currency.

The result is that markets start to link the fate of governments to the solvency of the banking system and the other way round. The doomed loop between banks and sovereigns increases the costs of credits for business and households in the Southern member states leading to less investment.

As such, the banking union—with its three pillars (i) the Single Supervisory Mechanism (SSM), which gives direct banking supervision to the European Central

[26]See Geeroms and Karbownik (2014, p. 3).

Bank, responsible for the direct supervision of the 123 largest banking groups in the European Union[27]; (ii) the Single Resolution Mechanism (SRM)[28,29,30] and (iii) the

[27]The Single Supervisory Mechanism (SSM) was established following the adoption of Regulation (EU) No. 1024/2013 of 15 October, which gave the ECB the power to oversee significant credit institutions in the euro area countries and other States which, although not having adopted the euro as their currency, wish to be part of this collaboration,

[28]under which, since January 2016, resolutions must be primarily financed by shareholders and bank creditors—in applying the "bail-in" principle according to which losses should firstly be borne by the hareholders and the creditors and not use State funds—and may, as a supplement, receive financing through the Single Resolution Fund (SRF), resulting from banking sector contributions made by banks over the next 8 years and which, when they reach the funds target-level, will enable it to hold about 55 billion EUR, or about 1 % of covered deposits in the euro area.

The Single Resolution Mechanism (SRM) is intended to prevent the resolution of banks affecting systemic stability and the financial situation of the countries in which they operate. Under the terms of the SRM, it is up to the ECB to trigger the resolution process and decide whether a bank is at risk of bankruptcy, as a result of Regulation (EU) No. 806/2014 of the European Parliament and of the Council of 15 July, establishing uniform rules and procedures for the resolution of credit institutions and certain investment firms under a Single Resolution Mechanism and a banking Single Resolution Fund which amends Regulation (EU) No. 1093/2010.

In this context, the Directive 2014/59/EU of the European Parliament and of the Council of 15 May 2014, concerning bank recovery and resolution (BRRD), which provides for ways of resolving credit institutions without recourse to taxpayers being necessary.

In April, the European Parliament also approved the CRD IV package, consisting of the banking Directive 2013/36/EU on Capital Requirements (CRD) and Regulation (EU) No. 575/2013 concerning Capital Requirements (CRR) Tradutor: error no original? Requisites de Fundos Próprios duas vezes. This new package transposed into Community law the prudential capital requirements for credit institutions and investment firms, reinforcing the rules of capitalization and liquidity of banks, the rules on remuneration practices and incentives for granting credit, in particular to SMEs.

[29]It is intended that in the future, this will be the European fund to ensure the resolution of financial system entities.

It should be noted that to access this fund, the "toxic" banks should apply losses to their main creditors, including senior debt holders (something not found in the large redemptions in this crisis).

This implies that the central authority, the Single Resolution Board (SRB)—independent agency of the European Union which became operational in January 2016—is in the final instance responsible for the decision to initiate the resolution of a bank and to exercise directly the resolution function in relation to all institutions subject to the direct supervision of the ECB or with cross-border activity in the euro area, while at the operational level, the decision will be executed in cooperation with the national resolution authorities.

All this encapsulates a central problem of the Banking Union, namely its lack of democratic legitimacy.

[30]We therefore agree with those who say that the single resolution mechanism cannot be seen as the magic bullet capable of solving systemic risk issues. The European Union is totally inexperienced in this field, as in the past, bank failures were resolved without recourse to resolution mechanisms, either through public intervention (the case of Ireland or Sweden in the early 1990s) or nationalisations (see the case of BPN in Portugal). Thus, see Véron and Wolff (2013, p. 2).

Single Deposit Insurance Fund[31,32] emerges from the framework of OCA theory in two ways: (1) the absence of a banking union can be a reason for important asymmetric shocks due to sudden capital flow reversals, or alternatively, (2) a well-functioning banking union can be an important instrument to accommodate such shocks.[33]

On the other hand, the banking union has the unique feature of increasing private and public risk sharing.

A full banking union will first of all increase financial integration by harmonising regulation (single rulebook, single supervisory mechanism, resolution plans, etc.), stimulating private financial flows and private risk sharing (depending on the nature of the financial flows), and increasing the correlation of income and/or the degree of openness.

## 4 The Insufficiencies of the European Banking Union

Various genetic defects were observed when setting up the Banking Union. Let us look at those that seem the most important.

First, the Banking Union does not have, regarding the single resolution mechanism, a legal basis in the text of the Treaties.[34]

---

[31]The Single Deposit Insurance Fund (SDIF) was created following the approval of Directive 2014/49/EU on deposit insurance systems, which contributes, along with the SRF and the European Stability Mechanism (ESM), to the third pillar of the Banking Union. On the possible creation of this mechanism in the context of the banking union, see Gros and Schoenmaker (2014, pp. 529–554).

The aim with this mechanism is to harmonise the rules on deposit insurances established at a national level so that a Member State has a deposit system that achieves a capitalisation level corresponding to 0.8 % of covered deposits, within 10 years.

However, at the present time, the third pillar has not moved forward with the European Union having limited itself to ratifying the conditions under which this fund should operate in each country.

[32]For a discussion on the realisation of the three pillars of the banking union, see Pisani-Ferry et al. (2012).

[33]See Geeroms and Karbownik (2014, p. 10).

[34]It involved, in order to harmonise prudential supervision—the 1st pillar—Article 114 of the TFEU as the appropriate legal basis. In addition, to establish the single supervisory mechanism, Article 127, paragraph 6 of the TFEU was invoked.

However, there are well-founded doubts regarding the resolution mechanism.

Indeed, the establishing of this mechanism—unlike the supervisory mechanism—is not expressly provided for in the text of the Treaties, which to some extent is connected to the fact that any resolution mechanism especially applicable to banks should be considered as an alternative to the insolvency regime which is still a matter dealt with by the Member States—unlike what happens, for example, in the USA.

Admittedly, it is the case for some, that the legal basis for the establishment of the single resolution mechanism can be implicitly extracted from Article 114 of the TFEU concerning the harmonisation of legislation among Member States.

On the other hand, politically, the Banking Union is devoid of democratic legitimacy. This point has already been examined by the European Parliament.[35]

To all this, it should be added that the Banking Union reinforced the ECB's powers and the type of democratic scrutiny to which this institution will be submitted remains to be determined.

This is, basically, seeking to answer the old Latin question: *Quis custodiet ipsos custodes?*—Who watches the watchers?

It is indeed the case that it is accepted that the actions of the ECB can be appealed to the Court of Justice.[36]

However, there is still some lack of accountability to which the ECB is subject, knowing that the TFEU only provides, in Article 284, paragraph 3, for the ECB to annually send to the European Parliament, the Council, the Commission and also the European Council a report on the activities of the ESCB and on monetary policy.

Finally, the Banking Union will never be complete without a true Economic and Monetary Union.

The truth is that the European Union tried, through establishing the Banking Union, to close the Economic and Monetary Union, believing that in this way it would remedy its shortcomings which had been revealed by the 2007/2008 financial crisis.

It turns out, however, that the EMU theoretical framework is not yet closed, since the following have yet to be achieved: (i) political union, (ii) a true union of capital, (iii) an institutional regulation model for the financial system which is uniform and consistent between the Member States, (iv) an institution which, effectively, ensures, the functions of lender of last resort (LOLR) and, finally, ensuring effective forms of (iv) accountability and liability within the actual Banking Union.

These deficiencies were observable already in 2012, when the then President of the European Council, Herman Van Rompuy, in a report entitled "Towards a genuine Economic and Monetary Union", set out his vision of a stable

When reading Regulation No. 806/2014—which created the Single Resolution Mechanism and the banking Single Resolution Fund—it can be seen that it was approved by taking into account precisely Article 114 of the TFEU.

It turns out that this regulation does not explicitly provide competences to the Union in this area.

Most doctrine considers it essential to revise the Treaties in this respect, so that the Banking Union is not, at the outset, doomed by the lack of an appropriate legal basis regarding the single resolution mechanism. On the lack of a suitable legal basis in the TFEU for the creation of the single resolution mechanism, see Véron (2013, pp. 5–7).

[35]It should be recalled that the Parliament was directly involved in the legislative process that led to the creation of the banking union but it had only an advisory role in relation to the legislation concerning that matter. See Howarth and Quaglia (2013, p. 119).

[36]See Article 271, paragraph d) of the TFEU which awards competence to the CJEU to hear disputes concerning the implementation of obligations under the Treaties and the Statutes of the ESCB and of the ECB by the national central banks. See Duarte (2006, pp. 149–176).

and prosperous Economic and Monetary Union based on four constituent elements[37]:

(i) An integrated financial framework to ensure financial stability, particularly in the euro area, and to minimize costs for European citizens resulting from situations involving bank resolutions;
(ii) An integrated budgetary framework (...) involving coordination (...), better enforcement and commensurate steps towards the common issuance of debt securities. This table may also include different forms of budgetary solidarity;
(iii) An integrated economic policy framework with sufficient mechanisms to ensure the implementation of national and European policies that promote sustainable growth, employment and competitiveness (...);
(iv) Ensure the democratic legitimacy and accountability necessary for decision-making within the EMU, based on the joint exercise of sovereignty in aspects of common policies and solidarity.

Now, if we can say that the Banking Union seeks to answer the first constitutive element of the (new) Economic and Monetary Union—creating a (more) integrated financial framework, which will minimize the costs for European citizens—the truth is that the remaining three components have yet to be achieved.

Where are the (i) measures leading to common issuance of debt securities and forms of budgetary solidarity, including a true federal budget to provide for dealing with asymmetric economic shocks such as those already observed?

Where is (ii) the integrated economic policy framework to ensure national and European policies that promote sustainable growth, employment and competitiveness?

And finally, where is the (iii) the legitimacy and democratic accountability necessary for decision-making in the EMU?

Because of all of this, it can be said that the Banking Union is still wobbly.

## 5 Towards a More Perfect Banking Union?

The construction of the Banking Union meant that the big banks have ended up being supervised by the European Central Bank and the others left to the supervision of the national central banks (although, of course, subject to common prudential supervision rules, approved by the European Union), all in an area that shares the same currency.

This reality will mean, in this area too, the (undesirable) maintenance of a European Union operating at differing speeds, similar to what happens in the euro area: on the one hand, the large banks and small and medium-sized banks and, on the other, the banks of the euro area and the banks from outside the euro area.[38]

---

[37] See President of the European Council, Herman Van Rompuy (2012).

[38] Raising a similar issue, see Howarth and Quaglia (2013, pp. 114–117).

If we share the same currency—the Euro—and, consequently, monetary policy has ceased to belong to the Member states, why have a single resolution mechanism for large banks and another one for small and medium banks, governed by separate entities—the ECB on the one hand, and national central banks, on the other?

Here a further element of discussion can be introduced, which is often overlooked or undervalued, namely the institutional architecture of regulation of the financial sector, questioning whether, at the national level, it makes sense for the supervisor simultaneously to have resolution competences, as is the case in most Member States, particularly in Portugal or, from another perspective, discuss the most appropriate models for the European Union; if this is a single or integrated model, the tripartite model or indeed the so-called twin peaks model and what the consequences of each of these choices is for the functioning of the Banking Union or the supervision of financial conglomerates.

Here, it can always, at the outset, be stated that no model is perfect and that with the emergence of the financial crisis, they have all revealed flaws.

In this context, it is crucial to ensure consistency of accountability of financial sector regulation—enabling this to be asserted before national parliaments and the European Parliament (particularly in the way the supervision of large banking groups is carried out)—and liability—because if this is already established in the TFEU in relation to the ECB, in the context of banking union (cf. Article 340 of the TFEU) this must exist, in parallel, at the national level, since Member States cannot take refuge in their institutional regulation models to remove responsibility from the national regulator as sometimes seems to occur, particularly in the Member States that have continued to adopt the tripartite model of financial sector regulation.

It is just that, at a time when the boundaries between the financial system regulators have been diluted, due to the emergence of financial conglomerates, globalisation or actions in several original markets, by operators (consider, for example, investment funds that have been acquiring banks or insurance companies), the specific allocation of responsibility to the financial sector regulators may also be diluted, particularly when we think of the tripartite model of regulation.

The freedom that the European Union grants to Member States in this area is known, with the Union itself, based on the tripartite model, having conceived embryos of trans-European regulatory bodies, integrated into the new European System of Financial Supervision (ESFS): the European Securities and Markets Authorities (ESMA), the European Banking Authority (EBA) and the European Insurance and Occupational Pensions Authority (EIOPA).[39]

[39]The three European financial supervision authorities, in operation since 1 January 2011, are independent although accountable to the European Parliament, the Council of the European Union and the European Commission. Apart from these three authorities (EBA, ESMA and EIOPA), the European System of Financial Supervision (ESFS) also comprises the European Systemic Risk Board (ESRB) as well as the Joint Committee of the European Supervisory Authorities and the national supervisory authorities. The objective of the European supervisory authorities is "to improve the functioning of the internal market by ensuring appropriate, efficient and harmonised European regulation and supervision", whilst the national supervisory authorities remain in charge

We can therefore speculate whether the freedom to define the internal institutional regulation model, granted by the European Union, should persist in the future.

We understand this to be so for a number of reasons.

Firstly, because the superiority of any of the aforementioned theoretical regulation models has not been demonstrated.

In some Member States who welcomed monistic regulation models, there have been serious flaws (knowing that the tripartite model can allow, in some cases, a subtle mutual monitoring by regulators).

On the other hand, the Banking Union cannot ignore the principle of subsidiarity stated in Article 4 of the TEU.

Nevertheless, it will be necessary, in the end, to affirm the possibility of imputing responsibility to the regulators.

Here, the adoption of common rules of responsibility for national regulators in the European Union, could be a positive path towards deepening banking union and, consequently, economic and monetary union, in order to complete a puzzle that is still to be finalised.

## References


Bellamy R (2012) The democratic deficit, social justice and the Eurozone crisis. In: Bellamy R, Staiger U (eds) The Eurozone crisis and the democratic deficit. UCL European Institute, London

Blanchard O, Wolfers J (2000) The role of shocks and institutions in the rise of European unemployment: the aggregate evidence. Econ J 110:1–33

Buiter W (1999) Alice in Euroland. J Common Mark Stud 37–2:181–209

Chari V, Dovis A, Kehoe P (2013) Rethinking optimal currency areas. Federal Reserve Bank of Minneapolis

De Grauwe P (2011) The governance of a fragile eurozone, CEPS working Documents, No. 346

de Grauwe P (2014) Economics of monetary union, 10th edn. Oxford University Press, Oxford

de Grawe P, Mongelli F (2005) Endogeneities of optimum currency areas: what brings countries sharing a single currency closer together? ECB Working Paper No. 468

Dellas H, Tavlas G (2009) An optimum-currency-area odyssey. Working Paper No. 102. Bank of Greece—Eurosystem

Duarte ML (2006) O Banco Central Europeu e o sistema judicial da união europeia: supremacia decisória e controlo da legalidade. In Estudos em Homenagem a Sousa Franco, III. Coimbra Ed., pp 149–176

European Commission (1990) One market, one money. An evaluation of the potential benefits and costs of forming an economic and monetary union. European Economy 44, Oct 1990

Frankel J, Rose A (1998) The endogeneity of the optimum currency area criteria. Econ J 108–449:1009–1025

Fukuyama F (1992) The end of history and the last man. Penguin, Harmondsworth


---

of supervising individual financial institutions. See esp. Regulation (EU) No. 1092/2010 of the European Parliament and of the Council of 24 November 2010 on European Union macro-prudential oversight of the financial system and establishing a European Systemic Risk Board.

Geeroms H, Karbownik P (2014) A monetary union requires a banking union. Bruges European Economic Policy Briefings No. 33–2014
Gonçalves JR (2010a) The Euro and the future of Portugal and of the European Union (O Euro e o Futuro de Portugal e da União Europeia). Wolters Kluwer, Coimbra Ed, Coimbra
Gonçalves JR (2010b) The sustainability of the Eurozone and the financial system regulation (A sustentabilidade da zona euro e a regulação do sistema financeiro). Competition and Regulation Review (Revista de Concorrência e Regulação—C & R) I-2: 289–320
Gros D, Schoenmaker D (2014) European deposit insurance and resolution in the banking union. J Common Mark Stud 52–3:529–554
Howarth D, Quaglia L (2013) Banking union as Holy Grail: rebuilding the single market in financial services, stabilizing Europe's banks and 'completing' economic and monetary union. J Common Mark Stud 51:103–123
Kenen P (1969) The optimum currency area: an eclectic view. In: Mundell R, Swoboda A (eds) Monetary problems of the international economy. Chicago University Press, Chicago
Krugman P (1993) Lessons of Massachusetts for RMU. In: Torres F, Giavazzi F (eds) Adjustment and growth in the European Monetary Union. CEPR, CUP, London, Cambridge
Mckinnon R (1963) Optimum currency areas. Am Econ Rev 53–4:717–725
McKinnon R (2004) Optimum currency areas and key currencies: Mundell I versus Mundel II. J Common Mark Stud 42–4:689–715
Mongelli F (2008) European economic and monetary integration and the optimum currency area theory. European Economy, Economic Papers, No. 302, European Commission
Mundell R (1961) A theory of optimum currency areas. Am Econ Rev 51–4:657–665
Mundell R (1973) Uncommon arguments for common currencies. In: Johnson H, Swoboda A (eds) The economics of common currencies. Harvard University Press, Cambridge
Pisani-Ferry J, Sapir A, Véron N, Wolff G (2012) What kind of European banking union? Bruegel Policy Contribution No. 2012/12. Available at: http://hdl.handle.net/10419/72098. Accessed Feb 2016
President of the European Council (Herman Van Rompuy) (2012) Towards a genuine Economic and Monetary Union. 5 Dec 2012. Available at: www.consilium.europa.eu/pt/workarea/downloadasset.aspx?id=17415&usg=AFQjCNGnh0c6RzX5cUdrR5623-0BCRvR2g
Tavlas GS (1994) The theory of monetary integration. Open Econ Rev 5(2):211–230
Véron N (2012) Challenges of Europe's fourfold union. Hearing before U. S. Senate on "The future of the Eurozone: outlook and lessons", 1 Aug 2012
Véron N (2013) A realistic bridge towards European banking union. Bruegel Policy Contribution 2013/09. Available at: http://hdl.handle.net/10419/106306
Véron N, Wolff GB (2013) From supervision to resolution: next steps on the road to European banking union. Bruegel Policy Contribution 2013–04. Available at: http://hdl.handle.net/10419/72128. Access Feb 2016
von Hagen J, Eichengreen B (1996) Federalism, fiscal restraints, and European Monetary Union. Am Econ Rev 86–2:134–138

# The (Future) European Unemployment Insurance and Its Role as an Automatic Stabiliser

**Miroslav Beblavý, Karolien Lenaerts, and Ilaria Maselli**

**Abstract** In this paper, we examine possibilities and limitations of a potential European Unemployment Insurance in alleviating impact of both symmetric and asymmetric shocks on national budgets and workers' welfare. We present various policy options and their assessment. In the paper, we first discuss the framework in which an automatic stabiliser would operate and present different options for such a stabiliser. We then focus on the idea of a European unemployment insurance, and review a range of proposals that have been made in this domain. We conclude by listing the challenges and strengths of a common insurance scheme. In terms of challenges, we consider the size, funding and stabilisation impact of the scheme, the countries involved, political feasibility and harmonisation and the issue of moral hazard and permanent transfers. We also explain how these challenges can be overcome.

**JEL Classification** E63 • H55 • J65

## 1 Introduction

Since the outbreak of the financial-economic crisis and the long recession that followed, academics and policy-makers have called for reform. Much attention has focussed on the shortcomings of the Economic and Monetary Union (EMU), which became painfully clear during the downturn. In the crisis, it became clear that traditional market-based mechanisms were inadequate. One solution that has been

---

This chapter draws on earlier work that the CEPS prepared on European unemployment insurance schemes. For more details, see Beblavý and Maselli (2014) and Beblavý et al. (2015a, b).

M. Beblavý (✉) • K. Lenaerts
Centre for European Policy Studies (CEPS), Bruxelles, Belgium
e-mail: miroslav.beblavy@ceps.eu; karolien.lenaerts@ceps.eu

I. Maselli
Conference Board, Bruxelles, Belgium
e-mail: ilaria.maselli@conference-board.org



N. da Costa Cabral et al. (eds.), *The Euro and the Crisis*, Financial and Monetary Policy Studies 43, DOI 10.1007/978-3-319-45710-9_17

put forward is the idea of introducing a supranational automatic stabiliser, in order to complete the EMU. This idea has also been taken up in the Four Presidents' Report and in the more recent Five Presidents' Report. Although a consensus has emerged that a stabiliser is needed, the debate on how this stabiliser should look like is still ongoing. One idea would be to introduce a European unemployment insurance scheme.

This chapter is devoted to a European unemployment insurance scheme and the role it could have as a supranational automatic stabiliser. It first explains what a supranational automatic stabiliser is and summarises the rationale for introducing such a mechanism. The chapter presents an overview of different potential stabilisation mechanisms and then continues with a more detailed discussion of the different proposals for a European unemployment insurance scheme. The chapter also points out the challenges of a European unemployment insurance, as well as its strengths.

## 2 What Is a Supranational Automatic Stabiliser and Why Does Europe Need One?

Before we start our analysis of a European unemployment insurance scheme and the potential that is has to serve as a stabilisation mechanism, we go back to the definition of an automatic stabiliser. The concept of an automatic stabiliser is an important one in the macro-economic literature. In this literature, an automatic stabiliser is considered to be *an economic policy that offsets fluctuations in national economy activity—both downturns and upswings—without intervention from the government or policy-makers* (In't Veld et al. 2012). There is a range of mechanisms and policies that can be regarded as automatic stabilisers on the basis of this definition. Well-known examples are taxes and transfer systems (e.g. unemployment benefits—which go up at times of crisis and go down in upswings). In this chapter, we focus on the latter. One example of a paper that proposes a mechanism based on taxation is Majocchi and Rey (1993). These authors suggest that a progressive tax, such as a carbon tax, can be used to achieve stabilisation. Automatic stabilisers can be set up at the national or supranational level, as would be the case for a European unemployment insurance scheme.

The idea of establishing a supranational automatic stabiliser in Europe is not new but the debate on this topic has clearly been reignited after the crisis. In fact, already in the 1970s it became clear that monetary unions all around the globe were equipped with important automatic mechanisms to offset fluctuations in economic activity (e.g. unemployment allowances and budgetary assistance to compensate a reduction in revenues, see Marjolin et al. 1975). For Europe and for the members of the EMU in particular, such a mechanism is vital (In't Veld et al. 2012). EMU countries can no longer fall back on monetary policy when hit by a shock and national fiscal policy is constrained by EU rules (e.g. the Stability and Growth Pact and the fiscal compact, which force countries to stay within certain debt and deficit limits). In such a scenario, a supranational automatic stabiliser is needed to ensure sufficient stabilisation (In't Veld et al. 2012). As economies become more integrated, national policy instruments become less effective.

In the academic literature, the rationale for a supranational automatic stabiliser has further been derived from spillover effects, current account imbalances and market failures (Beblavý et al. 2015b). When a country in a monetary union is hit by a shock, there may be *spillover effects* to its neighbouring countries or other members of the union (Majocchi and Rey 1993; Frankel and Rose 1998; Kalemli-Ozcan et al. 2001; Allard et al. 2013). In these circumstances, a supranational stabiliser may be needed to achieve stabilisation. *Current account imbalances* are a second issue, one that became highly relevant during the crisis. EMU members can no longer adjust exchange rates to account for imbalances. Instead, adjustments occur through a deflationary process, which can be buffered with an automatic stabiliser (Majocchi and Rey 1993; Guyon 2007). Interestingly, Emerson et al. (1990) argued that in a currency union, current account imbalances can be addressed through capital and labour adjustments. Goodhart and Smith (1993), however, provide evidence of *market failures*. In Europe, labour mobility is limited and there are downward wage rigidities, to name just one example (Majocchi and Rey 1993). In light of these issues, an automatic stabiliser is an essential tool for the EMU.

## 3 Potential Automatic Stabilisers

In the few last decades, a range of potential stabilisers have been examined. Beblavý et al. (2015b) present an overview of these mechanisms, which includes regional policy, public investment, a debt agency and taxation. A proposal for regional policy, for example, can be found in the report of MacDougall et al. (1977). MacDougall et al. (1977) developed a system of cyclical grants to local or regional governments. These grants are conditional on a region's economic performance. Padoa-Schioppa et al. (1987) proposed a similar idea. They suggest to subsidise the interest rate on private sector loans (conditional on the quality of programmes) and to provide grants (financed with structural funds, conditional on carrying out structural reform) to support less-developed regions and regions facing a downturn. Related work by Drèze and Durré (2014) focuses on public investment. Investment in social housing, renewable energy and transportation would be valuable for regions that are lagging behind. Beblavý et al. (2015b) do point out, tough, that investment can be difficult to carry out in practice. In addition, there has been a longstanding debate on whether investment can really be considered as a stabiliser due to the time lags it is associated with (e.g. to develop, approve and conduct projects).

Another proposal was put forward by Enderlein et al. (2013). These authors introduce the idea of a European debt agency that could issue its own bonds. Euro

Area members can issue part of their debt as bonds (up to 10 % of GDP). In a period of economic decline, this share can be increased to 20 % of GDP, on the condition that the country agrees to implement macro-economic and structural policies. Similar proposals have been discussed by Moesen and De Grauwe (2009), Allard et al. (2013) and Pisani-Ferry et al. (2013). Enderlein et al. (2013) further discussed the idea of setting up a European fund. This fund would be financed on the basis of contributions. It would pay out transfers to countries going through a crisis. Transfers are earmarked for a payroll tax reduction. Despite the lower multiplier that this approach would achieve, Enderlein et al. (2013) emphasise that its strength is that it does not undermine other government spending programmes.

The final supranational automatic stabiliser that we list is the European unemployment insurance scheme. In this system, benefits either are paid out directly to unemployed citizens (known as a 'genuine scheme'), or funds are transferred to national governments with the idea that these funds will be used to cover unemployment benefits ('reinsurance scheme'). In the past, several proposals for a European unemployment insurance scheme have been put forward. Generally, the scheme consists of three components, which can be combined in different ways. The components are: an enhancement of national unemployment insurance schemes (through minimum requirements), a spatial insurance component and an inter-temporal insurance component. By imposing minimum requirements on national schemes, their stabilisation capacity could be improved (e.g. by obliging countries to reach a coverage rate). Spatial insurance is true risk-sharing, across the participating countries. It is an important instrument to address asymmetric shocks. Inter-temporal insurance, which involves debt-issuing or deficits, is key to deal with symmetric shocks.

The debate on a supranational automatic stabiliser for Europe builds on four early reports on the future of the EMU, Marjolin et al. (1975), MacDougall et al. (1977), Padoa-Schioppa et al. (1987) and Emerson et al. (1990), which already discussed this idea. This idea first emerged in the 1970s, was revived in the 1990s and again resurfaced after the Great Recession. The Great Recession has put the idea of creating a fiscal capacity for the EMU back on the agenda. Academics and policy-makers have argued for an automatic stabiliser (see e.g. De Grauwe 2003, 2013; the Four Presidents' Report and the Five Presidents' Report).

Although several mechanisms were designed and presented in the past, none of these mechanisms was ever implemented. In order to better understand why, Beblavý et al. (2015b) interviewed some of the authors of these seminal reports. Overall, it seems that there was a broad consensus that market adjustment mechanisms would be sufficient to ensure stabilisation. In addition, many believed that in a monetary union asymmetric shocks would be less frequent and that current account imbalances could easily be tackled through capital and labour adjustments (Emerson et al. 1990). Other reasons are of a political nature. There was already a lot to discuss in light of the Maastricht criteria and a fiscal capacity was not regarded as sufficiently important. A related argument is that it was politically difficult to demand from national governments to cut their budgets while at the same time the European budget would be increased. Furthermore, an unemployment insurance scheme could not be embedded in the EU budget without a common authority having an influence on labour market reforms (Beblavý et al. 2015b). Another issue was the enlargement ahead. Finally, Beblavý et al. (2015b) also discovered that in the 1990s, it was difficult to imagine a large shock triggered by the financial sector.

## 4 Proposals for a European Unemployment Insurance Scheme

Generally, the literature on a European unemployment insurance scheme can be distinguished into two strands. A first set of studies have proposed a 'genuine' scheme, in which individual workers are insured (see Dullien 2007; Dolls et al. 2014; Jara and Sutherland 2014). This line of work is inspired by the Marjolin et al. (1975) report, which was the first study that proposed a European unemployment insurance. It paved the way for later research. The Marjolin et al. (1975) report presents a very detailed picture of what a common unemployment insurance could look like, how it could be financed and managed, and what its main advantages and challenges would be. The report concluded that a genuine European unemployment insurance could be a valuable instrument to achieve stabilisation and redistribution.

Within the set of genuine European unemployment insurance schemes, a distinction can be made between 'basic' and 'top-up' schemes. Basic schemes have received widespread support, whereas only very few studies regard top-up schemes as a viable option (Delpla 2012). The underlying idea of a basic genuine European unemployment insurance system is to create a scheme that (at least) partly replaces the existing national schemes. Genuine schemes are financed on the basis of contributions collected from employers and employees. Unemployment benefits are paid out directly to the unemployed. The same conditions, determining the benefit amount, duration and eligibility, apply to all workers across Europe. National governments can go beyond the European unemployment insurance scheme, for example in terms of coverage and generosity. In other words, national governments can top up the basic European insurance scheme.

The 'top-up' genuine European unemployment insurance scheme is of a very different nature. In this case, the idea is that an unemployed individual is guaranteed a minimum benefit. Importantly, 'minimum' refers to all dimensions of the insurance scheme, it is not limited to the benefit amount. For example, it also refers to the duration of the benefits and the eligibility conditions. When the national scheme is sufficient to meet these requirements, the European scheme does not intervene. In the opposite case, the European scheme covers the difference by topping up the national scheme. In the study of Delpla (2012), this idea is translated as follows: workers can choose between the European and the national insurance scheme if the national scheme is more attractive.

The second set of studies takes a different perspective. These studies investigate to what extent it is possible to set up a 'reinsurance' for national unemployment insurance schemes (Italianer and Vanheukelen 1993; Dullien 2013, 2014; Beblavý and Maselli 2014; Beblavý et al. 2015a, b). In this case, funds are collected from and disbursed to national governments. Reinsurance schemes only transfer funds when triggered. In most studies, a scheme is triggered when the unemployment rate exceeds a threshold level. A low threshold implies that the insurance scheme is triggered frequently and vice versa. Also in this system, the conditions that determine the pay-in and pay-out are similar across the countries. One crucial caveat is how the funds received are used by the government: are these funds earmarked to unemployment benefits or can governments choose how these funds are spent? The stabilisation capacity of the reinsurance scheme depends on this.

Regardless of whether a European unemployment insurance scheme is a genuine or reinsurance scheme, it is always composed of a *range of features that can take different values*. These are the features or building blocks that policy-makers have to keep in mind, when designing a European unemployment insurance. Some of these features can also be found in national unemployment benefits schemes while other features are generally only present in the European schemes. A first element to consider is *eligibility*: who qualifies for unemployment benefits? In national schemes, eligibility depends on several factors, including the nature of unemployment (voluntary or involuntary), the employment (how long has someone worked, vis-à-vis a reference period) or unemployment record, personal characteristics (e.g. worker or self-employed), etc. Eligibility conditions determine coverage, and hence have an impact on stabilisation. They can be strict or easy to meet. A second element is the benefit amount: how large are the benefits that an eligible unemployed worker receives? This amount is often calculated on the basis of a *reference wage* (e.g. gross or net, last or average wage) to which a certain *replacement rate* and *caps* are applied. Yet, there are countries in which unemployment benefits are flat-rated. A third feature is the *duration of the benefits*: how long are benefits paid out and does this vary over time? In many national schemes, benefit duration depends on the case (e.g. related to the age of an unemployed individual). Another point is whether there is a waiting period before benefits are paid out. All these features are used to determine the level and duration benefits in the genuine schemes and to establish who is eligible. In the reinsurance schemes, these features apply as well: governments receive an amount of transfers that is sufficient to support unemployed individuals who meet the eligibility conditions with a benefit amount that is calculated according to these criteria for a pre-defined duration.

Besides these features, European unemployment insurance schemes can have *experience rating, claw-back and cyclical variability*. Experience rating and claw-back are two instruments that link the pay-in into the scheme to the use of the scheme. Experience rating works ex ante, while claw-back operates ex post. Experience rating ensures that countries that use the scheme more, or that have a higher probability of doing so, have to pay more into the scheme. Claw-back tackles long-term imbalances vis-à-vis the scheme. If Member States have a negative cumulative balance (i.e. they have received more than they have paid into the fund), the scheme can adjust this situation by increasing the country's pay-in or demanding a supplementary contribution.

## 5 Challenges to a European Unemployment Insurance Scheme

A European unemployment insurance, however, would also be confronted with several challenges. In the literature, six main challenges were identified. These challenges, which are explored in depth by Beblavý et al. (2015b), are related to the financing, size and stabilisation capacity of the scheme, its political feasibility and the harmonisation needed, to which countries the scheme would apply, and the issue of moral hazard and permanent transfers.

When it comes to the *financing* of the insurance scheme, proposals include taxation, contributions paid by Member States and debt. Studies that have put forward a genuine scheme generally opt for the first solution, either in the form of a payroll tax (Dullien 2013, 2014) or a corporate tax (Pisani-Ferry et al. 2013). In both cases, there is a clear link between the individual and the scheme. Other work has promoted reinsurance schemes, in which transfers flow to the national government when the scheme is triggered (Italianer and Vanheukelen 1993; Beblavý and Maselli 2014; Dolls et al. 2014). In these studies, the scheme is financed through Member States' contributions. These contributions are expressed as a percentage of the country's GDP and can be funded through taxes or any other means that the countries choose. Although debt-issuing has been discussed in many papers, a consensus has yet to be reached on the desirability of this financing channel. Nonetheless, there are important arguments in favour of debt (e.g. Dullien 2013). A first argument is that debt-issuing is essential to deal with large, symmetric shocks, when the scheme likely has insufficient funds. Raising contributions or taxes at this time would put even more pressure on Member States that are already struggling. Such a strategy would undermine stabilisation, it instead is pro-cyclical.

A second dimension that has been much debated is the *size* of the European insurance scheme (i.e. the cost that it would entail). In most studies, the size of the European scheme is in line with that of the existing national schemes. Italianer and Vanheukelen (1993), for example, propose a scheme that would cost 0.5 % of GDP. These authors arrive at this estimate by multiplying the number of unemployed individuals by the average EU wage, applying a replacement rate of 70 %. In recent work, the features of the European scheme, such as the replacement rate and duration, are chosen so that they mimic those of (some of) the national schemes in Europe. Typically, the duration is 12 months (e.g. Dullien 2007, 2012, 2013; Beblavý and Maselli 2014; Dolls et al. 2014) and the replacement rate 40 % or 50 % (e.g. Dullien 2007, 2013; Beblavý and Maselli 2014; Dolls et al. 2014; Jara and Sutherland 2014; Beblavý et al. 2015a, b). The coverage rate either is determined endogenously (e.g. Dullien 2013; Dolls et al. 2014; Jara and Sutherland 2014) or it is set at 75 or 80 % (Beblavý and Maselli 2014; Beblavý et al. 2015a, b). The size of the European scheme will also depend on whether it is a genuine or a reinsurance scheme. In the second case, the scheme only pays out benefits when trigged and therefore a smaller scheme is needed. Across the literature, estimates appear to vary between 0.3 and 0.85 % of EU GDP.

Closely related to the size of the scheme is its *stabilisation impact* and how this is measured. Given the limited size of the European unemployment insurance scheme, one can expect that the scheme will contribute to macro-economic stabilisation but it will not be the full answer. Instead, other mechanisms are needed as well. In their recent paper, Beblavý et al. (2015b) identify three factors that determine a scheme's stabilisation capacity: the duration of the benefits and whether it can be extended in a severe crisis, the presence of a trigger, and the possibility to do redistribution. In the United States, unemployment benefits can be extended for a period of 6 months in the event of a severe shock. This idea can also be translated to the European context. Dullien (2007), for example, shows that such extended benefits substantially raise a scheme's stabilisation capacity. Brandolini et al. (2014) provide evidence for the other two features. These authors argue that in schemes that are conditioned by a trigger, transfers are only made in case of a major downturn—precisely when needed the most. This boosts the scheme's stabilisation impact. They further indicate that schemes that do allow for redistribution are more flexible, and hence also contribute more to stabilisation.

In the literature, the stabilisation capacity of a European unemployment insurance scheme has been measured in different ways. The measurement approach, however, may affect the estimated impact of the scheme (Beblavý et al. 2015b). In this regard, a first issue is whether one should consider the impact of the insurance scheme over the business cycle or during a recession? The stabilisation capacity of the scheme generally is larger in the latter case. A second issue is whether one should use the long-term GDP trend as a benchmark to weigh the stabilisation impact of the scheme against or whether past GDP is more suitable? Estimates usually are larger when past GDP is used. Another key question is one which countries one should focus: the average country or the country most strongly hit? In his paper, Dullien (2013) uses the long-term GDP trend and focuses on the stabilisation impact at times of recession. He obtains an effect of 11 % for the average country when the net balance of payments is used as a measure (vis-à-vis the change in aggregate income in the country). Italianer and Vanheukelen (1993) used the same approach in their paper and arrive at an impact of 20 % across Europe. Dolls et al. (2014) have also used a similar approach, but rely on the net sum of contributions paid and benefits received, divided by the sum of individuals' changes in employment income. Interestingly, these authors detected a stabilisation impact of 23–31 % for Greece, Ireland, Italy, Spain and Portugal in the recent crises. Beblavý and Maselli (2014) and Beblavý et al. (2015a, b) have criticised this approach, because it neglects fiscal multiplier effects. Nevertheless, the stabilisation impact reported in the literature seems to be important.

A fourth challenge to a European insurance scheme relates to the *countries that would be involved*: would the scheme be implemented for all EU countries or for the members of the Euro Area only? In the literature, both cases have been studied and arguments have been put forward in favour and against both scenarios. One clear advantage of extending the scheme to the EU is that this brings together a larger pool of countries to share the risk (Beblavý and Maselli 2014). Moreover, a common unemployment insurance would impose a minimum standard across Europe and stimulate convergence and solidarity. Nevertheless, recent work does suggest that the case for the Euro Area is particularly compelling. In the Five President's Report published in 2015, for example, the idea of introducing a supranational automatic stabiliser to complete the EMU is discussed. Another important conclusion is that, regardless of which group of countries is selected, participation in the scheme should be mandatory in order to avoid adverse selection (i.e. when only the countries with a higher probability to benefit from the scheme would participate, see Beblavý and Maselli 2014 and Beblavý et al. 2015a, b). Delpla (2012) is the only study that we are aware of that allows countries and citizens to opt out of the scheme.

*Moral hazard and permanent transfers* are another major challenge to a European unemployment insurance scheme. These issues are intertwined. Moral hazard seems to be inevitable in a monetary union where financial transfers flow from one economic region to another, especially when regions have policy powers (De Grauwe 2003). Indeed, a mechanism that supports countries in a downturn may reduce their incentives to carry out reforms. Moral hazard undermines the political legitimacy of the scheme. Vandenbroucke and Luigjes (2016) study the issue of moral hazard in the context of a European unemployment insurance. They investigate eight countries inside and outside of the EU that have a multi-tiered unemployment regulation. If a European unemployment insurance scheme would be introduced, it adds another layer on top of the existing national unemployment schemes. This may result in a highly complex structure, but can also encourage countries to adjust their national scheme. On the basis of their eight case studies, Vandenbroucke and Luigjes (2016) conclude that moral hazard cannot be avoided, but there are mechanisms that can be used to mitigate the issue. A first mechanism that serves this purpose is a trigger, which has two components: an indicator and a threshold. If a scheme is conditioned by a trigger, it only becomes active in the event of a shock. In other words, when the indicator surpasses the threshold, the European unemployment insurance scheme transfers funds to the government. To rule out permanent transfers, Beblavý et al. (2015b) argue that the indicator has to be tied to a rate of change in economic activity (e.g. the unemployment rate, so that every country can benefit) and that the threshold has to be sufficiently high (so that transfer are not permanent by definition). A second mechanism is claw-back, which is an instrument to reduce long-term imbalances vis-à-vis the supranational fund. If a country has received much more pay-outs from the fund than it has paid into the fund, a supplementary contribution may apply or the country's pay-in may increase (Dullien 2014; Dolls et al. 2014). Beblavý and Maselli (2014), for example, suggest that the pay-in of a country should go up if the negative balance is over 1 % of GDP. A third option is experience rating, which ties the pay-in to the use of the scheme (or to the likelihood of recurring to it). The report by Vandenbroucke and Luigjes

(2016) has identified a number of alternative mechanisms that have been used in countries with multi-tiered unemployment schemes. Some examples are financial incentives, centralisation, and minimum requirements. In light of these mechanisms, one has to keep in mind that the European unemployment insurance scheme would be an insurance. Some level of redistribution cannot be avoided. In addition, moral hazard may be the 'price to pay' to reap the benefits that such an insurance scheme could bring: stabilisation, social cohesion and economic growth are just a few examples.

The final challenge is *political feasibility and harmonisation*. These two topics are highly relevant, and closely intertwined. Moreover, the distinction between genuine and reinsurance schemes is of great importance here. Reinsurance schemes are conditioned by a trigger and involve a transfer of funds between the supranational scheme and the national government. This implies that when such a scheme is introduced, it leaves the existing national schemes largely intact. For genuine schemes, the situation is quite different. In this case, there is no trigger (the scheme functions continuously) and transfers flow between the scheme and individuals. Genuine schemes (at least partly) replace the existing national schemes. This means that in the genuine case, national governments have less flexibility to operate their own scheme when compared to the reinsurance scenario. In other words, genuine European unemployment insurance schemes are associated with a much higher need for harmonisation. However, as the existing national unemployment benefits schemes reflect national preferences, it seems likely that European schemes that require more harmonisation are politically more difficult to implement. In addition, especially in countries with a national scheme that differs substantially from the genuine European scheme, difficulties would emerge (e.g. in countries with a scheme based on voluntary insurance or a liberal welfare system). Harmonisation would be politically difficult especially when there are large differences in the objectives of the schemes.

In comparison to basic genuine European unemployment insurance schemes, the top-up schemes would require less harmonisation. One interesting example is the study by Delpla (2012), in which workers can choose between the European and the national scheme. Yet, top-up genuine schemes are associated with a range of other issues. For example, they may trigger a race-to-the-bottom in which countries adjust their national schemes to ensure that a larger part of the costs is covered by the European level. From the political perspective, these schemes may be less desirable because they do not provide a basic provision. Another example is that top-up schemes may also require frequent interactions between the European and national scheme, which are administratively hard to manage.

These divergences between reinsurance and genuine unemployment insurance schemes are also reflected in their legal and operational feasibility. Reinsurance schemes are much less demanding on both counts. From the legal perspective, they would cause few conflicts with constitutional law and would not require many amendments to ordinary national legislation. Operationally, these schemes would call for a small staff to manage the fund at the EU-level. In the Member States, they would rely on the existing framework, posing limited operational barriers. A different image emerges for the genuine schemes. In all EU Member States, these schemes would require changes in ordinary legislation. From the operational point of view, they would bring severe administrative issues. Politically, it appears that reinsurance schemes may be more feasible than genuine schemes If a European unemployment insurance scheme would be implemented, these legal and operational issues, which are found at both the country-level and the EU-level, would have to be addressed

Earlier research has provided evidence of the wide variation in national schemes across Europe, in terms of their set-up, generosity, duration, eligibility conditions etc. (Esser et al. 2013; Strauss et al. 2013). There are countless examples that illustrate this, we present a few of them here. While in some countries unemployment benefits are available only for unemployed workers, the self-employed are also covered in other countries. This difference has a major impact on the coverage of the scheme and its stabilisation capacity. A second example is the calculation method: countries can offer earnings-based or flat-rated unemployment benefits and a reference wage expressed in gross or net terms. There further are huge differences in the caps and the replacement rate used.

## 6 Strengths of a European Unemployment Insurance Scheme

Next to these challenges, a European unemployment insurance scheme also brings advantages that make it an interesting option to consider as a fiscal capacity for Europe. Beblavý et al. (2015b) list the following strengths: unemployment benefits are automatic and anti-cyclical, quickly provide a source of income to those hit the most, and have a high multiplier effect. Unemployment benefits could therefore also be regarded as a sign of solidarity and boost trust. A European unemployment insurance scheme further has the potential to foster labour mobility. Recent studies have confirmed that a European unemployment insurance scheme contributes to stabilisation, redistribution and crisis prevention. Moreover, the six challenges that are mentioned in the previous section can be mitigated or addressed. Moral hazard, for example, can be dealt with by introducing minimum requirements on the quality of benefits and activation (Vandenbroucke and Luigjes 2016). Such minimum requirements, in turn, may improve national schemes' stabilisation capacity and result in convergence. Next to this, a common insurance scheme could encourage countries to align their national schemes with the European scheme, again encouraging convergence. A final point is that a common unemployment insurance scheme would focus attention on unemployment and its social outcomes. Both have deteriorated in the post-2007 recession.

## 7 Conclusions

The financial-economic crisis has revealed the shortcomings of the Economic and Monetary Union and revived the debate on fiscal integration. While a consensus has been reached that a common fiscal capacity in Europe is needed, as evidenced by numerous academic studies. A European unemployment insurance is one potential stabiliser. It has important strengths, such as its high multiplier effect, and clearly contributes to stabilisation. Moreover, a European unemployment insurance scheme can support countries that can no longer fall back on market mechanisms (Beer et al. 2014). A major caveat is that such a scheme, due to its small size, can only be one instrument to achieve stabilisation in Europe. It is not the full answer. Other caveats are moral hazard, which is inevitable in any insurance scheme, and the fact that the implementation of the scheme is associated with a number of practical difficulties. Nevertheless, a European unemployment insurance is a very interesting option for a fiscal capacity for Europe.

## References

Allard C, Brooks PK, Bluedorn JC, Bornhorst F, Christopherson K, Ohnsorge F, Poghosyan T (2013) Toward a fiscal union for the Euro area. IMF Staff Discussion Note 13/09, Washington, DC

Beblavý M, Maselli I (2014) An unemployment insurance scheme for the Euro area: a simulation exercise of two options. CEPS Special Report No. 98, CEPS, Brussels, December

Beblavý M, Gros D, Maselli I (2015a) Reinsurance of national unemployment benefit schemes. CEPS Working Document No. 401, Brussels

Beblavý M, Marconi G, Maselli I (2015b) A European unemployment benefits scheme: the rationale and the challenges ahead. CEPS Special Report, 30pp, Brussels

Beer C, Köhler-Töglhofer W, Stiglbauer A (2014) A common European unemployment insurance—a much debated route toward European fiscal union. Monetary Policy & The Economy, Q4/14

Brandolini A, Carta F, D'Amuri F (2014) A feasible unemployment-based shock absorber for the euro area. Questioni di Economia e Finanza (Occasional Papers) No. 254, Banca d'Italia, Rome

De Grauwe P (2003) Economics of monetary union. Oxford University Press, Oxford

De Grauwe P (2013) Design failures in the Eurozone: can they be fixed? LSE 'Europe in Question' Discussion Paper No. 57/2013, London

Delpla J (2012) A Euro-wide conditional unemployment insurance. Paper prepared for the seminar "EU level economic stabilisers", Brussels, July

Dolls M, Fuest C, Neumann D, Peichl A (2014) An unemployment insurance scheme for absorbers for the Eurozone–deepening the debate on automatic stabilizers, Brussels, June

Drèze J, Durré A (2014) Fiscal integration and growth stimulation in Europe. CORE Discussion Paper No. 13/2013, Université catholique de Louvain

Dullien S (2007) Improving economic stability in Europe. What the Euro area can learn from the United States' Unemployment Insurance. Working Paper FG 1, German Institute for International and Security Affairs (SWP), Berlin

Dullien S (2012) A European unemployment insurance as a stabilization device –selected issues. Paper prepared for brainstorming workshop at the DG EMPL, Brussels, 2 Jul

Dullien S (2013) A euro-area wide unemployment insurance. Paper prepared for DG EMPL, Brussels

Dullien S (2014) Preventing permanent transfers under a European unemployment insurance: can a clawback mechanism be the answer? Presentation at the conference "Economic shock absorbers for the Eurozone: deepening the debate on automatic stabilisers", Brussels, 20 Jun

Emerson M, Gros D, Pisani-Ferry J, Reichenbach H, Italianer A, Lehner S, Vanheukelen M, Brandsma A, de Macedo J, Pearce J, Kröger J, Cabral A, Santos P, Ghymers C (1990) One market, one money. European Economy No. 44

Enderlein H, Guttenberg L, Spiess J (2013) Blueprint for a cyclical shock insurance in the Euro area. Notre Europe, Paris

Esser I, Ferrarini T, Nelson K, Palme J, Sjoberg O (2013) Unemployment benefits in EU member states. European Commission, Brussels

Frankel J, Rose K (1998) The endogeneity of optimum currency area criteria. Econ J 108 (449):1009–1025

Goodhart C, Smith S (1993) Stabilization. Eur Econ 5:417–456

Guyon T (2007) Should we worry about current account imbalances in a monetary union? Trésor-Economics No. 2, Paris, pp 1–8

In't Veld J, Larch M, Vandeweyer M (2012) Automatic fiscal stabilisers: what they are and what they do. European Economy, Economic Papers No. 452, Apr 2012

Italianer A, Vanheukelen M (1993) Proposals for community stabilization mechanisms: some historical applications. In: The economics of community public finance, European economy: reports and studies No. 5. European Commission, Brussels

Jara Tamayo HX, Sutherland H (2014) The implications of an EMU unemployment insurance scheme for supporting incomes. EUROMOD Working Paper No. EM5/14, ISER, Colchester

Kalemli-Ozcan S, Sorensen B, Yosha O (2001) Economic integration, industrial specialization, and the asymmetry of macroeconomic fluctuations. J Int Econ 55(1):107–137

MacDougall D, Biehl D, Brown A, Forte F, Fréville Y, O'Donoghue M, Peeters T (1977) Report of the study group on the role of public finance in European integration—volume I: general report. European Commission, Brussels

Majocchi A, Rey M (1993) A special financial support scheme in EMU: need and nature. Rivista di diritto finanziario e scienza delle finanze 52(2):161–204

Marjolin R, Bobba F, Bosman H, Brouwers G, Camu L, Clappier B, Foighel I, Forte F, Giersch H, Lynch P, MacDougall D, Markmann H, Peeters F, Shonfield A, Thysegen N (1975) Report of the study group 'Economic and Monetary Union 1980'. European Commission, Brussels

Moesen W, De Grauwe P (2009) Gains for all: a proposal for a common Eurobond. CEPS Commentary, Brussels, 3 Apr

Padoa-Schioppa T, Emerson M, King M, Milleron J, Paelinck J, Papademos L, Pastor F, Scharpf F (1987) Efficiency, stability and equity: a strategy for the evolution of the economic system of the European community. Oxford University Press, Oxford

Pisani-Ferry J, Vihriälä E, Wolff G (2013) Options for a Euro-area fiscal capacity. Bruegel Policy Contribution No. 2013/01, Brussels

Strauss R, Bontout O, Lejeune G, Ciesielska M, Di Girolamo R (2013) Paper on automatic stabilisers. European Commission, Brussels

Vandenbroucke F, Luigjes C (2016) Institutional moral hazard in the multi-tiered regulation of unemployment and social assistance benefits. CEPS Working Document No. 137, Apr 2016

# Part IV
# A Budgetary Union as a Way-out of the EMU Crisis: Is It Possible?

# Achieving Accountable Governance and Structural Reforms: Lessons from the Crisis in Europe

**Ehtisham Ahmad and Giorgio Brosio**

**Abstract** The global financial crisis of 2008 has severely impacted the functions and operations of different levels of government in Europe—requiring costly bailouts from national or supranational levels in some cases. A typical adjustment has been reductions in wages and benefits at different levels together with harmonization of fiscal policies across the EU and control of general government deficits (involving all levels of government). This highlights the incentive and governance problems associated with fragmentation of government. Overlapping responsibilities and absence of full information prevent effective governance and yardstick competition.

The paper offers a review of the recent processes of structural reform of subnational government in a number of EU countries, such as France, Spain, Denmark and Italy. The purely economic side of reform, i.e., achievable scale economies, and the political economy of reform, and more precisely the institutional constraints, are highlighted. With the exception of Denmark, the restructuring of levels and numbers of government has proved difficult. Meaningful reforms must address assignments and own-revenue responsibilities and transfers, together with the political economy of institutional reforms. This has lessons for large multi-level countries, such as Brazil, China, Indonesia and in South Asia.

## 1 Introduction

Among the preconditions for accountable governance at the sub-national level are the existence of clarity of responsibilities, adequate own-source revenues, a design of transfers that facilitates the delivery of similar levels of service at similar levels

E. Ahmad (✉)
LSE and University of Bonn, London, England
e-mail: s.e.ahmad@lse.ac.uk

G. Brosio
University of Turin, Turin, Italy
e-mail: Giorgio.brosio@unito.it



N. da Costa Cabral et al. (eds.), *The Euro and the Crisis*, Financial and Monetary Policy Studies 43, DOI 10.1007/978-3-319-45710-9_18

of revenue effort, and full information on the sources and uses of funds and the build-up of liability. Electoral (or yardstick) competition is not possible without these minimal criteria. Unfortunately, many of the requirements cannot be attained because of the fragmentation of levels and numbers of governments—largely part of the historical legacy in many European countries. The resulting system, with an absence of accountability, depended on direct central government financing of many functions, as well as the assumption of local liabilities that contributed to the severity of the financial crisis in Europe since 2008 (Ahmad et al. 2016). The resulting lack of accountability exacerbated the macro-fiscal crisis for general government in many countries and at the EU-level.

The response to the global financial crisis of 2008 has led to a focus on the reduction of the cost of operation of subnational governments, to contain their dependence on transfers and other fiscal assistance from the central government. Structural reform directed at shrinking the number of levels of government and/of the number of units at each level has been attempted in a number of countries. According to the intentions of the reform, economies of scale should have allowed savings in administration costs, while the reduction in the levels and numbers of governments at each level should lead to better accountability, as well as the containment of political costs. This set of reforms should also facilitate the harmonization of fiscal policies across the EU and control of general government deficits (involving all levels of government). The excessive disparities and fragmentation of subnational government also pose problems for harmonization of policies at the EU level.

The paper offers a review of the recent processes of structural reform of subnational government in a number of EU countries, such as France, Spain and Denmark. While we do not cover Portugal in this paper, the issues of the political economy of institutional change are similar.[1] The paper analyzes motivation and results, focusing both on potential economic savings from scale, and political economy and institutional constraints.

Structural reform is constrained by the number and strength of veto-players. Overcoming their opposition requires a global and negotiated approach, also

[1]In Portugal, due to the Troika Memorandum, an administrative reform was carried out in 2012–2013, and reduced several small 'freguesias' ('parishes'), from 4260 to 3092. This is the lowest layer of government. Initially, the MoU wanted to eliminate small municipalities as well (they correspond to 480), the 'munícipios' are the second layer. But this reform as been stopped due to local political resistance and it was then replaced by another political option: to create by law (new) municipalities' associations covering all the Portuguese continental territory. In fact, they now correspond to regions equivalent to the EU's NUTs III. In order to avoid overlapping problems, notably with the municipalities themselves, the law has given the associations powers in areas that typically involve 'network management', notably areas with high spillovers and or economies of scale (water supply, waste treatment, public transport, etc.), and that can be directly provided by intermunicipal governments or by enterprises (totally owned by the municipalities or with private capital as well). The next step—which might be challenged constitutionally—is to ensure that the governments of these associations (and of the metropolitan areas of Lisbon and Oporto) are directly elected (for the time being, they are chosen by and amongst the municipal leaders that are represented in the referred associations or areas).

involving own-source revenues and equalization transfers. Spain and France and Italy have implemented reforms within a short timeframe with the objective of fiscal consolidation. But established layers of government, such as the municipalities and the provinces, have evolved over decades with vested interests involving politicians and officials, and are almost immune to reform. In Greece the reform has been dominated by the severity of the financial crisis and the urgency of a rapid fiscal consolidation. Yet fundamental reforms have been circumvented through the establishment of SOEs financed by the center to provide local services, which however are designed to maintain employment levels.

Denmark represents a very interesting case, not only because it combines a pure proportional system of representation with a corporatist decision-making process, but also because its negotiated approach has produced far-reaching results with the drastic reduction of the number of municipalities, the elimination of counties, and their replacement by regions with clearly assigned responsibilities for health care. This has required a "package" approach with a rationalization of responsibilities, and non-distorting equalization transfers at the municipal level.

Our maintained hypothesis is that meaningful adjustments in spending assignments cannot be made without corresponding own-source revenues and equalization systems, as well as the political economy of institutional and governance reforms. Countries that try to disentangle spending responsibilities in isolation, just end up with unfunded mandates and a weaker federation as in Pakistan, or nothing really happens as in Germany.

## 2 The Impact of Fiscal and Political Institutions on Multilevel Structural Reform

The global financial crisis of 2008/2009 has the potential for deeper long-term impact on local governments than that experienced in the short term. As in the private sector, where deep crises catalyze the restructuring of firms and rationalization of employment, in the public sector the equivalent is the rationalization of the numbers of levels of government and their functions. Historically, multiple layers of administration were needed to ensure controls and national unity. Although medieval cities, or landed aristocracies, were the basic unit for service delivery, intermediate layers were necessary to ensure that tributes to the Emperor were paid, and that information on services delivered was effectively generated. These multiple layers have largely become redundant as the accurate flows of information on subnational entities can be ensured in real-time with new technologies that are now widely available. The multiple administrative layers have become an impediment to efficiency, and part of the reason lies in the vested interests of both the large numbers of officials concerned, as well as politicians that benefit from these arrangements.

In many EU countries, the costs of general government spending exceed 50 % of GDP (see Table 1). Financing this level of spending puts European companies at a disadvantage vis à vis competitors in other parts of the world, especially North America and China—although there have been attempts to shift from distortive taxation to the VAT in countries like Portugal to reduce the competitive disadvantages. However, this makes it more difficult to finance many layers of sub-national governments, doing more or less similar functions. Attempts to unravel the overlapping functions (both spending and revenues) in Germany during the period of the coalition government (from 2003 to 2007) largely failed, as the reforms were being discussed one by one, and different groups of Länder opposed each of the main measures. The debt-break on the Swiss model adopted as a compromise (as it is due to come into effect in 2019) may have unfortunate consequences for subnational investment (Milbradt 2016). Unlike the Cantons, German Länder do not have own-source revenues, and would have incentives to push down liabilities "under the carpet" at the municipal level (Spahn 2016).

A special case of political accommodation relates to the asymmetric arrangements for ethnically or economically distinct regions (particularly those with natural resources, as in Indonesia)—to persuade them to stay within the national boundaries. Spain and Italy provide examples in Europe. A difficulty is that these constructs are inherently unstable, and weaken discipline and accountability by leading to demands for "special treatment" in other regions, effectively negating yardstick competition, as is being witnessed in Catalunya, for example.

Structural reform can bring about a lower cost of provision of public services and greater efficiency, especially when it introduces clarity in the assignments and adequate own-source revenues at the relevant level for accountability. Of course, this assumes that all spending and the generation of liabilities are well-documented

**Table 1** Public expenditure by level of government in a sample of European countries. 2006–2013 (% of GDP)

| | | 2006 | 2007 | 2008 | 2009 | 2010 | 2011 | 2012 | 2013 |
|---|---|---|---|---|---|---|---|---|---|
| Denmark | Central | | 16.61 | | | | | | 19.37 |
| | Local | | 30.83 | | | | | | 35.37 |
| France | Central | 42.05 | 41.61 | 42.18 | 45.28 | 45.27 | 44.75 | 45.27 | 45.43 |
| | Local | 10.47 | 10.66 | 10.84 | 11.50 | 11.19 | 11.20 | 11.44 | 11.71 |
| Germany | Central | 27.73 | 26.42 | 26.78 | 29.35 | 29.30 | 27.06 | 26.92 | 27.05 |
| | State | 10.00 | 9.61 | 9.84 | 10.58 | 10.42 | 10.31 | 10.18 | 10.04 |
| | Local | 6.87 | 6.72 | 6.87 | 7.51 | 7.46 | 7.19 | 7.09 | 7.23 |
| Italy | Central | 32.92 | 32.50 | 33.10 | 35.48 | 34.69 | 34.59 | 36.02 | 36.19 |
| | Local | 14.77 | 14.33 | 14.78 | 15.73 | 15.22 | 14.59 | 14.43 | 14.36 |
| Spain | Central | 19.57 | 19.62 | 20.71 | 23.26 | 23.68 | 24.45 | 28.28 | 25.80 |
| | Regional | 13.78 | 14.01 | 15.07 | 16.46 | 16.07 | 15.70 | 14.50 | 14.17 |
| | Local | 5.03 | 5.40 | 5.49 | 6.22 | 6.08 | 5.54 | 4.88 | 4.84 |

Source: OECD, government at a glance, various years

(in a consistent manner across jurisdictions at the same level and across levels), and known in a timely manner.

Opposition to structural reform has its own peculiar political-economy related motivations. Critically, self-interested stakeholders reduce political/bureaucratic competition within the public sector. Central bureaucracies may resist further erosion of their powers that might come with a streamlining of functions (e.g., removal of overlapping competences). These adjustments are even more difficult when asymmetric arrangements are involved, as it is relatively easy to depict the reforms as an attempt to roll back the special benefits of autonomy, privileges or preferences.

On the other hand, the growing unpopularity of politicians and politics in many countries should facilitate reform. This is not only linked to the direct costs of salaries and benefits, but also the possibilities of rent-seeking that are facilitated by the weak information and monitoring systems. An increasingly costly, dysfunctional and inefficient system of public service provision results that yardstick competition cannot counteract. One redress is to reduce the cost of politics, particularly at local level. Caps on elected officials' remuneration and similar measures, such as reducing the size of local councils, impact directly on political costs. But the reduction in the number of government may be more effective.

However, structural reform is not an easy process, even where gains are evident (which is not always the case), with opposition from politicians and officials. The number of stakeholders is a (negative) determinant of reform. A smaller set of governments reduces the number of elected officials and employees. Table 2 presents various factors relevant for France, Spain and Denmark.

The characteristics and structure of national electoral systems are almost completely ignored in the political economy literature.[2] When electoral colleges for national elections coincide with local jurisdictions, the elimination of these local units will be strongly opposed also by national elected officials, who face a loss of the political capital they have built in their electoral constituency. The operation of this factor is clearly visible in the case of France, Spain and Italy, where reform has taken place not where it was more needed, but where it has proved to be politically easier.

[2]Ken Kollman (*The perils of centralization* 2013) develops a similar although distinct analytical path when he compares Westminster type democracies with presidential systems with reference to their effectiveness in preserving decentralization of government. Parliaments, when they have control of the executive and especially when they are elected according to majority (fist past the post) rule which establishes a strong tie with local interests, are resisting with more force the centralization push exerted by the central executive.

**Table 2** Election system of legislative chambers in France, Spain and Denmark

| | Number of representatives | Electoral districts | Election method |
|---|---|---|---|
| France: Lower House (Assemblée Nationale) | 577 | Are defined on the basis of population within existing Departments | Majoritarian, two stages |
| France: Senate (Sénat) | 348 | Are set up on the basis of equal population within existing departments | Indirect. 148,000 Grand electors (577 Members of the Lower House; 1870 Regional councilors; 4000 Department's councilors; 142,000 delegates of municipal councilors) |
| Spain: Lower House (Congreso de los Diputados) | 350 | Provinces. Statutory minimum: 102 MPs; two for each Province plus two to Ceuta and Melilla. Plus 248 MPs assigned to Provinces on the basis of the population | Proportional. With minimum threshold of 3 % |
| Spain: Senate (Senado) | Number is variable. Presently there are 266 Senators. 208 of them (four senators per Province) are elected popularly. 58 senators are appointed by the Autonomous Communities (one senator per Community plus one per 1,500,000 inhabitants) | Provinces for popularly elected senators Autonomous communities | Basically majoritarian for popularly elected senators. Partly proportional for the appointed senators |
| Denmark: Single Chamber (Folketinget) | 179 | 10 electoral colleges are built on the basis of population and density for the election of 135 members of Folketinget. 40 MPs, elected in a single national college to enhance proportional representation. Four MPs are elected in the Faroe Islands and Greenland | Strictly proportional |

Source: Senato della Repubblica Italiana (2013a, b), Folketinget (2011), and Montero et al. (1992)

**Table 3** Spain: public employees by level of government, 2014

| | Number of employees | as % of total |
|---|---|---|
| Central government administration | 536,499 | 15.1 |
| Autonomous communities, of which: | 1,284,026 | 36.2 |
| Education (tertiary excluded) | 531,030 | 15.0 |
| Health | 475,465 | 13.4 |
| Municipalities | 517,838 | 14.6 |
| Provinces | 59,326 | 1.7 |
| Universities | 147,115 | 4.1 |
| National total | 3,551,299 | 100.0 |

Source: Registro Central de Personal: Boletín Estadístico del Personal al Servicio de las Administraciones Públicas, January 2015

# 3 Spain

Spain illustrates the struggle for greater autonomy if not outright secession coming from Catalunya, and pressures for more central government control favored by national parties. Catalunya's demand for parity with the asymmetric arrangements for the Basque region would keep revenues in the richest region, exacerbating regional inequalities that the center would be unable to redress.

Spain has, with Italy and France, a highly costly system of government at five levels with a large number of units: 17 Regions (Comunidades Autonomas__ACs); 50 Provinces (Diputaciones Provinciales), and more than 8000 municipalities and about 1000 bodies of inter-municipal cooperation (mostly Mancomunidades, and a few Comarcas).

Autonomous Communities are by far the most important layer with a level of expenditure that is three times higher than that of local government. They are responsible also for education and health, the two largest areas of spending in contemporary states. Autonomous Communities alone employ more people that all other levels of government combined, central government included (Table 3). The size of Autonomous Communities shows an important variation with a minimum of 319,000 inhabitants in Rioja to a maximum of 8,400,000 in Cataluña.

Scale economies do not play a role in spending decisions (Fundacion progreso y democracia 2012—FPD) and attempts to curtail regional autonomy would be badly received. Municipalities try to collaborate on certain functions through Mancomunidades and, in some regions, with Comarcas. These agencies are frequently too small to be able to deliver substantial scale economies.

There is some agreement on the optimal size of municipalities. FPD (2012) and Hortas-Rico and Salinas Pena (2014) estimate around 20,000 inhabitants for general administration, decreasing considerably for the other functions. FPD (2012) takes into account Oates' zoo effect (Oates 1988): when the size of a local government increases the range of its functions also expands. Tiny municipalities cannot afford a zoo, but larger municipalities can, increasing the range of functions and expenditures. There are 7727 municipalities below 20,000, a structural rationalization would reduce Spanish municipalities to a few hundreds, or around the number of local government in the UK (418).

The 2008 crisis and bursting of the property bubble impacted Spanish subnational governments severely, given their dependence on taxes directly related to the property market. More precisely, the ACs are assigned registration tax on property, while municipalities levy a registration tax on sales of land and the building tax. These are among the most pro-cyclical taxes; during the construction boom revenues skyrocketed, and collapsed subsequently, severely affecting local service provision.

Corruption scandals involving elected officials increased the unpopularity of government, especially at sub-national levels. In 2005, 67 % of Spaniards considered ACs positively but by 2012 this fell to 56 % (Lagos and Solé Ollé 2016). Similarly, approval for decentralized assignments decreased from 58 % in 2005 to 32 % in 2012 (Liñeira Sanchez 2012). Support for recentralization of the functions rose from 8 to 22 % over the same period. These opinions stimulated the recentralization policy since 2011 by the governing Popular Party with the tacit support of the Socialist Party. Law of December 27, 2013 formalizes the recentralization push. It has three main components: (a) the clarification/re-definition of the competences of Municipalities and ACs to reduce overlapping: (b) creating new incentives for consolidation and merging of municipalities, (c) establishing ceilings on remuneration of local elected officials and the creation of local publicly owned companies (mainly utilities) and, (d) the transfer to Provinces of the competences for basic urban services, such as refuse collection, water provision and disposal in the municipalities smaller than 20,000 inhabitants, if they cannot match the efficiency of Provincial service provision, and subject also to the latter being able to guarantee the coordination of the various Municipalities or, alternatively, to take over directly the provision of the concerned services.

The clarification of the assignment of responsibilities is a necessary recurrent process in all decentralized systems. It introduces clarity in mandates. In Spain, the recurrent need of clarification of tasks between Regions and Municipalities derives from their same level of constitutional autonomy. This differentiates Spain, (and also Italy and Brazil) from classical federations, where local governments—Municipalities, Districts and Counties—are hierarchically subordinated to the States/Provinces. However, this generates conflicts between Municipalities and Regions over new responsibilities. Municipalities are closest to citizens with practically universal competence, whereas Regions try to ensure coordination of lower level governments.

The Spanish reform has two components. The first is to distinguish between functions directly assigned to Municipalities and those delegated by the Regions. In principle, Regions are free to delegate their functions but must cover the cost. The second component transfers from Municipalities to Regions all the competences in the areas of education, health and social services. This has been disputed (Suárez Pandiello 2013) because of higher proximity of municipalities to the beneficiaries, and to a possible lack of funds for the new regional competences.

Incentives for Municipal consolidation were used frequently but with limited success. The merging and creation of Municipalities is the responsibility of the ACs, that try to not antagonize Municipalities—the center does not share this political concern. The 2013 Law introduces incentives based on the increasing the Municipal share of national taxes. It also makes programs of inter-municipal cooperation more financially attractive. But at the same time it allows merged municipalities to maintain services at the deconcentrated level to maintain existing facilities located. This clearly reduces the cost reduction potential.

The introduction of limits on the remuneration of elected officials is similar to that in Italy and Greece. The Spanish law refers to both the absolute admissible remuneration and to the number of full time elected councilors and mayors. The norm aims at making public positions less attractive—with the reduction in both the number of mayors and their salaries.

The transfer of competences from small (less than 20,000 inhabitants) municipalities to the Provinces is by far the most important policy measure. It is hard to evaluate this policy at the present time, because of the number of factors involved in its success or failure.

The attempts to eliminate a redundant tier of government—Spanish Provinces—have failed. There has been no debate concerning the number or existence of provinces, that seem to have potentially gained strength (Diario de derecho municipal 2014). However, doubts linger about Provinces delivering new functions more effectively than Municipalities.

The resilience of Provinces is due to their role in the public administration and electoral systems. Proir to the creation of the ACs, Provinces were the basic administrative unit of the Spanish State. More importantly Provinces still form the electoral college for both the Lower House and of the Senate (see Table 2). Consequently, individual political careers and the organization of political parties are built around Provinces. Their elimination endanger the political capital accumulated by elected officials, as boundaries of electoral colleges would be quite likely redrawn.

There is no possibility of significant reforms of ACs, given the traditional aspiration to independence in the Basque Region, and the present steps taken by Cataluña to secede from Spain. Any move to reform ACs, not to speak of reducing numbers, would further inflame the secessionist tendencies.

Municipalities are the net losers, with a diminished role, although numbers are the same. There is a considerable skepticism about cost saving associated with the transfer of competences from the small municipalities to the Provinces, considering that in most cases Municipalities already participate in the Mancomunidades. These entities also need to be reformed for real efficiency gains. In the smaller municipalities the territorial dispersion of services cannot be avoided because of low population density (Acuña and Peñas 2013). Hence the increased size of the provider may not allow substantial cost cutting. In other words, scale economies are not related to provision but rather to production of services.

# 4 France

Despite the Napoleonic tradition of rational/modern governance, exported, with mixed success, to many countries including Italy and Spain, the present French system of decentralized government is referred to as a "millefeuilles" cake, to stress the high number of layers and complexity. France has:

36,767 Municipalities (Communes);
14,547 bodies of inter-municipal cooperation (Etablissements publics de cooperation intercommunale);
101 Departments (Départements) (including five Overseas Departments);
13 Metropolitan Regions (they were 22 before December 16, 2015) plus 5 Overseas Regions.

While Municipalities and Departments (which were created after the Revolution of 1789) have general and unrestricted competences, Regions, whose councils were first elected in1982, are assigned a limited range of responsibilities, mainly involving growth promotion, infrastructure and vocational schools.

Almost all (99.8 %) Municipalities engage in some form of cooperation: with the Etablissements publics de cooperation intercommunale, (EPCI) First, variously named EPCIs (Communautés de communes; Communautés d'agglomeration; Communautés urbaines and Métropoles) have own-tax powers. Their councils can determine the tax rates applied to the bases assigned to them (usually the local business tax, Taxe Professionelle). It has to be noted that the base of the local taxes, taxes on property: the Taxe foncière paid by the owner; and the Taxe d'habitation levied on the occupants, are shared between all levels of subnational government. In 2014 there were 2145 EPCIs. A second category has a slimmer structure and includes the so-called syndicates (Syndicats) that rely mostly on contributions from their members. They numbered 13,402 in 2014.

It is also worth noting that EPCIs employ 262,724 people in 2012 amounting to one/fourth of municipal employees (see Table 4). Between 1998 and 2012 their number has registered a fourfold increase (Conseil Superieur de la fonction publique territoriale 2013).

French subnational governments absorb a large and growing share of total public sector employment. Between 2002 and 2012 their number increased by 30 % against a reduction of 8 % in the number of central government employees (Rapport sur l'état de la Fonction Publique et les Rémunérations 2015).

The fragmentation of municipalities and its impact on cost, quality and completeness of public services is a continuous preoccupation of French governments. EPICs should have been able to ensure completeness of supply with, albeit with a questionable impact on costs.

There is no evidence of actually generating scale economies through associations (Frère 2013). Political explanations predominate. First, when two distinct municipalities join efforts for the provision of a service, they tend at the same time to expand the quality and the variety of their supply, with increasing costs that

**Table 4** France: public sector employees by layer of government, 2012

| | Number of employees | as % of total |
|---|---|---|
| Central government | 2,373,183 | 44.2 |
| Subnational government | 1,862,419 | 34.7 |
| Of which: municipalities | 1,025,232 | 19.1 |
| Intergovernmental cooperation bodies | 460,962 | 8.6 |
| Departments | 294,543 | 5.5 |
| Regions | 81,682 | 1.5 |
| Health sector | 1,136,973 | 21.2 |
| National total | 5,372,575 | 100.0 |

Source: Rapport sur l'état de la Fonction Publique et les Rémunérations (2015)

outweigh any agglomeration scale economies. A second phenomenon obstructs the evaluation of the impact of specific policies. The creation of new EPCIs usually arises when the central government assigns new tasks to municipalities and/or their associations. More specifically, EPICs are exploited by the central government to strengthen local action.

Municipal ineffectiveness may be directly linked to the opportunism of officials, who are free to decide with whom to associate and for what. Associations can be, and are, created on the basis of political (parties) affinities, or alternatively and more simply for defensive purposes, as with small rural municipalities that come together to avoid being absorbed by large urban municipalities, that would leave officials with practically no decision-making powers. Or, EPICs may be used to avoid undesired redistribution of revenue. Thus, rich municipalities associate among themselves to avoid using their tax base to finance the expenditure needs of poor municipalities. Summing up, creation and development of agencies of inter-municipal cooperation does not seem to have brought up real savings or improvements in service delivery.

As in Italy and Spain, successive French governments have tried to reduce fragmentation since the end of World War II, particularly in the years 1958, 1971 and 2010. Between 1959 and now the number of municipalities has decreased from 38,500 to 36,700 units mainly through the consolidation of small rural municipalities with the bigger contiguous urban municipalities. The 2010 reform to merge tiny rural municipalities was successful only in thirteen cases!

There are two forces opposing local reform in France. The first is the sheer number of persons interested to maintain the number of municipalities and of cooperation bodies—there are 1.3 million employees and 519,000 local councilors. Councilors have huge powers to oppose any reforms that disadvantages its members. Their veto power becomes practically absolute with the present French bicameral system. Reform of the Senate has made the representatives of Municipalities the basis for the election of Senators. Out of 148,000 grand electors of the Senate 142,000 are appointed among municipal councilors (Senato della Repubblica Italiana 2013a, b). Moreover, the French Senate plays a predominant role in the reform of the territorial structure of the state, and since the constitutional reform of 2003, territorial reform bills have to be read first by the Senate. Hence, it is not surprising that reform attempts since 2008 did not target municipalities, but rather Regions and Departments.

Law MAPAM (Modernisation de l'action publique et affirmation des Métropoles) of January 27 2014 introduced a new statute for metropolitan governments (Métropoles). This could transform the governance of the big urban areas (with more than 400,000 inhabitants), because the new Métropoles will be created by merging the existing Department with the Urban Community (Communauté Urbaine). Métropoles maintain their present weak institutional status, where the councils of the Municipalities that comprise them appoint the council. It has to be stressed that the creation of Métropoles does not lead to the suppression of Municipalities. It is too early to evaluate the effects of the reform. Articles appearing in the French press report the difficulties to getting the new entities started, with a lot of maneuvering by councilors as regards the formation of a governing coalition, while the new entities will have no more financial strength and autonomy than their predecessors.

Departments have again survived the present presidential administration's attempts to eliminate them. The prime minister announced their elimination in April 2014,[3] with the possibility of their continuation in rural areas and their fusion with the urban Metropoles. In June 2014 the President announced their elimination by the year 2020. Finally, in June 2015 the government announced the (quite diminutive) reform of Departments with three different and somewhat contradictory options: (a) their maintenance; (b) their merging with the Métropoles; (c) their merging with the associations of Municipalities.

Regions have paid the price of the reforms. The law of January 16 2015 mandated the aggregation of Regions by reducing their number from 22 to 13, through their merging and without any change affecting the Departments. The law was prepared and approved in an extremely short span of time with a quite surprising little discussion and practically no opposition. As a matter of fact, elections of the councils of the new entities took place in December 2015 and the new entities have started in January 2016. The government explains that the main motivation behind the consolidation of Regions has been increasing the effectiveness of their growth promotion policies.[4]

Recently, the French government (www.gouvernement.fr/action/la-reforme-territoriale) has also proposed to set a minimum threshold of 20,000 inhabitants for the EPCIs endowed with taxing powers. Presently, about three/thirds of them are smaller.

The French intergovernmental responses to the 2008 crisis were not sufficiently developed to be able to withstand or overcome the political power of the existing

---

[3]www.gouvernement.fr/action/la-reforme-territoriale; Dumont (2014) and Amabile et al. (2015).

[4]See the government website www.gouvernement.fr/action/la-reforme-territoriale. Consolidation of Regions would also have led to a similar consolidation of the regional agencies of the central government (13 Regional Prefects are replacing the present 22).

institutional establishment. Consequently, they have focused largely on symbolic gestures and no real efficiency gains or improvements in service delivery or governance should be expected.

## 5 Denmark

Denmark is a unitary state with two levels of subnational government: Municipalities and Regions. Denmark is one of the most decentralized countries in the world in terms of spending. The share of subnational government expenditure is almost the double than that of the central government, because of local responsibilities for social assistance and protection, particularly transfers to families, in addition to services for children, elderly and disabled persons. Denmark is almost unique in this respect. Social expenditure absorbs 56 % of the total, four times higher than the corresponding averages for Europe and the OECD countries (see Table 1). Before the 2007 reform, counties was responsible for the provision of health services, including hospital care; and also for secondary education, roads and regional transport. Municipalities were responsible for primary education.

Until 1970, there was no modern and efficient decentralized system of government in Denmark. There were 1394 Municipalities with urban municipalities regulated by the Ministry for Social Affairs and Rural Municipalities; by the 24 existing Counties. The 1970 reform reduced the number of Municipalities to 275 and Counties to 15.

There was little change during the following three decades, apart from a small number of mergers of Municipalities on the islands. There was also some discussion concerning the creation of Great Copenhagen, a metropolitan administration for the capital, and growing scepticism on the role of Counties. The central government continued, however, to transfer responsibilities to the municipalities, to reduce its financial burden, a familiar pattern of adjustment—push it down to lower political costs and visibility.

Denmark, as in other Scandinavian countries, has a corporatist tradition based on the combination of a proportional electoral system, and the involvement of all interest groups in the political decision-making process. The role of trade unions and business associations is particularly active. In the realm of intergovernmental relations, the corporatist model led to a growing role for associations of municipalities and counties.

Consequently, the structure and evolution of intergovernmental relations was determined, not only by central government executive and legislative actions, but also by big interest groups and by subnational governments represented by their associations. The stance of the latter can be, alternatively, purely defensive or proactive. The Danish political/decision-making process is inevitably complex. Reforms need careful and protracted preparation. Hence, the reform completed in 2007 was the result of actions started much earlier, with the appointment of a number of special committees with wide participation. Their tasks included the

**Table 5** Local expenditure by function Denmark and average EU and OECD countries: 2012

| | Denmark | OECD27 | EU28 |
|---|---|---|---|
| General administration | 4 | 15 | 17 |
| Economic affairs | 4 | 13 | 12 |
| Health | 22 | 18 | 13 |
| Education | 10 | 26 | 20 |
| Social assistance and protection | 56 | 12 | 20 |
| Other functions | 4 | 16 | 18 |
| Total | 100 | 100 | 100 |

Source: OECD (2015)

analysis of issues, singling out of tentative solutions, and their informal submission to the various stakeholders to gauge the amplitude of consent/dissent (Table 5).

A schematic history (see Ministry of the Interior and Health 2005) includes:

The Report of the Opgavekommissionen (Tasks Commission, literally) is published. It includes a deep analysis of the assignment of functions between the State, the Counties and the Municipalities.

The 2003 Report of the Sundhedsudvalget Kommissionen (Health Commission) contains an analysis of the future organization of the health system in view of the creation of the Regions.

The 2004 Report of the Strukturkommissionen (literally Structure Commission) appointed in the year 2002 with the mission of conducting a technical analysis of the structure of decentralized government and to advance reform proposals. Independent experts joined representatives of the central government and of local government in equal numbers. The main finding of the Report is the suboptimal size of Municipalities. More specifically, the Report suggested that the efficient size would be 20,000 inhabitants. The Report also suggests that the size of Counties was suboptimal and that their number should be reduced to 3–8 units.

The report suggests three alternative reform options. The first is based on a minimum threshold of 30,000 inhabitants for Municipalities, the transfer of a number of policy responsibilities to the Municipalities from the Counties and a consolidation of the latter, whose unique responsibility would remain hospital care. The second alternative would be to limit the minimum threshold for Municipalities to 20,000 inhabitants and the transfer of some central responsibilities to the Counties with a parallel reduction of their number. The third option includes, again, the elimination of the Counties the transfer of most of their functions, with the exception of hospital care, to the Municipalities, whose minimum threshold would have to be increased again to 30,000 inhabitants.

On April 2004, the national government after reaching an agreement with the two main political parties presented its own reform proposal. It was based on: (a) the elimination of the Counties and the transfer of hospital care to five newly created Regions, governed by elected councils, but devoid of any autonomous taxing power; (b) the consolidation of Municipalities targeted to reach minimum size of 20,000 inhabitants, implying a reduction of their number by two-thirds. A lower size was allowed, subject to the promotion of intercommmunal cooperation. The government proceeded to public hearings and promoted mergers of Municipalities with the intermediation of their Association.

An analysis of the interests that moved the various stakeholders is revealing. Big municipalities were clearly in favor of consolidation, both because urban growth had made their boundaries obsolete, and were worried of the growing central government interference in their affairs. The powerful Ministry of the Interior saw a big opportunity for further enhancing its own role.

Small municipalities were against, but were too few to organize effective opposition to reform (also the door opened to association had a mitigating impact on their opposition). Counties has already lost all their political sponsors, also because the transfer of hospital care to the Regions would have created a more centralized context where bargaining between interest groups, the fulcrum of any corporatist system, would have become easier and more determinant,

Also Counties has lost any link with the electoral system of the single Chamber. Denmark is divided—see Table 2—into ten electoral colleges, whose number is higher than that of the Regions, but lower than that of the old Counties. The size of electoral colleges is determined by the goal to expand as much as possible the proportional character of the electoral system. Last, but not least, the Association of Industrialists, that is a powerful partner in the decision-making process of the corporatist state, favored the increase in the size of Municipalities so that service provision could be devolved to private firms.

On January 2007 the reform was fully operational. Municipalities have well-defined and manageable responsibilities together with own-source revenues (see Table 6). There is an advanced equalization system in operation based on spending needs and revenue capacities. And, by and large, the institutions are efficient and report on a regular basis. This shows how careful attention to the political economy constraints and analysis and discussion of technical options, together with appropriate assignments, are needed for meaningful and politically sustainable reforms.

## 6 Conclusions and Lessons for Other Regions

In this paper we have tried to illustrate the interactions between intergovernmental policy design, institutions and political-economy constraints, and the pressure exerted by the 2008 crisis. The countries were chosen carefully because of some general lessons for other countries undergoing fiscal adjustment or strengthening decentralization. We focus on the structural reform of the decentralized system in three countries. In Spain and France the results have been limited.

The first set of lessons is from Spain, which had moved from a very centralized dirigiste system to democracy after the death of Franco, had tried to follow classic advice on spending and revenue assignments, including own-source revenues, and

**Table 6** Denmark: structure of decentralized government before and after reform

| | December 2000 | December 2007 |
|---|---|---|
| Number of regions. Main responsibility: hospital care | 14 | 5 |
| Regions average size in terms of population | 382,000 | 1,095,000 |
| Number of municipalities | 275 | 98 |
| Municipalities average size in terms of population | 19,500 | 56,000 |

Source: Compilation by the Authors on the basis of OECD (2015) and Ministry of the Interior and Health (2005)

equalization transfers. It also allowed an asymmetric arrangement to evolve for the Basque region that was in revolt. This was more or less the same pattern followed in Indonesia after decades of centralized rule, except that there were no own-source revenues, and local governments were largely financed by shares of natural revenues and equalization grants. An asymmetric solution emerged, given the insurgency in Acheh, where a higher share was retained by the districts and region in Acheh (similar case in E. Kalimantan). The attempt to "wash out" the larger shares by including actuals in the equalization formulae rather than standards, weakens incentives, and does nothing to avert demands for the same treatment elsewhere. In Spain also, the asymmetric arrangements for the Basque country are demanded by Catalunya, that has already voted to secede from Spain. This may not happen, but with full retention of revenues by the richest region, interregional inequalities are bound to increase, with a reduced ability of the central government to equalize.

The other fault line in Spain was the absence of full information on all the assets and liabilities being generated at the local level. This ability to "hide" transactions was also facilitated by considerable rent-seeking at the local levels. The explosion of liabilities following the crisis led to pressures to restructure, again falling at the lower levels.

In Spain regional reform was not an option, and could only result in further imbalances. Municipal consolidation was essential and inter-communal cooperation did not work. Reform is difficult also because of overlapping of competences between the national parliament and the ACs. Parliament assigns functions, but ACs govern Municipalities. The elimination of the Provinces is an obvious and recurrent goal of any reform, since these governments have ceded most of their competences to ACs. Given their political power, Provinces have strengthened gaining coordination functions, and there has been little overall restructuring or efficiency gains.

In France, reducing municipal fragmentation is considered as a necessity, along with the elimination of Departments. Not much has been achieved. Municipal fragmentation has not been reduced; Departments have been left untouched despite the repeated announcements of their elimination. Again, political economy concern prevail.

The Danish case is very different. The further consolidation of the Municipalities (here the main step was taken in 1970, with the fourfold reduction in numbers and, consequently, of likely opponents) and the search of a bigger sized layer of government for secondary education and health. A very well-planned process including technical analysis, elaboration and presentation of proposals and search for a wide consensus has allowed to further consolidate the Municipalities, to eliminate the Counties by transferring their competences for hospital care to the newly created Regions and most of their remaining functions to the Municipalities. Responsibility for secondary education has been assigned in 2007 to functional agencies subject to regulation by the central government. Danish local elected officials were able to display, during the reform, a political weight that was considerably lower than in France and Spain, since their number had already been reduced. Furthermore, electoral colleges had no further relation with the boundaries of local governments, their size having been considerably expanded to ensure a high as possible level of proportionality to parliamentary representation. At the same time, with a proportional system a large consensus among interest groups is needed to carry out reform. This is particularly the case of Denmark, where weak parliamentary majorities usually support national governments.

Empirical literature applied to the three countries and preparatory work done for the reform shows a surprising consensus about optimal size for Municipalities pinpointing to 20,000 inhabitants. This threshold is the reference point for the detailed reform proposals. In two cases out of three, Denmark and Spain, actual reform has targeted exactly this threshold. This seems to have more a political significance than an economic one. The three countries have different municipal systems, different economic and demographic conditions; and different systems of inter-municipal cooperation. The political significance refers to the fact the threshold, when implemented, would bring about a reduction of the number of municipalities to a manageable dimension—444 in France, 398 in Spain, 507 in Italy—that greatly reduces their bargaining power.

Cooperation agencies are a more accessible political solution, but seem to be much less cost effective than what is usually assumed, because of duplication of political and bureaucratic costs.

One might wonder, as a final point, about the possible role of the European institutions in structural reform. The current stance is that local government is an exclusive national competence. The only present regulation at this level is the European Charter of Local Self-Government issued by the Council of Europe that does not make reference to structural issues and that is de facto binding only for the accession countries. However, structural reform has a lot of political significance also from the point of view of macroeconomic and financial control.

Here, again, standards such as for reporting and provisioning for liabilities, such as PPPs, as well as coverage of State Owned Enterprises, would appear to be essential in light of the last economic crisis, the effects of which are still being felt. Indeed, national and sub-national stability pacts would likely not function without this use of information standards. This is a lesson that clearly transcends the EU area, and is equally relevant in Brazil, China, South Asia or Indonesia.

## References


(2008) Administrative reform—arguments and values. Nordregio

Ahmad E, Bordignon M, Brosio G (eds) (2016) Multi-level finance and the Euro crisis. Edward Elgar, Cheltenham

Amabile A, Bernard C, Épaulard A (2015) La Réforme territoriale et cohérence économique régionale, France Stratégie—13/05/2015—0-8. Journaux officiels, Paris

Assemblée Nationale (2015) Annexe au Projet de Loi de Finances pour 2015 Rapport Sur l'état de La Fonction Publique et Les Rémunérations. Journaux Officiels, Paris

Campus Acuña C, Lago Peñas S (2013) A necessary (but flawed) reform of local government. Informe IEB sobre Federalismo, 2013

Commissariat General a' l'Egalitè des Territoires (2015) Rapport sur les EPCI. La taille des EPCI, un levier d'action pour la politique. Journaux Officiels, Paris

Conseil Superieur de la fonction publique territoriale (2013) Etat des lieux de la fonction publique territoriale. Journaux officiels, Paris

Court des Comptes (2005) L'intercommunalité en France: rapport au Président de la République suivi des réponses des administrations et des organismes intéressés. Journaux officiels, Paris

Diario de derecho municipal (2014) Estudios y Comentarios, La Posición Institucional de las Diputaciones Provinciales a Partir de la Ley de Racionalización y Sostenibilidad de la Administración Local, Madrid

Dumont GF (2014) La Reforme Territoriale ou l'illusion Jacobine, Revue d'economie urbaine et regionale, September

Folketinget (2011) The parliamentary electoral system in Denmark. Folketinget, Copenhagen

Frère Q (2013) Le périmètre pertinent de l'intercommunalité: les apports de l'Economie Publique Working Paper, INRA, UMR1041 CESAER, Université de Bourgogne

Fundacion progreso y democracia (2012) El coste del Estado autonómico II: Administración autonómica y local. Fundacion progreso y democracia, Madrid

Hortas-Rico M, Salinas-Peña P (2014) Determinación de la escala mínima eficiente en la provisión de bienes públicos locales. Evidencia para los municipios españoles. Mimeo

Ken K (2013) Perils of centralization. Lessons from church, state, and corporation. Cambridge University Press, Cambridge

Lago-Peñas S, Solé-Ollé A (2016) Multi-level finance and governance in Spain: the impact of the Euro crisis. In: Ahmad E, Bordignon M, Brosio G (eds) Multi-level finance and the Euro crisis. Edward Elgar, Cheltenham

Lapuente Ginè V (2013) Reforma de la Administración Local en España. Informe IEB sobre Federalismo, 2013. Barcelona

Liñeira Sanchez R (2012) El estado de las autonomias en la opinion publica: preferencias, conocimientos y voto, 2012 Tesis Doctoral. www.tdx.cat/bitstream/handle/10803/96419/rls1de1.pdf?sequence=1

Milbradt G (2016) History of the constitutional debt limits in Germany and the new "debt brake"—experiences and critique. In: Ahmad E, Bordignon M, Brosio G (eds) Multi-level finance and the Euro crisis. Edward Elgar, Cheltenham

Ministry of the Interior and Health of Denmark (2005) The local government reform. Ministry of the Interior and Health of Denmark, Copenhagen

Montero J, Llera F, Torcal M (1992) Sistemas electorales en Espana; una recapitulacion, Revista espanola de investigaciones sociologicas

Oates WE (1988) On the nature and measurement of fiscal illusion: a survey. In: Brennan G et al (eds) Taxation and fiscal federalism: essays in honour of Russell Mathews. Australian National University Press, Canberra, pp 65–82

OECD (2015) Subnational governments in OECD countries: key data. 2015 edn. OECD, Paris

Senato della Repubblica Italiana, XVII legislatura, Ufficio ricerche (2013a) Sistemi Elettorali: Francia. Dossier, settembre 2013 n. 52

Senato della Repubblica Italiana, XVII legislatura, Ufficio ricerche (2013b) Sistemi Elettorali: Spagna. Dossier, settembre 2013 n. 51

Spahn PB (2016) Multilevel finance and the Euro crisis: the German experience. In: Ahmad E, Bordignon M, Brosio G (eds) Multi-level finance and the Euro crisis. Edward Elgar, Cheltenham

Suárez Pandiello J (2013) Un primer apunte sobre la reforma local. Informe IEB sobre Federalismo 13

www.gouvernement.fr/action/la-reforme-territoriale

# The Financing of the European Union Budget

**Herman Matthijs**

**Abstract** This article will deal with the working and the impact of the new council decision of 2014 concerning the system of own resources for the European Union (EU). It will analyse the system and compare it with the previous one of 2007. In addition, this article makes several comparisons concerning the effect of these own resources in relation to the member states of the Union. The national cost price of the EU is a very current item in many member states, where there is a discussion going on concerning the future of European integration.

## 1 Introduction

The financing of the European Union is based on a council decision concerning its own resources. For years there has been political discussion concerning the system. Is it fair and transparent enough? The present financing system has existed since 1970 and was updated in 2014. But the system is more and more under pressure through the expansion of member states and the growing differences in welfare between the EU countries. Another political discussion concerning the financing system of the European Union is the choice between own resources or contributions by the member states.[1]

This article examines the financing system of the European Union, which is based on the system of own resources: customs duties, value added tax and national contributions based on GNI (Gross National Income). The sources for this article are primary sources, namely the figures in the EU budget and secondly recent academic publications on this topic.

Specifically, this article pursues the following lines of inquiry:

---

[1]Matthijs (2014, pp. 9–21, 2015, pp. 458–467), Benedeto and Milio (2012), Cipriani (2014), and European Commission (2014).

H. Matthijs
Vrije Universiteit Brussel, Ixelles, Belgium

Universiteit Gent University, Ghent, Belgium
e-mail: herman.matthijs@ugent.be



N. da Costa Cabral et al. (eds.), *The Euro and the Crisis*, Financial and Monetary Policy Studies 43, DOI 10.1007/978-3-319-45710-9_19

What has been the evolution of own resources since 1970, the ranking of the financing of the EU budget by the member states per capita and the general funding, the new system of 2014 and the differences to the previous funding.

## 2 The Present Financial System

Since 1970 several systems have already been utilised for the financing of the EU budget. The European Council at Brussels held on 8 February 2013 laid the basis for a new financial system for the general budget of the European Communities, which ended in the council decision of 2014.[2]

The financial system of the European Union is always based on a council decision. This means that the member states are taking this decision. This is related to article 311 of the Lisbon treaty concerning the functioning of the EU, which also says that the arrangements relating to the union's own resources have to be made through a unanimous council decision. This has the consequence that each member state has a "veto" concerning the proposals for the modification of this system.

The system of own resources contains three kinds of own resources, namely:

- "Traditional own resources" (TOR)—these mainly consist of duties which are charged on the importing of products coming from a non-EU State.
- The resource based on Value Added Tax (VAT) is a uniform percentage rate that is applied to each Member State's harmonised VAT revenue.
- The resource based on "Gross National Income" (GNI) is a uniform percentage rate applied to the GNI of each Member State. Although it is a balancing item, it has become the largest source of revenue.

The EU budget also receives other revenues, such as taxes paid by EU staff on their salaries, contributions from non-EU countries to certain EU programmes and fines on companies that breach competition or other laws. These miscellaneous resources add up to around 2 % of the budget.

### *2.1 TOR*

TOR are related to the levies and other duties provided for under the common organisation of the markets in sugar. And mainly with the custom duties on imports levied at the external borders of the Union.

These common custom rates were determined in 1968, 2 years earlier than planned. Customs duties were mentioned in the Treaty of Rome as the primary

[2]Council Decision no. 335 of 26 may 2014 on the European Communities' system of own resources (Official Journal, Series L, no. 168, 7 June 2014).

source of finance for the expenditure of the European Economic Community. In 1988, the customs duties of the European Coal and Steel Community were added to these. With a harmonised customs duties system, the European Union is a customs union with a common tariff. This is not the case in a free trade organization, like EFTA (European Free Trade Association).

The customs administrations of the EU member states have to collect this money and 20 % of revenues remain in the national budget to cover collection costs. The new financial system of 2014 had reduced this collection cost by 5 %. This means that the national budgets of the member states lose money with this new system. In other words, the member states have to pay in the new system a percentage of 80 % in place of 75 % to the general budget of the Union. The only change is the decrease of the collection cost for the national treasuries from 25 to 20 %.

The agricultural levies were instituted in 1962 and were transferred to the Community through the decision of 21 April 1970 and these were originally taxes which varied according to the price in global markets and the price in the European market. But since the multilateral trade agreements of the Uruguay Round (April 1994), which were related to GATT (General Agreement on Trade and Tariffs) & WTO (World Trade Organisation) negotiations concerning more global free trade, these duties were taken up into Community rules of the EU. Since then, there are no distinctions anymore between agricultural levels and customs duties.

The assignment of customs duties as own resources to the financing of the EU budget is the logical consequence of the free movement of goods within the union.

## 2.2 *VAT*

Value Added Tax (VAT) was also established by the listed decision of 21 April 1970. The reason was that the traditional own resources were not sufficient anymore for financing the EU budget.

The VAT resources are the result of the application of a specific percentage on a uniformly established basis. In the period from 1988 to 1994 the basis was set at a maximum of 55 % of the GDP of the member states. From 1995 until the present this rate has been established at 50 %.

Through the decision of 1970 the maximum percentage that could be collected from VAT revenues was limited to 1 % of a specified tax base. The decision of 1985 on own resources increased this percentage to 1.4 %. This fact was related to the moment when the EU was enlarged through Spain and Portugal joining. This VAT increase was needed in order to fund the costs of enlargement. But the fourth decision on own resources (dated 31 October 1994) provided for a gradual return to the ceiling of 1 % in the 1995–1999 period for reasons of fairness. During this century this call-in percentage was reduced to 0.5 % (2000 decision) of the maximum level of the harmonized VAT base and further to 0.3 % (2007 decision).

In the new 2014 system this VAT rate is still fixed at 0.3 % for member states. However, the system of own resources for three countries, namely, the Federal

Republic of Germany, the Netherlands and Sweden specifies a rate of only 0.15 %. This new situation represents a status quo for the Federal Republic, but an increase for the Netherlands and Sweden (it was 0.1 %). Also in the old system of 2007, the Federal Republic of Austria had a VAT rate of 0.225 %, but this benefit disappeared in the new 2014 system.

The reduced VAT rate persists for Germany and also, but less advantageously, for the Netherlands and Sweden (−0.050 %). Austria is the greatest loser in the new VAT system (−0.075 %).

## 2.3 GNI

In the year 1988 with the then financial system, the "Gross National Income" (GNI) was introduced as the third own resource for the EU budget. This GNI was originally based on the "Gross National Product" (GNP). This resource was meant to replace the VAT resource as the way of balancing the budget. The same decision of 24 June 1988 set the ceiling for the total of own resources. In 1988 this was 1.14 % of GNP while in 1999 it was 1.27 %. The decision of 2000 extended the application of the European system of economic accounting introduced in 1995 (ESR 95, now version 2010) to the field of the EU budget. The notion of gross national product (GNP) was replaced by the idea of gross national income (GNI). The new decision thus replaced GNP with GNI for the determination of own resources. In order not to touch the amount of financial resources made available to the Communities, the ceiling for own resources as a percentage of the GNI of the EU was adjusted. The new ceiling was 1.24 % of the GNI of the EU, and this was confirmed in the decision of 2007 concerning own resources.

The GNI resources result from the application of a specific percentage which is determined every year in the context of the budgetary procedure through an assessment basis that consists of the sum of the gross national income of member states at market prices. They are equal to the difference between expenses and the sum of all other budget resources.

They play a key role because they finance not only the greater part of the budget but also determine the ceiling of the assessment base for VAT, the distribution of the financing of the UK rebate and the maximum amount of the total resources that the Community is allowed to collect.[3]

The new system concerning own resources determines that some countries will have a reduction of their GNI contribution to the EU budget. This involves the following member states: the Netherlands (−695 million euros), Sweden (−185 million euros), Denmark (−130 million euros) and Austria (−60 million euros but divided over the years 2014–2016). The latter case of the Federal Republic of

[3]Matthijs (2014, p. 13).

Austria is compensation for the loss in VAT reduction (supra). The global reduction for these four countries in 2016 represents a budget cost of 1120 million euros.[4]

## 2.4 *Comparison*

Figures given below show that the own resources system (TOR and VAT) has a considerably reduced share in total revenues. Originally, the intention in the 1970s was that the member-state should contribute to financing the European community through a system of own resources. Custom duties and VAT can certainly relate to this. However, the GNI contribution is in fact not an own resource in the meaning of the Luxembourg agreement.

This declining share in respect of traditional own resources (agricultural levies, customs duties and sugar contribution) has to do with the growing freedom of world trade and the associated policy of lower import duties.

The lower share of VAT has to do with the maximum percentage of 1.4 % that was imposed in 1985 and which by now has been reduced to the present 0.3 % for most of the member states or 0.15 % for three other EU countries.

Over the last 20 years the importance of the GNI resources has been constantly growing. This evolution is shown in the next table (Table 1).[5]

The idea of the 1970 treaty to introduce own resources has been modified by the present system, which is based on national contributions. Knowing that the GNI is not a real own resource, it should be admitted that the EU has left this political idea to finance the budget with its real own resources. The impact of the GNI is extremely high and has a share of three quarters of the global financing of the budget. Customs duties have lost more than half as a share and the impact of VAT, the only EU harmonised tax, is the great loser in this story with a present share below the customs duties.

# 3 The UK Rebate and Related Reductions

The first return in favour of the United Kingdom took place in the agreement of June 1984.

The question of "fair return" is related to the discussion about net contributors. This subject returned to the negotiating table of the European Council during the negotiations about the new financial system, but this rebate structurally remains.

As such, the correction mechanism in favour of the United Kingdom was maintained in the 2014 Council decision concerning own resources. This means

[4]Matthijs (2015, p. 462).

[5]*Ibidem*, p. 463.

**Table 1** Budget percentage

| | 1988 | 1990 | 1995 | 2000 | 2005 | 2015 |
|---|---|---|---|---|---|---|
| Sugar levies & customs duties | 28.5 | 26.1 | 19.3 | 15.3 | 11.3 | 12.2 |
| VAT resources | 57.2 | 59.1 | 52.2 | 38.1 | 14.0 | 11.4 |
| GNP/GNI resources | 10.6 | 0.2 | 18.9 | 42.3 | 73.8 | 75.3 |
| Miscellaneous—balance past year | 3.7 | 14.6 | 9.7 | 4.3 | 0.9 | 1.1 |
| Total | 100 | 100 | 100 | 100 | 100 | 100 |

that a modification is only possible if all the member states are in favour and this situation gives the United Kingdom a de facto and de jure veto. A modification of the UK rebate rules in the EU council decision is only possible through a unanimous agreement. This system is a rather complicated regulation.

First of all, the U.K. is reimbursed by 66 % of the difference between its contribution and what is received back from the budget. The calculation is based on its GNI and VAT.

In the 2015 budget[6] this rebate was 5.4 billion euros. In the present system concerning own resources, the rebate in favour of the UK is less attractive than in the former versions of this system.

The cost of the U.K. rebate is divided among the other EU member states in proportion to the share they contribute to the EU's GNI. Using as an example the 2015 budget, the UK has a share of 15.36 % in the GNI of the Union. This is the share which will be divided throughout the other 27 states. However, since 2002 this has been limited to 25 % of its normal value for Germany, the Netherlands, Austria and Sweden.

The practical calculation of this application in the new system of own resources results in the following figures (calculations based on the 2015 budget):

- Germany has a share of 21.51 % and that becomes 25.41 %, after the contribution of the UK share. However, the Federal Republic has an exemption of three quarters (¾ of 25.41 % is 19.06 %). The final financing scale for Germany in relation to the UK rebate is 6.35 %;
- The same calculation is made for the Netherlands (4.58/5.41 % and −4.06 = ¾ becomes 1.35 %), Sweden (3.23/3.81 % and −2.86 % = ¾ becomes 0.95 %) and Austria (2.39 %/2.82 % −2.11 % = ¾ becomes 0.7 % as its share);
- e.g. Belgium has a share of 2.9 % and without the UK share this becomes 3.43 %. This country has to pay more (1.54 %) in relation to the ¾ exemptions for the four members. Finally, the Belgian financial amount is 4.96 % or 269 million euros of the 5.4 billion for the UK rebate;
- e.g. Portugal has a share of 1.21 % and without the UK share it becomes 1.43 %. In relation to the exemptions for the four member states, the Portuguese share increases by 0.64 % until 2.07 % or 112 million euros of the total rebate amount.

[6]Definitive adoption of the EU budget 2015 by the European Parliament (17th December 2014), in: Official Journal edition: L no. 69, 13 March 2015.

Finally, the cost of the UK rebate (5.4 billion euros in 2015) is divided over the 27 other member states with the listed reductions for the Federal Republic of Germany, the Netherlands, Sweden and Austria. Considering the calculations, the 5.4 billion euros rebate is paid by: France (27 %), Italy (19.8 %), Spain (12.91 %), Germany (6.35 %), Poland (5.02 %), Belgium (4.96 %), Denmark (3.36 %), Finland (2.5 %) etc.

It is remarkable that three southern countries are paying the greatest share in this rebate cost and together this amounts to nearly 60 % of the rebate total. Even with the ¾ reduction, Germany is still the fourth payer in this compensation system. However, the German share is a lot smaller than the three largest contributors to the UK rebate.

## 4 Calculations

The following table gives an overview of the ranking of the member states by per capita "contribution" (in Euros) for the budget years 2006 and 2015, on the basis of own resources.

Bulgaria and Romania were not member states in 2006 and Croatia has been an EU member since 1 July 2013 (Table 2).

The year 2006 was the period before the financial crisis and, per capita, the Benelux and Scandinavian states were the most important contributors to the EU budget along with France and Germany. However, the new member states, since 2006, are all less important contributors. In the year 2006 all the new member states, except Cyprus, were behind the 15 member states from 1995 with exception of Portugal.

The difference between Luxembourg and the last (Latvia) is a factor of 10.28!

In the next table the same calculation is made for the 2015 financial year. It should be pointed out that this 2015 calculation was still made on the base of the 2007 own resources system, which was still the base for the budget (Table 3).

It is noteworthy that two countries (i.e. Belgium and Luxembourg)—that are home to the large majority of the European institutions—are among the top five per capita contributors in 2006 and the top three in 2015.

What is also remarkable is that the twenty-first century expansion of the Community to include ten Southern and Eastern European countries in 2004 and the 2007 expansion with Romania and Bulgaria cannot be regarded as a financial success for the EU budget.

The Republics of Cyprus, Slovenia and Malta are the only member states in the 2015 ranking which have a higher capita level than two old members, namely Portugal and Greece.

In the two rankings the EU-15 from 1995 are still at the head with the exception of Portugal and Greece.

**Table 2** Per capita contribution in 2006

| | | |
|---|---|---|
| 1. | Luxembourg | 535 |
| 2. | Denmark | 355 |
| 3. | Ireland | 327 |
| 4. | Sweden | 290 |
| 5. | Belgium | 276 |
| 6. | France | 274 |
| 7. | The Netherlands | 260 |
| 8. | Austria | 259 |
| 9. | Finland | 258 |
| 10. | Germany | 236 |
| 11. | Italy | 230 |
| 12. | Spain | 198 |
| 13. | United Kingdom | 179 |
| 14. | Cyprus | 172 |
| 15. | Greece | 162 |
| 16. | Slovenia | 139 |
| 17. | Portugal | 129 |
| 18. | Malta | 108 |
| 19. | Czech Republic | 92 |
| 20. | Hungary | 84 |
| 21. | Estonia | 69 |
| 22. | Slovakia | 67 |
| 23. | Poland | 60 |
| 24. | Lithuania | 58 |
| 25. | Latvia | 52 |

Source: EU budget figures and population figures in CIA fact book

The difference between Luxemburg and Bulgaria in the 2015 calculation is a multiplication of 9.63 %. The newest members are all at the bottom of the ranking list.

Compared to 2006, Ireland and Greece have lost places in the ranking. This is due to the financial crisis.

Even with the reductions for Austria, Germany, the Netherlands and Sweden, these four countries have stayed in the top ten of the ranking.

The most important contributors are still the three Benelux countries, the three Scandinavian members, Germany, France, Austria and Ireland.

Below, the calculation is given concerning the share of the member states in the EU general budget in relation to several own resources, namely TOR, VAT and GNI contribution.

This table gives the ranking in terms of state percentage share in EU budget financing between 2002 (15 members), and the years 2006 (25 members) and 2010 (27 members) to the year 2015 (28 members) (Table 4).

Germany was and is still the greatest contributor to the Union. But the German share has been reduced following the EU expansion and the correction in favour of

**Table 3** Per capita contribution in 2015

| | | |
|---|---|---|
| 1. | Luxembourg | 607 |
| 2. | Denmark | 488 |
| 3. | Belgium | 475 |
| 4. | Sweden | 415 |
| 5. | Netherlands | 395 |
| 6. | Finland | 379 |
| 7. | Austria | 371 |
| 8. | Ireland | 358 |
| 9. | Germany | 354 |
| 10. | France | 341 |
| 11. | Spain | 294 |
| 12. | Italy | 271 |
| 13. | UK | 252 |
| 14. | Slovenia | 197 |
| 15. | Cyprus | 195 |
| 16. | Malta | 189 |
| 17. | Portugal | 167 |
| 18. | Greece | 166 |
| 19. | Estonia | 162 |
| 20. | Slovakia | 145 |
| 21. | Czech rep. | 143 |
| 22. | Lithuania | 137 |
| 23. | Latvia | 133 |
| 24. | Poland | 111 |
| 25. | Croatia | 107 |
| 26. | Hungary | 103 |
| 27. | Romania | 77 |
| 28. | Bulgaria | 61 |

Source: EU budget figures and population figures in CIA fact book

the Federal Republic. Through this, the difference with France was reduced and this country has always had an equal share in the financing of the EU.

The 'juste retour' principle operates in favour of the British treasury and the UK, since the middle of the former decade, has been a smaller contributor than Italy. This country has also had an equal share over these years but over the last years we have seen the influence of the financial crisis. The same remark can be made for Spain.

If we group these countries by date of accession what is noteworthy are the following facts (2015 figures from the preceding table):

- The six founder members still contribute 58.55 % of the funding;
- The three member states that joined in 1973 are contributing 15.32 %.
- The southern expansion of the 1980s with the accession of Greece in 1981 and the two main countries of the Iberian Peninsula (1986) accounts for 10.82 %.

**Table 4** Ranking in terms of state percentage share in EU budget financing

| | 2002 (%) | 2006 (%) | 2010 (%) | 2015 (%) |
|---|---|---|---|---|
| Germany | 24.44 (1) | 20.56 (1) | 19.53 (1) | 20.84 (1) |
| France | 16.72 | 16.43 (2) | 16.73 (2) | 16.52 (2) |
| United Kingdom | 14.27 | 12.38 (4) | 10.87 (4) | 12.08 (4) |
| Italy | 13.03 | 13.69 (3) | 13.34 (3) | 12.13 (3) |
| Spain | 7.73 | 8.93 (5) | 9.33 (5) | 8.20 (5) |
| Netherlands | 6.48 | 5.20 (6) | 5.03 (6) | 4.89 (6) |
| Belgium | 3.97 | 4.01 (7) | 4.02 (7) | 3.92 (7) |
| Sweden | 2.73 | 2.72 (8) | 2.28 (9) | 2.95 (9) |
| Austria | 2.47 | 2.15 (11) | 2.19 (10) | 2.32 (10) |
| Denmark | 1.97 | 2.09 (12) | 2.17 (11) | 2.02 (11) |
| Greece | 1.63 | 2.20 (10) | 2.15 (12) | 1.34 (12) |
| Portugal | 1.46 | 1.36 (15) | 1.37 (14) | 1.29 (14) |
| Finland | 1.45 | 1.48 (13) | 1.58 (13) | 1.52 (13) |
| Ireland | 1.40 | 1.38 (14) | 1.25 (15) | 1.22 (15) |
| Luxembourg | 0.25 | 0.24 (20) | 0.25 (22) | 0.25 (24) |
| Poland | – | 2.34 (9) | 2.64 (8) | 3.16 (8) |
| Czech Republic | – | 1.02 (16) | 1.23 (16) | 1.12 (16) |
| Slovakia | – | 0.38 (18) | 0.66 (19) | 0.58 (19) |
| Hungary | – | 0.91 (17) | 0.76 (18) | 0.76 (18) |
| Slovenia | – | 0.29 (19) | 0.36 (20) | 0.30 (22) |
| Lithuania | – | 0.22 (21) | 0.25 (23) | 0.30 (23) |
| Latvia | – | 0.13 (23) | 0.15 (25) | 0.15 (25) |
| Estonia | – | 0.10 (24) | 0.13 (26) | 0.15 (26) |
| Cyprus | – | 0.16 (22) | 0.18 (24) | 0.12 (27) |
| Malta | – | 0.05 (25) | 0.06 (27) | 0.05 (28) |
| Romania | – | – | 1.15 (17) | 1.14 (17) |
| Bulgaria | – | – | 0.34 (21) | 0.33 (21) |
| Croatia | | | | 0.33 (20) |

- The 1995 expansion which saw the accession of Sweden, Finland and Austria, has in relative terms been financially favourable. These three member states contribute 6.79 % to the EU budget.

The conclusion is that the 15 member states that acceded in the period from 1951 to 1995 still account for 91.48 % (2015 figures) of the national contributions to the EU budget.

This makes it clear that the accession of the new members has certainly not brought any budgetary windfalls.

It also provides a clear indication concerning the differences in prosperity between the 15 members, which joined in the preceding century and the 13 new member states in this century. Poland, with 40 million citizens, is the greatest contributor from the new group, with a share of 3.16 % and an eighth place in the ranking, but after Belgium!

The influence of the economic recession and financial crisis have reduced the shares of the PIGS (Portugal, Italy, Greece and Spain) countries regarding their contributions to the EU budget.

Remarkable is the impact—with 9.06 % (2015 figures) of the three Benelux countries which is greater than that of Spain. The less attractive system of the British rebate is shown in this table concerning the British share between the years 2010 and 2015.

## 5 Policy Problems

The idea of the EU commission for more and new own resources for the EU budget has created a few noteworthy policy problems concerning this item. Creating more money for the union at a time when most of the member states are having to tighten their national budgets is a difficult political prospect. Is focusing on more appropriations in all policy fields for the future budget, with the exception of natural resources, a realistic proposition?

Article 311 of the TFEU contains the procedure concerning a new system of own resources. It is still the case that the council after consulting the European Parliament takes a unanimous decision concerning the own resources system. This means that new types of own resources or a change in the present system (e.g. a reduction in the GNI) is only possible if all the member states in the council are in favour. This situation both de facto and de jure provides a veto for each member state in the European Union. Furthermore, the unanimity rule becomes a standard procedure for fiscal affairs in EU procedures.

Several states are not in favour of changing the present system, such as the United Kingdom because of its rebate, and corrections for the Netherlands Denmark, Sweden, Austria and Germany, etc. As such, the unanimity rule is not a factor leading to a fast change to the present decision-making. Article 314 TFEU also demands approval from the Parliaments of the member states according to their national ratification procedures. Nevertheless, this veto position of the members is logical in an international organization where the political base is essentially a confederation.

Related to the commission question concerning a review of the system of own resources most of the states will have objections to providing more money to the European budget which is an understandably coherent response if these members have to tighten their public budgets. In terms of politics it is not so simple to ask the public for important financial savings in national public finances and at the same time to agree to spend more money on Europe.

The second idea of the commission is to change the GNI system through VAT own resources. This kind of thinking is acceptable for the members if the state budgets do not to spend more revenue on the EU budget.

The EU budget exists to fund the common policies that member states have agreed should be handled at the EU level (e.g. agriculture). The budget expresses solidarity between all states and regions. In addition, budget finance interventions complete the internal market.

However, the present system of own resources is very complicated with an important share of GNI contributions in place of the own resources. The present system is not a transparent model with the completed corrections for several states in the calculation of the VAT, the GNI and the UK rebate.

A new system of own resources demands a simplification of the rules. The current funding rules have evolved not only in response to the need for more accountability on how public money is spent but also to take account of previous problems.

## 6 New Member States?

The EU expansion of this century certainly did not involve the wealthy states on the European continent. Most of the 12 new members are states with a level of prosperity lower than the EU average.

Interesting for the EU budget would be new members with a high standard of living. Which European states are still available? The answer is the following countries: Norway and Switzerland.[7] These two countries are today member of the European Free Trade Association (EFTA). Besides these two countries, Liechtenstein and Iceland are also members of this organisation.

Nowadays, both countries make contributions to EU agencies and programmes—Norway via the European Economic Area (EEA) and Switzerland on a bilateral base with the Union. In comparison with the EU, the EEA does not cover the following EU policies:

- Common agriculture and fisheries policies;
- Customs union;
- Common trade policy;
- Common foreign and security policy;
- Justice and Home affairs[8];
- Economic and Monetary Union (EMU).

Following the Porto treaty of 1992 concerning the EEA, Norway has to pay yearly grants to the new EU member states. In addition, the Swiss confederation has created budget grants for these new members. Both countries are financing several EEA activities and the 12 new EU member states from this century. The total

[7]H. Matthijs, The budget cost for the member states of the European Free Trade Association., American International Journal of Research in Humanities, Arts and Social Sciences., issue 6, vol. 1, 2014, pp. 11–18.

[8]The four EFTA member states are joining the Schengen area.

amount for these two countries is about 500 million euros a year, which is cheaper than full membership of the union.

The conclusion is very clear: EU membership for Norway and Switzerland would cost these countries a lot more than their membership to EFTA/EEA. In line with the GDP of these two countries, they would be net payers to the Union. Concluding the EU membership of these two countries would have a very positive effect on the EU budget but the status of being a net payer is certainly not an argument for these countries to campaign for EU membership.

The 2015 EFTA general budget[9] is fixed at 22 million CHF, which is divided over the four members with the following shares: Norway (55.91 %). Switzerland (40.54 %). Iceland (2.61 %) and Liechtenstein (0.94 %).

## 7 Conclusion

The 2014 own resources decision formalises the existing trend towards making the GNI contributions the main source of financing for the General Budget of the European Union. For almost 40 years this budget has been compromised by the "fair return" principle, which works in favour of the United Kingdom. In the meantime, special arrangements have also been allowed for the Netherlands, Sweden, Denmark, Austria and Germany.

Decisions concerning own resources continue to be subject to unanimous approval. This means that each member state must give its approval to any change. That is the problem when it comes to changing anything concerning this decision.

In the 1970s and 1980s the idea was to raise an EU tax to fund the EU budget. This concept has now been entirely abandoned. The funding of the budget continues to rest very largely on the shoulders of the first 15 member states. The accession of the 12 new member states can hardly be regarded as a financial success.

The new commission proposal has returned to the original idea of own resources. VAT is an excellent means for financing this EU budget. A reduction of the GNI and the replacement by a higher VAT collection would be in line with the conclusions of the Fontainebleau European council of 1984 to contain the contributions of those member states that would otherwise face a budgetary burden which is excessive in relation to their relative prosperity.

Europe needs a new, fairer and more transparent system. Since the 1970 Luxembourg agreement the Union has not done anything with VAT as an own resource. This VAT is related to the financial health of the member states and a fixed share of this indirect tax can form the base for a long term financing plan for the general EU budget.

---

[9]EFTA (2015, p. 10).

The EU budget is necessary and has a pan-European logic not a national one. Its comparatively small size allows it to be concentrated where it delivers high EU added value. This budget does not seek to fund interventions that the member states could finance by themselves.

However, the demand from the EU Commission for more financial revenues is a controversial question at this time of budgetary discipline. Indeed, the EU is asking the member states to put an end to budget deficits and debts in their public finances. Already in 2012 the European Union required member states not to have a deficit in their public finances of more than 3 % of their national GDP.

Given this, the final question is the following one: are the member states in agreement to go back to the situation of own resources related to an increase in revenues at the moment when nearly all the states have had to undertake financial reconstruction measures.

It is up to the EU council to take a decision concerning this issue. However, member states like the UK, France, Germany, the Netherlands and Finland are not in favour of the demand from the Commission for more revenues. Even in November 2012, Denmark opposed the question from the EU Commission of more contributions to the budget.

The present system of own resources is too complicated and needs to be replaced by a more transparent version.

In fact, the European Union can use some more affluent new member states to finance its budget, but knowing the net payer situation in these countries future membership would appear to be out of the question.

## References

Benedeto G, Milio S (2012) European Union budget reform. Palgrave, London

Cipriani G (2014) Financing the EU budget. Rowman & Littlefield, London

European Commission (2014) European Union public finance, 5th edn. Publications Office of the European Union, Luxembourg

EFTA (2015). EFTA, Brussels, p 10

Matthijs H (2014) Who pays the budget of the European Union. Scott J Arts Soc Sci Sci Stud 18 (2):9–21

Matthijs H (2015) De nieuwe financiering van de begroting van de Europese Unie. SEW tijdschrift Europees en economisch recht, nr. 10, oktober 2015, pp 458–467

# Toward a Closer Union in Europe: Elusive Mirage or Reality Within Grasp?

**George Kopits**

**Abstract** In the wake of the euro debt crisis, there have been multiple initiatives to repair the EU structure and governance, focused on the existing financial and fiscal framework. On the financial front, major steps—albeit still under construction—are taken toward unifying and strengthening banking regulation, supervision and resolution. By contrast, on the fiscal front, efforts in redesigning the existing framework so far have not been matched by progress toward unification. Likewise, practically no headway has been made in merging other key policy areas, such as defense, internal security, or external relations, as envisaged in the Treaty of Maastricht. Beyond taking inventory of what has been accomplished, the chapter explores the prospects and tasks for further political and fiscal integration—in line with well-known guiding principles, including subsidiarity and solidarity.

## 1 Introduction

Recent developments, notably, the recent euro debt crisis, the military confrontation in Ukraine, and the immigration crisis, serve as tangible reminders of the need for accelerating the pace of unifying Europe. Moving toward a deeper European Union (EU) is no longer merely material for visionary speeches by political leaders, or just a thought experiment to be carried out by policy analysts within the confines of think tanks and academic circles. Instead, unification should become a central focus of policymakers and elected officials throughout Europe, and particularly in the core member countries, with the support of careful technical preparation, replacing improvised coordination at numerous, often hastily organized,

---

An earlier abridged version of this paper was presented at a Public Finance Dialogue seminar, in the German Federal Ministry of Finance, Berlin. The author is indebted to seminar participants and an anonymous referee for useful comments. But he alone is responsible for all views expressed.

G. Kopits
Woodrow Wilson Center, Washington, DC, USA

Portuguese Public Finance Council, Lisbon, Portugal
e-mail: george.kopits@wilsoncenter.org

 
N. de Costa Cabral et al. (eds.), *The Euro and the Crisis*, Financial and Monetary Policy Studies 43, DOI 10.1007/978-3-319-45710-9_20

governmental summits, as unfolding developments and threats demand a common policy stance.

Within the narrower context of the euro debt crisis, there have been multiple initiatives to repair the EU structure and governance, focused on the existing fiscal and financial framework. In addition, there seems to be a renewed willingness expressed by some European leaders in forging a closer union in these areas, seen by some as the path toward a political union, to be backed by democratic legitimacy. On the financial front, major steps are taken toward unifying and strengthening banking regulation, supervision and resolution, yet with considerable scope for further steps, notably, in creating a risk-priced common deposit insurance scheme. By contrast, on the fiscal front, the efforts in redesigning the Stability and Growth Pact have not been matched by progress toward unification. And, so far, compliance with the revised Pact by certain major EU members remains the weak link of the fiscal framework. If past behavior continues, these efforts can be characterized as nothing more than "tinkering around the edges."

The purpose of this chapter is primarily to examine the scope and limits for political and fiscal unification within the EU. The chapter begins with a review of some antecedents to the current situation, as well as of future challenges facing the EU, which set the stage for stepped-up unification. This is followed by a discussion of the guiding principles for a political union, inspired by the literature on assignment of responsibilities in a multi-level federal system, and as reflected in the EU statutes and structure. In the light of these principles, the chapter focuses, first, on the extent and manner of unifying budgetary outlays, and then, on the choices and design of tax harmonization, unification, and government financing. Subsequently, it addresses key political economy aspects that may promote or prevent completion of the union in the spirit of the Treaty of Maastricht. To conclude, the chapter summarizes the outlook and tasks for further European integration.

## 2 Background

The Treaty of Maastricht represents a landmark decision in establishing the foundations of a truly unified Europe. It enacted multiple steps toward integration in the monetary, fiscal, security and foreign policy dimensions. Of these, only monetary unification materialized under a common currency area. It was understood that fiscal discipline, labor market flexibility, and effective banking supervision, are necessary conditions for a well-functioning common currency area.[1] According to the theory of optimum currency areas, asymmetric shocks need to be offset by fiscal

[1]As illustrated by the crisis, the fiscal condition becomes imperative lacking an area-wide banking union consisting of effective banking supervision and uniform deposit insurance across member countries. Otherwise, impaired banks eventually need to be recapitalized directly or indirectly by the host government, compounding its debt burden.

and wage adjustments, absent the exchange rate as a shock absorber.[2] But the importance of fiscal discipline in EU member countries was underscored by a high degree of fiscal sovereignty, fragmentary banking supervision and relatively rigid labor markets within the euro area. Hence, to ensure that the fiscal condition would be met and to avoid free-rider behavior, a set of fiscal rules, consisting of ceilings on the general government deficit and debt, along with the no-bailout provision specified in the Treaty, was adopted under the Stability and Growth Pact (SGP) for all EU member countries.[3]

It was widely acknowledged that the fiscal rules under the Pact were well designed, except for the lack of effective enforcement,[4] which eventually proved to be the Achilles' heel of the Pact.[5] Indeed, most member governments, including the largest among them (France and Germany), violated the rules and breached the so-called excess deficit procedure, without incurring the financial sanctions prescribed by the statutes. During the Great Moderation, and the accompanying easy access to financing, some peripheral member governments had adopted an expansionary procyclical fiscal stance, which, in combination with the one-size fits-all monetary policy—that was expansionary for these countries—and with lax banking supervision, fueled asset price bubbles and a private sector boom. The expansionary monetary and fiscal policy stance, coupled with weak banking supervision, rendered these member countries highly vulnerability to shocks.

When the financial crisis metastasized across Europe, in 2008–2010, the most vulnerable euro area member countries, suffered a sudden stop in capital inflows, following a period when neither the EU institutions nor the financial markets had exercised adequate surveillance of macroeconomic and fiscal fundamentals. To contain the crisis, supported with financial assistance from the European Central Bank (ECB) and the European Commission (EC), jointly with the International Monetary Fund (IMF), these countries (Greece, Ireland and Portugal, followed by Cyprus) undertook large-scale stabilization programs, which were met with mixed

[2]For a comprehensive analysis of the application of the theory, see De Grauwe (2003), and for empirical evidence on whether the necessary conditions are met in the euro area, see Pasimeni (2014).

[3]Chari and Kehoe (2009) formalized, in theoretical terms, the need for such fiscal rules in a monetary union.

[4]This was the assessment of the EU fiscal rules by Buti and Giudice (2002) on the basis of seven of the eight criteria of good practice formulated in Kopits and Symansky (1998), namely, definition, transparency, adequacy, consistency, simplicity, flexibility, efficiency, and enforceability.

[5]Criticisms that the Pact lacked an insurance device or that it was too rigid can be easily dismissed. Collective insurance proposed by Schelkle (2005) would have created added moral hazard and, as argued by Münchau (2016), it would have been inherently inconsistent among sovereign states. Contrary to the criticism of rigidity, leveled for example by Wyplosz (forthcoming) among others, the binding deficit ceiling has been sufficiently flexible to accommodate even significant output shocks. Given tax progressivity, for most EU members, 1 % percent decline in GDP was estimated to lead to an automatic deterioration in the budget balance equivalent to roughly 0.5 % of GDP. Thus, it would take 6-percentage-point fall from trend GDP (that would anyway trigger a waiver under the Pact) to push the budget from balance to excess deficit.

success.[6] A number of valuable lessons were learned from the crisis for preventing the emergence of systemic risks in the financial sector and for strengthening the fiscal rules, hopefully paving the way toward a closer union in banking and public finances.

Substantial progress has been achieved in the financial sector, starting with the 2012 summit meeting of European leaders who agreed to create a banking union within the euro area, extended on a voluntary basis to the rest of the EU membership as well.[7] The agreement was followed up with the establishment of the Single Supervisory Mechanism (SSM) and the Single Resolution Mechanism (SRM). These new institutions have taken over central supervisory functions through application of stress tests to major banks and of resolution of insolvent banks, in cooperation with national governments and banking supervisory authorities. As well, they are supported by a set of banking regulations and directives under new EU legislation, including on capital adequacy requirements, recovery and resolution procedures, and deposit guarantees. The common resolution scheme, effective since January 2016, is still *en rodage*. Implementation of the scheme in Italy and Portugal, with some banks holding sizable share of nonperforming loans in their portfolios, has yet to be completed in an orderly manner.[8] However, the banking union remains incomplete without establishment of a joint deposit insurance scheme. Although an essential component of the banking union and indispensable for the prevention of a future crisis, the proposed European Deposit Insurance Scheme (EDIS) is held in abeyance due to open opposition mainly by Germany and the Netherlands.[9] To be sure, for the deposit insurance to be viable and free of moral hazard, it must be properly calibrated as a risk-priced scheme.

In comparison to the steady progress toward a banking union, modifications of the fiscal framework have been rather modest. At the national level, most member governments have enshrined in their fundamental statutes (organic legislation or constitution) key elements of the reformed EU fiscal framework, namely, the structural budget balance rule, with some variations. Many of them have also established an independent fiscal institution to monitor compliance with the rules, as well as independent macroeconomic forecasts as an input for, or control over,

[6]For an analysis of the pre-crisis period and the stabilization programs, see Mayer (2012), Sinn (2014), and Kopits (2017).

[7]For a detailed account, see Veron (2015).

[8]For a critical assessment of the ongoing resolution process, see Sebastiao (2016). Difficulties encountered in the resolution of insolvent banks without government capital injections, under the present regime, stem from the failure of banks to disclose that it can be much riskier to hold bank bonds than bank deposits. As a last resort, after having exhausted the bail-in from shareholders and bondholders, the European Stability Mechanism (ESM) may recapitalize banks under a restructuring program, while the Single Resolution Fund (SRF) would be expected to coordinate financing by banks to this effect.

[9]However, a timetable for implementing such a scheme has been proposed in the Five Presidents' Report by Juncker and others (2015).

official budgetary forecasts. The degree to which these fiscal watchdogs conform to best practice varies across countries.[10]

The extent of national ownership and effective political support for these innovations remains to be tested. Beyond the enactment of the rules-based framework in national legislation, in practice member governments need to adopt the framework in a simplified and transparent manner that places accountability at the decision-making level. For this purpose, it is necessary to distinguish between policy rules and operational rules, and between indicative and binding rules. Views are converging toward establishing a framework in which the principal policy rule is the debt ratio rule, while an expenditure rule is the binding operational rule—for which the finance minister or the budget director could be held accountable—and the structural balance rule is treated as an indicative rule, given the difficulty of estimating reliably the latter in real time. Such a framework is broadly compatible with the reformed SGP, with the advantage of being more enforceable in practice.[11] In most member countries, it is essential that this approach be accompanied with political commitment to tackle structural reforms—to ensure sufficient fiscal space within the envelope of the medium-term objective (MTO)—and embodied in concrete measures outlined in the annual Stability Program.

Presumably, rather than fear of financial or legal EU-level sanctions for noncompliance, member governments will become increasingly sensitive to market perceptions, reflected in sovereign bond spreads and to evaluation by credit rating agencies, which since the outbreak of the crisis seem to be more alert to macro-fiscal fundamentals. Market pressures, however, have yet to be fully felt again beyond the eventual phase-out of the sovereign quantitative easing by the ECB that currently dampens spreads on government paper. In any event, enhanced fiscal discipline and structural reforms should not be undertaken to avert possible sanctions from the financial markets or from the EU authorities, but for regaining stability and growth.

It is, however, at the level of EU institutions that the most important lessons of the crisis need to be learned and implemented. The ECB has become aware of the importance of differentiating among sovereign collateral by taking into account each government's credit rating. Hopefully, it will also manage to take into account cross-country inflation rate differences when formulating monetary policy. Furthermore, it is now in charge of a unified macroprudential approach to systemic risk across member countries through the newly established European Systemic Risk Board (ESRB). A major challenge ahead will be to wind down quantitative easing as soon as the risk of deflation subsides. In principle, the European Stability Mechanism (ESM), as the principal financial tool of crisis management, including banking resolutions within the euro area, in the context of the evolving banking union, can help alleviate the need for bank recapitalization by member

[10]See the analysis and country cases in Kopits (2013).

[11]See the proposals by Kopits (2014) and Andrle and others (2015).

governments. All these steps should contribute not only financial and price stability, but also to sound fiscal policymaking.

The EC, under the leadership of the Eurogroup, is expected to continue to play a pivotal role as guardian of the reformed SGP. The 2011–2013 revisions, intended to strengthen the design of, and compliance with, the Pact (contained in the so-called six-pack, two-pack, and an intergovernmental treaty), included granting increased independence and inspection authority to Eurostat. In principle, the emphasis on the structural balance or surplus, replacing the balance or surplus over the cycle, allowance for overruns on account of structural reform measures, and adoption of a numerical yearly reduction in the debt ratio, are welcome steps. In practice, the difficulty of measuring these metrics in real time may render them ineffective. Moreover, the increased complexity of the rules poses a major challenge for compliance with the reformed fiscal framework.[12]

A promising tool of enforcement is the MTO to hold governments accountable to their commitments. Apart from the complexity of the existing framework that will need streamlining for greater simplicity and transparency, the critical challenge for the EC will be effective enforcement of the framework through the European Semester, and ultimately, through rigorous peer review within the Eurogroup. The recent decision of allowing the governments of France and Italy further deferral of compliance with the MTO has been disappointing in this regard.

Nevertheless, it is increasingly recognized by government leaders and policy analysts that the next major step for future crisis prevention and management in the euro area, and possibly throughout the EU, is the creation of a closer fiscal union.[13] Two prominent elder statesmen, Valery Giscard d'Estaing (2014) and Helmut Schmidt (2014), view this as a moment of truth for the Union. They contend that following a linear progress toward unification, peaking with the Treaty of Maastricht, the EU has been bogged down in a circular process without direction, which contributed to the euro debt crisis. In their opinion, this is the last chance to move toward unification in the euro area, thereby preserving the integrity of the area and the Union. Alternatively, the EU is likely to weaken and disintegrate.

## 3 Guiding Principles

Arguably, the euro debt crisis, followed by diplomatic and military confrontations abroad, and more recently, the immigration crisis, provides a vivid illustration of the high stakes for the EU in "hanging together or falling apart." In all, a quantum leap toward fiscal union can only be discussed in the broader context of a political

[12]European Commission (2013a, b) is intended to help navigate through the maze of rules, regulations, and practices, which currently underlie the SGP.

[13]See, for example, Allard and others (2013).

union. As a corollary, the principles for a fiscal union are derived from those that guide the establishment of a political union.

These principles can be summarized under three general headings, namely, subsidiarity, solidarity, and fairness, which explicitly or implicitly are in conformity with basic EU official documents; also, they can be found in many federal systems around the world.[14] In turn, these principles are supported by a number of specific criteria, including efficiency, transparency, flexibility, and operational feasibility, which need to be addressed when applying the principles in various areas of public finance. The principles guide the assignment of responsibilities and functions, as well as the allocation of resources to carry out those functions, among government layers within a federal system—broadly in conformity with the traditional theory of fiscal federalism.[15] However, responsibilities and resources cannot be assigned without observance of certain degree of sovereignty at lower levels of government, highlighted in Sect. 6 below. National or subnational sovereignty, in fact, sets the ultimate limit to unification.

The subsidiarity principle—borrowed from Catholic social teaching—is recognized as essential for further political and fiscal EU integration, including by German finance minister Schäuble.[16] Under this principle, a function should be located at the lowest level of government where it can be performed most efficiently, with no externalities outside the jurisdiction of that government. Higher levels of government (national, supranational), should have a subsidiary role, performing only tasks that be cannot be performed efficiently at lower (subnational, municipal, local) jurisdictions.

According to the subsidiarity principle, educational, cultural, sanitation, and police protection, are primarily the responsibility of local governments. Whereas the judicial system and communications are solely the responsibility of the national government, social security and assistance, including healthcare, may be shared with subnational levels of governments. Within the broader multinational EU context, international relations, defense, environmental protection, and immigration, with significant spillovers beyond national boundaries (much like monetary policy and banking regulation), should be carried out by a supranational authority, rather than by national or local governments. Currently in the euro area, apart from monetary policy, which is firmly under the authority of the ECB, and some progress toward creating a single banking regulation, supervision, and resolution, all the other responsibilities remain with national or subnational governments by virtue of either formal arrangements or improvisation under stress.

---

[14]See Escolano and others (2015) for a recent survey of practices in federal systems around the world.

[15]These principles broadly overlap with the three basic branches or functions of government, popularized in the classic treatment by Musgrave (1959). From that perspective, the stabilization and redistribution functions should be assigned to the highest government level, while the allocation function can be decentralized to lower levels.

[16]See Lamers and Schäuble (2014).

In foreign policy, the High Representative of the Union for Foreign Affairs and Security Policy is tantamount to hardly anything more than a ceremonial function. In the confrontation with Russia over Ukraine and Crimea, including the ensuing sanctions, EU member governments were at times in disarray before agreeing to rather fragile concerted action. It has been only under the umbrella of NATO, rather than the EU, that member governments have been able to adopt a strategic posture. Reaching a unified position has been even more elusive with respect to the unfolding immigration crisis, absent a common institutional umbrella.

In line with single market requirements, as well as the subsidiarity and solidarity principles, responsibility for EU-wide telecommunications, transportation, and energy distribution, is to be shared by the supranational and national authorities. Although the trans-European networks—with legal basis in the Treaty on the Functioning of the European Union—represent an ambitious initiative in these areas, progress in financing and implementation has been modest.

Solidarity is required among member countries to compensate for differences in economic and social structure and in standards of living—largely due to failure to completing real convergence within the Union. The solidarity principle includes risk sharing given the members' uneven vulnerability to various asymmetric economic shocks; *mutatis mutandis*, this may be extended to protection from uneven noneconomic shocks, including climate-related shocks, or from uneven threats to internal security and national defense. From the outset, the EU budget served as an income-equalization scheme for allocating Structural and Cohesion Funds to disadvantaged regions within the Union. The Stability and Growth Pact (SGP) allows for an escape clause from compliance with the budget deficit ceiling in the event of a significant and prolonged recession. The European Stability Mechanism (ESM) and the Outright Monetary Transactions (OMT) can be regarded as vehicles for risk sharing in term of their role in providing financial assistance conditional on an adjustment program of a member country, under EU tutelage.

Fairness, closely related to the solidarity principle, is aimed at equalizing the net costs and benefits among member countries, taking into account income and wealth differentials. This involves primarily burden sharing by member governments through the funding of the EU budget in proportion to their economic strength and size, mainly as determined by major sources of tax revenue.

## 4 Public Expenditure

The functions typically identified as the responsibility of the highest authority, under the subsidiarity principle, determine the expenditures of the supranational government. Accordingly, outlays on foreign affairs, defense, environmental and border protection should be centralized in an expanded EU budget.[17] However,

[17] See Alesina, Angeloni, and Schucknecht (2005) on application of the subsidiarity principle in the EU.

there are multiple collateral benefits from centralizing these functions besides greater efficiency derived from the subsidiarity principle. For one, economies of scale would accrue particularly from a common and flexible defense posture by foregoing duplication in weapons procurement and by adopting an enhanced strategic approach. In addition, free-rider behavior by some member governments would be reduced or eliminated, by pooling expenditures under a unified defense policy.[18] All told, the size of centralized expenditures would amount to less than an additional 5 % of GDP, replacing a larger level of outlays by most national governments on the same functions, insofar as economies of scale and efficiency gains materialize.

A logical extension of the subsidiarity principle is the assignment of macroeconomic stabilization to the supranational authority—much like in the case of monetary policy, assigned to the ECB—to counteract cyclical, regional, country-specific or asymmetric shocks, regardless of their source.[19] In this regard, the proposal for a fiscal union put forth recently in the so-called Five Presidents' Report authored by the heads of the five major EU institutions,[20] envisaged as the next stage in the evolution of EMU, is a welcome initiative. Although without specifying the source of financing, the report proposes centralization of the fiscal stabilization function—assigning the responsibility for formulating the aggregate fiscal stance to the newly established European Fiscal Board (EFB). In the present circumstances, the yet to be named decision-making authority could launch a large-scale, time-bound, and targeted fiscal stimulus within the euro area, on the basis of the EFB's recommendation.

This function would encompass primarily, but not solely, government spending on public investment and on active labor market programs, with direct or indirect repercussions across member economies. Expenditures would be deployed on major infrastructure and research and development projects, manpower training, labor mobility, and housing subsidies. They could include tax expenditures, for example, to induce firms to hire and/or train the unemployed. Such outlays, whether through the budget or the tax system, would not merely stimulate aggregate demand, but more important, contribute to supply, that is, to long-term potential growth. The overall impact of these expenditures would, of course, be much more significant if they were subject to the additionality criterion, much like it is applied to disbursements from the Structural Funds.

These expenditures need to surpass by an order of magnitude the scope, resources, and time horizon of the European Investment Bank (EIB), as well as a number of short-term budgetary allocations to cope with various emergencies and uncontrollable events, such as the migration crisis. There is a range of instruments

[18]Under their continued neutrality status—a relic of the cold war—Austria, Finland, Ireland, and Sweden so far have benefited from defense spending of neighboring EU member governments under the NATO umbrella.

[19]See footnote 14.

[20]See Juncker and others (2015).

that provide such funding in a flexible manner from various sources, including unallocated of unused resources from existing facilities, including from the Structural Funds.[21] The European Fund for Strategic Investment (EFSI), an initiative launched by EC President Juncker at the outset of his term is an example of such an ad hoc scheme.[22]

Centralizing the stabilization function at the aggregate level is entirely consistent with the subsidiarity and solidarity principles. Recessionary conditions prevailing in some member countries have repercussions throughout the Union. Social unrest and emergence of extreme political movements in one member country cannot be ignored in other member countries, since they may cause, partly through contagion, severe and long-lasting distress and instability in the euro area as a whole. Euro area-wide stabilization would be a win-win solution, conferring widespread multiple benefits: a major euro-wide expansionary impulse and a strengthened institutional architecture, with negligible moral hazard for member governments. Highly indebted member countries would regain some fiscal space under the SGP deficit ceiling, with room for implementing structural reforms that socially and politically may be difficult to undertake.

Assignment of the macro-stabilization function to the supranational level would provide much-needed means to coordinate fiscal policy with a single monetary policy for the euro area. Although at this juncture perhaps observationally equivalent, such an approach would differ from placing responsibility for stabilization on individual member countries that have sufficient fiscal space,[23] including through one-off measures, as recommended by various authors.[24]

## 5 Public Revenue

The guiding principles for unification outlined above are applicable in the revenue area as well, though in a somewhat different form than in expenditure assignment. The High Level Group on Own Resources (HLGOR) (2014), tasked with identifying potential sources of financing the EU budget, listed a number of criteria that overlap with, or are derived from, the foregoing guiding principles. The main

[21]Mijs and Schout (2015) evaluate critically these facilities under the flexibility criterion promoted by the European Parliament, attributable in part to the unwillingness of some member governments to commit additional resources to the EU budget on a permanent basis.

[22]The EFSI is envisaged to finance €315 billion in investments from private sources (equivalent about 1½ % of GDP), leveraged with €21 billion from the EU budget and the EIB, over a 3-year period.

[23]The governments of Germany and a few other countries resist launching a fiscal stimulus that would be procyclical, given full capacity utilization in their economies.

[24]Giavazzi and Tabellini (2014), for example, propose discretionary fiscal stimulus through tax cuts, to be followed by eventual compensatory expenditure cuts, to be coordinated with the ECB's expansionary monetary stance.

criteria are efficiency, fairness, equity, sufficiency, stability, transparency and simplicity of the source of revenue or financing. Although the relevance of most of these criteria is obvious, there are some that deserve to be highlighted.

Efficiency is to be interpreted both as allocative efficiency, or rather the elimination or minimization of distortions in commodity and (real and financial) factor flows across member countries, and as administrative efficiency, that is, capacity in raising revenue. Efficiency obtains under the benefit principle of taxation, which is consistent with the subsidiarity principle on the expenditure side. According to the benefit principle, tax assignment should reflect the incidence of a tax where it finances expenditures that benefit individuals who bear the tax burden. Thus, strictly speaking, only taxes on (mainly immovable) property and user fees assigned to the local government are least distortionary and meet unequivocally the benefit principle—assuming sufficient administrative capacity, for example, in the form of an adequate registry.[25] On this basis, indirect taxes and payroll taxes may overlap or be shared among national and subnational jurisdictions. Income taxation is perhaps most amenable for taxation at the national or supranational levels, but without preempting partial capture by subnational governments.

Fairness refers to equitable burden-sharing in terms of each member's net contribution to the EU budget, according to some measure of the ability to pay; but it can also be applied to fairness in tax competition among member governments. In either case, fairness should insofar as possible avert moral hazard. Equity is an all-encompassing criterion that is reflected in tax incidence. And, of course, the revenue raised or shared from various sources should be sufficient and stable to cover common expenditures. Transparency and simplicity in the tax system are essential in fostering efficiency and fairness. In addition to these general criteria, the subsidiarity principle, limited by a significant degree of national fiscal sovereignty, characterizes the EU architecture.

However, the issue of tax harmonization within the EU must be addressed before exploring the extent and types of taxes, or other sources of financing, that lend themselves to support the central EU budget under these criteria. In fact, quite apart from the resource needs of a unified budget, tax harmonization is recognized as a necessary ingredient to completing the single market. As envisaged in the Single European Act of 1987, taxation was to be harmonized sufficiently to ensure efficiency and prevent tax-induced distortions in the functioning of the market. Tax harmonization is relevant primarily for the most mobile effective tax bases, especially capital and commodities.[26] For the sake of efficiency and transparency, priority was assigned to tax base harmonization, along with minimum tax rate harmonization.[27] Harmonization on both counts has been accomplished for the

[25]For a succinct discussion of tax assignment and country practices, see Norregaard (1997).

[26]Given the lesser mobility of labor, there is no attempt to harmonize the bases or rates of payroll taxation, including in the form of social security contributions. Property taxes on real estate imposed on the least mobile base, are the least distortionary, and thus not a candidate for harmonization.

[27]For a comprehensive treatment of EU tax harmonization, see the papers by Bovenberg, de la Fuente, Gardner, and Horne, in Kopits (1992).

value-added tax (VAT) and excises. Also, taxation of interest from savings has been harmonized, along with compulsory exchange of information among tax authorities. But practically no progress has been made in harmonizing the base of the corporate income tax, leaving the door open to opaque tax competition among member countries. Against this backdrop, as an added attempt to create a more neutral, transparent and equitable approach to corporate taxation, for multinational firms operating across national jurisdictions, the Commission proposed a directive on a common consolidated corporate tax base (CCCTB), which to date does not seem to have had any traction for implementation in member countries.[28]

In a recent investigation, European Commission staff sought to identify the types of taxes that are amenable for unifying or for revenue sharing.[29] To this effect, potential revenue estimates were prepared for the following: value-added tax (VAT), excise duties, emission trading, seigniorage, the proposed financial transactions tax (FTT), the proposed CCCTB, savings income taxation, user charges, and possible taxes on financial activities (FAT) and carbon emission.[30] Of all these possible sources, not all of which have a harmonized base, the highest potential revenue obtains from the VAT, the FTT, the CCCTB, user charges on transport, and savings income taxation, in descending order. In view of the effectively harmonized base and potential revenue yield, as well as the broad and equitable base, at present the VAT and savings taxation are the most amenable candidates for financing permanent expenditures in the EU budget.

Unlike ordinary EU budget expenditures, expenditures targeted at macroeconomic stabilization, which by their very nature are temporary, could be financed with eurobonds issued by the supranational authority. These bonds would not be used to mutualize existing legacy public debt of member governments. The interest cost would be minimal inasmuch as these bonds finance public spending during recessions, to be wound down during expansionary periods. Moreover, the ECB would not have to refrain from sizable acquisition of such bonds, regardless of each member's capital key currently used to allocate monetary financing under the quantitative easing program.

[28]See European Commission (2011).

[29]See Fatica and Mourre (2016).

[30]Bénássy-Quéré and others (2014) recommended the FAT (levied on profits and wages in the banking sector, equivalent to a sectoral VAT) as a complement to banking regulation, with its revenue yield earmarked to the SRF. Beyond a predetermined level, revenue could accrue to the central EU budget.

## 6 Political Economy Aspects

The foregoing discussion of the way toward a closer union is couched in terms of principles laid down in EU statutes and invoked repeatedly by EU leaders, and grounded in the traditional literature on fiscal federalism. Also called first-generation theory of fiscal federalism, this literature implicitly assumes that public decision-making is predicated on the objective of welfare maximization at each government level and political stability among governments. Over the past decades, a new second-generation theory evolved which, drawing on public choice models, incorporates utility- and budget-maximizing behavior at each government level, exploiting asymmetric information regarding preferences and constraints of its constituents vis-à-vis other participating governments within the federation.[31] The second-generation theory seems to provide a viable political economy explanation for the centrifugal forces that the EU is experiencing as it confronts quasi-existential challenges.

The euro debt crisis, followed by the military and diplomatic confrontation over Ukraine, the ensuing sanctions toward Russia, and more recently, the relentless immigration from the Middle East, all contain valuable lessons for the future of the Union above and beyond the immediate remedies that have been cobbled together to cope with each challenge, while preserving some semblance of integrity. As discussed, some of these lessons have been internalized, with a view to strengthening macroeconomic governance, foremost toward a closer union in the financial sphere. By and large, governance within the euro area can be said to be more robust than before the crisis, though with considerable scope for further improvement especially on the fiscal front.

However, any progress toward creating a union in the fiscal and the other areas inevitably must be built on the foundations of a closer political union. In fact, the latter is indispensable to paving the way to a fiscal union. In this regard, the thesis put forth by Giscard d'Estaing (2014), that budgetary convergence and tax harmonization and unification will evolve organically—though admittedly requiring some technical fine-tuning—and eventually will lead the way to a political union, within the euro area, seems a like placing the cart before the horse. If history is any guide, there has been practically no progress in enlarging the central EU budget, in harmonizing tax bases or rates, except over a brief period after the enactment of the Treaty or the Single European Act. By the same token, neither national armies (except under NATO) nor foreign policymaking have been merged. At most the latter two functions have been briefly coordinated on an ad hoc basis (for example, in the case of military support for the Libya operation).

The challenges of transferring key functions from national governments to the supranational government cannot be overstated. Although most of the statutory authority for unification in these areas can be found in the Treaty, including in

[31]For a comprehensive review of the literature on the two theoretical strands of fiscal federalism, see Oates (2005).

security and foreign relations (Title V), political resistance has become ever stronger over time. Merging defense budgets across member countries is bound to be a protracted process, even in the shadow of the confrontation with Russia over Ukraine. By comparison, activating the common macroeconomic stabilization function in the euro area might be relatively easy to reach through a fast-track procedure, as envisaged in the Five Presidents' Report, in view of the need for averting a bleak economic and social outlook.

Given constraints stemming from cultural and economic diversity among member countries, it would be unrealistic to expect that major steps toward a closer political union in the euro area can be accomplished in less than a generation. To be sure, completion of the banking union—by centralizing deposit insurance—should be feasible well within that interval, against the backdrop of the recent crisis. But if the United States can serve as an example, it may take up to three generations to establish and enforce the essential elements of a consistent institutional framework, including compliance with an unwritten but effective no-bailout clause, for a well-functioning federal system, under the principles outlined above, along with some risk pooling.[32] Admittedly, even under exceptionally favorable circumstances, tensions and unresolved issues are likely to prevail among member states well beyond that period.

Realization of a closer union is unimaginable without sufficient political will, acceptance, and democratic legitimacy, which are difficult to garner at a time when centrifugal political forces have been on the rise across the continent, more or less since the proposed constitution failed to gain ratification. Clamoring for a referendum on EU membership across an increasing number of countries—following the British example—may in fact contribute to erosion of popular support for the Union and of the values that had been enshrined in the Treaty. While the Five Presidents' Report recognizes the need to promote legitimacy through a more active legislative role for the European Parliament, it fails to address, and reach out to, the source of legitimacy vested in national and subnational parliaments.

It is not, however, inconceivable that because of an unanticipated tipping point, these forces may be reversed over time, under some common economic, climatic, or security threat, perceived by the population at large.

## 7 Concluding Remarks

Following the linear evolution of a political, economic and monetary union in postwar Europe, which culminated in 2005 with the abandonment of the draft constitution, we are witnessing a nonlinear stop-go process toward further

[32]In his Nobel lecture, Sargent (2012) provides a comprehensive economic analysis of the history of U.S. fiscal unification in an embryonic federal context, spanning the period between the 1790s and the 1840s.

integration. Distracted by the Eastern enlargement and by a sense of complacency stemming from the Great Moderation, the EU leadership and institutions have been unprepared to tackle the challenges posed by the euro crisis, a diplomatic-military setback, and the immigration crisis. Efforts to strengthen the institutional underpinnings have been often met by unabashed resistance from some member governments—driven by inward-looking political movements that undermine these efforts. Against this backdrop, and in the light of the guiding principles for a coherent federal system as well as the impediments to their application, we can draw at least five summary observations as regards the prospects and tasks for further integration.

First, the nonlinear process is likely to prevail, laced with multiple improvisations. Major progress toward unification can only be expected occasionally, in the event (or under the threat) of an existential crisis—possibly exacerbated by dissenting pressures from internal fringe movements—that concentrates the attention of the political class. A case in point is the advent of the banking union, launched at the mid-2012 summit, owing to market turbulence and to the negative feedback loop between banks and sovereigns.

Second, meaningful deepening of the Union will be achieved within core groups of countries within concentric memberships, such as the euro area and as the Schengen area. Inevitably, EU member countries that for various reasons are unable or unwilling to join such groups will need to be excluded, lest they derail deeper integration. Countries that choose to exit the Union or a subgroup (say, via referendums) may, over time, elect—and be allowed—to reenter when a majority of their populations perceive that the advantages of membership outweigh the disadvantages.

Third, a closer fiscal union, comparable to completion of the banking union, must go hand in hand with a closer political union, nurtured by a broad consensus and resolve. It is practically inconceivable that expansion of the EU budget to encompass defense and foreign relations can be accomplished without an overarching political agreement. Statutory authority alone, albeit enshrined in the Treaty, is not sufficient to drive integration on these fronts, as experienced over the past two decades.

Fourth, any illusion about reaching a complete fiscal union is entirely misplaced. Indeed, even in an advanced federal system—embodying a relatively high degree of subsidiarity and solidarity—subnational governments retain considerable fiscal sovereignty.[33] As reflected in the experience of federal systems around the world, a perpetual tension prevails between the central government and decentralized governments in multiple economic and noneconomic spheres—along the lines of the second-generation theory of fiscal federalism. The lesson for the EU is to alleviate the tension by drawing as much as feasible from the deep-rooted

[33]In the United States, for example, state governments are constitutionally immune from bankruptcy under the 11th amendment. By contrast, local governments can avail themselves of Chap. 9 of the bankruptcy code.

legitimacy of lower levels of government. Ultimately, the task at hand is to balance interests at the supranational, national and subnational levels.

Finally, faced with continued high unemployment rates, financial fragmentation, zero-lower-bound interest rate, lackluster economic activity, against the backdrop of declining productivity growth and aging labor force, throughout much of the euro area, it is imperative to complement the extraordinary quantitative and qualitative easing pursued by the ECB with imminent action on two fronts—besides complying with the fiscal rules under the Pact. Foremost, member countries that experience eroding competitiveness need to step up the liberalization of product and labor markets. In addition, for the euro area as a whole, it is necessary accelerate the adoption of an aggregate fiscal stance by endowing the EU budget with a common stabilization function financed with the issuance of eurobonds.

## References

Alesina A, Angeloni I, Schucknecht L (2005) What does the European Union do? Public Choice 123(3):275–319

Allard C, Koeva-Brooks P, Bluedorn J, Bornhorst F, Christopherson K, Ohnsorghe F, Poghosyan T (2013) Toward a fiscal union for the Euro area. IMF Staff Discussion Note SDN/13/09, September

Andrle M, Bluedorn J, Eyraud L, Kinda T, Koeva-Brooks P, Schwartz G, Weber A (2015) Reforming fiscal governance in the European Union. IMF Staff Discussion Note SDN/15/09, May

Bénássy-Quéré A, Trannoy A, Wolff G (2014) Tax harmonization in Europe: moving forward. Les notes du conseil d'analyse économique, no. 14, July

Buti M, Giudice G (2002) Maastricht fiscal rules at ten: an assessment. J Common Mark Stud 40 (5):823–848

Chari VV, Kehoe P (2009) On the need for fiscal constraints in a monetary union. J Monet Econ 54 (8):2399–2408

De Grauwe P (2003) Economics of the monetary union. Oxford University Press, Oxford

Escolano J, Benedek D, Jin H, Mulas Granados C, Nozaki M, Pereira J, Rota Graziosi G, Sinn L, Torres J (2015) Distribution of fiscal responsibilities in federations. In: Cottarelli C, Guerguil M (eds) Designing a European fiscal union: lessons from the experience of fiscal federations. Routledge, International Monetary Fund, New York

European Commission (2011) Proposal for a Council Directive on a Common Consolidated Corporate Tax Base (CCCTB). COM(2011) 121/4, Brussels

European Commission (2013a) Building a strengthened fiscal framework in the European Union: a guide to the stability and growth pact. European Economy Occasional Papers 150, May

European Commission (2013b) Vade mecum on the stability and growth pact. European Economy Occasional Papers 151, May

Fatica S, Mourre G (2016) Own resources for the EU budget: an exploration of alternative revenue instruments. Paper presented at the 18th Banca d'Italia workshop on public finance: current issues in fiscal policy, Rome, Mar 31–Apr 2

Giavazzi F, Tabellini G (2014) What macroeconomic policies for the Eurozone? VoxEU, 25 Sept

Giscard d'Estaing V (2014) Europa: La dernière chance de l'Europe. XO Editions, Paris

High Level Group on Own Resources (2014) First assessment report. Brussels, Dec 14

Juncker J-C, Tusk D, Dijsselbloem J, Draghi M, Schulz M (2015) Completing Europe's economic and monetary union. European Commission, Brussels

Kopits G (ed) (1992) Tax harmonization in the European community: policy issues and analysis. Occasional paper 94, International Monetary Fund, July
Kopits G (ed) (2013) Restoring public debt sustainability: the role of independent fiscal institutions. Oxford University Press, Oxford
Kopits G (2014) Ireland's Ireland fiscal framework: options for the future. Econ Soc Rev 45 (1):135–158
Kopits G (2017) Managing the Euro debt crisis. In Odor L (ed) Rethinking fiscal policy after the crisis. Cambridge University Press, Cambridge
Kopits G, Symansky S (1998) Fiscal policy rules. IMF occasional paper 162, International Monetary Fund
Lamers K, Schäuble W (2014) More integration is still the right goal for Europe. Financial Times, Sept 1
Mayer T (2012) Europe's unfinished currency: the political economics of the Euro. Anthem Press, New York
Mijs A, Schout A (2015) Flexibility in the EU budget: are there limits? Clingendael report. Netherlands Institute of International Relations, The Hague
Münchau W (2016) The Eurozone cannot escape political and fiscal union. Financial Times, Jun 6
Musgrave R (1959) The theory of public finance: a study in public economy. McGraw-Hill, New York
Norregaard J (1997) Tac assignment. In: Ter-Minassian T (ed) Fiscal federalism in theory and practice. International Monetary Fund, Washington, DC
Oates WE (2005) Toward a second-generation theory of fiscal federalism. Int Tax Public Financ 12:349–373
Pasimeni P (2014) An optimum currency crisis. Eur J Comp Econ 11(2):173–204
Sargent TJ (2012) Nobel lecture: United States then, Europe now. J Polit Econ 120(1):1–40
Schelkle W (2005) The political economy of fiscal coordination in EMU: from disciplinarian device to insurance arrangement. J Common Mark Stud 43(2):371–391
Schmidt H (2014) Preface. In: Giscard d'Estaing V (ed) Europa: La dernière chance de l'Europe. XO Editions, Paris
Sebastiao M (2016) Banking Union: the quest for a new financial regulation paradigm. Paper presented at the seminar on Uniao Bancaria: a Nova Fronteira da Regulacao Financiera na Uniao Europeia, Catolica Lisbon School of Business and Economics, Jan 25–26
Sinn HW (2014) The Euro trap: on bursting bubbles, budgets, and beliefs. Oxford University Press, Oxford
Veron N (2015) Europe's radical banking union, Bruegel essay and lecture series. Bruegel, Brussels
Wyplosz C (2017) Fiscal discipline in a monetary union without fiscal union. In Odor L (ed) Rethinking fiscal policy after the crisis. Cambridge University Press, Cambridge

# The Scope for a Budgetary Union in the European Monetary Union

**Oscar Bajo-Rubio and Carmen Díaz-Roldán**

**Abstract** In the scenario of the Economic and Monetary Union of the European Union (EU), where the EU budget is not able to play the role of a centralized fiscal policy instrument, proposals for a budgetary union have been widely discussed. As a contribution to the debate, in this chapter we will discuss the macroeconomics of a monetary union focusing our analysis on the scope for coordination of budgetary policies. When using the public deficit as policy instrument, we will identify the full cooperation of fiscal policies with a budgetary or fiscal union. The results will allow us to explore the role that fiscal integration can play in reducing the incidence and severity of future crises, and will also allow us to derive under which circumstances a budgetary union would not be advisable. In particular, we will show to which extent a fully coordinated fiscal performance of the Eurozone's members should be complemented with fiscal discipline, a zone-wide system of transfers, or an automatic mechanism to ensure the stability of the Eurozone.

## 1 Introduction

The formation of a monetary union means, for the countries involved, losing the exchange rate (now irreversibly fixed) and national monetary policy (that becomes the responsibility of a common central bank) as stabilization tools in order to cope with macroeconomic shocks. However, according to the theory of optimum currency areas pioneered by Mundell (1961), the occurrence of asymmetric shocks (i.e., those requiring a different optimal policy response within each member country) means a potential impediment to the successful working of a monetary union. Since a monetary policy that is now common to all the member countries of the monetary union cannot be the right tool to cope with asymmetric shocks, the cost of losing national monetary policies would be smaller the more integrated are

O. Bajo-Rubio (✉) • C. Díaz-Roldán
Facultad de Derecho y Ciencias Sociales, Universidad de Castilla-La Mancha, Ronda de Toledo, s/n, 13071 Ciudad Real, Spain
e-mail: oscar.bajo@uclm.es; carmen.diazroldan@uclm.es

 
N. de Costa Cabral et al. (eds.), *The Euro and the Crisis*, Financial and Monetary Policy Studies 43, DOI 10.1007/978-3-319-45710-9_21

the economies of the countries forming the monetary union. This is so because, within highly integrated countries, the evolution of their economies would be much synchronized, and therefore less likely the occurrence of asymmetric shocks (Alesina and Barro 2002).

Regarding the case of the European Union (EU), the Economic and Monetary Union (EMU) launched in 1999 did not contemplate establishing a common fiscal policy. In this way, fiscal policy was mostly assigned to national governments, with some intergovernmental coordination mechanisms addressed to monitor the evolution of public finances. The resistance to the development of fiscal instruments at the Eurozone level can be explained in terms of concerns of moral hazard (Guerguil 2015). As a result, while strongly integrated in economic, regulatory and monetary matters, the EU seems to be weakly integrated in budgetary matters (Prud'homme 2015).

This contradiction between monetary integration within the Eurozone and the persistence of national fiscal policies has proven to be a major obstacle faced to the current crisis, which has led to several authors to point to the need of some kind of fiscal union; see, e.g., Enderlein et al. (2012) or Allard et al. (2013). The concept of fiscal union could involve fiscal federalism among the member countries; where fiscal federalism is concerned with the allocation of public expenditures and revenues across the different government levels, i.e., central and sub-central. Bordo et al. (2013) identify several conditions necessary for a fiscal union to work properly, namely: a credible commitment to a no-bailout rule; independence of revenues and expenditures reflecting the preferences of the member countries; a well-functioning system of transfers to be used in times of distress; and the ability to learn from past mistakes and adapt to changing economic and political circumstances.

In particular, given the insufficiency of the current adjustment mechanisms in the face of country-specific shocks in EMU, establishing an insurance mechanism able to provide an automatic stabilization has been recently proposed in, e.g., Enderlein et al. (2012), Wolff (2012) or Allard et al. (2013). Specifically, the central budget should provide a stabilizing effect in an automatic way, through direct transfers and progressive taxes. In this way, when a particular member country (or a region within a country) suffers a recession not affecting the others, net transfers of the central government to that country (or region) would increase: this is the insurance function of the central budget. The proposal of such an instrument is something recurrent in the literature, dating back to Kenen (1969), within the theory of optimum currency areas; and has been developed thereafter in, e.g., Goodhart and Smith (1993), von Hagen and Hammond (1998) or Bajo-Rubio and Díaz-Roldán (2003).

In addition to the implementation of an insurance mechanism, some other measures aimed to develop a budgetary or fiscal union have been proposed in the recent literature; see, among others, Dullien and Schwarzer (2009), Majocchi (2011), Marzinotto et al. (2011), Fuest and Peichl (2012), Henning and Kessler (2012), Enderlein et al. (2012), or Bordo et al. (2013). Some of these measures are as follows:

- Fiscal discipline of the member states of EMU.
- Mechanisms for crisis resolution and rescue of the member states.
- Joint guarantee of the public debt.
- Creation of a federal European central government with its corresponding budget and treasury.

In general, all these proposals would require several institutional changes, such as reinforcing the role of the European Parliament, creating a supranational authority on taxes, or funds guaranteed by different budget rules. The particular role played by fiscal rules has been discussed, e.g., in Ballabriga and Martínez-Mongay (2003), Debrun et al. (2008), or Wyplosz (2013), to name a few.

In this chapter, we will focus on the scope for coordination of budgetary or fiscal policies. The economic environment will be a macroeconomic scenario describing a large monetary union. In such a context, and given the interaction between the involved economies, we will define two polar cases regarding the implementation of fiscal policies, namely, the individual decision of each country at a national level, and the coordinated decision at a supranational level (i.e., the monetary union). As our main assumption, we will identify the full cooperation or coordinated solution with the fiscal union. The intuition is that in the coordinated solution all the member states of the union conduct their fiscal policies using the government deficit in the same way, ignoring idiosyncratic issues. The results will show us that, when dealing with country-specific shocks, fiscal policies coordination (i.e., a fiscal union) will not be advisable.

## 2 A Macroeconomic Model for a Large Monetary Union

From a theoretical point of view, the macroeconomic interactions between a monetary union (such as EMU) and the rest of the world can be described by a two-country model. However, and assuming for simplicity a monetary union made up of two countries, the macroeconomic interactions between the monetary union and the rest of the world would be described by a three-country model; where the monetary union constitutes a block against the rest of the world, but also a two-country model by herself. In this case, we will be modelling a large monetary union.

The first attempt to extend the standard macroeconomic model for an open economy, i.e., the Mundell-Fleming model, incorporating a fully specified supply side, to the case of a monetary union, was made in Bajo-Rubio and Díaz-Roldán (2011). Specifically, we started from the standard two-country Mundell-Fleming model with perfect capital mobility (Mundell 1964), extended it to incorporate the supply side in a context of rigid real wages (Sachs 1980), and allowed for a common money-market equilibrium condition. From here, the effects of a number of shocks, both common to the union and country-specific, were analysed in the novel macroeconomic framework given by a monetary union.

The basic model in Bajo-Rubio and Díaz-Roldán (2011) was later modified in Bajo-Rubio and Díaz-Roldán (2015) where, instead of the standard depiction of the money market, it was assumed that the central bank of the union followed a monetary policy rule based on inflation targeting (Taylor 1993). Such an assumption can be justified on the grounds of the enormous development experienced by financial innovation, which makes highly unstable the demand for money, and hence the traditional working of monetary policy, based on the control of the supply of money. The model in Bajo-Rubio and Díaz-Roldán (2015) was developed for the case of a small monetary union, i.e., when the rest of the world is not modelled and simply taken as exogenous; and was used to illustrate the interactions within the Eurozone across her member countries.

In this chapter, however, we will consider instead the case of a large monetary union, i.e., when the rest of world is modelled in the same way as the member countries of the monetary union. Then, this model will be integrated into an optimization framework, where the fiscal authorities of the member countries of the union can choose whether following an independent fiscal policy, or coordinate instead their fiscal policies. We will follow here the approach of Díaz-Roldán (2000), but assuming that the central bank of the union follows a monetary policy rule.

The model is a three-country aggregate demand-aggregate supply model describing a large monetary union formed by two symmetric countries, where the rest of the world is modelled in the same manner. The monetary authority (i.e., the central bank) of the union follows a Taylor-type monetary rule in order to achieve the goal of price stabilization (i.e., inflation targeting). We assume that a country would agree joining a monetary union only if the monetary policy of the union is anti-inflationist enough. In addition, in order to highlight this, the monetary policy rule is assumed to have the only objective of inflation targeting; the latter assumption tries to proxy the kind of monetary rule followed by the European Central Bank.

By solving the model, we obtain reduced-form equations for the output levels and inflation rates of the two countries of the union and the rest of the world. These reduced-form equations depend on their fiscal policy instruments, as well as on (exogenous) country-specific shocks to aggregate demand (to consumption, investment, trade balance, and money market) and supply (to wage- and price-push factors, labour force, and productivity). All shocks can originate in any of the two member countries of the monetary union, or in the rest of the world; in the latter case, they will be called external shocks.

In particular, in the reduced-form equations:

- A **contractionary supply shock** (i.e., an exogenous increase in wages or prices, or a decrease in labour force or productivity), independently of its origin (i.e., each member country of the monetary union or the rest of the world) leads to an **increase in inflation** and a **decrease in output** in both the union and the rest of the world.

**Table 1** Coefficients of the reduced form of the model

| | | Demand shocks | | Supply shocks | | External shocks | |
|---|---|---|---|---|---|---|---|
| | | Country 1 | Country 2 | Country 1 | Country 2 | Demand | Supply |
| Output | Country 1 | + | – | – | – | – | – |
| | Country 2 | – | + | – | – | – | – |
| | Rest of the world | – | – | – | – | + | – |
| Inflation | Country 1 | + | + | + | + | + | + |
| | Country 2 | + | + | + | + | + | + |
| | Rest of the world | + | + | + | + | + | + |

Note: + and – indicate that the change in the endogenous variable (output or inflation) has the same and the opposite sign than the shock, respectively
Source: Own elaboration from Díaz-Roldán (2016b)

- An **expansionary fiscal policy** or an **expansionary demand shock** (i.e., an exogenous increase in consumption or investment, an improvement of the trade balance, or an expansionary monetary policy) always lead to an **increase in inflation** in both the union and the rest of the world. However, the effect on output depend on the country of origin of the shock (i.e., each member country of the monetary union or the rest of the world), since **output increases in the country of origin of the shock, but decreases in the other two countries**.

The latter result (i.e., the transmission to a country of a shock originated in another country with the opposite sign) is called in the literature the *beggar-thy-neighbour* effect. Specifically, when countries follow a monetary policy rule and are particularly concerned with inflation targeting, the *beggar-thy-neighbour* effect prevails, so that the interest rate and exchange rate channels dominate over the trade balance channel, and demand shocks are transmitted abroad in an asymmetric way, i.e., with the opposite sign. The ultimate reason would be the stronger response of the interest rate to any disturbance that may occur under inflation targeting and a monetary policy rule.

In Table 1, we can see the signs of the coefficients of the reduced form of the model, which indicate the way of transmission of the shocks.

## 3 The Optimization Problem

Given the country's economic structure, summarized in the corresponding reduced-form equations of the model, the fiscal authorities of each member country of the monetary union will proceed to minimize both changes in output, with stabilization purposes, and changes in the government deficit, in order to achieve budgetary discipline. On the other hand, regarding inflation, we will assume full delegation of prices control to the monetary authority of the union; accordingly, the government deficit will be the only demand policy instrument available at the country level. In such a situation, the optimal (fiscal) policy would be the optimal level of the government deficit compatible with the stabilization target.

As we have seen in the previous section, when the monetary authority (i.e., the central bank of the union), is anti-inflationist enough and follows a monetary policy rule with the only objective of inflation targeting, an output increase in a member country of the union results in an output decrease in the other (see Table 1). As a result, the public deficit of each country behaves as a complementary strategic tool of fiscal policy for the other country. This happens because a fiscal expansion in a country, which leads to a fall in output in the other country, makes the latter to stimulate her aggregate demand via fiscal policy, thus avoiding the possibility of a recession in the monetary union as a whole.

Under the individual solution, each country minimizes separately her loss function, i.e., the changes in her budget deficit (the policy instrument) and output changes, in response to both shocks and changes in the other countries' deficit. On the contrary, under the cooperative solution the two member countries of the union minimize jointly a weighted average of their loss functions.

When solving the problem individually, each fiscal authority chooses the level of government deficit that counteracts the non-desired effects of the shocks, but ignoring the reaction of the other country's authority. However, when the countries coordinate their actions, their fiscal authorities jointly choose as response the level of government deficit that internalizes (i.e., takes into account) the reaction of both of them. The individual (i.e., non-cooperative) solution is the best one from an individual point of view, whereas the coordinated solution is optimal from a social point of view. Yet, sometimes a conflict arises since the cooperative solution does not coincide with the non-cooperative one.

Accordingly, the desirability of the cooperative solution against the individual solution will depend on the nature of the externality, or side effects, that the implemented fiscal policy (i.e., a change in government deficit) provokes on the output of the other country. When the externality has the same sign of the shock, the cooperative solution does not offset the adverse side effects, but reinforce them. In particular, for external shocks (i.e., shocks originated in the rest of the world), as well as for the common monetary shocks of monetary unions, cooperation is the best solution, since it offsets the side effects on output. On the contrary, in the face of country-specific shocks (i.e., shocks originated in any of the two member countries of the monetary union), coordination is not helpful.

The first line of Table 2 shows the signs of the effects of all possible shocks hitting output (the endogenous variable relevant for stabilization) in country 1 (the information would be symmetric for country 2), as shown in Table 1. In turn, lines 2 and 3 show the signs of the effects of all shocks in the individual and the cooperative solution of the optimization problem, respectively. If we compare these signs, we can easily see that for any kind of external disturbance cooperation is the best solution, since it counteracts the effects on output. In the case of country-specific demand shocks originated in the other country, cooperation is not advisable since it reinforces the effect of the shock. Finally, regarding country-specific

**Table 2** Reduced form of the model, competitive and cooperative solutions for country 1

| | Demand shocks | | Supply shocks | | External shocks | |
|---|---|---|---|---|---|---|
| | Country 1 | Country 2 | Country 1 | Country 2 | Demand | Supply |
| Output | + | – | – | – | – | – |
| Individual solution | – | + | + | + | – | – |
| Cooperative solution | – | – | + | + | + | + |

Note: + and – indicate that the change in output has the same and the opposite sign than the shock, respectively
Source: Own elaboration, from the equations in Díaz-Roldán (2016b)

demand shocks originated in the own country, as well as any country-specific supply shocks, both the individual and cooperative solutions offset the effects of the shock. However, it can be proved that in these cases coordination is not advisable, since the coefficients of the individual solution are lower, in quantitative terms, than those of the cooperative solution; see Díaz-Roldán (2016b) for the technical details. The reason is that a lower coefficient in either the individual solution or the cooperative solution means, other things equal, a lower change in the government deficit, which is always preferable since the viewpoint of the fiscal authorities.

Therefore, according to our results, the desirability of a fiscal union depends on the origin of the shocks to deal with. Cooperation among the fiscal authorities of the member countries of the monetary union would be counterproductive against country-specific demand and supply shocks originated within the union. This occurs because, when a country uses the budget deficit as the policy instrument, the externality or side effect given by the policy response of the other country have the same sign than the shock; and, as a result, the coordinated policy action reinforces the undesired effects of the shock. On the contrary, for any external shocks coming from out of the union, as well as for common shocks in general (e.g., the common monetary shocks of monetary unions), the externality or side effect given by the policy response of the other country has the opposite sign than the shock. Hence, the cooperative solution requires a lower change in the budget deficit than in the case of the competitive solution.

Our results are in line with those of some related contributions. For example, Sánchez (2013) analyses the role of monetary stabilisation in a currency union of small open economies. He finds that demand-side shocks hinder stabilization in the monetary union, unless the business cycles of the member countries are perfectly synchronised. Due to the interaction between monetary and fiscal policies, the central bank of the union reacts to the fiscal deficits of the member countries in proportion to the contribution that each country's fiscal deficit makes to aggregate demand determination, which results in individual countries' deficits that are only partially offset. In addition, for country-specific supply-side shocks, a currency union of small open economies underperforms the case of no monetary union. Since the countries' fiscal authorities aim at mitigating the consequences of the shock, this results in a higher increase in the interest rate as the common central bank reacts to larger government deficits.

From another point of view, Allard et al. (2013) stress that in EMU, when facing the current crisis, the side effects from the policies implemented by individual countries were not sufficiently taken into account. In turn, Bajo-Rubio and Díaz-Roldán (2015) analyse the performance of EMU in the light of macroeconomic modelling, although they do not deal with the possibility of coordinated policies. Regarding the consequences of country-specific shocks to the union, a redistribution of the effects is found for individual countries: sometimes with an opposite sign and offsetting them, and sometimes with an ambiguous effect on the other country. This leads to a debate on how the effects of economic policies aimed to deal with country-specific shocks in the Eurozone are actually allocated across member countries.

## 4 Conclusions

In this chapter, we have analysed the scope for coordination of fiscal policies in a large monetary union. The analysis has taken as reference the scenario of EMU, where the EU budget is not able to play the role of a centralized fiscal policy instrument as in federal countries.

The results have shown that there are situations where the coordination of budgetary or fiscal policies is not advisable. Specifically, these are the cases where the coordinated solution requires performing a further change in the fiscal deficit (either an expansion or a contraction) as compared to the uncoordinated solution. This would make difficult to minimize changes in the budget deficit, i.e., a variable that is used as policy instrument although is at the same time an objective of the fiscal authorities.

Summing up, when fiscal authorities are concerned with the budget deficit as an objective, a budgetary union (understood to mean full coordination of fiscal policies) would not be always advisable. On the contrary, in a monetary union where the central bank is concerned with inflation targeting, coordination of fiscal policies would be helpful only when the probabilities of suffering common shocks, as well as external shocks, are higher.

When including the public deficit as an objective, fiscal authorities would try to minimize simultaneously both changes in output (aimed to stabilization) and in the fiscal instrument. Minimizing the instrument (i.e., the budget deficit) implies giving more importance to reaching a deficit target than to offsetting the effect of macroeconomic shocks. This might explain the reluctance to establishing limits on the use of budget deficits in monetary unions; see, e.g., Buiter et al. (1993) or, more recently Perotti (2013) and Díaz-Roldán (2016a).

According to our results, cooperation is not helpful when the member countries of the monetary union show asymmetries, leading to country-specific shocks that force fiscal authorities to use different fiscal policies to deal with them. In such a case, which could be representative of the Eurozone member countries, the particular fiscal performance should take into account the specific features of the involved economies.

The main policy implication we can derive is that a common budgetary policy, i.e., the full coordination of fiscal policies, cannot be the right answer to deal with country-specific shocks. This conclusion is in line with Mundell's (1961) regarding monetary policy: if a common (monetary) policy responds to any asymmetric shock affecting to a particular region, it will necessarily hurt the other regions. To conclude, recall that the results in this chapter refer to the *discretionary* component of fiscal policy, and do not preclude the introduction of a fiscal policy instrument acting as an automatic mechanism aimed to offset those country-specific shocks that might eventually affect the member countries of EMU; see Bajo-Rubio and Díaz-Roldán (2003).

## References

Alesina A, Barro RJ (2002) Currency unions. Q J Econ 117:409–436

Allard C, Brooks PK, Bluedorn JC, Bornhorst F, Christopherson K, Ohnsorge F, Poghosyan T, IMF Staff Team (2013) Toward a fiscal union for the euro area. IMF Staff Discussion Note 13/9

Bajo-Rubio O, Díaz-Roldán C (2003) Insurance mechanisms against asymmetric shocks in a monetary union: a proposal with an application to EMU. Rech Econ Louvain 69:73–96

Bajo-Rubio O, Díaz-Roldán C (2011) Macroeconomic analysis of monetary unions: a general framework based on the Mundell-Fleming model. Springer, Berlin

Bajo-Rubio O, Díaz-Roldán C (2015) Macroeconomic linkages in the European Union. In Tache I (ed) The European Union and the challenges of the new global context. Cambridge Scholars Publishing, Newcastle, pp 208–232. Available at SSRN: http://ssrn.com/abstract=2746918

Ballabriga F, Martínez-Mongay C (2003) Has EMU shifted monetary and fiscal policies? In: Buti M (ed) Monetary and fiscal policies in EMU. Interactions and coordination. Cambridge University Press, Cambridge, pp 246–272

Bordo MD, Jonung L, Markiewicz A (2013) A fiscal union for the euro: some lessons from history. CESifo Econ Stud 59:449–488

Buiter W, Corsetti G, Roubini N (1993) Excessive deficits: sense and nonsense in the Treaty of Maastricht. Econ Policy 16:57–100

Debrun X, Moulin L, Turrini A, Ayuso-i-Casals J, Kumar MS (2008) Tied to the mast? National fiscal rules in the European Union. Econ Policy 23:297–362

Díaz-Roldán C (2000) Coordination of fiscal policies in a monetary union. Working Paper DEFI 00/09, AEEFI-FEDEA

Díaz-Roldán C (2016a) Fiscal performance in monetary unions: how much austerity should be allowed? Panoeconomicus (in press)

Díaz-Roldán C (2016b) Monetary and fiscal performance in large monetary unions. Mimeo, Universidad de Castilla-La Mancha

Dullien S, Schwarzer D (2009) Bringing macroeconomics into the EU budget debate: why and how? J Common Mark Stud 47:153–174

Enderlein H (coordinator), Bofinger P, Boone L, de Grauwe P, Piris J-C, Pisani-Ferry J, Rodrigues MJ, Sapir A, Vitorino A (2012) Completing the euro: a road map towards fiscal union in Europe. Report of the "Tommaso Padoa-Schioppa Group", Notre Europe, Paris

Fuest C, Peichl A (2012) European fiscal union: what is it? Does it work? And are there really 'no alternatives'? CESifo Forum 1:3–9
Goodhart CAE, Smith S (1993) Stabilization. Eur Econ Rep Stud 5:417–455
Guerguil M (2015) Can the eurozone prosper without a fiscal union? IEB's Report on Fiscal Federalism and Public Finance'15, Institut d'Economia de Barcelona, pp 11–12
Henning CR, Kessler M (2012) Fiscal federalism: US history for architects of Europe's fiscal union. Bruegel Essay and Lecture Series
Kenen PB (1969) The theory of optimum currency areas: an eclectic view. In: Mundell RA, Swoboda AK (eds) Monetary problems of the international economy. The University of Chicago Press, Chicago, pp 41–60
Majocchi A (2011) Towards a European Federal Fiscal Union. Perspectives on Federalism 3, No. 1, E-78-98
Marzinotto B, Sapir A, Wolff GB (2011) What kind of fiscal union? Bruegel Policy Brief 2011/06.
Mundell RA (1961) A theory of optimum currency areas. Am Econ Rev 51:657–665
Mundell RA (1964) A reply: capital mobility and size. Can J Econ Polit Sci 30:421–431
Perotti R (2013) The 'austerity myth': gain without pain? In: Alesina A, Giavazzi F (eds) Fiscal policy after the financial crisis. The University of Chicago Press, Chicago, pp 307–354
Prud'homme R (2015) The European budgetary union: necessary and impossible. IEB's Report on Fiscal Federalism and Public Finance'15, Institut d'Economia de Barcelona, pp 9–10
Sachs J (1980) Wages, flexible exchange rates, and macroeconomic policy. Q J Econ 94:731–747
Sánchez M (2013) Monetary-fiscal wage interactions in a multi-country currency union. J Econ Integr 28:507–524
Taylor JB (1993) Discretion versus policy rules in practice. Carn-Roch Conf Ser Public Policy 39:195–214
von Hagen J, Hammond GW (1998) Regional insurance against asymmetric shocks: an empirical study for the European Community. Manch Sch 66:331–353
Wolff GB (2012) A budget for Europe's monetary union. Bruegel Policy Contribution 2012/22
Wyplosz C (2013) Fiscal rules: theoretical issues and historical experiences. In: Alesina A, Giavazzi F (eds) Fiscal policy after the financial crisis. The University of Chicago Press, Chicago, pp 495–525

MIX
Papier aus verantwortungsvollen Quellen
Paper from responsible sources
FSC® C105338

If you have any concerns about our products,
you can contact us on
**ProductSafety@springernature.com**

In case Publisher is established outside the EU,
the EU authorized representative is:
**Springer Nature Customer Service Center GmbH**
**Europaplatz 3, 69115 Heidelberg, Germany**

Printed by Libri Plureos GmbH
in Hamburg, Germany